Library of
Davidson College

THE
GRENVILLE PAPERS.

VOL. II.

THE
GRENVILLE PAPERS:

BEING

THE CORRESPONDENCE

OF

RICHARD GRENVILLE EARL TEMPLE, K.G.,

AND

THE RIGHT HON: GEORGE GRENVILLE,

THEIR FRIENDS AND CONTEMPORARIES.

EDITED, WITH NOTES,
By WILLIAM JAMES SMITH

VOL. II.

AMS PRESS
NEW YORK

Reprinted from the edition of 1852, London
First AMS EDITION published 1970
Manufactured in the United States of America

International Standard Book Number:
  complete set: 0-404-06150-8
  volume 2: 0-404-06152-4

Library of Congress Catalog Card Number: 72-119154

AMS PRESS, INC.
New York, N. Y. 10003

CONTENTS

OF

THE SECOND VOLUME.

1762.

	Page
Mr. Fox to Mr. Grenville. *November* 11.—Sir Charles Hardy and the Expedition to Brest. Care should be taken that no Action occurred after the signing of the Preliminaries of Peace	1
Mr. Grenville to Mr. Fox. *November* 11.—Sir Charles Hardy's squadron to go to sea. The Admiralty cannot put a stop to hostilities until after the exchange of the ratifications	1
Earl Temple to Mr. Wilkes. *November* 13	3
Earl Temple to Mr. Wilkes. *November* 21.—The assertion that Mr. Pitt approves of the Peace is untrue. Cannot sufficiently admire the *North Briton* of this week: it is unanswerable, as founded on stubborn facts	3
Mr. Wilkes to Earl Temple. *November* 23.	4
Earl Temple to Mr. Wilkes. *November* 25.—Satirical remarks upon the state of parties. Pitiful appearance of our grand Administration	5
Earl Temple to Mr. Wilkes. *November* 28.—Thanks for the competent idea he gives him of the humours of St. Stephen's Chapel. The *glorious* and *lasting* Peace	7
Admiral Rodney to Mr. Grenville. *December* 4.—Description of the West India Islands	9
Countess Temple to Earl Temple. *December* 17.—The King, Lord Bute, and the Duke of Devonshire	21
Earl Temple to Mr. Wilkes. *December* 26.—His kind correspondence makes time pass pleasantly in the country. The Militia disembodied	22
Earl Temple to Mr. Wilkes	24

VOL. II. b

1763.

Page

Admiral Rodney to Mr. Grenville. *February* 1.—The comparative value of some of the West India Islands to England and France. St. Lucia and Martinico very sickly. Serpents and venomous animals abound in them, which are not to be found in other islands. Requests a grant of uncultivated land in St. Vincent's 24

The Earl of Egremont to Mr. Grenville. *February* 12.—Reflects upon the Duke of Bedford for allowing the King's Ministers to receive the earliest information that the Treaty was to be signed from the French Ambassador 29

The Earl of Bute to Mr. Grenville. *February* 13.—Communication from M. de Nivernois, that everything was agreed on respecting the Definitive Treaty of Peace 29

The Earl of Buckinghamshire to Mr. Grenville. *February* 19.— Satisfied with his residence at Moscow, and with the attention which he receives from the Empress 30

The Earl of Egremont to Mr. Grenville. *March* 2 . . . 31

The Earl of Bute to Mr. Grenville. *March* 25.—Cabinet difficulties 32

Mr. Grenville to the Earl of Bute. *March* 25.—Expresses his warm sense of the friendship and good opinion which has induced Lord Bute to recommend him to the King as First Commissioner of the Treasury. Enters minutely into the state of parties. Lord Shelburne's youth and inexperience in business a great objection to his appointment as Secretary of State. Desires Lord Bute to reconsider his resolution to retreat at this critical moment of the King's affairs 33

The Earl of Bute to Mr. Grenville. *April* 1.—He has desired Lord Shelburne to call upon Mr. Grenville : still thinks his services would be useful, as he can, better than any one, prevent Fox's people from going over to the enemy 40

Mr. Jenkinson to Mr. Grenville. *April* 3 41

Countess Temple to Earl Temple. *April* 5.—Mr. Walpole admires her verses on Lady Mary Coke. Lord Waldegrave has the small-pox 41

Mr. Stanley to Mr. Grenville. *April* 7.—Declines the offer of being a Lord of the Treasury, or to make demands of other preferment *that may suit him better:* requires specific proposals of employment more worthy his acceptance . . . 42

Count de Viry to Mr. Grenville. *April* 8.—Congratulations upon his advancement 44

Mr. Jenkinson to Mr. Grenville. *April* 8 45

	Page
The Earl of Halifax to Mr. Grenville. *April* 18.—Draft of the King's Speech	45
Mr. Jenkinson to Mr. Grenville. *April* 20.—Lord Clive. Dinner at Wildman's. The West India Merchants	46
Mr. Jenkinson to Mr. Grenville. *April* 28.—Lord Luxborough and his title	48
Earl Verney to Mr. Grenville. *April* 29.—Offers his services .	49
Mrs. Grenville's account of the Christening of Lord Egremont's son: the King and Queen being sponsors in person. *May* .	50
The Earl of Egremont to Mr. Grenville. *May* 1.—Despatches from Paris. Alarming secret letter from Mr. Neville . .	52
The Earl of Egremont to Mr. Grenville. *May* 3.—Lord Temple is to be forbid the Court	52
Mr. Wilkes to Earl Temple. *May* .—Pamphlet on the *Seizure of Papers*	53
The Duke of Grafton to Earl Temple. *May* 3.—Reasons for declining Mr. Wilkes's request to become bail for him. Explains his motives for visiting him in the Tower . . .	53
The Earl of Halifax to Earl Temple. *May* 7.—Dismissal from the Lord Lieutenancy of Bucks	55
Mr. Wilkes to Earl Temple. *May* 15	56
Mr. Wilkes to Earl Temple. *May* 25.—Begs the loan of 200*l*. more	57
The Duke of Bedford to Mr. Grenville. *May* 25.—Address of the Merchants of the City of London on the Peace . .	57
General Townshend to Mr. Grenville. *May* 30.—Complains that his Regiment of Militia has been refused its pay . .	58
Mr. Wilkes to Earl Temple. *June* 5.—Asks for a last sum of £400 or £500	59
Mr. Wilkes to Earl Temple. *June* 11.—The approaching trials. Hopes within a fortnight to congratulate him on the explicit declaration of a Court of Justice, in favour of the liberty of the subject	60
Mr. Wilkes to Earl Temple. *June* 18.—Cause of the Printers against the Messengers. Mr. Sergeant Glynn, and Mr. Dunning. Charles Townshend	62
Mr. Wilkes to Earl Temple. *June* 30.—Exonerating himself from a charge relative to the Militia accounts . . .	63
Mr. Almon to Earl Temple. *July* .—Account of the proceedings against him in the Court of King's Bench, for the *Letter on Libels*	65
Dr. Samuel Johnson to Mr. Grenville. *July* 2.—Applies for the quarterly payment of his pension	68
Mr. Welbore Ellis to Mr. Grenville. *July* 3.—Allowance to	

b 2

	Page
General Conway for extraordinary expenses during the March of the Army from the German Cantonments	68
Mr. Wilkes to Earl Temple. *July* 7.—Congratulations on the result of the Trials of yesterday	70
Mr. Wilkes to Earl Temple. *July* 9.—Law proceedings. *The North Briton*: desires his Lordship's opinion as to reprinting No. 45. The King is enraged at his insolence. Begs for another sum of 500*l*.	71
Mr. Wilkes to Earl Temple. *July* 15.—Quarter Sessions at Aylesbury. Lord Le Despencer proposes an Address to the Crown on the Peace. Proceedings and discussions thereon	76
Mr. Wilkes to Earl Temple. *July* 23	78
Earl Temple to Mr. Wilkes. *July* 24.—On the business of the Printers, and their Actions against the Secretaries of State	78
Mr. Edward Weston to Mr. Grenville. *July* 25.—Desiring to be recommended to the King for a reward for past services .	79
Mr. Wilkes to Earl Temple. *July* 26.—Begs to submit the produce of his Press in Great George Street. *The North Briton* will appear without any Advertisement. Proposes a short visit to Paris	80
Mr. Wilkes to Earl Temple. *August* 2.—His reception at Canterbury and Dover. English Sailors no enemies to Wilkes and Liberty. Arrival at Paris. The Duke of Richmond .	82
The Earl of Egremont to Mr. Grenville. *August* 3.—The King's extraordinary behaviour to himself and Lord Halifax. Desires Mr. Grenville's opinion and advice	83
Mr. Grenville to the Earl of Egremont. *August* 4.—Unsettled state of the Administration. Marks of superior influence proposed alterations in Government concealed from the Ministers. Advises a continuance in office, rather than an immediate resignation, which might facilitate any intended arrangement	85
The Earl of Egremont to Mr. Grenville. *August* 6.—Encloses a letter from the Lord Chancellor. Continued uncertainty of the situation. The King's manner placid and gracious . .	88
Mr. Calcraft to Earl Temple. *August* 10.—Enquires by what channel communication may be had with Mr. Pitt, if it should be necessary during his Lordship's absence. Hopes to see him soon, and desires secrecy	90
Earl Temple to Mr. Calcraft. *August* 12.—In reply to the foregoing	91
The Earl of Egremont to Mr. Grenville. *August* 12 . .	92
The Earl of Halifax to Mr. Grenville. *August* 26.—He shall proceed with the business of his office as if nothing had hap-	

1763. CONTENTS. ix

Page

pened, and insinuates his wish that Mr. Grenville should do the same 92
Mr. Grenville to the Earl of Halifax. *August* 27.—Cold reception from the King, and no information as to what was settled or intended. Expresses warm indignation against the *North Briton* of to-day 93
Mr. Grenville to the Earl of Halifax. *August* 27.—Mr. Pitt was with the King near two hours 95
Mr. Grenville to the Earl of Halifax. *August* 28.—Sent for by the King. A new scene opened, in consequence of Mr. Pitt's extraordinary terms 97
The Earl of Halifax to Mr. Grenville. *August* 29.—Considers it important that Mr. Grenville should be informed by the King whether Mr. Pitt proposed the extravagant conditions as his own, or whether he was authorized to do so by the Duke of Newcastle 98
Mr. Wilkes to Earl Temple. *August* 29—He is detained in Paris. Notice of Lord Egremont's death. The French Ministry unanimous in praise of Lord Bute. Proceedings of the Parliament of Rouen. France considered to be on the eve of a great Revolution 98
Mr. Elliot to Mr. Grenville. *August* 31.—Lord Bute steady in his purpose of retirement, and in his determination of resigning the Privy Purse 101
The Earl of Sandwich to Mr. Grenville. *August* 31.—Lord Weymouth's visit to Trentham, of a political nature . . 102
Mr. Welbore Ellis to Mr. Grenville. *September* 2.—Offers his services to be at the head of the Admiralty . . . 102
Mr. Grenville to Lord Strange, and the Marquess of Granby. *September* 3.—Full particulars of the late negotiation with Mr. Pitt, and the causes of its failure 104
Mr. Grenville to the Duke of Leeds. *September* 3 . . 107
The Earl of Sandwich to Mr. Grenville. *September* 3.—The Duke of Bedford approves of the present system, and will give it every support in his power 108
Mr. Grenville to the Duke of Bedford. *September* 5.—Hopes that His Grace may be prevailed upon to give his name, as well as his weight and influence, to the support of the King's Government, at the head of his Council 108
Mr. Grenville to the Earl of Egmont. *September* 5 . . 110
The Duke of Bedford to Mr. Grenville. *September* 6 . . 111
Mr. Wilkes to Earl Temple. *September* 6 112
Mr. Horace Walpole to Mr. Grenville. *September* 7.—In favour of Mr. Grosvenor Bedford, Collector of Customs at Philadelphia 113

	Page
Mr. Grenville to Mr. Horace Walpole. *September* 8.—In reply	113
Mr. Grenville to Mr. Welbore Ellis. *September* 8.—Communicates the arrangements which have rendered him unable to execute his wishes with regard to the Admiralty. The King's approbation of his services in his present situation	115
Sir John Phillips to Mr. Grenville. *September* 8.—Thanks for the account of Mr. Pitt's negotiation and its failure. Relates a conversation with the King, at a recent private audience	117
Mr. Charles Townshend to Earl Temple. *September* 11.—Convinced that in the late negotiation, the measure did not break upon a real objection to the extent or nature of the terms and changes suggested by Mr. Pitt. The Duke of Bedford as President of the Council consents unwillingly, hates his Colleagues, and despises the Cabinet	120
Mr. Grenville to Mr. Stuart Mackenzie. *September* 16	122
Mr. Wilkes to Earl Temple. *September* 16.—Encloses some correspondence with Mr. Murray, relating to a challenge he had received from Captain Forbes	124
The Chevalier D'Eon to Mr. Grenville. *September* 19.—Relating to some wine detained at the Custom-House	124
The Earl of Hertford to Mr. Grenville. *September* 20.—M. D'Eon and his wine	125
Mr. Grenville to the Earl of Northumberland. *September* 22.—The King's resolution with regard to grants in Ireland. Meeting of Parliament in November	126
Mr. Wilkes to Earl Temple. *September* 27.—Unhappy in the belief that Lord Temple disapproves of his conduct	129
Earl Temple to Mr. Wilkes. *September* 28	129
Verses by Earl Temple addressed to Mr. Wilkes	130
Mr. Wilkes to Earl Temple. *October* 1	131
Mr. Charles Townshend to Earl Temple. *October* 3.—Political rumours	132
Mr. Grenville to Lord Strange *October* 15.—Requests him to move the vote of censure against Mr. Wilkes, at the ensuing meeting of Parliament	134
Mr. Grenville to the Bishop of Hereford *October* 18.—In reply to the Bishop's desire of being appointed Dean of Windsor in case of a vacancy	136
Mr. Wilkes to Earl Temple. *October* 18.—The approaching Trials against Wood and Webb, for seizure of papers. Governor Johnstone. State of his subscriptions. Wishes to raise 3000*l.* on his estates. Asks the present loan of 400*l.*	137
Sir John Fielding to Mr. Grenville. *October* 19.—Necessity of increasing the number of Horse Patrole	141

Earl Temple to Mr. Wilkes. *October* 20.—Sends a draft for 500*l*.	142
Mr. Charles Townshend to Earl Temple. *October* 21.—Mr. Grenville's account of the late negotiation is illustrated with comments and anecdotes prepared and communicated by the King's order	143
Sir Francis Blake Delaval to Mr. Grenville. *October* 24 .	144
Mr. Grenville to the Marquess of Carnarvan. *October* 25.—Requests that he will move the Address at the ensuing meeting of Parliament	145
Mr. Grenville to the Earl of Northumberland. *October* 28.—The King's opinions and concessions with regard to the Pensions and Grants in Ireland, for lives or years	146
Lord North to the Earl of Halifax. *October* 30.—The enclosure alluded to in the following letter	151
The Earl of Halifax to Mr. Grenville. *October* 31.—Enclosing a letter from Lord North, who expresses unwillingness to be put forward in the measures against Wilkes . . ,	152
Mr. De Grey to Mr. Grenville. *November* 1.—Desires to be appointed Attorney or Solicitor General in the event of a vacancy, occasioned by the resignation of Mr. Yorke . . .	153
The Earl of Sandwich to Mr. Grenville. *November* 5.—Proposed complaint in the House of Lords against Wilkes. Libel on Bishop Warburton. Wilkes has been constantly watched since his return from France. Sends Mr. Grenville the reports made to the Secretary of State, by the persons employed for that purpose, from the 31st of October to the 2nd of November	153
Lord Clive to Mr. Grenville. *November* 7.—Dispute with the East India Company	160
The King to Mr. Grenville. *November* 15.—Suggests a slight alteration in his Speech. Wilkes's impudence is amazing	161
The King to Mr. Grenville. *November* 16.—Debate of yesterday. General Conway's conduct. Proposes instant dismissal .	162
The King to Mr. Grenville. *November* 16.—Thanks for congratulation. Expressions of approbation . . .	162
The King to Mr. Grenville. *November* 18 . . .	163
The King to Mr. Grenville. *November* 18.—The Speaker's illness most unlucky	163
The Earl of Sandwich to Mr. Grenville. *November*.—Mr. Pitt in consultation with Lord Shelburne and Mr. Calcraft .	163
Countess Temple to Earl Temple. *November* 20 . .	164
The King to Mr. Grenville. *November* 23.—Remarks upon the irregularity of the Debate, and the evil of breaking the Orders of the House	165

The King to Mr. Grenville. *November* 24.—Anxious to be informed respecting the Debate of this day 165
The King to Mr. Grenville. *November* 25.—Rejoices at the majority in favour of Ministers.—Proposed dismissal of General Conway, Mr. Fitzherbert, &c. 166
Mr. Grenville to the Earl of Northumberland. *November* 26.— Expresses the confidence reposed by the King and the Ministers in the discretion and wisdom of his Administration in Ireland, and desiring to give him free scope for the public benefit at this conjuncture 166
The Earl of Sandwich to Mr. Grenville. *November* 27.—The Duke of Bedford and the Hessian Protocol 169
Admiral Rodney to Mr. Grenville. *November* 28.—Desires to succeed Admiral Townshend as Governor of Greenwich Hospital, in the event of a vacancy 170
Lord Egmont to Mr. Grenville. *December* 3.—The State of the Navy of England, as compared with that of France. . . 171
General Townshend to Mr. Grenville. *December* 4.—Offers his services in support of order 175
General Conway to Mr. Grenville. *December* 4.—Desires an interview upon a subject in which his honour and character are deeply concerned 176
Mr. Grenville to General Conway. *December* 4.—Appoints a meeting, but requests it may be understood that he has no proposition to make 177
General Conway to Mr. Grenville. *December* 4.—It was in consequence of having received a message by Mr. Walpole that he supposed Mr. Grenville was desirous of seeing him . . 178
Mr. Grenville to General Conway. *December* 4. . . . 179
Lord North to Mr. Grenville. *December* 13. Examination of the Surgeons respecting Mr. Wilkes 180
Lord Clive to Mr. Grenville. *December* 13.—Desires Mr. Grenville's mediation in his dispute with the East India Company. The Company have acquired all their possessions by force of arms.—The ingratitude of the Directors afflicts him more than their injustice 180
Lord Clive to Mr. Grenville. *December* 21.—The same subject . 183
Mr. Wilkes to Earl Temple. *December* 25.—Upon his landing at Calais. He intends returning to England by the 14th of January 185
Mr. Grenville to the Earl of Hertford. *December* 26.—Mr. Bunbury as Secretary of the Embassy.—M. de Guerchy and his wine.—Mr. Wilkes's departure for Paris 186
Earl and Countess Temple to Mr. Horace Walpole. *December* . 189

1763-1764. CONTENTS. xiii

Page

Mr. Grenville's Diary, entitled "Some account of Memorable Transactions since the Death of Lord Egremont." . . 191
Mrs. Grenville's Narrative of Events from November, 1763, to January, 1764 242

1764.

The Earl of Hertford to Mr. Grenville. *January* 4.—General Conway's conduct in Parliament. Mr. Wilkes at Paris: attentions which he considered necessary to show to him . . 247
The Rev. Dr. Francis to Mr. Grenville. *January* .—Expressing obligations for being recommended to the King for a pension of £300 a year 250
Mr. Stuart Mackenzie to Mr. Grenville. *January* 10.—Reception of the Hereditary Prince by the Opposition 251
Mr. Horace Walpole to Countess Temple. *January* .—Opinion of her Poems 252
Mr. Wilkes to Earl Temple. *January* 16.—Anecdote of the Chevalier D'Eon; sends a suppressed pamphlet called the *Anti-Financier* 253
The Rev. Dr. Francis to Mr. Grenville. *January* 19.—Thanks for favours received 254
The King to Mr. Grenville. *January* 20 255
The Earl of Sandwich to Mr. Grenville. *January* 27.—The first Cabinet dinner 256
Mr. Horace Walpole to Countess Temple. *January* 28.—Limited impression of her Poems to be printed at the Strawberry Hill press 256
Mr. Grenville to the Earl of Hertford. *January* 28.—Mr. Bunbury. General Conway's opposition. M. de Guerchy and his wine 257
The Earl of Hertford to Mr. Grenville. *February* 11.—Complains of disrespect shown to him as Ambassador, by the Custom-House Officers 260
The King to Mr. Grenville. *February* 14 261
Mr. Grenville to the King. *February* 15.—Account of the Debate in the House of Commons 261
The Earl of Bath to Mr. Grenville. *February* 16.—Desirous of communicating some scheme 264
Mr. Glover to Mr. Grenville. *February* 16.—Suggestion on Parliamentary tactics 265
Mr. Grenville to the King. *February* 18.—Account of the last night's debate 266
The King to Mr. Grenville. *February* 18 267
Mr. Wilkes to Earl Temple. *February* 25.—Resignation to his fate.

	Page
Determined to make no submission. Employed in writing a Treatise on the English Constitution and Government	267
Memorial to Mr. Grenville in favour of Dr. Shebbeare. *February* 29	270
Lord Clive to Mr. Grenville. *February* 29.—The East India Directors and General Colland	273
The Earl of Northumberland to Mr. Grenville. *March* 2.—His desire of giving the most effectual support to Mr. Grenville's Administration	274
General Townshend to Mr. Grenville. *March* 4.—Advises the offer of a reward from Government for the discovery of the author of a letter relative to Wilkes's jury	277
M. de Guerchy to Mr. Grenville. *March* 6.—Solicits permission to consult the Archives of the Exchequer for documents relating to the History of France	278
Mr. Grenville to the Earl of Mansfield. *March* 7.—Desires to succeed Lord Hardwicke as a Governor of the Charterhouse	279
The Earl of Mansfield to Mr. Grenville. *March* 7	279
The Lord Chancellor to Mr. Grenville. *March* 31	280
Mr. Grenville to the Lord Chancellor. *March* 31.—Upon the question of sending M. D'Eon out of the kingdom	281
The King to Mr. Grenville. *April* 2	284
Mr. Grenville to the King. *April* 2	284
Lord Hyde to Mr. Grenville. *April* 3	285
Mr. Grenville to the King. *April* 4.—On the subject of M. D'Eon	285
Lord Hyde to Mr. Grenville- *April* 8	287
Chevalier D'Eon to Mr. Grenville. *April* 9.—Gratitude for protection from his enemies	288
Lord Hyde to Mr. Grenville. *April* 9.—Affairs of the Post Office. Precedents relating to the case of M. D'Eon	289
Lord Egmont to Mr. Grenville. *April* 16.—State of the Navy	290
The Earl of Mansfield to Mr. Grenville. *April* 16.—Approves of the Draft of the King's Speech	292
Mr. Grenville to the Earl of Egmont. *April* 16.—Expenses of the Navy	293
Countess Temple to Earl Temple. *April* 17	295
Mr. Grenville to the Earl of Hertford. *April* 18. The King's displeasure at General Conway's conduct. His dismission determined upon	296
Countess Temple to Earl Temple. *April* 19	299
Mr. Jenkinson to Mr. Grenville. *April* 21.—General Conway's dismission. Lord Fife, and the Surveyor of the Board of Works	299

Page

The Earl of Sandwich to Mr. Grenville. *April* 23.—The Duke of Bedford requires the Red ribband for Colonel Draper . . 301

Mr. Jenkinson to Mr. Grenville. *April* 23 302

The Duke of Bedford to Mr. Grenville. *April* 25.—Dissatisfaction at the Red ribband having been given to Lord Clive instead of Colonel Draper 303

The Earl of Sandwich to Mr. Grenville. *April* 25.—The Duke of Bedford and the Red ribband.—Suggests that an addition should be made to the Order of the Bath 305

The Earl of Hertford to Mr. Grenville. *April* 26.—Disapproves of General Conway's conduct, but regrets that he should have been treated with such unusual severity 307

Mr. Jenkinson to Mr. Grenville. *May* 1 309

Lord Clive to Mr. Grenville. *May* .—His determination not to return to India without full powers 310

Lord Vere to Mr. Grenville. *May* 3.—Recommends his brother for the Bishopric of London 311

The Bishop of Peterborough to Mr. Grenville. *May* 5.—Upon his translation to the Bishopric of London 312

The Bishop of Gloucester to Mr. Grenville. *May* 5.—Desires to be recommended to the King for the See of London . . 313

Mr. Grenville to the Bishop of Gloucester. *May* 8 . . . 314

Princess Amelia to Countess Temple. *May* 10.—Acknowledges the presentation of her Poems, recently printed at Strawberry Hill 315

The Bishop of Gloucester to Mr. Grenville. *May* 11 . . 316

Countess Temple to the Princess Amelia. *May* 11 . . . 316

Lady Hyde to Mr. Grenville. *May* 14.—Solicits Mr. Grenville to recommend to the King that the Earldom of Clarendon should be conferred upon Lord Hyde 317

Mr. Grenville to Mr. Thomas Pitt. *May* 15.—Defending himself from the report circulated by Mr. Walpole that he had asserted that if General Conway voted in Parliament according to his conscience, he was unfit to have any command in the King's Army 320

Mr. Thomas Pitt to Mr. Grenville. *May* 25.—In reply . . 324

Mr. Cadogan to Mr. Grenville. *May* 25.—The Duke of York finds his income inadequate to his expenses, and is in present want of about 4000*l*. 327

Mr. Grenville to the Duke of York. *May* 25.—The King has ordered the sum of 4000*l*. to be paid to Mr. Cadogan for the use of the Duke 328

Lord Vere to Mr. Grenville. *May* 26.—The Duke of St.

Albans' patent of Hereditary Registrar of the High Court of
Chancery 329
Anonymous to Mr. Grenville. *May* 27.—Upon Dr. Terrick's
promotion to the See of London 330
The Earl of Hertford to Mr. Grenville. *May* 29.—Desires to
be recommended to the King for promotion to the rank of
Marquess 331
Lord Vere to Mr. Grenville. *May* 29.—Upon the subject of
King Charles the Second's grant to the first Duke of St. Albans 332
Countess Temple to Lady Harriet Campbell. *June* .—Sends a
copy of her Poems for the Princess of Hesse . . . 333
The Comte de Guerchy to the Duc de Praslin. *June* 5.—Complains that his "habit de gala," intended to be worn on the
King's birthday, has been detained in the English Custom-house 334
Mr. Horace Walpole to Mr. Thomas Pitt. *June* 5.—Upon the
report of a conversation with Mr. Grenville relative to the
dismission of General Conway 335
The Earl of Sandwich to Mr. Grenville. *June* 6.—Conference
with the French Ambassador on the subject of the payments
for the maintenance of French Prisoners in England . . 344
Mr. Thomas Pitt to Mr. Horace Walpole. *June* 10.—General
Conway and Mr. Grenville 346
Mr. Grenville to the Earl of Hertford. *June* 12.—The King has
no intentions at present of making any promotions from the
Earl's Bench 352
Mr. Grenville to Mr. Thomas Pitt. *June* 19.—Mr. Walpole's
explanation relative to Mr. Grenville and General Conway . 353
Mr. Grenville to the Lord Chancellor. *June* 20.—Relating to the
arrest of the French Ambassador's servant 360
Count Haslang to Mr. Grenville. *June* 22.—The Custom-House
officers have detained his clothes 361
Lady Harriet Campbell to Countess Temple. *June* 23.—Princess Amelia's intention of visiting Stowe on the 23rd of July . 362
Sir John Fielding to Mr. Jenkinson. *June* 26.—Amazing good
effects of the Horse Patrole 363
Countess Temple to Lady Harriet Campbell. *June* 26.—The
Princess Amelia's intended visit to Stowe 364
The King to Mr. Grenville, *June* 26 365
Mr. Grenville to the King. *June* 26.—The arrest of the French
Ambassador's servant 365
Sir John Fielding to Mr. Jenkinson. *June* 28.—Encloses an account of robberies in the fields near Tyburn and Tottenham-
Court Roads 366

Page

Mr. Jenkinson to Mr. Grenville. *June* 28 368
Mr. Whately to Mr. Grenville. *June* 29.—Great fire at Lisbon.
Mr. Pitt at the King's Levée 369
The Earl of Halifax to the Comte de Guerchy. *June* 29.—Commanded by the King to express his regret at the circumstances attending the arrest of his servant 370
The Earl of Sandwich to Mr. Grenville. *June* 30 . . . 371
Mr. Jenkinson to Mr. Grenville. *July* 2.—Important resolutions of the French Government. The Stamp Act. Revenue at Quebec 372
The Earl of Sandwich to Mr. Grenville. *July* 3.—Reports of a change of Administration 376
The Earl of Halifax to Mr. Grenville. *July* 3.—The French Ambassador and his privilege 377
The Lord Chancellor to Mr. Grenville. *July* 3 . . . 378
Mr. Grenville to the Earl of Halifax. *July* 4.—The French Ambassador. The Spanish Government and the Logwood Cutters 379
Mr. Grenville to the Bishop of Gloucester. *July* 5.—Death of Mr. Allen of Prior Park 381
Mr. Jenkinson to Mr. Grenville. *July* 5.—The Sheriff of Banff. Trial of M. D'Eon 382
The Duke of York to Mr. Grenville. *July* 7 384
Mr. Jenkinson to Mr. Grenville. *July* 9.—Lord Warkworth's marriage. Sir John Fielding and the Horse Patrole. Mr. Pitt's reception at the Levée 384
The Earl of Fife to Mr. Grenville. *July* 11.—Appointment of a Sheriff in Banffshire 387
Mr. Stuart Mackenzie to Mr. Grenville. *July* 15 . . . 388
Mr. Grenville to the Earl of Sandwich. *July* 16.—Conference with M. de Guerchy 390
Mr. Grenville to the Earl of Hertford. *July* 20.—Various points of discussion and dispute with the French Ambassador . . 392
The Marquess of Carnarvan to Mr. Grenville. *July* 21.—Resigns his Lord Lieutenancy in consequence of Mr. Stanley being appointed Governor of the Isle of Wight 399
Mr. Grenville to the Marquess of Carnarvan. *July* 22 . . 401
General Conway to the Secretary at War. *July* 22.—Complains of Libels upon him in the printed Papers, which seem to be under the protection of Government 403
Mr. Welbore Ellis to General Conway. *July* .—In reply to the foregoing 405
Account of Princess Amelia's visit to Stowe. *July* 23 . . 406
Mr. Grenville to the Earl of Halifax. *July* 23 . . . 409
The Earl of Halifax to Mr. Grenville. *July* 23.—Letter from

1764.

Page

Lord Hertford to the Duc de Choiseul. Intention of the late French Arrêt 410

The Earl of Hertford to Mr. Grenville. *July* 28.—Conversation with the Comte de Guerchy, and the Duc de Praslin. Necessitous state of the French finances. Desires that Mr. Hume should be Secretary to the Embassy 410

The Earl of Sandwich to Mr. Grenville. *August* 4.—Lord Buckinghamshire having desired his recall, now wishes to prolong his stay at St. Petersburg. Mr. Macartney appointed to succeed him. Lord Hertford's memorial 415

The Earl of Sandwich to Mr. Grenville. *August* 8 . . . 417

The Earl of Halifax to Mr. Grenville. *August* 8.—Interview with M. Blosset respecting the French proposals of payment for the Prisoners. Turk's Island 418

Mr. Grenville to the Earl of Halifax. *August* 9 . . . 422

Mr. Grenville to the Earl of Sandwich. *August* 9 . . . 423

The Duchess of Queensberry to Countess Temple. *August* 13 . 424

Mr. Charles Townshend to Earl Temple. *August* 14.—Sends his Pamphlet : the " Defence of the Minority " . . . 426

Mr. Almon to Earl Temple. *August* 14.—Enclosing several pamphlets lately published. *The North Briton*. Conduct of the Lord Chief Justice and the Juries, on the late Trials . 428

The Earl of Sandwich to Mr. Grenville. *August* 22 . . 431

Mr. Grenville to Mr. Jenkinson. *August* 22 . . . 432

The Earl of Sandwich to Mr. Grenville. *August* 29.—Whether money should be given for the support of what is called our party in Sweden 434

Mr. Grenville to the Earl of Sandwich. *August* 31.—Necessity of immediate measures with regard to the Logwood Cutters. Our Squadron at Jamaica should be reinforced . . 435

The Earl of Halifax to Mr. Grenville. *September* 9.—The French Court promise ample satisfaction for the outrage on Turk's Island 436

Mr. Wilkes to Earl Temple. *September* 9.—Introduces M. de Beaumont, who desires to pay his respects to Lord Temple and Mr. Pitt 437

Mr. Grenville to the Duke of Bedford. *September* 12.—Lord Hertford's despatches. Restitution of Turk's Island . 438

The Lord Chancellor to Mr. Grenville. *September* 18.—Opinion upon the questions pending with the Court of France . . 439

The Earl of Sandwich to Mr. Grenville. *September* 22.—State of the Navy in France and Spain 441

The King to Mr. Grenville. *September* 22 441

Mr. Charles Townshend to Earl Temple. *October* 4.—Hopeless

	Page
state of the Duke of Devonshire. Political consequences which must necessarily ensue upon his death	441
Mr. Charles Townshend to Earl Temple. *October* 6.—Illness of the Duke of Cumberland. Mr. Grenville's opinion of the state of political parties. Mr. Townshend considers that delay and indecision are ruin, and that some resolution should immediately be taken by the Opposition	442
Lord Clive to Mr. Grenville. *October* .—Voyage to India. Rio Janeiro: Description of the fortifications	445
Lord Holland to Mr. Grenville. *October* 14.—Solicits the office of Comptroller of Customs at New York, in favour of Mr. O'Brien, the actor, who had eloped thither with Lord Ilchester's daughter	447
Mr. Morton to Mr. Grenville. *October* 15.—Conversation with one of the leaders of Opposition, who would be inclined under favourable circumstances to discontinue adverse measures, and become a supporter of Government	448
Sir Richard Lyttelton to Mr. Grenville. *October* 15.—Acquittal of Colonel Johnston by the Board of General Officers. Expresses a desire to resign the Government of Minorca	449
Earl Temple to Mons. Michell. *October* 18.—Complimentary, on his return to Prussia, and reception by the King, at Potsdam	450
Mr. Nugent to Mr. Grenville. *October* 20.—Asks that his son may be made Governor of the Castle of St. Mawes. Society at Bath. Duke and Duchess of Bedford. Mr. Prowse, Lord Strange, &c.	452
Mr. Wilkes to Earl Temple. *November* 1.—Resolution of retirement and economy. Intends to devote himself to the compilation of the *History of England* since the Revolution. Churchill and Cotes at Boulogne	454
Mr. Harris to Mr. Grenville. *November* 2.—Recommends Mr. Stuart to succeed Hogarth as Pannel Painter to the King	457
Mr. Almon to Earl Temple. *November* 12.—A weekly paper to be established by the Opposition. Horace Walpole. General Conway. The Minority and the Lord Mayor's feast. Death of Churchill. Mr. Legge's papers on the Hampshire Election	457
Mr. Whately to Mr. Grenville. *November* 14	460
Memorandum by Mr. Grenville relating to a negotiation with Mr. Charles Yorke. *November* 14	461
Mr. Grenville to the Lord Chancellor. *November* 16	462
The Lord Chancellor to Mr. Grenville. *November* 16.—The King's early yet sound judgment. Conversation with Mr. Charles Yorke	463

CONTENTS. 1764.

Page

The Lord Chancellor to Mr. Grenville. *November* 19.—Another conference with Mr. Yorke 464
Dr. Hay to Mr. Grenville. *November* 19 464
Mr. Jenkinson to Mr. Grenville. *November* 20.—Mr. Charles Townshend's political conversation and intentions . . . 465
The Earl of Sandwich to Mr. Grenville. *November* 23.—Encloses a letter from Lord Townshend on his attachment to the Government 466
The Lord Chancellor to Mr. Grenville. *November* 26.—Relating to Mr. Charles Yorke, and the patent of Precedency to be granted to him 467
Mr. Grenville to the Lord Chancellor. *November* 26.—Mr. Charles Yorke 469
Mr. De Grey (Solicitor-General) to Mr. Grenville. *November* 30. —On the late appointment of the Master of the Rolls . . 471
Mr. Grenville to Mr. De Grey. *November* 30 472
The Reverend Dr. Markham to Mr. Grenville. *December* 4.— Respecting the Deanery of Rochester, which was promised to him in the event of a vacancy 474
The Lord Chancellor to Mr. Grenville. *December* 14 . . 476
Earl Temple to Mr. Wilkes. *December* 21 · . . . 476
The Earl of Mansfield to Mr. Grenville. *December* 24.—On the report of a Civil Government and Judge being sent to Canada . 476
The Earl of Sandwich to Mr. Grenville. *December* 27.—The Duke of Bedford's strong objection to the appointment of Bishop Robinson to the Primacy of Ireland. The Duke of Grafton and the Thetford Election 479
Mr. Grenville's Diary of Memorable Transactions (continued from page 242) 481

CORRIGENDA.

VOL. II.

Page 24, line 13, *for* 1782 *read* 1762.
„ 44, line 21, *for* amis *read* ami.
„ 125, line 5, *for* supplié *read* supplie.
„ 166, line 16, *for* Nothumberland *read* Northumberland.
„ 176, line 19, *for* partiality *read* impartiality.
„ 262, note [2], *for* Lord William *read* Lord Frederick.
„ 265, note [1], *for* one side *read* our side.

THE GRENVILLE PAPERS.

THE RIGHT HON. HENRY FOX TO MR. GRENVILLE.

November 11, 1762.

DEAR SIR,—The important question you asked yesterday was not, as I heard, resolved; and if so, Sir Charles Hardy must set out under the orders you mentioned.

Should the expedition from Brest set out after the Preliminaries were known to have been signed, Lord Mansfield rightly said, it would be insidious, and no matter how ill they were treated. But should Sir Charles Hardy, setting out after we know the Preliminaries are signed, intercept Mons. de Blenac, what would our conduct be esteemed, and how much must we regret, and how would His Majesty blame us, for the loss of what lives should, in such a case, be destroyed on either side.

Your own sense of the importance of this consideration will excuse my putting you in mind of it. I am, dear Sir, yours ever, H. Fox.

MR. GRENVILLE TO MR. FOX.

Admiralty Office, November 11, 1762.

SIR,—I return you my thanks for the honour of your letter, which I received this morning. The subject of it is, as you truly observe, very important, and for that reason I so earnestly press to have the opinions of the King's servants upon it, that I might lay them before His Majesty. Some of them gave their advice openly whilst you was there, and I asked many of the others separately, and found that all those whose sentiments I could collect, agreed in advising that Sir Charles Hardy's squadron should go to sea, agreeably to the former orders. Lord Bute, to whom I likewise spoke, told me that, as he saw what the opinion of the Council was, he thought it necessary for me to go to the King and inform His Majesty of it immediately, that no time might be lost; which I did accordingly, and received his directions to recall the order by which they were to be stopped, and to let them proceed in pursuance of their former instructions. I obeyed those directions last night, and consequently the question is now determined, and I hope very properly, as we could not leave a French squadron at sea in the Channel with all our trade coming home, and liable to be captured, by the very words and intention of the Preliminary Articles, with a superior force of our own lying in harbour. As for Monsr. de Blenac, Sir Charles Hardy's squadron is too much superior to his to admit of a combat if they had met; which, however, is at present out of the question, as by letters received to-day from Sir Charles Hardy, it appears that M. Blenac, with his five ships of the line, got into Brest, since our squadron was obliged to leave the coast of France.

I cannot help observing to you that, by the Preliminary Articles, hostilities are to cease *after the ratification of the Preliminaries*, which the Council were yesterday unanimously of opinion must be construed *after the exchange of the ratifications;* and consequently, until it is signified to us from the Secretary of State, by the King's command, the Board of Admiralty cannot take any notice of them, or put a stop to hostilities at sea.

I am, with great regard, &c., &c.

GEORGE GRENVILLE.

EARL TEMPLE TO MR. WILKES.

Stowe, November 13, 1762.

WHAT shall I say to my dear Colonel from these regions of solitude, and profound ignorance of what is transacting and to be transacted in the gloomy regions of town? Is it all pitiful submission, or is there a spark of real spirit and virtue left in this country?

With what face can the patrons of the Auditor and of the Briton seize and confine the Monitors? Monitoribus asper! the contents of your letter do not please me; I must think it is impossible to happen, if anything is impossible in these times.

I beg you to weigh your own conduct very maturely. You have to deal with a very strange world. I may possibly hear again from you soon. My hands are almost frozen, as I am just returned from riding, but my heart dictates to me that I am warmly, my dear Colonel's most faithful and obedient TEMPLE.

EARL TEMPLE TO MR. WILKES.

Stowe, Sunday night, November 21, 1762.

I SET pen to paper again, my dear Marcus Cato, to converse with you for a few moments, and to condole with you that a fresh fit of the gout has seized Mr. Pitt.

I received a letter from him this evening, in which he laments his situation, and the unrelenting persecution of that cruel enemy. He was in town, it seems, on Wednesday; but your intelligence concerning the interview I should think not well founded, as he does not in the least glance at it.

I find they have been industriously circulating that he approves of the Peace, which is a d——d l—.

I cannot sufficiently admire the North B——[1] of this week: it is unanswerable, as it is founded in stubborn facts, which cannot be controverted, and they are ably, concisely, and most forcibly put together. If the storm rises, I quit Stowe and leave my Abele walk more than half cut down; the finest alteration I ever made. I find by the public papers, and servants' intelligence, that Lord Lincoln[2] has resigned; the enclosed is a letter of warm and most cordial congratulations, which, if the account of his resignation be true, I will beg you to send him, if not, please to return it me, when next you write. Jemmy is here, and all Stowe salute you with the highest applause, affection, and esteem. Adieu, good night, the curtain drops, and I am going to sleep.

MR. WILKES TO EARL TEMPLE.

Great George Street, Tuesday, November 23, 1762.

MY LORD,—Yesterday was a white day in my calendar, for it brought me the happiness of two letters from Stowe. The letter enclosed I sent.

[1] The *North Briton*, No. 25. It contains an elaborate defence of Mr. Pitt's war policy.

[2] He resigned his place as a Lord of the Bedchamber. He held the lucrative office of Auditor of the Exchequer *for life*.

We are all most impatient for your Lordship's arrival in town; and my Lord Mayor desires me to transmit to you the warmest wishes of the few upright in Israel. The scene is amazingly changed, and I think, tho' the fog is so thick, the prospect clears up in a surprising manner. I have but a moment to say how important we all think it to the common cause to have Lord Temple soon among us. I am, my Lord, &c., &c.

JOHN WILKES.

Lord Litchfield came to me at Court last Sunday, and entered into a good deal of chat in his usual easy manner.

Mr. Hogarth is said to be dying, and of a broken heart. It grieves me much. He says that he believes I wrote that paper[1], but he forgives me, for he must own I am a thorough good-humoured fellow, only *Pitt-bitten.*

EARL TEMPLE TO MR. WILKES.

Stowe, November 25, 1762.

MY DEAR COLONEL,—Since you give so kind a denomination to the days that bring you the trouble of my correspondence, even when the letters are doubled upon you, Friday shall not pass without your receiving this, and in it some observations, some Q.

First, then, let me remark what a pitiful appearance our grand administration makes at the outset, in not being able to find, by way of decoration, any better tools, wretched indeed, than the wooden Lord Carysfort[2], and

---

[1] The *North Briton*, No. 17. On the publication of Hogarth's print called the *Times*. Hogarth did not die, however, until 1764.

[2] John Proby, first Lord Carysfort. The Address was moved by him, and seconded by Lord Charles Spencer, not by Sir John Phillips.

that quintessence of dulness, Sir J. P.; which shall I admire most, his dulness, or the infamy of standing out foremost in the support of B——, and called to it by F—x? *Proh pudor!*

In the House of Lords it seems Lord Egmont[1] leads the dance; the man, in all the creation, once most detested by Leicester House—more detested, if possible, than Fox himself. The Earl of N[2]. condescends to be Chamberlain to the Queen, when his name had been upon the honourable list of resigners. The Duke of M.[3] to cover an infamous conclusion of a war more glorious than than that which was so *feloniously* disgraced by the Treaty of Utrecht.

The liberty of the Press most signally attacked in the case of the Monitors, by way of sample for all the popular acts of B—— ministry, when the *talons* are full grown.

Now Q., what number of persons, and what great names of the House of Commons attended Mr. Fox at the private meeting on Tuesday? Was Mr. Yorke there? Did Lord Barrington wait upon Mr. Paymaster? What appearance was there at the Cockpit? How many Peers did homage to Lord Bute at his house last night? Of what remarkable great men did that meeting consist? Have Beckford, Gascoyne[4], yourself, and many others thundered in the Capitol? Is the

---

[1] John Perceval, second Earl of Egmont, in the peerage of Ireland, and first Baron Lovel and Holland in the English peerage. His son was the Prime Minister Spencer Perceval.

[2] Hugh Smithson, Earl of Northumberland. He was created Duke of Northumberland in 1766, and died in 1786.

[3] The Duke of Marlborough was made Lord Chamberlain.

[4] Bamber Gascoyne, M.P. for Malden. He had declined an offer of a place at the Board of Trade, and attached himself to Mr. Pitt. He was subsequently a Lord of the Admiralty, and died in 1791.

voice of your thunder gone forth into all parts? How passed it in our virtuous house? Answer me these questions satisfactorily, and renew the orders of *real* friends for me to come up, and however contrary it may be to plan, and to opinion, and to inclination, yet I am not that presumptuous kind of personage as not to yield to real friends.

Mr. Pitt lies now in bed, tortured with a most violent fit of the gout; God knows when it will end; when it begins so early in the winter, it generally lasts very long.

I hear they talk of 50 in our house, 150 in yours, men of spirit: how many of the neuter gender, and what majority is depended upon, I hear not.

Why stop the resignations? How fares it with his Grace of Rutland? I don't wonder Lord Litchfield should talk with you so easily. I thought it impossible he could take that matter up in our house, and surely his present conduct is more wise, and I think superior. Thus have I poured forth rudis indigestaque moles, having an opportunity of conversing with you in private by means of my servant who carries this to town. All Stowe are much yours, and most particularly your affectionately devoted   TEMPLE.

What says the Body of *your friends*, the Torys?

EARL TEMPLE TO MR. WILKES.

Stowe, November 28, 1762.

I AM very thankful to my dear Senator, for I write to you in all capacities, when I reflect upon your goodness in sparing so much time as was requisite to give me a very complete idea of the humours of St. Stephen's Chapel. I honour and admire Beckford as much as I think the great Charles (a North Briton, perhaps a North British, hero) derogated from every principle of policy but that of downright submission. Sir John is again grown, in my opinion, a man of some parts, and even vivacity, from not seconding the motion, as Lord Vere, Lord Charles Spencer's father-in-law, informed us he was to do, so lately as by Tuesday's post: from which I collect that some sudden alteration must have been made.

I am astonished to find the Preliminaries are only to be laid in *due time*, not *forthwith*, before Parliament. I wonder this *equitable, glorious, and lasting Peace* should be as yet ashamed to show its head. I remember the famous or infamous Convention was just as modest, and puffed to be just as excellent.

I could make several observations upon this speech, but will reserve them to breathe the air of London. I fear if you was to show your face in Edinburgh you would not be much better received than His Majesty of the Isle of Bute in the streets of London, so I wonder not at your having a fellow feeling. I know this letter is to be read before it gets into your hands; if my sentiments are worth knowing, I think them not worth concealing, and so let them please themselves, whilst I please myself with repeating assurances to you that I am most affectionately yours, &c., &c. T.

Not one voice of the N. party to echo Mr. B———'s expression of infamous ——— ? After all, I am not much in the wrong to stay in the country.

ADMIRAL RODNEY TO MR. GRENVILLE.

Martinique, December 4, 1762.

DEAR SIR,—Yesterday a vessel from Cork brought me the very agreeable news of your being appointed First Lord of the Admiralty. Among the many congratulations you will receive on this occasion, I am sure the friendship you have long honoured me with will induce you to believe none are more sincere than mine, being convinced the public will find integrity and justice preside at the head of naval affairs; and I have at the same time the satisfaction of knowing His Majesty has been most graciously pleased to bestow on my particular friend so great and honourable an employment.

Whether you still continue Secretary of State, or removed to the Admiralty, I flatter myself you will take it as a mark of my regard, if I endeavour, in the best manner I am able, to lay before you the state of affairs in this part of the world, and to make you perfectly master of the situation of the principal islands, and their utility in regard to a future war.

Your own goodness of heart in the perusal will cause you to reflect, that 't is the plain narrative of a seaman who endeavours to give the best intelligence he can to a Minister and a friend: happy if his account can point out anything advantageous to his King or country.

The Caribbee Islands from Grenada, the southernmost, to Anigada, the northernmost, form a very extensive chain, and require many more ships and small armed vessels to protect them in time of war, than if they were fewer and larger. They extend from the latitude of twelve degrees to the latitude of nineteen degrees north; they lay in the form of a crescent; its arch to windward, the centre of which is Martinique; which gives it this very great advantage over all the other islands, that, being the weathermost, it can attack them with more facility than it can possibly be attacked, the wind blowing perpetually from the East, and the almost constant lee currents rendering it extremely difficult to get to windward in these seas.

This happy situation, its numerous harbours, safe roads, and fertility of soil, gives it the preference of all the other islands: it has four harbours capable to receive the largest ships of war. Fort Royal and Sac Marine to leeward, Trinity and Sac Robert to windward, besides many small harbours, and the great Bay before the town of St. Peter's, the present seat of commerce.

Many of the principal gentlemen from the English Islands have had the curiosity to visit it; from them I learn that, if inhabited by old British subjects, in a very few years it would produce two hundred thousand hogsheads of sugar; the late Intendant of this island likewise acquainted me that during his Administration it had one year produced one hundred thousand; and as the French are far behind the English in the art of agriculture, if His Majesty should retain this island at the Peace, there would soon be a very surprising increase in its productions, seventy thousand negroes being wanted for cultivation, with which the island would be almost instantly supplied from Barbadoes, and our other islands. The eagerness and strong inclination of almost all the principal inhabitants of the British Islands to purchase estates and settle here, is scarce to be credited; they all look upon the retention of Martinique as their only security in case of a future war.

The next island to the northward and to leeward withal is Dominique, seven leagues' distance. It is a continued range of mountains, which cause an almost perpetual rain, is extremely unhealthy, as our troops which took possession thereof too fatally experienced. It has no harbour, and but one good bay, called Prince Rupert's, where His Majesty's ships employed in these seas used to wood and water at. From its vicinity to Martinique and Guadaloupe, it would be impossible to induce any people to settle it but them who were left in possession of one or other of those large islands.

About north-west from Dominique, at ten leagues' distance, and to leeward, is the island of Guadaloupe, which some self-interested merchants who have hired estates in the said island, and are in hopes of possessing, should it be ceded at the Peace, have laboured to represent as more advantageous to Great Britain than Martinique; but the very article of its being to leeward, and the island extending in length from the north-east to the south-west, and the trade wind constantly blowing from the east, causes such a sea upon the shore, as to make its principal place of commerce a dangerous and open road; whereas the more happy situation of Martinique, which extends from the north-west to the south-east, has a smooth sea on its shore for near sixty miles, the length of the island.

Guadaloupe has one good harbour, called Point Peter, capable of receiving the largest ships of war, but unfortunately is situated to leeward of a continued and very extensive range of swampy land, which must ever cause it to be extremely unhealthy; whereas the carènage at Fort Royal, in Martinique, is to windward of the swampy ground, and never receives any bad effects from it, but during the hurricane months : the swamp itself is but a few acres, and, in any other hands but the French, would long since have been made as healthy a spot as any in the island.

From the observations I made sailing round Guadaloupe, I judge that Island and Grand Terre to be equal in bigness to Martinique. From its having been conquered upwards of three years (in which time forty thousand negroes have been imported), its production must have been very much increased. It is certainly a very fine island, extremely fruitful, and still capable of great improvements; has no one advantage over Martinique, but that of having sooner submitted to His Majesty's arms, and thereby enjoyed the benefits of commerce and importation of negroes to improve their estates; while, on the other hand, the inhabitants of Martinique have been kept in a perpetual alarm, their slaves taken from the cultivation of their land to be employed on the fortifications, and themselves obliged to assemble in arms, dreading and expecting the fatal attack. This makes it impossible as yet to make any just calculation of the difference of produce between the two islands, either of which are far superior to all the English islands united.

I beg you will not impute my seeming partiality to Martinique as being partly a child of my own. I should look upon myself as infamous, should I attempt to deceive a Minister, who must be supposed to form his conceptions of places from accounts transmitted him, from those best acquainted therewith; you will please to take notice that I speak throughout this as an officer of the Marine on the spot, who has had time to make his observations on the very great advantage accruing to a maritime power, from being in possession of a weathermost island in these seas. A late instance is a sufficient proof of the importance of such a situation: the rendezvous for the fleet and army, destined for the attack of Martinique, was first ordered at Guadaloupe. Had so fatal an order taken place, Martinique had never been conquered, as it would have been impossible for so great an armament to have turned to windward in these seas, against the wind and currents, part of the few troops that were sent from Guadaloupe having been drove to leeward as far as St. Christopher's.

Immediately on my arrival at Barbadoes (being made acquainted with Sir Jeffry Amherst's intention of sending the troops from America to Guadaloupe, and foreseeing the fatal consequences of such a rendezvous) I instantly despatched a number of frigates with the most positive orders to the Commanding Officer of the Convoy, to join me with the troops at Barbadoes, notwithstanding any former orders he might have received; the consequence of which was that all the fleet and army were assembled to windward, and were thereby enabled to put His Majesty's commands in execution.

Next to Guadaloupe, to the north-westward and to leeward, at about twelve leagues' distance, lie what are called His Majesty's Leeward Islands; Antigua. Monserrat, Nevis, St. Christopher's, and a cluster of islands called the Virgins. The principals islands have been entirely cleared of wood for many years, and cultivation carried to its greatest extent throughout the whole. I cannot help owning to you my astonishment, when (according to my duty) I visited them, to find how very insignificant they appeared to me in comparison to the French islands, the whole united not being near equal in bigness to Guadaloupe or Martinique; but I was more surprised to observe their defenceless condition, and the almost impossibility of making them otherwise than an easy prey to an enemy who might happen to be superior at sea in this part of the world; no strong forts, no redoubts, no difficult passes to dispute with an enemy, and only a number of sea batteries calculated to keep off privateers from plundering, and to deceive the inhabitants themselves in case of a real attack, whereon little or no resistance could be made, as all the islands abound in many safe and good landing places; and the country being entirely open, renders it an easier prey to an active enemy, who might sweep the whole, and retire with its plunder, before the news of such an attack could possibly reach Europe.

You will please to take notice, my dear Sir, that I do not speak of the present time, when His Majesty's arms are triumphant in these seas, and in possession of the enemy's capital island, but only point out what may be the consequences at the beginning of a future war, should the French be then in possession of Martinique, Guadaloupe, and have a superior squadron in these seas, which, notwithstanding the vigilance of the best Administration, may happen to be the case, as a squadron from Brest may have done all the mischief before a superior one could arrive from England, unless the certain destination of such a squadron should be known, the difficulty of which you are best acquainted with.

As I have given you the best description in my power of the Islands to the northward of Martinique, I shall now proceed to describe those to the southward 'till I end at Grenada, the extremity of His Majesty's empire in these seas.

South of Martinique, at seven leagues' distance, is the Island of St. Lucia; it has several good ports and safe roads for shipping; it extends from the north-north-east to the south-south-west, about forty-five miles in length, twelve or fourteen miles in breadth; its inhabitants of all sorts (when taken) were computed at one thousand; it is as yet very little cleared, which makes it subject to much rain, is reckoned very fruitful, and capable of the same productions as the other islands; but what makes its chief value is its excellent harbour called the Little Carènage, a draught of which I transmitted at the conquest to Lord Anson; it is one of the best in the West Indies, on the lee side of the Island, and impossible to be attacked by shipping if fortified. It will receive ships of war of the greatest draught of water, having seven fathom close to its shore, and a Cove wherein a first-rate may be careened, but 'till the adjacent country be cleared of wood, it must, like all the other places in the West Indies, be unhealthy.

The French were so sensible of the utility of this harbour, that immediately on receiving information of Mr. Boscawen taking the *Alcide* and *Lys*, Mr. Bompart, then Governor of this Island, took possession thereof, and caused it to be fortified, going himself to see his orders put into execution, and at the same time gave notice to the Governor of Barbadoes and the Leeward Islands, that he had so done. The fortifications still remain, upwards of thirty pieces of heavy cannon mounted thereon, and might have given us much trouble could the enemy have afforded troops for the defence; at present all the cannon are spiked, as no garrison has as yet been settled in the Island.

The chief motive for the eagerness of the French to possess this island, proceeds from its vicinity to Martinique, and the excellence of the aforementioned port: should they be possessed of both islands, they would deprive England of every harbour in these seas capable of giving annoyance. This Island alone being the greatest check upon the French, should they ever repossess Martinique, it being in sight of the Bay of Fort Royal, and only a few hours' sail distance; next to the possession of Martinique, this Island will certainly be of the greatest consequence to a Maritime Power.

South-west of St. Lucia, at nine leagues' distance to leeward, lies the Island of St. Vincent, about forty miles in length, and twelve in breath; it extends from the north-east to the south-west, is a mountainous island, extremely fruitful, and abounds in rivers of excellent water; it has no harbours, but several good bays capable of receiving ships of the greatest burthen. This island affords a striking instance of the dependence to be laid on French Treaties; for notwithstanding they were obliged by the last Treaty of Peace to withdraw their subjects from the neutral Islands, and pretended they had given instructions accordingly, yet, nevertheless, they not only encouraged their subjects to settle upon this island, but a Governor and proper Magistrates for each district were commissioned, and acted by authority of the French General of Martinique; whereby the island is become very opulent, produces great quantities of cocoa, coffee, and cotton (the French having wisely prohibited their planting any sugar), has about two thousand inhabitants, exclusive of the Indians, who amount to near the same number, and inhabit the weather side of the island. This island in the whole is reckoned as wholesome and fruitful as any of the Caribbees.

South-west from St. Vincent's, about twenty-five or twenty-six leagues' distance, is the Island of Grenada, between which are a chain of islands called the Grenadillos, some of which are inhabited.

The Island of Grenada is as large as Barbadoes, about thirty miles long, and of an unequal breadth; it extends north-east and south-west, its harbour, called the Carènage, is to leeward, and, though small, capable to receive ships of the greatest draught of water. The island itself is mountainous; and from the quantity of wood still remaining thereon, is subject to much rain, which occasions its being so extremely sickly, as to be proverbial among the other islands: the effect must cease with the cause, and when cleared of wood, be as healthy as the others: it is reckoned the most fruitful among all the Caribbees, and produces the best and finest sugars: as yet 't is but very indifferently peopled with whites: its situation makes it the key to that part of the Spanish Main called the Caraccas, all ships bound to Cumana, Laguira, Porto Cavallo, or other places on that coast, being obliged to pass in sight of this island; but, from its situation being seventy leagues to leeward of Martinique, it can never be a proper place for the rendezvous of His Majesty's ships in these seas during a French war, it being reckoned a remarkable good passage for a clean frigate to beat up from thence to Martinique in ten days, and then provided the currents are not strong to leeward. There are other harbours in this island which I shall cause to be surveyed.

Thus, Sir, I have endeavoured to give you an insight

into His Majesty's Islands in these seas, and if I have forebore mentioning the Island of Barbuda to the northward of Antigua, and Deseada, Marigalante, and the Saints in the neighbourhood of Guadaloupe, it is because they are of little consequence, the first belonging to Sir William Codrington, and only proper for cattle; the others small, and appendages on Guadaloupe.

Thirty leagues to windward of this chain of islands is Barbadoes, the weathermost of all the West India Islands; has been many years entirely cleared, and fully planted. Its inhabitants are more numerous than all the other islands, and are at an extraordinary expense in raising their sugars, the whole being the produce of the dung made by their cattle; the natural earth of the island, being very near the rock, has long since been worn out, and from the great expense attending cultivation, there is scarce an estate throughout the whole island unincumbered with debts. Its inhabitants are eager to possess, and would soon settle a new colony.

About forty leagues to the southward of Barbadoes, between the latitude of eleven and twelve degrees north, lies the Island of Tobago, extending from the north-east to the south-west, forty miles in length, and about ten in breadth.

This island is entirely overrun with wood, and unsettled. On my arrival in these seas, I caused it to be taken possession of, in His Majesty's name: it has many good anchoring places, and well watered; the land in general mountainous: its situation makes it of consequence, being a weathermost island situated near the Island of Trinidada and the Spanish Main, and is the first land made by the Spanish ships coming from Europe, who are bound to the coast of Caraccas: it is the place, likewise, from whence the inhabitants of Barbadoes are supplied with mill timber, and, in any other hands but the English, would be of infinite detriment to that island.

A squadron cruizing off Tobago, and another off Porto Rico, must of course intercept all vessels whatever bound to any part of the West Indies.

Thus, Sir, I have taken the liberty to explain as well as I am able the situation of the islands in these seas, and have ventured to give you my present opinion thereon; but whatever measures His Majesty and the Administration may think proper to take on restoring peace to Europe, my inclination as well as duty will always lead me to submit with humility, and support those measures with my voice in Parliament.

I must now beg, Sir, you will cast an eye on the small force I command in these seas, far inadequate to the protection of the great extent of Islands committed to my charge.

I flattered myself, when the expedition was ended at the Havannah, and a certainty of the French squadron returning from St. Domingo to Europe, that seven or eight sail of the line might have been ordered to join me from Sir George Pocock's fleet, but a small frigate dispatched to me by him, after a passage of two months, has deprived me of any hopes of a reinforcement from that quarter.

The necessity of a strong squadron being in these seas during the continuance of the war, I am sure will appear to you highly necessary, when you reflect on the situation of those islands, being the frontier of all the West Indies, and if attacked from Europe, cannot possibly receive in time any succours from Jamaica; whereas a strong squadron in these seas can always afford a speedy succour to any island to leeward, attacked by an enemy who may have passed these seas, as all armaments whatever from Europe are obliged to do. The smallness of the garrison in this island reduced by sickness, and the nature of the French inhabitants, are uneasy under any government but their own, and who, notwithstanding the vigilance of the few frigates remaining under my command, still carry on a correspondence with the enemy's privateers.

A few days since, one of them landed a party of men, and repaired to the house of a principal inhabitant of the island, where he was entertained at dinner, and remained several hours, though the said inhabitant was one of the Council, and might have acquainted me in two hours of the enemy's being landed, yet he delayed the intelligence 'till the next morning, by which time the privateer and all the crew were in my power, having been taken by one of the vessels under my command, and am determined they shall never have it in their power to land again during this war on Martinique, having given directions (since my command in these seas) never to exchange any men belonging to the French privateers, but to send them prisoners to England, which I hope in time will entirely clear these seas of such vermin.

I wish I could say my health was established, but for some time since the climate has continued to disagree with me; but, however, if my endeavours to do the duty of my station meet with the approbation of His Majesty and the Administration, I shall think myself extremely happy.

You will do me but justice in believing me to be, with the utmost sincerity and respect, &c., &c.

G. B. RODNEY.

COUNTESS TEMPLE TO EARL TEMPLE.

December 17, (1762.)

THE Parliament does not meet till the 20th of January, and I desire you will send the post-chaise for me to be at Stowe the Tuesday after Christmas-day. I really do not like to be so long without you; this is no grimace, for indeed it is not pleasant. There have been this day several coming in and turning out; three have kissed hands, and the places are all to be filled up in a moment. It is believed, and given out, that even to a hundredth cousin of those that have not behaved well are to march out of the most trifling places; it is well if our two window-peepers won't be called upon.

Mr. Ellis is Secretary at War; Mr. Rigby, Treasurer of Ireland; Lord Charles Spencer is Outranger of Windsor Forest with something else, that comes in for twelve hundred per annum.

My Lord and Lady Vere mighty uppish; some sarcasms thrown at my head, and Mr. Brand came in for a snub pretty often, because he did not entirely agree with them. My Lord Vere thinks it perfectly right that they should take away the smallest place, and make a thorough clearing, for it was always done in all Ministrys: Lord George[1] and Mr. Brand denied it, and said it was impolitic and foolish to go so far as those trifling places, it would raise a flame for nothing; Lord Vere said the Duke of Newcastle did it; they both answered it

[1] Lord George Sackville.

was no such thing. I find there are people that think if Mr. Pitt had not said he was a single man, Charles Townshend, cum multis aliis, would never have voted for the Peace, and that it was impolitic to make that declaration when there was no occasion for it. Cunningham[1] will come to you to dinner Monday or Tuesday.

Mrs. Ryde was here yesterday, she is acquainted with a brother of one of the yeomen of the guard, and he tells her the King cannot live without my Lord Bute ; if he goes out anywhere, he stops when he comes back to ask of the yeomen of the guard if my Lord Bute is come yet, and that his lords, or people that are with him, look as mad as can be at it. The mob have a good story of the Duke of Devonshire[2], that he went first to light the King, and the King followed leaning upon Lord Bute's shoulder, upon which the Duke of Devonshire turned about and desired to know which he was waiting upon. I really believe you will see a great flame rise soon, for certainly there is a general discontent, notwithstanding all the places and money they have given away. Adieu, my dearest Lord.

EARL TEMPLE TO MR. WILKES.

Stowe, December 26, 1762.

Many thanks to my dear Colonel for his kind correspondence, which has only the ill effect of making me pass my time more agreeably in the country; in all other respects it is most laud*able*, charit*able*, and ami*able*.

[1] Colonel James Cunningham, afterwards Adjutant General of Ireland. See *Junius*, Letter xl.
[2] At this time Lord Chamberlain.

I had a letter the other day from a person, to inform me that the exchange made with Sir Richard Lyttelton, had been conducted with all gracious*ness*, kind*ness*, and friendli*ness*, that is omne quod exit in ess, you see I am endeavouring all I can to accommodate myself to the Court style, but I fear I am too old and too wrongheaded to succeed, and may probably step into my grave before I have learnt the modern A B C.

Our Militia is disembodyed somewhat irregularly, owing to a mistake in Major Lowndes, founded, as it might well be, in some words of Mr. Ellis's order from the War Office, not very clear, and very likely to mislead.

In short I received the King's orders for that purpose by Friday night's post, and sent directions early yesterday morning accordingly, when my servant met Major Lowndes returning to Winslow, not re infectâ, but factâ, this is a small slip, but of no consequence; by the order from the War Office the men are to keep their clothes. I suppose the commanding officer will have writ to you upon this subject at large, and therefore I quit it.

All accounts both from town and country agree, that the popular detestation does but increase, far from diminishing, in consequence of the *incorrupt* testimony of both Houses. For my own part, if I was the only man in both Houses of Parliament who would never countenance or assist in laying such ignominious fetters upon my country, I should be but the more proud, and never less alone than when alone.

You see I have not made good use of my time in town, and as to my discretion, who would make such a declaration in black and white, and call in for witnesses the Clerks of the Post Office?

I admire the silence of the City of London, that

sweet nightingale who has lost her voice, but who was ready to have sung such a ditty in the Grand Signor's ears as would have resounded to their immortal honour in every part of the kingdom: why this did not happen early may with propriety be asked of somebody.

I believe the Gentleman you mention, as well as other of your true friends, does wish you at—the Devil.

I hear with pleasure various testimonies concerning the great credit you have gained, and there is no note that sounds more sweetly in the ear of your affectionate friend and humble Servant, T.

EARL TEMPLE TO MR. WILKES [1].

———, (1782.)

THE Two Butterflies, by a Lady, is exceedingly beautiful; we dare to lay it at Churchill's door, which is panegyric indeed, but if mistaken conceal the suspicion. I like much better that living immortality which your friend will bestow upon you, than that sort which the Bagshot pistol might have provided for you; but it has likewise given you its share of living immortality. We mean that the Butterflies is the production of one of the Archbishop of Canterbury's fine women. I am scarce awake, so excuse incoherence.

ADMIRAL RODNEY TO MR. GRENVILLE.

Martinique, February 1, 1763.

DEAR SIR,—I have been favoured with your letter by Mr. Kendall, and am happy that I could so soon

[1] This letter is not dated; but was evidently written soon after the duel between Wilkes and Lord Talbot. Of the Poem to which it alludes, or of the *fine woman* supposed to be the author of it, I have no information.

obey your commands; the *Lynx* coming here without a Lieutenant gave me an opportunity of providing for him, which I hope will meet with your approbation.

Was it fair to appoint a Captain in the room of Rear Admiral Swanton? A Captain promoted to the rank of Admiral in foreign parts has always, since I have been at sea, been looked upon as a fair vacancy. I remember at Lisbon, when Sir Tankred Robinson was promoted to a Rear Admiral, Sir John Norris filled up the vacancy; the same was done under Mr. Matthews in the Mediterranean, when Sir William Rowley was promoted, and in this climate, 't is a sad disappointment to the Admirals' Lieutenants, but I am sure 't is owing to the critical time that occasioned its being done now, and I shall always submit with pleasure to your decisions.

Could I have conceived that the time of signing the Preliminaries had been so near, I would not have troubled you with my description of the Leeward Islands, but would have reserved my information till I had the honour of seeing you, and since the affair was ended before you could possibly be justly informed, I shall endeavour all in my power to supply you with arguments in favour of keeping Dominique in preference to Saint Lucia, at least such as seem most interesting in this part of the world, and which I find to be the constant topic of conversation among the French, who alledge that England's being in possession of Dominique, will be of infinite detriment to Martinique and Guadaloupe, as it will cut off their communication in war, and carry on a very large clandestine trade with the said Islands in peace, by supplying them with India goods, Negroes, and provisions at a much cheaper rate than the Dutch from

Eustatia, the former island being only two or three hours' sail distance, and the Dutch Island far to leeward; that notwithstanding people will be unwilling to turn planters in Dominique, yet many merchants will be induced to settle thereon, in hopes of smuggling the produce of the French Island, by which means the French King will lose their duties, and the nation the benefit of carriage; how far this sort of trade may be thought proper to be allowed, is entirely out of my sphere; besides, if Prince Rupert's Bay should be fortified, and the country in that neighbourhood cleared of the wood, it would not only be the means of inducing people to settle there, but would likewise be the most proper rendezvous for His Majesty's ships in time of war, and entirely cut off the communication between the two great islands. Nothing will induce people to settle the neutral Islands so soon as a strong Fort in each, but of all, Saint Vincent's is the most cleared, and the best, as you will perceive by the quantity of its produce, which I enclose, and on which you may depend, is short of its real value.

Saint Lucia is extremely sickly, and must continue so from its numerous swamps, is at present entirely over-run with woods which abound in serpents, none of which will live either at Dominique or St. Vincent's: you may laugh at this assertion, but I have been assured of it by many, and what is more surprising is, that notwithstanding Martinique and St. Lucia have infinite numbers of serpents and other venomous animals, none are to be found in the other islands.

I hope we shall receive orders relative to Indians on St. Vincent's. Their chiefs should have some presents, and an assurance of the King's protection, or I foresee the

French will cause them to be troublesome. They have not been to pay their respects as yet to the Governor of Martinique, which used to be their annual custom, and although I have invited them often, they have declined it under some frivolous excuse.

It will be necessary that three or four companies of soldiers should be quartered in that Island, in order to be cheque on the inhabitants and Indians, and to protect the King's revenue. I can venture to say that St. Vincent's, in a few years, will yield as much or more produce than any other of the English Islands, and if the uncultivated land is to be given away, I hope His Majesty will permit me to have a lot, which, though of very little service to me, may be of use to my posterity. I hope for your friendship in obtaining it, and have taken the liberty to mention the place I could wish to have, as 't is entirely overrun with timber, no people inhabiting that part of the island, and was some years since made a present to the Governor of Martinique by the Indians, but he never settled it. My reason for desiring some land in the conquered Islands proceeds not only from a desire that my name may be remembered in a part of the world where I was honoured with the chief command of His Majesty's fleet in a prosperous war, but likewise from a desire to gain to my posterity some solid advantage, as Fortune, though so very favourable to me in the execution of His Majesty's commands, has not smiled upon me in other respects, and I believe no conquest was ever made with such little advantages to the chief. I can assure you, upon my word of honour, that my share, on the entire reduction of Martinique and the other islands, only amounted to seven hundred pounds sterling, by which means I was consideraby out of pocket by the expense I was obliged to be at, and though I have never suffered any ship to be idle, but have constantly kept them at sea, and in those stations most likely to distress the enemy, yet the prizes that have been taken have been but little more than sufficient to maintain the rank and figure I am obliged by my station to keep up. I may properly say, that the conquest of Martinique has been twenty thousand pounds loss to me, as it deprived all French ships coming into these seas; but I had rather have lost forty thousand pounds than not have succeeded in obeying the King's commands, and I am sure you, who know me, are convinced that my ambition in doing the duty of my station is in my mind far beyond any other consideration.

Pardon me for thus troubling you with my affairs, and permit me, at the same time, to tell you that I am fully convinced 't is to your friendship that I owe the rank His Majesty has bestowed upon me, and for which I shall ever think myself much indebted to you.

I am now fully employed in surveying the coasts of the conquered Islands, and hope, by the observations that will be made, the said islands may again be conquered when a future war makes it necessary. Adieu! dear Sir, and believe me to be, with the utmost sincerity and respect, &c., &c. G. B. RODNEY.

Memorandum. — St. Vincent's — The Mornagaron, near to the north part of the island, contains about four hundred French acres of very good land, is well watered by two rivers which run on each side, is entirely overrun with wood at present, and has no inhabitant on it. 'T is bounded on one side by the Rivulet Mornagaron, on the other by the Rivulet Walilabie.

THE EARL OF EGREMONT TO MR. GRENVILLIE.

Saturday morning, (February 12, 1763.)

DEAR SIR,—Perhaps the Duc de Nivernois has sent you word that the Treaty was to be signed as yesterday; if not, I would not leave you a moment ignorant of the news after I had it. Ever yours most faithfully,

EGREMONT.

What think you of the D. of B.[1], who lets the King's Ministers be informed by the French Ambassador of the appointment to sign the Treaty[2]?

THE EARL OF BUTE TO MR. GRENVILLE.

South Audley Street, February 13, 1763.

LORD BUTE presents his compts. to Mr. Grenville, and acquaints him that he has received an account from the Duke of Nivernois that everything was agreed with respect to the Definitive Treaty, on Tuesday last, the 8th instant, and that they intended to sign as on Thursday last.

M. de Nivernois received this intelligence by a Courier last night, and though Mr. Grenville may have already had an account of it, Lord Bute could not deny himself the pleasure of congratulating him upon it.

[1] The Duke of Bedford.
[2] Mr. Neville arrived from Paris on the 15th instant with the Definitive Treaty, and was immediately accompanied by Lord Egremont to an audience of the King. See the *Bedford Correspondence*, vol. iii. p. 199, for an interesting letter from Mr. Neville, describing his reception at Court.

THE EARL OF BUCKINGHAMSHIRE[1] TO MR. GRENVILLE.

Moscow, February 19, 1763, N.S.

DEAR SIR,—I received your most kind letter of the 7th of January just as my packet was making up, or should not have neglected that first opportunity of thanking you for it. My friends in England have neglected me a little since my absence, so that I have hardly received any information but from the public papers, yet what news has reached me gives me particular pleasure; a glorious peace concluded, and those I most interest myself for, in honourable, and I will flatter myself agreeable, situations. Though Muscovy is not exactly England, I am not in the least dissatisfied to find myself here, nor shall I think of soliciting my recall, so long as my services here can be agreeable to His Majesty, 'till the state of my own private affairs shall make my return to England absolutely necessary. It is a pleasure to me to think myself not quite an idle man, and I should be most completely happy could I flatter myself that the utmost exertion of my abilities might merit the approbation of my most gracious master. Two favours I most earnestly entreat of you: the first, that if any part of my conduct is disapproved of, you would let me know it to the full extent; the second, that if it is thought His Majesty's affairs in this country are not well conducted, and that the public suffers through my fault, that no personal regard to me may be a reason with you or any of my friends for keeping me here.

---

[1] Lord Buckinghamshire was at this time Ambassador at the Court of Catherine the Second.

My brother's[1] desire of leaving this place has given me great uneasiness upon his own account; it is, however, a satisfaction to me that I have in this, and in every instance, done my best for him.

Lady Suffolk must have talked with you upon the subject, and acquainted you with my wishes, which, in the uncertainty I was under, I hardly knew how to mention myself.

Her Imperial Majesty has hitherto treated me with an attention which every foreign minister must wish to deserve from the Sovereign of the country where he resides.

When you have a little leisure, let your good nature remind you how very agreeable a few lines from you will be to, dear Sir, your most affectionate, &c., &c.

BUCKINGHAM.

THE EARL OF EGREMONT TO MR. GRENVILLE.

Wednesday evening, 7 o'clock, (March 2, 1763.)

DEAR SIR,—I send you a more extraordinary letter[2] than has yet come from that extraordinary personage His Majesty's Ambassador in France; pray return it

---

[1] George Hobart, M.P. for Beeralston, afterwards third Earl of Buckinghamshire. He was Secretary to the Embassy.

[2] The letter referred to has not been preserved, but probably that from Lord Bute to the Duke of Bedford, dated March 3rd (*Bedford Correspondence*, vol. iii. p. 212), is upon the same subject as that from his Grace to Lord Egremont, viz., that the ratification of all the contracting Powers, including Portugal, should be exchanged at the same time, without regard to any dispute still subsisting with the King of Sardinia. It may have been observed that Lord Egremont seldom loses an opportunity of showing his ill-will towards the Duke of Bedford, and it would appear from a passage in Mr. Neville's letter above mentioned, that the Duke was not unaware of it.

when you have read it, because I want to get it copied for answering, before it circulates any farther. Ever yours, &c. EGREMONT.

THE EARL OF BUTE TO MR. GRENVILLE.

(March 25, 1763.)

MY DEAR GEORGE,—I have communicated to our common friend Elliot, the general points that passed between us[1]. I did it on purpose that he might know my regard for you, and that he might carry you my final determination without incurring the suspicion that frequent visits bring with them, in this most critical minute. I still continue to wish for you preferable to other arrangements, but if you cannot forget old

[1] The retirement of Lord Bute had therefore been the subject of previous conversations with Mr. Grenville; it had been long under deliberation, and had been decided upon much earlier than has hitherto been suspected. So much secrecy was observed, that when it became publicly known, two or three days only before it happened on the 8th of April, it was generally supposed, even by the best-informed persons, to be a very sudden resolve. He seems to have been invested with absolute power for the formation of the future Cabinet, which was to be completely arranged before his own resignation took effect. Mr. Adolphus, on the authority of private information, states, that on this occasion a place in the Cabinet was offered to Pitt, but that he insisted on terms with which the King could not in honour comply. This report, however, is not confirmed by any information to be found either in the Grenville or Chatham correspondence. Horace Walpole alludes to it in a letter to Mr. Montague: "They wished, too, to have had Pitt, if they could have had him without consequences." Walpole has also asserted that the Treasury and the seals of the Exchequer were first offered by Lord Bute to Fox, and refused by him; but it seems most probable that Lord Bute was, for reasons of his own, sincere in his wish for Mr. Grenville as "*preferable to other arrangements;*" and that Fox was only the alternative he should have had recourse to, in case Mr. Grenville had declined the offer, and he should have been obliged to put "*other things in agitation.*"

grievances, and cordially take the assistance of all the King's friends[1] that are determined to give it; if Lord Egremont's quitting the seals, or Shelburne having them, are obstacles to your mind at present insurmountable, I must in a few hours put other things in agitation, in which case, I again repeat, I expect the strictest honour, and that what has passed may convince you of my friendship, affection, and opinion.

MR. GRENVILLE TO THE EARL OF BUTE.

Admiralty Office, March 25, 1763.

MY DEAR LORD,—You will easily believe that, since I saw you yesterday, I have thoroughly considered the very important matters that were the subject of our conversation, as far as I have been able to do it from what you then opened to me.

I am extremely happy that you have communicated what passed between us to our friend Mr. Elliot, and that you have given me this opportunity of explaining my sentiments to you, in consequence of your letter; which is the more necessary, as it seems to me that I had not sufficiently done it before, or that in some respects you had misunderstood them.

I have, however, the pleasure of thinking, from the very kind and affectionate expressions you make use of towards me, that you are fully convinced how warm a sense I have of this high mark of your friendship and good opinion, in your recommendation of me to the

---

[1] The designation of certain persons as *the King's friends* was a phrase much commented upon hereafter *as a nickname*. I do not know whether Lord Bute invented it, but this is the first time I find it used in this correspondence.

King to be First Commissioner of the Treasury, and that in this respect my sentiments are not mistaken.

I feel most truly the infinite importance of that great office, at this critical minute; nor can I ever forget this signal proof of the confidence you repose in me, and of the honour you do me in this destination of me to fill it. I will make myself as worthy of it as I can, and endeavour, if possible, to deserve it, by giving you the unreserved dictates of my heart.

You tell me "that you still continue to wish this preferable to any other arrangement, but that if I cannot forget old grievances, and cordially take the assistance of all the King's friends that are determined to give it; if Lord Egremont's leaving the seals, and Lord Shelburne's having them are obstacles in my mind at present insurmountable, you must in a few hours put other things in agitation, in which case you expect the strictest honour."

I do assure you, my Lord, no grievances whatever, either old or new, as far as they relate personally to myself, shall, in my mind, ever stand a moment in competition with what I owe to the King, or prevent me from acting with those whom His Majesty shall call into his service.

As to Lord Egremont quitting the seals, you will not wonder at my saying that I can be no instrument in it, unless it is done entirely with his own consent and approbation; but, to answer your question directly, his leaving that situation will be no insurmountable obstacle to me, if he himself shall agree to it, which your Lordship knows, from the secrecy you so strongly exacted from me, and which I have religiously complied with, I have no means to inform myself of.

With regard to the other part of your question, relating to Lord Shelburne's being appointed Secretary of State, the difficulties arising from that arrangement at this time are not founded upon any *personal* considerations of my own, which I beg leave, in a business of this moment, to lay entirely out of the question; and I do solemnly protest to you, they shall not weigh with me in the decision of it; but it imports me thoroughly to consider, and from my duty to the King, and my regard to your Lordship, to state to you a much more interesting question, which it is essentially necessary for us both to give the utmost attention to; I mean, how far that appointment will affect the carrying into execution that system, which the King thinks of forming for his future government, and which (whoever is employed in it) must at present unavoidably be attended with great difficulties.

For this purpose you will allow me to represent to you the objections which will be made to this part of the arrangement in the House of Lords, the House of Commons, and the public. These will arise from Lord Shelburne's youth, his inexperience in business, by having never held any civil office whatever, and from his situation and family, so lately raised to the Peerage, however considerable both may be in Ireland.

The envy and jealousy of the old Peers, many of whom are already trying to band together, must naturally be excited to the highest pitch by a distinction of which, in most of its circumstances, there is, I believe, no example in our history.

The pretensions of such as now hold offices of the second rank in the House of Lords will be raised to a degree that cannot be gratified, and their disgust and disappointment will either break out into an open resistance, or at least prevent any cordial support.

In a discussion of this kind, it will be absolutely necessary to know the sentiments of individuals, which the secrecy you require makes it impossible for me to do; and, therefore, obliges me to represent things as they at present appear to me.

You will consider how far this appointment will meet with the cordial approbation of all or any of those from whom in that House, this system must expect assistance; from Lord Halifax, Lord Egremont, Lord Chancellor, Lord Mansfield; from Lord Egmont, Lord Marchmont, Lord Denbigh, &c.; from the Duke of Bedford, Lord Gower, and all their friends.

I know not their sentiments, and therefore cannot decide upon them; but as far as my own uninformed judgment goes, I cannot persuade myself that many of these, even of the most congenial, would bear Lord Shelburne's being put at once over their heads, with satisfaction or content.

In the House of Commons the same jealousies and uneasinesses will probably arise, and I see very few, if any, of the considerable persons there, whose approbation and hearty concurrence with this measure could be depended upon.

I cannot at present believe that it would be agreable to the country gentlemen of any denomination, either Whigs or Tories, nor to those who for many years have holden distinguished offices of Government, even if the majority of them should acquiesce under it, which I think uncertain. As to Mr. Charles Townshend, it will certainly throw him into immediate opposition.

What impression it will make upon many others I will not say, but I fear not a favourable one.

I will not specify individuals, as I may be deceived, nor would I have done it in the House of Lords, if you had not mentioned the particular situation there, as an inducement to you for this nomination.

In the public, popular clamour will undoubtedly be raised, and from many motives will be industriously propagated as much as is possible, and the graver and more sober part of mankind will be surprised and offended at the novelty of this step in all its circumstances.

These, my Lord, are some of the most obvious difficulties, which, I apprehend, cannot fail of being aggravated at this critical juncture, upon the appointment of a person so young and so unknown in public business.

They seem also to carry the greater weight with them at a time when so large a body of the nobility are ostentatiously combining themselves in a public avowed opposition: a measure on their part which surely makes it advisable in Government to place in the first offices at least such persons as may be free not only from real, but even plausible objections.

Do not believe, my Lord, that they arise in me from personal prejudice only. Were Lord Shelburne the dearest friend I have in the world, I do protest I would advise him for his own sake to decline for the present the high office of Secretary of State, and to accustom the public by degrees to see him acting in business in some office lower than what is now proposed. In such a situation he might ripen for the seals, so as to take them whenever His Majesty shall be disposed to give them, without that offence which such a sudden and unprecedented elevation I think must occasion[1].

I flatter myself you will believe I am too sensible of the King's goodness to me, to pretend to put any negative upon those whom he shall approve. I do not presume to suggest who is the most proper for that high office. I make no objection to any one who is, in the public eye and opinion, big enough to fill it; if Lord Egremont leaves it, whether it be Lord Gower, or any other person of that connection whom the King shall wish to bring forward, or of any other connection which is most agreeable to His Majesty: but what I have said is from a real sense of my duty, and of my honour. I may possibly be mistaken, though my conviction is strongly otherwise, and I should indeed be wanting to both, if, before I entered upon such a situation, I did not state to you my opinion upon those parts of the system which have been opened to me, and upon the means proposed for carrying it into execution. If your Lordship had allowed me to consult with some of those who must bear the greatest share in it, I should then have either verified my opinions, or, from being convinced, should have changed them. But since I am not at liberty to do this, I must entreat you in the mean time to inform yourself how this will be received by the principal persons you mean to confide in, and to ask the cool opinion of neutral and indifferent people. If they concur with me, I am confident you will not desire

---

[1] Mr. Grenville's objections to the appointment of Lord Shelburne were the cause of an alteration in the arrangements proposed by Lord Bute. Lord Shelburne was made first Commissioner of Trade and Plantations, and Lord Halifax became the Colleague of Lord Egremont as Secretary of State.

me to give a more positive or final answer with regard to the part I am to bear in a system which could not then be formed in the manner it is proposed. For if the public in general, a great part of the nobility, and some of the leading persons in the House of Commons, should be indisposed to this appointment, your Lordship must see that my saying I am ready to bear any part, could be of no service whatever: but if it shall appear that what I have said upon this occasion is not well founded, and that the most essential of these difficulties do not occur, I shall be glad that I have been mistaken, and the conviction that I have been so, must necessarily alter my sentiments upon this subject, and you will then certainly find me, as you always have done, desirous and happy to devote myself to the service of my King and my country, thinking it the greatest honour that can befal me, if I could do it with any degree of success in that high and important situation to which the King's goodness, and your Lordship's friendship, has destined me.

Upon the whole, whether I bear any part in this transaction or not, which perhaps may be of little consequence to the public welfare, yet, let me beseech your Lordship, from your affection and duty to the King, and from what you owe to yourself and to your country, to give this subject a thorough examination before you determine upon a matter of this infinite moment, that if you still persist in your former resolution of retreat[1] (which I most earnestly wish you if possible to re-consider), the establishment which the King shall now think fit to make in his Government, may be such a one

[1] A still stronger reason for believing that Lord Bute had long determined upon retirement, and that it was his own desire.

as will reflect honour on your Lordship who advised it, and give that permanency and stability which, in the present crisis, is essentially necessary to his Administration.

I am now only to ask pardon for the length of my letter; this interesting subject made it unavoidable, and I have explained my sentiments thus fully to your Lordship, not only that you might be apprized of them, but that you may be enabled to represent them in their true light to the King, if he should ever condescend to enquire about them, and that he may not think me more unworthy than I am of his Royal favour: give me leave to add, that I esteem it a peculiar happiness that they will be transmitted through the channel of a friend so partially disposed to me, and to whom I feel myself so sensibly obliged upon this occasion.

I am, my dear Lord, with the truest regard and attachment, your most affectionate, &c.

GEORGE GRENVILLE.

THE EARL OF BUTE TO MR. GRENVILLE.

Friday, half-past 4, (April 1, 1763.)

DEAR GEORGE,—I just write two lines to tell you, that nothing could be handsomer, more respectful to the King, or more cordial to yourself, than the language of Lord Egremont and Lord Halifax; they seemed to approve extremely of the arrangement I flung out, and entered thoroughly into the necessity of a strict union, not only amongst yourselves, but with all the other parts of the defenders of Government, and this as the only means of supporting the King's independency.

I have since seen Shelburne, who, in the handsomest manner, wished to be omitted, that the ground might be enlarged by more necessary people; this, however, I don't think safe, for he can better prevent Fox's people from going off to the enemy, in case of accident to the latter[1], than any man now living; but I desired him to call on you on Monday at eleven, and then to speak to you without reserve, and you will talk to him solely on the ground I was on this morning. Jenkinson will attend you when you please. Adieu! my dear George. Yours, &c. BUTE.

MR. JENKINSON TO MR. GRENVILLE.

South Audley Street, April 3, 1763.

DEAR SIR,—I have told Lord Bute what you said to me concerning Lord Digby[2]. It appeared to give him great uneasiness. He said that he had mentioned to the King last night all he had said to you, and what you had said in return to him, so that he hopes you will not wish any change on this head, as it would hurt the whole system. I have, &c. C. JENKINSON.

THE COUNTESS TEMPLE TO EARL TEMPLE.

April 5, (1763.)

MY letter must be no longer than to tell you I am glad you are well; I am just come from Princess

[1] He means, I presume, in case Fox should be so extremely offended that the Treasury had not been offered to him, as to go into opposition. According to Walpole, Fox was greatly enraged with Lord Shelburne for having so long concealed from him Lord Bute's intended resignation.

[2] He was appointed a Lord of the Admiralty.

Emily's[1] Court; have since writ out my verses upon Lady Mary to send. Her Royal Highness was much upbraided by her for letting other people see them and never showing them to her. It is too long a story to tell you, but Mr. Walpole[2] has got them, admires them much as an impromptu, and shows them to everybody.

Poor Lord Waldegrave[3] is in a bad way with the small-pox, and she is with child.

I am to undress before dinner, and it is almost four. I am, &c., &c. A. T.

MR. HANS STANLEY TO MR. GRENVILLE.

Paulton's, April 7, (1763,) half-past 1, A.M.

SIR,—I think it my duty not to delay my answer a moment, as I should be very unwilling that His Majesty's arrangements should suffer the least retardment on account of any attention paid to me.

The persons to whom you succeed must, Sir, have given you very imperfect informations, if they have not told you that I rejected the removal into the Treasury[4]

[1] Princess Amelia, fourth daughter of King George the Second. Lady Temple lived in great intimacy with her for many years.

[2] Walpole in a letter to Montague, on the following day, says, "Here are six lines written extempore by Lady Temple on Lady Mary Coke, easy and genteel, and almost true :—

"'She sometimes laughs, but never loud;
She's handsome too, but somewhat proud :
At Court she bears away the belle;
She dresses fine, and figures well:
With decency she's gay and airy;
Who can this be but Lady Mary?'"

[3] He died in a very few days. His widow was a niece of Horace Walpole; she was afterwards remarried to the King's brother, the Duke of Gloucester, by whom she had the late Duke of Gloucester and his sister the Princess Sophia.

[4] He was now a Lord of the Admiralty, and was offered a removal to the Treasury Board.

as an offer not worthy my acceptance; the slightest call to the business of the Admiralty, or of Parliament, should, Sir, have brought me to London, but I cannot leave my house, which happens at this time to be full of people of the first distinction, in order to return you this answer by word of mouth, which I now give in writing, or to form in conversation demands of other preferments, *that may suit me better.* Any such proposal must be made specifically to me; it will then receive a plain negative or affirmative.

I have served my country in a manner to which every Court in Europe has done justice except my own. I have since, from a sense of my duty, supported that Administration which had neglected me. My desire of showing my profound and loyal veneration to the person of the King solely, joined to my resolution of never taking any part that should have the least appearance of faction, has alone prevented my laying the office I actually hold at His Majesty's feet. I have drawn a line above the Treasury, nor will I ever alter my present situation, unless it be to retire from public business, or to rise to an equality with those who are my juniors in office, and in no other light my superiors. Lord Halifax, who has long honoured me with his friendship, knows all my sentiments on this subject. Lord Bute himself is not an entire stranger to them. Whenever I am so happy as to deserve such a share in the King's attention as will call me to offices in which I have an opportunity of doing myself credit, no party or combination whatever shall shake my zeal and courage. I am conscious I shall show the world that such a favourable opinion of me has not been misplaced; meanwhile I shall trouble no present or future Minister with any solicitation;

I may be again slighted; I have not, I will not be refused.

I am persuaded that your own good understanding will show you how improper and superfluous it is, to say more on my own circumstances; as to your part of this affair, Sir, I beg you will accept my congratulations on your advancement, and my sincere thanks for the civilities you have been pleased to show me at the Admiralty. I am, with the most respectful esteem, &c., &c. Hans Stanley.

THE COMTE DE VIRY[1] TO MR. GRENVILLE.

Londres, ce 8 Avril 1763, à 8 heures du matin.

Monsieur,—Je suis persuadé que vous êtes trop convaincu de mes sentimens pour vous, pour que vous ne me fassiez pas la justice de croire que personne ne prend plus de part que moi aux témoignages distingués que sa Majesté Britannique va donner publiquement aujourd'hui, de la haute estime qu'elle a pour votre personne, pour vos talens, et votre grande sagacité: si ma santé ne me retenoit pas toujours chez moi, je vous serai allé embrasser à ce sujet comme un amis, en attendant que je vous rends ensuite mes devoirs comme Ministre, ce que je ne manquerai pas de faire aussitôt que je le pourrai. Je prie mi ledi Grenville d'agréer mes sincères et respectueuses félicitations. Je vous demande la continuation de votre amitié. J'ai l'honneur d'être, avec un attachement très respectueux, &c., &c. De Viry.

[1] The Sardinian Ambassador.

MR. JENKINSON TO MR. GRENVILLE.

South Audley Street, April 8, 1763.

DEAR SIR,—I delivered to you a few days ago, by Lord Bute's desire, a memorial in favour of Mr. Fall, who has served as a shipwright at Antigua, desiringth at he may be *superannuated*. Mr. Fall sends word that Mr. Cleveland[1] raises an objection, because he has not served in the fleet the full time required by the Order of Council, when, as he says, this order was never meant to extend to those who serve in the yards, which is his case, and that Lord Bute has been told that Dr. Hay is of the same opinion. Lord Bute ordered me to mention this to you, and at the same time observe, that he has this promotion very much at heart, if it could be contrived without impropriety.

I have the honour to send you enclosed a list of the lawyers that are in the House, as you desired. I have, &c., &c.   C. JENKINSON.

THE EARL OF HALIFAX TO MR. GRENVILLE.

Great George Street, Monday, half-past 5,
(April 18, 1763.)

DEAR SIR,—Weston has sent me the enclosed copy of to-morrow's speech; does he mean that it is for the King's use, or have you sent orders to him to copy over another for His Majesty, in the hand the King wishes?

I forgot to tell you that one of our Cabinet Councillors to-day seemed to doubt whether the phrase of *forming*[2]

---

[1] M.P. for Saltash, and Secretary to the Admiralty.

[2] The word was retained; "I acquainted you with my firm resolution to *form* my Government," &c. &c.

Government on the plan of strict economy is a proper one. I own I see no objection to it, as a new formation of the plan of Government must necessarily take place in time of peace, but if you think there is any weight in the objection, the verb *conduct*, instead of *form*, will answer the purpose. I am, &c. DUNK HALIFAX.

Upon recollection, I am happy my brother Secretary is with you, that I may know your joint opinion.

MR. JENKINSON TO MR. GRENVILLE.

London, April 20, 1763.

DEAR SIR,—Nothing material has occurred since you left us.

I saw Lord Clive this morning. He seems to think that Sullivan[1] will do all he can to obstruct their proceedings, but he does not appear to be afraid of him. He was full of the strongest expressions of gratitude to you, said that you might depend on Mr. Walsh[2] and Crabb Bolton[3], but said that the latter was a great rogue.

He talked to me much about Mr. Strachey[4], and wanted a particular account of his character.

I have been to several of Strachey's friends, and am

---

[1] Lawrence Sullivan had been made Chairman of the East India Company through the influence of Clive, to whom he was now in opposition.

[2] John Walsh, an East India Director, and M.P. for Worcestershire; he had formerly been Clive's Secretary.

[3] He was M.P. for Worcester, and afterwards Deputy-Chairman of the East India Company.

[4] Henry Strachey became private Secretary to Lord Clive, and accompanied him to India. He was subsequently joint Secretary of the Treasury, one of the Under Secretaries of State, and Master of the Household. He was made a Baronet in 1801, and died in 1810.

authorized to say so much in his favour, that I am convinced he will take him. I spoke to him as you ordered in favour of Mr. Daniel. He says that Mr. Sullivan has left such a load upon them, that they have hardly an office to dispose of; that he would speak, however, to Mr. Pierce to do what he could.

I saw Lord Bute this morning, he was very easy and cheerful ; he spoke to me of poor Bentley[1], lamented his poverty, increased by a family of six children, and extolled his merit, and seemed to wish that something was done for him.

I have not yet had an opportunity of talking to Mr. Mackenzie, but find Lord Sandwich saw him yesterday, after you did, and thinks him disposed to be reasonable.

I shall get Colonel Draper talked to, I hope with success.

There was yesterday a great dinner at Wildman's[2], by way of taking leave. I have not yet heard the particulars of what passed.

Mr. Long and Mr. Payne, West India merchants, yesterday came to me to complain that our men of war,

[1] Richard Bentley, son of Dr. Bentley, the eminent classical scholar. He is now chiefly remembered as Horace Walpole's friend and correspondent, but he had talents and accomplishments of a very high order, accompanied, however, by eccentricity and want of worldly prudence which led him into pecuniary difficulties. He was indebted to the patronage of Lord Bute for some appointment in the Customs, which he appears to have lost upon the retirement of the latter; but he retained a pension of five hundred pounds a year. He made some designs for an edition of Gray's poems, printed by Walpole, at Strawberry Hill, and he wrote a Drama called the *Wishes*, and a satirical poem, in which he ridiculed Lord Temple, Wilkes, and others; but its merit extorted praise even from Churchill himself.

[2] A Tavern, kept by one Wildman, in Albemarle Street; at this time much frequented by the minority, and where they subsequently established a Club, called *the Coterie*.

under the orders they had received from hence to prevent contraband trade, had interrupted our commerce with the Spanish Main; they said that fresh instructions were going from the Admiralty, and they wished that great care was taken in the manner of wording them, so as not to include the commerce to the Spanish Main. I told them that I was convinced it was not within your intention to include that: that I could do nothing till you came to town; unless that I could persuade the Admiralty to delay sending any fresh instructions till they had had an opportunity of consulting you: with this they appeared contented. I have, &c., &c. C. JENKINSON.

MR. JENKINSON TO MR. GRENVILLE.

South Street, April 28, 1763.

DEAR SIR,—The paragraph which follows is what I mentioned to you this morning, and made part of a letter I received last night from Lord Bute.

"I was surprised this morning with a letter from Lord Luxborough[1], thanking me for his title. I wrote to His Majesty about it, who says that Fox had asked it of him five months ago, and that Lord Halifax had brought it to him as a thing both Fox and I had recommended. I may have mentioned the request, but certainly not intending to have it done; but Halifax has took me otherwise. I mention this to you, that a thing

---

[1] Robert Knight, created in 1749, Baron Luxborough, in the Irish Peerage: he was now advanced to the Earldom of Catherlough, and died a few months afterwards, when the peerage expired. He was M.P. for Great Grimsby.

I don't care at all about may not be an occasion of jealousy."

I have since seen Lord Bute, and said to him what you desired me. I will tell you the result to-morrow. I have, &c., &c. C. JENKINSON.

EARL VERNEY[1] TO MR. GRENVILLE.

Curzon Street, 29th April, 1763.

SIR,—I understand, from my friend Mr. Burke[2], that you were pleased to mention the old acquaintance there has been between us. I certainly have not had any disinclination to you, and my whole life has shown how much I have been inclined to forward the business of the Crown; but I have now the mortification to see every other person get all they ask, while I only am marked out ignominiously as unworthy of His Majesty's least attention.

If His Majesty was made acquainted with my services, I have not the least doubt that I should not be thus disgraced; and I am sure if you were acquainted with the whole of my conduct, you would see that personally you ought to be satisfied with it. I should be very happy if, after all, I should owe my success to an old acquaintance, and I certainly should not prove an ungrateful nor, I think, quite an unprofitable friend; but

---

[1] Ralph Verney, Viscount Fermanagh, and second Earl Verney in Ireland. He died in 1791, when the Peerage became extinct.

[2] William Burke. He was soon after M.P. for Great Bedwin, through the interest of Lord Verney; and he was Secretary to General Conway while he held the seals of Secretary of State. He afterwards went to India. Walpole says of him, that "as an orator he had neither manner nor talents, and yet wanted little of his cousin Edmund's presumption." He died in 1798.

you cannot expect that, after having sincerely served His Majesty at a critical time, and now finding all his servants absolutely decline even to represent my services to him, I shall be in a hurry to rely again upon distant promises.

I never shall ask anything unreasonable, and (if not too troublesome) I will wait upon you, whenever you will give me leave, to explain more fully the whole. I am, with great respect, &c. VERNEY.

(*In Mrs. Grenville's handwriting*[1].)

LORD EGREMONT'S youngest son was christened May —, 1763. The King and Queen stood in person. Lord Northumberland, Chamberlain to the Queen, was the other godfather.

Lady Egremont sat upon her bed, two great chairs were placed on the right side for the King and Queen (N.B., this was wrong, the chairs ought to have been placed one on one side, and one on the other); the rest of the chairs were all moved out of the room. The ladies invited to the christening were Lady Aylesford[2], Lady Northumberland[3], Lady Weymouth[4], and Mrs.

---

[1] Inserted as a specimen of Court Ceremonial of the time.

[2] Wife of Heneage Finch, third Earl. She was the daughter of Charles, Duke of Somerset, by his second wife, Lady Charlotte Finch, daughter of Daniel, Earl of Winchilsea and Nottingham.

[3] Lady Elizabeth Seymour, daughter of Algernon, Duke of Somerset, and wife of Sir Hugh Smithson, who had succeeded to the Earldom of Northumberland.

[4] Wife of Thomas Thynne, third Viscount Weymouth. She was Lady Elizabeth Bentinck, daughter of William, second Duke of Portland. She died in 1825, at the age of 91.

Grenville. The men were Lord Thomond[1] and Mr. Grenville. The Queen came first; Lord Egremont met her in the hall, and led her up stairs. Lady Aylesford and Lady Northumberland went down to meet her at the bottom of the stairs; Lady Weymouth and Mrs. Grenville staid by Lady Egremont. Her attendants were, Lady Bolingbroke[2] in waiting; the Duchess of Ancaster[3]; four maids of honour; two bed-chamber women; Lord Harcourt, Master of the Horse; Lord Northumberland, Chamberlain; a Page; gentleman ushers, &c. The King was met in the same manner by Lord Egremont, who carried the candle before him. He was attended by Lord Gower, Chamberlain; Lord Hertford, in waiting; a Groom of the Bedchamber, &c., &c.

The Bishop of Bristol[4] performed the ceremony. Lady Aylesford brought in the child, and served the Queen with cake and caudle upon a salver, kneeling, with a napkin on her arm. Lord Egremont did the same to the King.

They went away in the same manner that they came, after having stood a good while talking to Lady Egremont, and afterwards to all the ladies and gentlemen. Lord Cockermouth and all the rest of the children were called into the room when the Queen asked for them, and staid there all the rest of the time. There was

[1] Percy O'Brien, second son of Sir William Wyndham; he inherited the Earldom of Thomond from his uncle. He died, unmarried, in 1774.

[2] Better known as Lady Di Beauclerc; she was Lady Diana Spencer, eldest daughter of Charles, second Duke of Marlborough. Her marriage with Lord Bolingbroke was dissolved in 1768, and she remarried the Honourable Topham Beauclerc.

[3] Wife of Peregrine Bertie, third Duke of Ancaster.

[4] Dr. Newton, Author of *Dissertations on the Prophecies.*

cake and caudle, &c., for the attendants in Lady Egremont's dressing-room.

The children were all in the octagon room, where Lady Blandford[1] was, undressed, and in private, to see the King and Queen.

THE EARL OF EGREMONT TO MR. GRENVILLE.

3 quarters past 3, (May 1, 1763.)

DEAR SIR,—I have this moment received a dispatch from Paris, and in it a most extraordinary and alarming secret letter from Mr. Neville[2].

I have sent the whole to the King. Pray let me have a quarter of an hour with you this evening. I am ever, &c.
E.

THE EARL OF EGREMONT TO MR. GRENVILLE.

4 o'Clock, (May 3, 1763.)

DEAR SIR,—We have carried the point we talked of yesterday, *nobody*[3] is to be forbid the Court. Ever yours, &c.
EGREMONT.

---

[1] Lord Egremont's mother-in-law; second wife and widow of Sir William Wyndham.

[2] I find nothing in the Grenville Papers relating to the contents of this letter.

[3] Over the word *nobody* is written in Mr. Grenville's hand, *Lord Temple*. The date is supplied by the same hand. This may relate to his intended dismissal from the Lord Lieutenancy of Bucks, which took place on the 7th instant. It could not mean literally that Lord Temple was forbidden to appear at Court, because we shall see that he accompanied Mr. Pitt to the King's Levée about three months after this time, when he was distinguished by His Majesty's speaking *one sentence* to him. Mr. Pitt being at the same time honoured with *two*.

MR. WILKES TO EARL TEMPLE.

Saturday Morning, (May 1763.)

MY DEAR LORD,—I hope by two to have the excellent pamphlet[1] *on the Seizure of Papers* ready to submit to your Lordship's perusal.

I shall have the honour of attending your Lordship at that hour, or after the Opera, or at any hour more convenient or agreeable.

I am, with an esteem and gratitude no words can reach, my Lord, your Lordship's most obliged and devoted
JOHN WILKES.

THE DUKE OF GRAFTON[2] TO EARL TEMPLE.

Bond Street, May 3, 1763.

MY DEAR LORD,—I sit down to open my situation to your Lordship with much less apprehension than I should do to most of my friends, since I have seen so

---

[1] A letter in the form of a Pamphlet, written anonymously by Lord Temple, and addressed to the Earls of Egremont and Halifax, upon the *Seizure of Papers*. One of the Printers, who was examined upon the trial of Wilkes, stated that this was the *second* production of the private press which Wilkes had established at his house in Great George Street, and that it was printed from a Manuscript *revised* by Mr. Wilkes. He now presents to Lord Temple the first complete copy of the Pamphlet, the contents of which I shall hereafter have occasion to notice.

[2] Augustus Henry, third Duke of Grafton. Taking into consideration the manner in which Wilkes had been patronized and encouraged by Lord Temple, who had besides offered upon this occasion to become his bail for any amount, however large, and considering also the friendship which the Duke of Grafton had hitherto professed for Wilkes, we may form some notion of the anger with which this letter was probably received by Lord Temple. I regret that I have not been able to find a draught of the reply.

many instances of your goodness, I may say, particularly to me.

A letter from Mr. Wilkes, which I enclose, came to me while I was out a riding this morning. Your Lordship will see the purport of it; and as it is now too late to send him in time my answer, I flatter myself you will add this to many other obligations, and that you will tell him how I stand circumstanced the first time you either see or write to him. In short, my Lord, I went, as I think every acquaintance is almost bound to do, to see Mr. Wilkes in his confinement, to hear from himself his own story and his defence, and to show that no influence ought to stop the means of every man's justifying himself from an accusation, though it should be of the most heinous nature.

Hearing the shyness of lawyers in general to undertake his cause, as also the manner (perhaps unwarrantable) of his confinement, I was more desirous than ever to show that, as far as my small power could extend, no subject of this country should want my countenance against oppression.

But, my Lord, when I look upon myself as called in to bail, though it had been for the person in the world who had the most right to have asked that sort of favour from me, I must nevertheless have trod very warily on ground that seemed to come any ways under the denomination of an insult on the Crown.

That, my Lord, is and always has been a rule laid down by me, which I will most religiously observe, that nothing in which I engage against His Majesty's Ministers, whom I disapprove, shall ever be carried on by me with the shadow of offence against his person or family.

The consistency of my character will, I hope, therefore be my excuse to him; I am confident it will be to your Lordship, which *I most* desire.

I might add to this, that on talking this point over with my relations, I have given them my opinion, and assured them that my meaning was only to go as far as I have here represented to your Lordship, to whom I have the honour to be, with every sense of honour, esteem, and respect, &c., &c. GRAFTON.

P.S. I am authorized to say that the same motive induced Lord Villiers[1] to go, who accompanied me to see Mr. Wilkes.

THE EARL OF HALIFAX TO EARL TEMPLE.

St. James's, May 7, 1763.

MY LORD,—The King has commanded me to acquaint your Lordship that His Majesty has no further occasion for your service as Lord-Lieutenant and Custos Rotulorum of the County of Buckingham. I am, my Lord, your Lordship's most obedient humble Servant,

DUNK HALIFAX[2].

---

[1] George Bussy, afterwards third Earl of Jersey.
[2] This *strictly official* and very formal letter was no doubt intended to be as contemptuous as possible. It is written in a clerk's hand, and signed only by Lord Halifax. The following lines were written by Lady Temple on this occasion:—

> " To honour virtue in the Lord of Stowe,
> The power of courtiers can no farther go;
> Forbid him court, from council blot his name,—
> E'en these distinctions cannot rase his fame.
> Friend to the liberties of England's state,
> 'T is not to Courts he looks to make him great:
> He to his much-lov'd country trusts his cause,
> And dares assert the honour of her laws."

MR. WILKES TO EARL TEMPLE.

Sunday, May 15, (1763.)

MY DEAR LORD,—I flew off in a tangent on Friday in a hack post-chaise to Hounslow, then obliquely steered my course to this hospitable house, the master[1] of which desires his best compliments. I am very happy with him, and mean to continue so 'till Tuesday morning, if I receive no commands from your Lordship.

Saturday's Public Advertiser, I see, contains a literary remark on the Georgics, which I communicated to Mr. Lloyd[2].

Churchill[3] talks of printing Talbot's letters to justify me against a stupid charge in the Daily Advertiser, but I have wrote to him to stop it. I am, under increasing obligation, &c., &c. JOHN WILKES.

---

[1] Probably Humphrey Cotes, a very intimate friend of Wilkes's. He was of a good family, but now a wine merchant in St. Martin's Lane, and a very busy politician. His brother, Admiral Cotes, was M.P. for Great Bedwin. The name of the place from whence this letter was dated appears to have been purposely torn away.

[2] Robert Lloyd, son of Dr. Pierson Lloyd, one of the Masters of Westminster School. He was the author of a Poem called *The Actor*. Churchill having been educated at Westminster School, and being afterwards Curate of St. John's, was always intimate both with father and son. The latter, like Churchill, led an irregular and dissolute life, and it ended in a few weeks after the death of Churchill, and at about the same age as his equally unfortunate friend.

[3] Charles Churchill " once the Reverend," as Hogarth styled him: the well-known author of the *Rosciad*, and other poems, which display very considerable, but, unhappily, misapplied talent. His acquaintance with Wilkes commenced in 1762, and from congenial tastes soon ripened into extreme intimacy. They were associated in the production of the North Briton, in which Lord Temple also is said to have assisted. Churchill's career was brief and wretched. He went over to Boulogne, accompanied by Cotes, on a visit to Wilkes, in October, 1764, and, being attacked by fever, died there, after a few days' illness, in his 34th year.

MR. WILKES TO EARL TEMPLE.

Great George Street, May 25, Wednesday (1763).

My Lord,—I am prevented, by a message from Gardiner, waiting on your Lordship this morning.

I entirely approve of all your Lordship's reasonings, yesterday, and shall conform to the soundest judgment I ever knew.

The enclosed letter I submit, to be sent, or corrected, or put in the fire. It obviates an objection which is for ever making to me.

My press and Mr. Phillips's[1] actions cost me so much more than I imagined, that I will beg the loan of 200*l.* more, if it is perfectly convenient to your Lordship.

I hope to settle all this account before Michaelmas, for I only opiniâtre one point, that a *public* concern ought to be carried on by the *public* purse, not by any one Nobleman, though by far the most respectable of the kingdom. I am ever, &c., &c.   JOHN WILKES.

THE DUKE OF BEDFORD TO MR. GRENVILLE.

Paris, May 25, 1763.

Dear Sir,—I was yesterday favoured with your letter, and I take the first opportunity of assuring you how sensible I am of His Majesty's great goodness to Mr. Neville, in being pleased to confer on that gentleman the place of Paymaster of the Pensions whenever I shall judge it can be done without any inconvenience to myself. I see of none that can possibly happen with regard to the borough of Tavistock should it take place

[1] An attorney, and, according to Wilkes, a very great rogue.

immediately, more especially as Mr. Neville's seat in Parliament will not be vacated 'till after having kissed His Majesty's hand for his employment, which I suppose cannot be before the Earl of Hertford's [1] arrival here, as some one must necessarily be left here after my departure from this place.

I think myself much obliged to you, Sir, for the part you have been pleased to take in this affair.

The Address of the Merchants of the city of London [2] gives me great satisfaction, as I think it must to every good subject of His Majesty, as it is a strengthening to the hands of Government, and is but a just tribute to His Majesty on his having given general peace to Europe.

I am, dear Sir, with great truth, &c.   BEDFORD.

THE HON. GENERAL TOWNSHEND TO MR. GRENVILLE.

Derham, May 30, 1763.

DEAR SIR,—I am sorry to give you this trouble, but as our regiment of Militia, which has been assembled here since the 23rd of this month, has been refused its pay by Mr. Vere, one of the Receivers General for this county, I submit it to you, if a regiment assembled by Act of Parliament, and I may say with great truth of it, most ambitious to deserve His Majesty's approbation, and that of their countrymen, does not deserve at the same time a little more attention than that which Mr. Vere is pleased to honour it with, and which the other

---

[1] Recently appointed Ambassador to the Court of France.
[2] See Mr. Grenville's letter on this subject, in the *Bedford Correspondence*, vol. iii. p. 230.

battalion has received from the other Receiver, Mr. Balderston.

I hope you will be so good as to send your orders to Mr. Vere that the officers may not be obliged to advance that money, which, unless I am much misinformed, a Receiver of a county can generally very well do if they please, it being pretty generally allowed that they make no trifling perquisites of what they have in hand. I beg leave to enclose Mr. Vere's letter, and am, Sir, with great respect, &c., &c.   GEO. TOWNSHEND.

MR. WILKES TO EARL TEMPLE.

Aylesbury, Sunday, June 5th (1763).

MY DEAR LORD,—I have most successfully got through the fine list of patriotic toasts, and the nasty wine of this borough. I have only a little headache, but poor Churchill is half dead. He was so violent against my Lord Mayor[1] at Missenden, that I was forced to drop that part of my toast, and only to drink the City of London.

Our late Lord Lieutenant and Mr. Pitt had three cheers each.

I had the honour of being escorted into the town by every man who had, or could hire, a horse, and if I have the honour of being expelled, the declaration is universal that I shall be re-chosen.

Mr. Hopkins very obligingly came to us.

My subscriptions I find increase, but little money is paid in, though many gentlemen have sent for numbers of tickets to dispose of: I am worse off than the Duke

[1] Alderman Beckford.

of Newcastle, or anybody; for I cannot be in anybody's debt, without reading a history of it in the Public, &c. I have paid Mr. Beardmore[1] 150*l*., and he wants 250*l*. more. If I do not put your Lordship to inconveniences, I should beg a last sum of 400*l*. or 500*l*., 'till I can call in my new scrip, and by Michaelmas my plan is to settle the whole, either from the Public purse or from my own private fortune. I make no apology to Lord Temple. I am proud to have an obligation to Lord Temple, and I have none to any other man, nor will I even to my Prince.

I am, with infinite regard, my Lord, &c., &c.

JOHN WILKES.

MR. WILKES TO EARL TEMPLE.

Great George Street, June 11, 1763.

MY LORD,—When Stowe presents so enchanting a scene to your eye, I cannot think of diverting it for more than a few moments by any account of the bustle of the Capital. Everything legal wears the most smiling aspect, and every mean art which has been used to protract justice has proved ineffectual, and I believe the trials will come on the end of next week.

I am not enough versed in the jargon of the Court to

---

[1] Arthur Beardmore, an attorney in the city: he was Lord Temple's confidential "man of business," and it appears that he was also employed by Wilkes. As Under Sheriff, it was his duty to see the sentence of the pillory carried into execution upon Dr. Shebbeare, in 1758, for writing his *Sixth Letter to the People of England*, and he was prosecuted and fined 50*l*., with two months' imprisonment, for having indulged the doctor upon that occasion by allowing him to stand *on* and not *in* the pillory. Beardmore was himself a political writer, and a very busy meddler in the under current of city politics.

descend to particulars, but I was charmed with the account Sergeant Glynn[1] gave me of the state of the cause.

I lead a very philosophical life: I rise early, and pass the day alone, or only with one or two friends. I have never lost sight of the great object of the liberty of the subject at large. All my researches are directed to that great point; and if I have at present the misfortune of finding that your Lordship cannot approve, so much as I wish, some particulars of my conduct, I trust that the dénouement will fully justify, not only to so great candour as your Lordship possesses, but to the world, however artfully prejudiced against me, all points of real importance. Several of the Militia officers of Bucks invited themselves to dine with me on Thursday, and notwithstanding the very intrinsic merit of the new Lord Lieutenant and Colonel drawn into the common focus of Lord Le Despencer, I was very glad to find that the old Lord Lieutenant and Colonel had left a pleasing desiderium behind them, and though they had lost all their power, yet retained more than a shadow of authority.

The business increases fast upon me, so that I have no chance of eloping into Buckinghamshire for the next ten days. I hope within the fortnight to congratulate your Lordship and every true lover of liberty on the explicit declaration of a Court of Justice in favour of the liberty of the subject.

Your Lordship has so lately left town, that I can

---

[1] The well-known Advocate and friend of Wilkes. Lord Chatham, in a letter to Calcraft, thus speaks of him. "Mr. Sergeant Glynn has just left me. I find him a most ingenious, solid, pleasing man, and the spirit of the Constitution itself. I never was more taken by a first conversation in my life."

have no news to write, for I hope it is none that I am with the utmost respect and gratitude, &c., &c.

JOHN WILKES.

I beg my sincerest respects to Lady Temple.

MR. WILKES TO EARL TEMPLE.

Great George Street, June 18, 1763.

MY LORD,—I was infinitely charmed with your Lordship's letter from Stowe, for it told me the most agreeable news I can hear—of your perfect health, and of my continuing, where I am most ambitious of being, in your favourable opinion. Such a testimony I value as I ought, and that alone would be sufficient to buoy up spirits worse than mine are, under the load of calumny of late so maliciously propagated against me. I think, however, the thousand tongues of scandal are at present still, and a good deal of fulsome panegyric has for several days succeeded.

I believe that I shall experience all the douceurs of the law, without either the smart or the delay of it. I passed yesterday three hours with Sergeant Glynn, Mr. Dunning[1], Mr. Baynam, and Mr. Gardiner. Mr. Beardmore has already given your Lordship the full detail of it. I have only to add a particular about Mr. Leach, the Printer's man. Their cause against the Messengers certainly comes on next Friday, and there is but one opinion respecting all those actions.

Stowe was always rich in virtue, but now it is the galaxy. In the great list, however, which your Lord-

---

[1] Afterwards Lord Ashburton.

ship mentions, I do not hold Mr. Ch. T.[1] a *fixed* star, though he is a very bright one.

I have so much better an opportunity than the post, that I shall now only add one truth, which I am desirous that all the world should know, that I am your Lordship's most obliged, &c.   JOHN WILKES.

MR. WILKES TO EARL TEMPLE.

Great George Street, Thursday, June 30 (1763).

MY LORD,—I confess that it has ever been my ambition to gain the approbation, and to secure the good opinion of the wise and virtuous. It is impossible, therefore, for me to be indifferent as to the sentiments your Lordship may entertain of my conduct in every particular. On the contrary, I most passionately wish to have the sanction of your good opinion, and the ratification of the most unerring judgment I ever knew.

Colonel Wilkes does not now, indeed, serve under the Earl Temple as Lord Lieutenant, but his esteem for his Lordship is founded on a personal knowledge of so many and great virtues, that he is peculiarly attentive to secure that approbation which he most values. My character, my Lord, has been most wickedly and maliciously attacked, on account of my conduct as Colonel of the Bucks Militia, and particularly in respect to the clothing of the regiment[2]. May I, therefore, trouble

---

[1] Charles Townshend: his vacillation and love of change were notorious.

[2] The accounts correctly stated, and accompanied by the vouchers, showed a balance of 146*l*. due to Wilkes as Colonel of the Bucks Militia.

your Lordship, in the cause of a gentleman very highly injured, to cast your eye over the enclosed account. I am not sure that it takes in all my disbursements, but I am certain that it is right as far as it goes.

I likewise take the liberty of enclosing another little account, which respects a very worthy man, Mr. Lewellyn[1]. I hope that as Colonel I may claim some small degree of merit, but I know that I am in every particular blameless.

I am so deeply engaged with Sergeants, Counsellors, Attornies, &c., that I shall not be able to eat a single strawberry out of my own garden, nor, what I more regret, be able to pay my devoirs at Stowe before the Quarter Sessions. I shall dine at Aylesbury the 13th, and should be indeed happy there, if I had the honour of Lord Temple's company.

From the *County town*, I mean to pay my respects to the good town of *Buckingham*, and as I hear that I am on the Grand Jury for *Aylesburyshire*, I will not fail my duty there; my head-quarters, to talk still in the military, being fixed at Stowe, unless I am told of a proscription, which would indeed mortify me.

I beg my very respectful compliments to Lady Temple. I am ever, &c., &c.   JOHN WILKES.

I have given the Adjutant the enclosed account for Lord Le Despencer, the Lieutenant Colonel, the Major, and every Captain. The Vouchers were examined by the Major and the Adjutant. I have likewise sent it to the Agent.

[1] He was the Surgeon to the regiment.

MR. ALMON[1] TO EARL TEMPLE.

Sunday, July —, 1763.

MY LORD,—The Court of King's Bench having found it impossible to pass judgment upon me, did on Tuesday last discharge the whole process relating to the attachments, and at the same time Webb brought into Court a new accusation of contempt; upon which Norton moved for another writ of attachment against me.

The part of the *Letter on Libels,* upon which they have now laid fingers, is from pages 108 to 120, being all the paragraphs beginning *Or if a Chief Justice, &c.,* and some of Webb's people have sworn that they all mean Lord Mansfield.

As soon as this extraordinary motion was made, I directly consulted with Serjeant Glynn and Mr. Dunning: they were now convinced that what I told them a

---

[1] Almon began life as a journeyman printer, and having had a tolerable education, he was soon employed by the booksellers in sundry small compilations and pamphlets on temporary subjects. He was engaged by the printer of the Gazetteer, in 1761, at a fixed salary, to assist in the production of that paper, and soon after published a review of Mr. Pitt's Administration, which he dedicated to Lord Temple, and this led to an introduction and subsequent patronage. Lord Temple made him known to the Duke of Newcastle, the Duke of Devonshire, Lord Rockingham, and other leaders of the Whig party; and about this time he became a very frequent visitor in Pall Mall, and was so confidently trusted by Lord Temple, as to be called *Lord Temple's man.* After he was established as a bookseller in Piccadilly, he published some of the best political pamphlets of the day. Some account of Almon's life and correspondence was printed in a small volume entitled *Memoirs of an Eminent Bookseller;* it was not published, and is now of considerable rarity. Almon died on the 12th December, 1805; and, by a singular coincidence, as regards their connection with *Junius,* on the same day as Henry Sampson Woodfall.

fortnight before was but too true, viz., that the Court not being able to make that one paragraph (which they had taken notice of before, and which they pretended alluded to the alteration of Mr. Wilkes's record) a contempt, would shift the ground of accusation to another part of the book, and punish for something else, particularly for what was said concerning the *habeas corpus*.

The same person who gave me this information, also assured me that what the Court intended to do this term, was to commit me to next November term, and then pass sentence. Both Sergeant Glynn and Mr. Dunning now gave credit to this information, as the first part of it had already proved true, and the remainder was in a right channel for being also verified. To defeat, therefore, the excessive malice of the faction, they both sincerely advised me, as the only means to avoid a six months' useless imprisonment, to leave London immediately, and not return till the end of term, which is next Wednesday.

The day of showing cause upon this new business was fixed for Saturday, and Mr. Dunning remarked upon it that if Webb's runners could not serve me *personally* with the rule of Court, there would of course be no showing cause, and it must of necessity go off to next term, when in all probability the intended punishment would be greatly mitigated. I took their advice and left London that evening. To increase my misfortune, my wife was next day taken in labour, and all my affairs thrown into confusion. Since Tuesday my house has been constantly beset with Webb's and Carrington's gangs.

On Saturday, when to all appearance the Court of King's Bench was up, two of the judges being gone and most of the lawyers, Norton[1] skulked out of a corner, and suddenly made a motion to make the leaving of the rule at my house of the same effect as serving me personally with it; for he said I knew of it, and kept out of the way to avoid it.

An affidavit was read of my having been watched last Tuesday (a few hours after the motion that day was made) from my own house to Sergeant Glynn's and Mr. Dunning's, but in coming back the spy lost me. The truth is I did not come back, and before the rule was ready to be served I was out of town.

What the Court did on this new motion was, they ordered a rule to show cause on Tuesday next, why a rule left at my house should not be deemed *good service*. So that now there are *two* rules to show cause upon.

On Saturday night (for I had regular information of everything that passed) I consulted again with Mr. Dunning, and there is no doubt but he will do the best he can for me on Tuesday, to get the matter put off to next term; it being of too much importance, and the change not only new, but too long to be properly weighed and considered in a few days.

This will be the groundwork of his argument, and he hopes to be successful; but still he thinks it best for me to keep out of the way till term ends, as it is impossible to tell what the Court will do, and he could not have imagined they would have done what they have. In general he says that this whole affair on the part of the prosecution is so scandalous, and so infamous,

---

[1] Sir Fletcher Norton, at this time Solicitor General. He was made Attorney General in December following; became Speaker of the House of Commons on the resignation of Sir John Cust in 1770, and soon after his retirement in 1782 he was created Lord Grantley. He died in 1789.

that in all his life he never saw or heard anything equal to it.

I beg pardon for troubling your Lordship with this long letter, but presuming your Lordship would be glad to know this business, I took the liberty of writing; and I hope, when it is proper for me to come to town, to have the inexpressible pleasure of congratulating your Lordship on having it once more in your power to serve this greatly injured and unfortunate country. I am, my Lord, your Lordship's most grateful and most obedient Servant, J. ALMON.

DR. SAMUEL JOHNSON TO MR. GRENVILLE.

July 2, 1763.

SIR,—Be pleased to pay to the bearer seventy-five pounds, being the quarterly payment of a pension[1] granted by His Majesty, and due on the 24th day of June last, to Sir, your most humble Servant,

SAM. JOHNSON.

MR. WELBORE ELLIS[2] TO MR. GRENVILLE.

Pope's, July 3, 1763.

DEAR SIR,—Pursuant to your desire I send you enclosed the present and the proposed plan of Quarters in the West, which His Majesty hath approved of.

[1] It was granted from Midsummer, 1762. The honour of having recommended Johnson to Lord Bute as a proper recipient of a pension from the King, as a reward for his literary merit, belongs to Mr. Wedderburne, afterwards Earl of Rosslyn, and Lord High Chancellor. When Johnson called to thank Lord Bute, the latter distinctly told him, "It is not given to you for anything you are to do, but for what you have done."

[2] Secretary at War. He was afterwards Lord Mendip. Walpole,

I also send you enclosed a letter from Mr. Conway; in order to explain it, I am to inform you again of what I mentioned to you some time past, that, at his and Lord Granby's request, His Majesty had thought it reasonable to grant him 5*l.* per diem in addition to his pay of Lieut. General, from the time of his being stopped by the King's order at Brussels, to the day of his landing; in consideration of the extraordinary expense he was put to during the march of the army from the German cantonments to the frontiers of the Generalité, their long encampment there, their march through that country, and their embarkation, as during all that time he acted as Commander-in-Chief, and principally conducted the several transactions with the States-General, relative to the passage of those troops through their territories.

He is allowed two Aid-de-Camps, as Lieut. General on the Staff; but as he has made no charge of Secretary during these transactions, he desires that Mr. Hotham, whom he used as Secretary, should be allowed ten shillings a day by warrant from the period mentioned, to the landing of the troops.

I have endeavoured to put this off, but he now returns to the charge, to which my answer in substance was, that this not being a matter of course, he must apply to you, for you must necessarily stop the warrant, if it should be granted, until you was satisfied of the reasons for granting it; that I would lay his request before the King, but it would not have its effect without your concurrence, so that I suppose you will soon hear of it, and

---

writing at this time to Mr. Montagu, says: " I saw his (Lord Holland's) jackall t'other night in the meadows—the Secretary at War, so emptily-important, and distilling paragraphs of old news with such solemnity, that I did not know whether it was a man or the Utrecht Gazette."

I thought it right to apprize you of the state of the case, that, being master of it, you may act therein as you shall think most fit. I have the honour to be, &c., &c.

W. ELLIS.

I ask your pardon, but I find that I have left Conway's letter in town on my table, but I am persuaded that I have stated the case exactly, and, when I return, I will show you the letter, which is very short.

MR. WILKES TO EARL TEMPLE.

Great George Street, Thursday, July 7, 1763.

MY LORD,—I beg to congratulate your Lordship, as a steady friend to liberty, on the glorious verdicts which the English juries of yesterday and to day have brought in[1].

I have the most entire satisfaction in every part of the transaction.

The iron rod of oppression was lifted very high, but a few honest Englishmen have saved their country.

The joy of the people is almost universal. The trial of yesterday lasted near twelve hours. I found almost as much difficulty to get to the King's Arms, where we dined, as I did to get from Westminster Hall to George Street, and the people were almost as loud in their applauses. The two days have been most propitious to liberty, most honourable to me.

---

[1] The jury found a verdict, with three hundred pounds damages, for the plaintiff, who was one of the journeymen printers taken into custody by the King's messengers under authority of the General Warrant. The action was tried before Lord Chief Justice Pratt.

The Chief Justice is adored, and Serjeant Glynn has increased a very great stock of reputation.

I have only time to add that I am, with the justest regard, my Lord, &c., &c.   JOHN WILKES.

Seven more of the printer's men have commenced actions.

MR. WILKES TO EARL TEMPLE.

Great George Street, Saturday, July 9, 1763.

MY DEAR LORD,—I have now an opportunity, by my own servant, of writing to your Lordship beyond the possibility of the wickedness or even impertinence of an abandoned minister's coming at a sacred private correspondence, the very first essence of which is, that it is between the two correspondents only, and unfit, unfair, and in the highest degree hazardous to one of them at least.

The trials of last Wednesday and Thursday have demonstrated to me where the strength of our cause really lies; for the merchants, as I had ever the honour of submitting to your Lordship, are firm in the cause of liberty. They refused to bring in a special verdict, though the Chief Justice wished it, and the Attorney General[1], Solicitor General, and three Sergeants, repeatedly urged it.

Pratt begged more time; said he was ready, if they desired it, to deliver his opinion, but wished not to be driven to it so soon. The Jury perfectly understood the nature of special verdicts, and withstood all solicitations. They only answered, *My Lord, we are unanimous*

[1] Mr. Charles Yorke.

not to bring in a special verdict; we desire to bring in a general verdict under the direction of your Lordship.

The City are warmly my friends, and talk of 20,000*l.* damages to me. The Administration are stunned, and poor Webb [1] is really an object of compassion.

In the course of the proceedings the Chief Justice was amazingly great.

The cause only determines that a warrant of that nature, *illegally executed*, entitles to damages; but Pratt declared that he would not consider the Secretaries either as Justices or Conservators of the Peace. The origin of their power, he said, was uncertain; he believed it rested on prescription. In the pleadings the Attorney General highly condemned the *North Briton*, for private scandal, for attacking public characters, for creating disunion between England and Scotland—*the major part of which he believed well affected*—and said that lenity had been mistaken for weakness, that the attack had at last reached the Throne itself, the sacred person of the King; talked of the *brevity which became Royalty, &c.;* that he had exhibited an information against me, to which I did not think fit to appear voluntarily; that it ill became him to act contrary to the jurisdiction of a Supreme Court, to take out the compulsory process; that the King acquiesced; that this question was between Government and faction, between order and confusion, &c., in defence of the King's personal honour; with an infinite deal of other trash. He was personally very civil. The Solicitor General very decent, and in his way polite, except to the Jury.

The effect these causes have had on the public is amazing, and the Bill of Exceptions is universally con-

---

[1] Philip Carteret Webb, Solicitor to the Treasury.

demned as tyrannical. Any printer, except the cautious Mr. Wilkes, will now print anything. My spirit is applauded, for having first dared to attack Secretaries of State. All our friends here are in raptures, Spanish Charles Townshend[1], Walsh,[2] Cotes, &c.

By the Bill of Exceptions I understand that though there can be no new trial, yet the Court of Common Pleas may set the whole aside, from defects of law forms; that an appeal still lies from thence to the King's Bench, and then to the House of Lords. I am told that the whole has been excellently well conducted.

I have several times seen Glynn and Dunning. Glynn desires that Dunning may direct all the steps, and he comes this morning to settle the farther progress of it. They both lament that Beardmore mistook them at consultation. There is a jealousy in Beardmore as to Phillips[3], but I know the fatal consequences of it, and the printer's success must make Mr. W. infinitely cautious in all his proceedings.

I hear from all hands that the King is enraged at my insolence, as he terms it: I regard not his frowns nor his smiles. I will ever be his faithful subject, never his servant.

Churchill has stolen some of my ideas :—

> " I cannot truckle to a fool of state,
> Nor take a favour from the man I hate."[4]

Hypocrisy, meanness, ignorance, and insolence, cha-

---

[1] So called, because he had been Secretary to the Embassy at Madrid, and to distinguish him from his more celebrated cousin of the same name.

[2] M.P. for Worcester.

[3] The two attorneys before mentioned.

[4] These lines are from Churchill's *Epistle to Hogarth*, which was first published about this time.

racterize the King I obey. My independent spirit will never take a favour from such a man. I know that I have neither the lust of power nor of money; and if I leave my daughter less dirty coin, I will leave her more honest fame. I trust, next to her own virtue, her greatest honour will be derived from her father. I am every day more and more philosophic and retired. I live to the world, not with the world. I am my own man, and Lord Temple's. If I have any talents which can please, they shall ever be dedicated to his service[1]: I know that next winter I shall be *wholly* the man of business, and indefatigable in it; yet all my pursuits shall be directed, all my studies drawn to the focus he prescribes. Many things I formerly found very difficult are now quite easy, and I can for a day together pore over journals and votes, as well as hear trials in Guildhall, from 9 to 9.

The North Briton is almost finished. I wish to know your Lordship's opinion about printing No. 45 in the volumes. My name does not appear. I have cured the paper by a variety of extracts of the Duke of Argyle's speech, of Lord Carteret's, of Mr. Shippen's, of Mr. Pulteney, now EARL OF BATH'S, &c., &c.; King James's first speech, *Servant of the People, &c.;* Lord Oxford's trial, *Falsehood in the mouth of Majesty, &c.*

If 45 does not appear in the volumes, the idea the public has of my spirit is lost, and Government never seized the impression of No. 45 before.

I own that I much incline to it, but I wait your Lordship's better judgment.

I expect your Lordship's congratulations on my won-

[1] Quod spiro et placeo, si placeo, tuum est.—HORACE.

derful prudence, and general reformed state: I do not now myself fear a relapse.

I have printed 2000 copies of the North Briton. There are not 120 subscribers. They will be sold at half a guinea. I am not a little out of pocket by such a bold undertaking, but North Briton and Wilkes will be talked of together by posterity, and the work is, I believe, the most just and animated account of last year's politics at home.

I have tired your Lordship, but I cannot conclude without two requests I have to make, the first of which is at my heart. It is that your Lordship would give me leave to go for a month to Miss Wilkes at Paris. Her heart, she says, is set upon it—so is mine; but I will not go without your Lordship's consent. I submit even this to Lord Temple.

The other is that I find every art is exerted to create unnecessary expenses, and to increase the old ones. Only ninety guineas have been yet paid in, but many subscriptions are out. I have this cause at heart, and I feel the spirit of Hampden in it, but I have not his fortune. I believe the causes, &c. will in time pay themselves, else I shall. In the meantime 500*l*. I must contrive to get, and, after your Lordship's goodness, I even blush to mention it. I will not, therefore, enclose any note now, nor can I wish that your Lordship should be put to any inconvenience.

I trust, on the winding up of the whole affair, your Lordship will approve every particular, the most minute of which I shall beg humbly to submit.

May I beg (by my servant, who is to come to George Street) your Lordship's opinion about No. 45 being inserted in the volumes; I must determine before I leave town.

I believe Mr. Walsh and Mr. Hopkins both dine with me at Aylesbury on Wednesday. How happy should I be if Lord Temple could!

I beg, my Lord, to add my highest respects to Lady Temple, and that I am ever your Lordship's most obliged, &c., &c. JOHN WILKES.

A motto and some lines of mine.
* * * * * often here.
(*The postscript is imperfect.*)

MR. WILKES TO EARL TEMPLE.

Aylesbury, Friday, July 15 (1763).

MY DEAR LORD,—Mr. Churchill, Mr. Thornton, and I, came to this renowned borough Wednesday noon. Yesterday we assisted at the solemnity of the Quarter Sessions, where the new Lord Lieutenant made his appearance. Everything in Court passed as usual, but on our adjournment to the George, Lord Le Despencer made a short speech on the excellence of the Peace, and the propriety of addressing the Crown on that occasion.

After his Lordship had finished I objected against the proposal, said I could have wished that a proper and decent notice had been given the County; that as it was known that there was a diversity of opinion, such a notice was in all fairness and candour absolutely necessary; that I was frank to declare there, as I would everywhere else, that I thought the Peace very inadequate to, &c., insecure, and that I would not sign an

Address which contained an approbation of the Peace, for which I trusted the Ministers who had signed it would be impeached, &c., &c. Mr. Hopkins spoke next, and enlarged upon the impropriety of entering into that question when no public notice had been given of it, and Lord Le Despencer had only desired *his* friends to come to support it. Lord Le Despencer denied this, but afterwards confessed that at Oxford he had desired several of his friends to meet him at Aylesbury. Lord L. D. declared he thought the Peace absolutely necessary for us, and he knew so, and that it was a good Peace.

Dr. Taylor spoke a little, and very absurdly. A plain majority appeared, but there was no division. A copy of the Address was then read, and Mr. Charles Lowndes objected to the *abhorrence and detestation* part, of *seditious practices, insults on the honour of the Crown, &c.*

At last the Lord Lieutenant signed, Lord Boston, Sir William Bowyer, Sir Wm. Lee, Sir John Vanhattem, Mr. Drake, Mr. Freeman, Mr. R. Lowndes, Mr. Dashwood, Mr. Waller, Mr. Hampden, Mr. Knapp, Mr. Hanmer, &c.; on the other hand, Mr. Hopkins, Mr. Ch. Lowndes, Mr. Scottowe, Mr. Bell, Mr. Ball, Dr. Stevens, Mr. Pugh and I, in that room, with a few more in the next, refused to sign it.

I am sorry that I cannot pay my duty at Stowe before Sunday evening, but Mr. Walsh cannot come out of town 'till Saturday noon, when Mr. Churchill and Mr. Thornton go into Hampshire.

Messrs. Hopkins and Walsh, with Mr. Wilkes, hope to wait on Lord Temple on Sunday evening.

The post waits, 'till I have the honour of subscribing myself, my dear Lord, &c., &c.   JOHN WILKES.

MR. WILKES TO EARL TEMPLE.

Great George Street, Saturday, July 23 (1763).

MY LORD,—On my return to town I have had the happiness of finding that the City of London, and County of Surrey, are almost unanimous in the great cause of Liberty. The noble spirit and animation of the people is beyond description, and the *Bill of Exceptions* is almost universally considered as an infamous attempt to render the sacred verdicts of juries of no effect.

Mr. Onslow[1] has just left me in high spirits, eager for Thursday's Croydon battle. He promises to write your Lordship the history of the day.

The opinion of the public is that the present Administration will not subsist many days: they have long survived the good opinion, if they ever had any share of it, of their countrymen.

The post only now gives me time to acknowledge the very particular obligations I received at Stowe: every motive, both public and private, will ever bind me to be, with the justest esteem and regard, my dear Lord, &c., &c. JOHN WILKES.

EARL TEMPLE TO MR. WILKES.

Stowe, July 24, 1763.

MY DEAR SIR,—On talking over the business of the Devils[2], your friends, it is a Q. here whether it may not

---

[1] George Onslow, only son of the celebrated Speaker of the House of Commons. He was at this time M.P. for Surrey. In May, 1776, he was created Baron Cranley, and having succeeded to the title of Baron Onslow, by the death of his cousin, the third Lord, he was made Viscount Cranley and Earl of Onslow in 1801, and died in 1814.

[2] The printer's men.

be right for them to bring provisional actions with notice against the Secretaries of State; for in case the Bill of Exceptions should prevail, the six months will be elapsed, and their worships, the sage Secretaries, will escape the Devils scot free. The whole fund of their damages, if successful, will abundantly answer even all the expenses which Webb can accumulate. I should be obliged to you for a copy of Kearsley's[1] information.

I rejoice to hear the public stand in town so favourable.

I am always happy in showing myself affectionately, your faithful and obedient Servant, TEMPLE.

MR. EDWARD WESTON TO MR. GRENVILLE.

Park Place, July 25, 1763.

SIR,—I propose setting out at five to-morrow morning for my house at Somerly near Brigg, in Lincolnshire, as well for the sake of my health, which very greatly wants such a dissipation, as of some necessary affairs.

I have left in my Lord Halifax's hands my humble petition to the King, and the reasons upon which it is founded, and have most earnestly entreated his Lordship that the hearty recommendation of my request, which he has most obligingly promised, may not be deferred. I now ask the same favour of you, and have the satisfaction of being able to promise myself, from all the assurances of your kindness and friendship, that you will not refuse me. I beg such a viaticum for the remaining and last stage of my laborious journey, as may enable me to travel with comfort and convenience

[1] The publisher of the North Briton.

to the end of it. I have seen many munificent provisions made; I could almost presume to say, as St. Paul does, that I have laboured more abundantly than them all, and the reward which I have obtained for my long and painful services to the Crown in the Secretary's office is 275*l.* per annum, with the honourable title of Gazetteer. What my time in this world may be, I cannot know, but the daily threatenings of the stone, with the increase of my other infirmities, which must and will very soon put an end to my political life, will, without doubt, shorten the natural one too. Retirement, air, exercise, and above all, ease of mind, may, by God's blessing, still preserve me some years for the benefit of my family. It is what I must have recourse to, whether I succeed in my present supplication or no. It is true that I can live upon what I shall have left, but upon a narrow, confined, and niggardly plan, if I would save anything; not as one might reasonably hope to live, who has served three great kings with constant approbation, and has lived in the confidence of so many Ministers of State; nor as one whom Mr. Grenville condescends to call his friend.

I am, with all possible esteem and respect, and (if I may use so familiar language to a First Commissioner of the Treasury) with the sincerest affection, dear Sir, &c., &c. E. WESTON.

MR. WILKES TO EARL TEMPLE.

Great George Street, Monday, July 26th (1763).

MY DEAR LORD,—I am highly honoured by your Lordship's obliging favour from Stowe of the 24th. I have sent to Mr Beardmore to give him the full idea of what is proposed, that he may lay it before the Sergeant and Mr. Dunning.

I beg to submit the produce of the press in Great George Street. The French book is indeed most excellent, but is not published, nor ever to be [1].

The North Briton will walk the town quietly; no advertisement whatever of its appearance. Not a scrap, nor the least symptom of it remains here, but the dull Epsom ballad (of Mr. Mawbey's)[2] my press has groaned under.

I cannot resist a violent temptation. The voice of Prudence forbids me, but the voice of Nature and Miss Wilkes calls me for a few days only to Paris. I blush, and—deteriora sequor.

I hope, after a very short stay, to find this Cerberean, *Athanasian* Administration, routed, as I did the last.

As to my own little concerns, I shall sacrifice all revenge, all interest, all plans of dèdommagement against Lord Egremont, and Halifax, &c., the moment your Lordship wishes it, whom I leave the most entire

---

[1] From the evidence given on Wilkes's trial by Michael Curry, one of the printers employed, I find that the following works were printed at the private press in Great George Street:—

1st. The latter part of an Affidavit relating to the Loan, for which see North Briton, No. 42.

2nd. Lord Temple's pamphlet on the Seizure of Papers.

3rd. The Essay on Woman: Universal Prayer: the Dying Lover to ——: and Veni Creator paraphrased.

4th. The octavo edition of the North Briton.

5th. The Poem called the Battle of Epsom, by Mr. Mawbey.

The above were all printed between March and July, 1763. There is no account of "the French Book" mentioned above.

[2] Joseph Mawbey, at this time M.P. for Southwark. He was a very wealthy vinegar-manufacturer at Vauxhall. In 1765 he was made a Baronet. He was the author of several poetical effusions in the Gentleman's Magazine. He died in 1798.

and absolute master of my conduct, engagements, &c. I will serve under your Lordship, and under no other man. My obligations to your Lordship are indelibly engraven on a grateful heart. On my return I will be the most indefatigable politician of this country, and in a cause I have ever had at heart, that of Liberty.

I am proud to find myself every day increasing in the opinion of my countrymen, but much more to be honoured as I am, by Lord Temple.

This little excursion, though it is to give me the sight of my beloved daughter, yet hangs heavy on me from the idea of your disapprobation. I trust, however, to my own good conduct to redeem it, for I must be more than forgiven by your Lordship.

My grateful respects ever attend Lady Temple. I am, &c., &c.   JOHN WILKES.

MR. WILKES TO EARL TEMPLE.

Paris, Tuesday, August 2 (1763).

MY LORD,—I have indeed left the land of liberty for a short time, but I have not left behind me in England the liveliest sense of the many distinguished favours I have received from your Lordship, which will ever remain equally the objects of my justest pride and warmest gratitude.

I left London Tuesday morning the 26th, and reached Paris on the Saturday morning following. I had the happiness of finding Miss Wilkes in perfect health; she gave me the most sincere testimonies of real affection, many, many tears of joy.

I was received at Canterbury and Dover with many

marks of regard, and I found the true glory and stability of our country, the English sailors, no enemies to *Wilkes and Liberty.*

I saw the Duke of Richmond on my route. He was just returned from the Court, which is at Compiegne. His Grace told me that the King asked many questions about me. I find that I am not without friends, even among this nation; but I trust that every fair account from Paris will bear testimony to my discretion and reserve, two virtues I find growing upon me.

Miss Wilkes joins with me in the most respectful compliments to Lady Temple. I am, &c., &c.

JOHN WILKES.

I am at the Hotel de Saxe, Rue du Colombier, Faubourg St. Germain.

THE EARL OF EGREMONT TO MR. GRENVILLE.

Piccadilly, Wednesday afternoon (August 3, 1763).

DEAR SIR,—The transactions of this day have been more extraordinary than any of the preceding ones. Lord Halifax spoke for half an hour, as well and as temperately as man could do; exactly upon the same plan you had spoke yesterday, saying that there were but two parts to be taken after the answer of Lord Hardwicke[1], the one to stand by and support his[2]

[1] Lord Egremont had been desired by the King to offer Lord Hardwicke the post of President of the Council, which had not been filled up since the death of Lord Granville. Lord Hardwicke, however, declined it upon the plea of his political connections, and his wish not to be separated from the Duke of Newcastle and others of his party. See an account of his conferences with Lord Egremont, in *Harris's Life of Lord Hardwicke*, vol. iii. p. 369.

[2] The King's.

Administration, the other to form another by taking in the Opposition: pressed him to resolve soon, that we were equally prepared to fight the battle to the utmost, if he decided for the first, or to retire if he decided for the latter; after turning this all the ways that eloquence could dictate or invent, no answer at all was made; and what was more remarkable, and contrary to whatever had appeared before, when Halifax talked of his giving support and confidence, and paused upon those words, not even the usual general assurances were given; and when he said that sure he could not mean to take in the whole body, and yield to the invasion of those he had detested, and paused upon that, the usual disclaiming of that was also suppressed, and nothing but obstinate silence.

The same thing happened to me when I spoke, and a resolution not to give even a civil evasive answer was the whole of the behaviour. I must say, one so insulting and uncivil I never knew, nor could conceive could be held to two gentlemen.

We propose trying again to-morrow, and in the meantime Lord Halifax writes to my Lord Chancellor. I write this to you desiring to know your thoughts upon this should it continue, whether we should never see him, except about office business, 'till your return, or whether we should (if so used for a constancy) put an end to it, and declare our inability to stay upon that foot. Pray be so good as to send back the messenger that we may hear by Friday before the Levée. I am, &c., &c.
                                                    EGREMONT.

MR. GRENVILLE TO THE EARL OF EGREMONT.

Wotton, Thursday morning, August 4, 1763.

MY DEAR LORD,—Your letter of yesterday was delivered to me by the messenger last night between ten and eleven.

The account contained in it was, indeed, as unsatisfactory and as unpleasing as is possible, but it was so exactly similar to that which I gave you and Lord Halifax of what had passed with me on Tuesday upon the same subject, that I was not in the least surprised at it. I see no alteration whatever, and supposing it to stand on the same footing as this transaction was then left upon, your Lordships have been fully apprized of my sentiments with regard to a question of this very great importance, and of the reasons upon which they were founded.

I have since considered it more fully, and am still of the same opinion that no final step should be taken until the option which has been given shall be determined one way or the other.

To wait ten days or a fortnight, if it is wished, for the decision of an alternative which has been so temperately and so firmly stated, is certainly more decent than to insist upon the conclusion of it in eight-and-forty hours[1].

This proposition seems to me equally true, whether we think it uncertain how this matter is to end, or whether we believe it to be absolutely settled.

In the former case such a hasty step would really

---

[1] After Lord Hardwicke's refusal, the King had desired an interval of ten days for consideration, before he took a final resolution with regard to the future arrangement of the Administration.

determine against us what is uncertain, and would make us answerable for the consequences; in the latter it would furnish the pretence which those that have advised a measure so dishonourable either in a public or private light, may probably wait for, and will certainly avail themselves of.

It will be urged, as a justification of this conduct, after the solemn engagements entered into, and the repeated assurances given to us, that it was owing to our precipitation alone, and that it was our own act which forced on and rendered unavoidable, what otherwise would never have been consented to. It will change our ground entirely. We entered into the King's service, called to it from principles of duty and respect, to hinder the law from being indecently and unconstitutionally given to him. We have continued in his service upon these principles; let us leave it with the same, and let us not *be complained of* as the authors of that very measure of which we have so much right *to complain*, and have sacrificed so much to prevent.

I do not see what inconveniency or impropriety the giving way to the King's wishes by this short delay will, in the present circumstances, be attended with. I call it a short delay, for, from the nature of this transaction, the decision of it cannot be long depending. There is no particular act of Government now in agitation which you are called upon to execute or to refuse. What are the motives, then, that are to be assigned for putting an end to the situation? The want of confidence and communication, the evident marks of that superior influence[1] to which it is owing, and the desire not to facilitate a change that you disapprove by giving time to concert it?

[1] Lord Bute.

If all the circumstances of this great alteration in Government shall continue to be concealed from us, the complaint of want of confidence and communication will be still much stronger than it is, the marks of that superior influence still more evident, and our conduct, in consequence of them, will stand, if possible, upon better ground.

Our continuance in our respective offices will not, I think, facilitate this change; on the contrary, it must embarass those that *treat*, and those that are *treated* with, whereas our immediate resignation would be a dereliction or abdication, that must force a settlement upon their own terms, and would, to a certain degree, justify the person treating, and *them* for treating with him. If any arrangement has been thought of, it would carry it into immediate execution with advantage. If none has yet been considered, it would furnish the best argument for surrendering at discretion.

Such, my dear Lord, are my thoughts upon the question you have stated to me, which, as you have desired to know them, I have again repeated. I will add to them only one consideration more. You tell me Lord Halifax has writ to my Lord Chancellor, which I am extremely glad of; but, after having writ to him, it would surely be improper to make any *declaration* of your resolution not to continue, beyond what you have already made without his participation, as it is impossible for him to take any step (whatever his inclinations may be) 'till he sees the King, and shall be authentically informed of His Majesty's intentions with regard to the supposed alterations in his Government.

I shall be impatient to hear his answer to your communication, as well as the result of the further trial which you propose making to-day. You will see, by what I have writ, how strongly I am of opinion that you should wait for the King's answer, which (if you continue to see him upon the office business, as I should wish you would) cannot, I think, be long deferred; if it is given before I have the pleasure of seeing you here, or that you otherwise think it necessary, I will come to town whenever you send to me.

My kindest and most affectionate compliments wait upon Lady Egremont and Lord Halifax.

I am ever, &c., &c.   GEORGE GRENVILLE.

THE EARL OF EGREMONT TO MR. GRENVILLE.

Petersham, August 6, 1763, half-past 8.

DEAR SIR,—I send you one more messenger because Halifax desires it, to transmit the enclosed copy of the answer to Lord Chancellor. As it contains absolutely nothing to assist or determine our judgment, perhaps it was scarce worth a courier, but he wished you should see how unusually cautious and dry our friend is upon this great occasion; however, I should draw from it that he had had no communication of this before; and hope, that from his presumption that it must be public in a few days, he will not make it so.

I sent you word by a post letter how placid and gracious the behaviour had been to me at St. James's on Thursday, of which I availed myself to settle all my American affairs, that I at all cared for: quorum unus is Mr. Whichcot's relation Mattison.

Friday I did not go, but my colleague (then recovered from his cold, &c.) did, and the words he wrote me of that day's Closet were as follows :—*All was kindness and affability in the Closet to-day; but not a word passed on the great question.*

I have known, I think certainly, that nothing has passed in point of negotiation with the Duke of Bedford, at least, I am sure nothing has transpired to my Lord Chamberlain[1]; and I am equally sure nothing has passed with your relations[2]; but whether any proposal may not have been already, or intended to be extended by other hands, I cannot tell; should rather fancy it is so intended to be, for I think nothing will make the fluctuating mind of the chief spring[3] of all this confusion resolve to do fairly by us, but absolute necessity and fear; most probably when it will be too late.

This uncertain situation cannot, I hope, last long, and at your return I trust it will be explained one way or the other, and that we shall be either public or private men.

I hope to have the pleasure of seeing you some time Thursday or Friday by noon. I am ever, &c.

EGREMONT.

THE LORD CHANCELLOR TO THE EARL OF HALIFAX.

(*Enclosed with the foregoing letter.—A copy, in Lord Egremont's hand.*)

August 5, 1763.

MY DEAR LORD,—I return many thanks for your obliging attention to me, in communicating to me so

---

[1] Lord Gower, the Duchess of Bedford's brother.
[2] Mr. Pitt and Lord Temple. Up to this time no negotiation had commenced.
[3] Lord Bute.

critical and so extraordinary a piece of intelligence, which, however secret at present, must in its nature be public in a very few days, and which in itself reveals its consequences.

It is a subject too tender to be wrote upon farther; I, therefore, conclude with one truth, that I am with true regard, &c., &c. HENLEY.

MR. CALCRAFT[1] TO EARL TEMPLE.

August 10, 1763.

MY LORD,—Your Lordship will probably be surprised at this letter[2], but you will, I hope, allow me so far to presume on our last conversation, as to ask through what channel in your absence some communication may

---

[1] John Calcraft was originally a Clerk in the War Office. He became an Army Agent, and, under the patronage of Fox, contrived to amass a very large fortune. At this time he held the office of Deputy Commissary General of Musters. His letters in the *Chatham Correspondence* show that he lived for many years in the most intimate confidence of Mr. Pitt and Lord Temple, and he was the medium of their reconciliation in 1768. He died in 1772.

[2] It marks the commencement of the negotiations between Lord Bute and Mr. Pitt. Calcraft was employed by Lord Bute, through the medium of Lord Shelburne, to open a communication with Pitt, and he was also desired to write to the Duke of Bedford, Lord Gower, and others of that connection. In a letter from Rigby to the Duke of Bedford (*Bedford Correspondence*, vol. iii. p. 236), it will be seen that Calcraft went to Hayes on the 15th, and had an interview of three hours' duration with Mr. Pitt, who said he should decline coming into employment without the whole of the Whig party. Mr. Grenville's authority (see *Diary, infra*) says, that Pitt was willing to treat, but that he would not engage if the Duke of Bedford was to have an office in the Government, although it appears the Bedford party were now willing to act with Mr. Pitt. This transaction of Lord Shelburne's was altogether unknown to Mr. Grenville at the time; but the King subsequently acknowledged it, and promised that nothing of the sort should ever happen again.

be had with Mr. Pitt, if I should hear it wished for, and to assure your Lordship no improper use shall be made of such confidence: in return I must entreat the favour of your Lordship to keep this letter an entire secret on your part, as it shall ever remain on mine, and believe me, I would neither wantonly nor improperly trouble you. I send it by a private messenger, who will bring any answer you may be pleased to honour me with; and when I have the pleasure of seeing your Lordship, you shall have the reasons for this address fully explained by him, who is with great truth and respect, your Lordship's most obedient and most humble Servant, J. CALCRAFT.

EARL TEMPLE TO MR. CALCRAFT.

Hackwood, August 12, 1763.

SIR,—Your letter of the 10th instant reached me here in my way to the West; and though I confess I do not collect with sufficient precision the extent of what is meant to be conveyed by it, yet it bears such obliging marks of your friendly regards to me, that I cannot but regret that my journey upon business will not permit me to hope that I can have an opportunity of seeing you very soon.

As to my opinion which you desire to know with regard to the channel by which some communication may be had with Mr. Pitt, if it should be wished for, all I can say on so delicate a subject is, that I have always thought that in any matter which really imports the public good, the most natural and direct way of going is the best.

I understand Mr. Pitt will be returned to Hayes about the beginning of next week, and that he is not likely to make any distant excursions for the rest of the summer.

Permit me to add that I shall on all occasions take a particular pleasure in showing you every mark of regard in my power, and that I have the honour to be, with great truth, &c., &c. TEMPLE.

THE EARL OF EGREMONT TO MR. GRENVILLE.

Friday, August 12, 1763.

DEAR SIR,— . . . . . Nothing new here, but bad accounts from Russia. I think our friend the Earl of Bucks has spoiled our affairs at that Court, as Sir Charles Williams did some years ago; with less excuse, as the other could at least plead a very good one for acting like a madman. Adieu! ever yours.

EGREMONT.

THE EARL OF HALIFAX TO MR. GRENVILLE.

Great George Street, Friday evening, (August 26, 1763).

MY DEAR SIR,—You probably will judge better on your own affairs than I can do for you, but I cannot go with ease out of town without telling you that I cannot agree in opinion that it would be right to ask the King to-morrow whether you should, or should not, go on with your Treasury business; it would look, I think, too much like asking your discharge, and bear the appearance of ill humour. As to myself, I shall go on with the business of both Secretaries' offices, just as if nothing new had happened. I am, &c., &c.

DUNK HALIFAX.

MR. GRENVILLE TO THE EARL OF HALIFAX.

Downing Street, August 27, 1763, 4 o'clock.

MY DEAR LORD.—I have just now seen the King, and have followed your advice in saying nothing about going on with the business of the Treasury, and in doing nothing that had the appearance of ill humour.

Mr. Pitt was with His Majesty at the Queen's House when I came in, and stayed near two hours. I do not know the particulars, but by what I collected, the measure is fully taken[1].

---

[1] The author of a criticism in the Quarterly Review upon the *Chatham Correspondence*, has observed that it is still a mystery why the negotiation between George the Third and Mr. Pitt for the formation of a Ministry to displace George Grenville, which appeared to be so amicably arranged on the 27th of August, 1763 (Saturday), was so suddenly broken off and abandoned on the Monday following.

The chief authority which has been hitherto relied upon for an account of this transaction is a letter from Lord Hardwicke to his son Lord Royston, dated a few days afterwards, in which he professes to give a true relation of the circumstances, having heard the whole from the Duke of Newcastle, and subsequently *de source* from Mr. Pitt. All other accounts are, in general, founded upon Lord Hardwicke's letter, in which he has designated it as "the most extraordinary transaction that ever happened in any Court in Europe, even in times as extraordinary as the present."

In this statement we have all that is known of Mr. Pitt's version of his interviews and conversations with the King, for there is nothing in the *Chatham Correspondence* which throws any stronger light upon the matter in question. Even Horace Walpole does not pretend to give an entire account of the negotiation, of which he says, "No transaction was ever involved in more contradictions and mystery, for though the retainers on both sides spoke out, and amply, their narrations disagreed materially, and the exact truth was never fully known."

In these papers will be found Mr. Grenville's relation of the circumstances derived *de source* from the King himself, and vouched by his authority.

The interview between Lord Bute and Mr. Pitt was arranged by the Lord Mayor (Beckford), at the request of the former. It took place on Thursday evening, the 25th of August, at Mr. Pitt's house in

This is all that I can say to you upon this subject 'till we meet. I am, &c., &c. GEORGE GRENVILLE.

Jermyn Street, and it may be inferred that in the conversation which ensued, Lord Bute was not then displeased at the terms which Mr. Pitt proposed for coming into office, because he stated that from those terms he could not depart, and therefore if the King could not consent to them, he had better not see him.

Upon Lord Bute's report, however, of this conversation to the King, Mr. Pitt was commanded by a note from His Majesty to attend him at the Queen's House on the Saturday following.

In this audience, which lasted three hours, the King listened with great patience and attention to the whole of Mr. Pitt's plan; and the latter affirmed that in general, and upon the most material points, the King appeared by his manner and many of his expressions to be convinced. At the conclusion Mr. Pitt was desired to wait upon His Majesty on the Monday following, in order to confirm the preliminaries which had been thus commenced for the new arrangement; and as Mr. Pitt had been fully impressed with the sincerity of Lord Bute, so he also believed that the King was " in earnest," and all that is known from other sources tends to corroborate this opinion. Mr. Pitt therefore left the Royal presence with the full persuasion from the King's manner and behaviour that "the thing would do." He went the next morning to Claremont to communicate with the Duke of Newcastle upon the subject; he wrote to the Duke of Devonshire and the Marquess of Rockingham to desire their attendance in town, and the Duke of Newcastle undertook to write to Lord Hardwicke for the same purpose. The Duke of Cumberland having heard of the negotiation, concluded, by a letter from Lord Albemarle to the Duke of Newcastle, that the steadiness and unanimity of the party had brought everything about to the satisfaction of Mr. Pitt.

Mr. Grenville, who went into the King's Closet immediately afterwards, and found his Majesty *a good deal confused and flustered*, says, "My interview was short, and no notice was taken of the audience which preceded mine;" he adds, "I have since heard from other hands that *carte blanche* is given, which account tallies with such observations as I could make;" and again, "I do not know the particulars, but from what I collected the measure is fully taken."

Another circumstance, too, strengthens still more the belief that the King was "in earnest" on this occasion. The significant manner of his taking leave of Mr. Grenville, as if he were parting with a man whom he should not again receive in his official capacity:— " the King said, with emotion, 'good morrow, Mr. Grenville,' and

MR. GRENVILLE TO THE EARL OF HALIFAX.

Downing Street, August 27, 1763.

MY DEAR LORD,—I really can tell you no particulars which you do not already know. My interview was repeated it again a second time, which was a phrase he never had used to him before."

Besides, it would perhaps be doing injustice to the character of George the Third, if it were supposed that he could, or would, endeavour to use so much dissimulation as would deceive the profound sagacity and experience of Mr. Pitt.

Lord Bute had an interview with the King on Saturday evening, and remained with him until a late hour, and was with him again early on Sunday morning, and then went to Kew, "where he saw Mr. Elliott and Mr. Jenkinson, who had a long discourse with him, in which they terrified him so much upon the consequences of the step he had persuaded the King to take, that he determined to depart from it, and to advise His Majesty to send to Mr. Grenville."

Thus it will be perceived that it was not the extravagant demands of Mr. Pitt which had alarmed the King, but that it was the wavering timidity and irresolution of Lord Bute which caused the abandonment of this negotiation. Mr. Jenkinson and Mr. Elliott were both in his most intimate confidence; the one had been his private Secretary, and was now a Secretary of the Treasury, the other Treasurer of the King's chambers; both of them had places to lose, and both of them were equally the intimate friends of Mr. Grenville, and therefore no doubt they would employ the strongest arguments in their power to work upon the fears of Lord Bute, to make him "afraid to think what he had done," and induce him to advise the King to send again for Mr. Grenville, and give up the idea of any extensive change in the Government.

The King, who it is evident was completely and entirely under the guidance of Lord Bute, readily adopted his views, and the same afternoon "Mr. Grenville received a message from the King to come to him at 8 o'clock in the evening. When he came, he found the King in the greatest agitation: His Majesty told him he had seen Mr. Pitt, explained to him the terms which he had demanded, that they were too hard, that he could not think of complying with them, and that he had, therefore, once more sent to Mr. Grenville to tell him he wished to put his affairs into his hands, that he gave him the fullest assurances of support, &c., &c."

This being settled, there was still the pending audience of Mr. Pitt very short, and no notice was taken of the long audience that preceded mine. I have since heard from other hands that *carte blanche* is given, which account tallies with such observations as I could make. I feel most sensibly the indignation you so warmly express against the North Briton of to-day. I think the present situation

fixed by the King for the day following, to be disposed of, and which, no doubt, His Majesty considered would be somewhat embarassing. Lord Bute, therefore, in order to do his part in breaking to Mr. Pitt the change which had taken place, sent Mr. Beckford early on Monday morning, to express his regret that the negotiation had failed by the high terms demanded, and offering other terms, which however Beckford could not prevail upon Mr. Pitt to listen to.

"Observe," says Mr. Grenville in his *Diary*, "that this extraordinary offer was made by Lord Bute after the King had told Mr. Grenville that he looked upon the negotiation with Mr. Pitt as over."

And now comes what Lord Hardwicke calls " the catastrophe of Monday." The King received Mr. Pitt very graciously, and the audience lasted near two hours. The King began, that he had considered of what had been said, and mentioned certain proposals, *still proceeding upon the supposition of a change.* Mr. Pitt hesitated objections; assured the King that affairs could not be carried on without the great families who had supported the revolution government, and other great persons, of whose abilities and integrity the public had had experience, and who had weight and credit in the nation ; that he should only deceive His Majesty if he should leave him in an opinion that he could go on, or make a solid administration upon any other foot. "Well, Mr. Pitt," said the King, " I see (or I fear) this won't do. My honour is concerned, and I must support it." And thus ended the conference :—"*Sic finita est fabula,*" says Lord Hardwicke.

Mr. Pitt subsequently affirmed to his friends that if he were examined upon oath, he could not pretend to say upon what this negotiation brake off, whether upon any particular point, or upon the general complexion of the whole ; but that if the King should assign any particular reason for it, he will never *contradict it.*

Lord Shelburne, who was instrumental in commencing this negotiation, in writing to Mr. Pitt at its termination, " felicitates him personally and very sincerely on a negotiation being at an end, which carried through the whole of it such shocking marks of insincerity, and if it had taken another turn, must have laid a weight on his shoulders of a most irksome nature, on account of the peculiar circumstances attending it."

may very probably occasion more productions of the same infamous nature, which I agree with you in wishing to see directed rather against the living than the dead. I am, &c., &c. GEORGE GRENVILLE.

After having sealed this letter I have this moment received yours, dated at eight o'clock this evening, and have opened this to answer your questions.

My reception was a cold one, and no proposition was made, or seemed likely to be made, either relative to you or to myself; nor could I, by any means, obtain information of what was already settled or intended.

I scarce know how to form an opinion of the ecclesiastical vacancies, or those which remain in America, 'till some further trial is made about them. Adieu, my dear Lord.

MR. GRENVILLE TO THE EARL OF HALIFAX.

Downing Street, August 28, 1763.

MY DEAR LORD,—The King sent to me to come to him at the Queen's House, at eight o'clock this evening, and has kept me till half an hour ago. A new scene has been opened in consequence of the extraordinary terms demanded yesterday.

I am desired to inform you of this without delay, and I beg you will come to town as early as you possibly can to-morrow, that I may apprize you of the state that things are in, and that we may concert together what is to be done. I am, my dear Lord, &c., &c.

GEORGE GRENVILLE.

THE EARL OF HALIFAX TO MR. GRENVILLE.

Great George Street, Monday evening,
7 o'clock (August 29, 1763).

DEAR SIR,—It has occurred to me that it is very material that, in your conversation with the King this evening, you be positively informed whether Mr. Pitt proposed his extravagant conditions as his own, or whether he was authorized to do so by the Duke of Newcastle and the rest of the opponents[1]; perhaps they will disavow his unreasonable proposition; and if so, we may break the opposition and leave those worthy gentlemen, Lord Temple, Mr. Pitt, and their attached friends, in the lurch.

I fear this can't be done, and that what has passed has been in concert; however, I think it is of great consequence that we should be assured of this fact.

I shall expect you when you come from the King, and am, my dear Sir, &c., &c.   DUNK HALIFAX.

Pray inform yourself as particularly as you can on this head, on which much may depend.

MR. WILKES TO EARL TEMPLE.

Paris, Monday, August 29 (1763).

MY LORD,—I had the honour of transmitting to your Lordship the last week an exact detail of what passed

[1] It was not likely that Pitt would condescend to make conditions upon the authority of the Duke of Newcastle; but Lord Halifax was speculating upon the possibility of detaching the Duke of Newcastle, Lord Hardwicke, the Duke of Devonshire, and some others, from the party of Mr. Pitt and Lord Temple.

here between Captain Forbes[1] and me. I flatter myself that it met with the sanction of your Lordship's approbation, as it has with that of our countrymen here, and of all the French. The account I had to settle with Lord Egremont, which has dwelt on my mind ever since (and I told the Governor of the Tower the particulars of the treatment, and my resolution), is at length in another way put an end to, and, as a Frenchman would say, il m'a joué un vilain tour.

I am now, therefore, a free man, entirely at Captain Forbes's service, if he pleases to call upon me in a way becoming a gentleman; and I will attend him with his second anywhere in the Empress Queen's dominions, or out of the territories of France. I have not since heard of him, and I believe Paris is too expensive for his pocket.

I am detained here much beyond my intention, for I find the house in which Miss Wilkes is, does not quite answer my plan of her education; and I need not mention to your Lordship how much in my heart her welfare rises superior to every other consideration. The moment I have settled this business, I shall return to England.

I was at Compiegne for three days. I visited Mr. Neville, who returned my visit the next day.

He is come back to Paris, but I have not yet seen him.

The Ministry here, I am told, are unanimous in

---

[1] A Scotchman who accosted him in the streets at Paris, and insisted upon his fighting a duel with him, because he had written against his country. Wilkes promised to indulge him, but that he was then under an engagement of a similar nature with Lord Egremont. That affair, however, was terminated by the melancholy end of Lord Egremont, who died very suddenly on the 21st instant.

encomiums, the most extravagant which can be imagined, on the virtue of the Scottish Minister, in which the Paris world is not at all duped.

The preparations making everywhere demonstrate what is meant by this. The Parliament of Rouen has made the strongest remonstrances against the new taxes, and refused the register.

The Duke of Harcourt attended them in the King's name, and commanded the clerks to make the entry. No man uttered a syllable, and the Parliament went away, leaving only the Duke and his Private Secretary in the House. The Secretary then made the entry. Soon after, the Parliament returned, and *ordered the entry to be erased from their books.*

This is a new and the boldest step which has yet been taken. Four regiments of horse are on their march there. Two other Parliaments have followed the example of that of Rouen. The distress in the provinces is risen to a great height. Paris is as gay as usual. The five last years the Government have been at the expense of several public shows in the city, &c. for the people. The most sensible men here think that this country is on the eve of a great revolution.

I hear from Mr. Churchill that he has several poems on the stocks; particularly one for next winter, an *Epic*, to be called *Culloden*.

My favourite will be *Liberty*, an epistle to her darling son, *Earl Temple*. I am ever, with the truest devotion and gratitude, &c., &c.   JOHN WILKES.

Miss Wilkes joins with me in the most respectful compliments to Lady Temple.

MR. GILBERT ELLIOT TO MR. GRENVILLE.

August 31, 1763.

DEAR SIR,—I was very sorry I could not be at Court this day, but, as I was desired to go to the country with Lord Bute, I thought I might be of more use there. I find him steady in his purpose of absolute retirement, and of not at all meddling in any business or arrangement: he also assured me he was determined to quit the Privy Purse, and I suggested to him that I supposed the King would consult with you about the filling it.

He seems extremely desirous that you may be armed with every degree of power so necessary at this juncture[1]. I am ever, &c.
G. E.

---

[1] Lord Bute must have been in a state of great perplexity at this moment, when he found that all his projects had failed, and chiefly by his own irresolution. Perhaps Mr. Elliot was desired by the King to go out of town with Lord Bute, and as he (Mr. Elliot) was certainly desirous that Mr. Grenville should remain in office, he might think he should be more useful there in keeping Lord Bute steady to his purpose of interfering no further in the Ministerial arrangements. This letter is important, because it at once settles a question respecting which there has been much misrepresentation. It proves that Lord Bute's retirement from Court was the result of his own resolution, and that it had not, *at this time*, been urged upon the King by the Ministers as a stipulation for their retaining office. There can be little doubt that they earnestly wished for his absence, but Mr. Grenville's language to the King for some time after was only to the effect that his retreat was necessary in consequence of the great ferment there was against him in the country. It is certain they had hitherto shown no desire to effect his removal by any attempt to force or restrain the King's inclinations upon the subject. Neither was he, as Walpole has reported, *deprived* of the office of Keeper of the Privy Purse; he resigned it very shortly after, and the circumstances of Sir William Breton's appointment to succeed him are fully related in Mr. Grenville's Diary. Lord Bute went out of London to reside permanently at Luton in Bedfordshire (an estate he had recently purchased), on the 5th of October.

THE EARL OF SANDWICH TO MR. GRENVILLE.

Almack's, Wednesday, 7 o'clock (August 31, 1763).

Dear Sir,—I find that Lord Weymouth[1] set out yesterday for Trentham[2]; knowing his connections, I am persuaded it is a political visit, particularly as he was engaged to go there with me (if things had remained quiet), and never sent to know whether I had changed my mind, or would be of the party. My friend Lord March[3], whose zeal cannot be too much applauded, will set out for the same place early to-morrow morning, in order that Lord Gower may hear the true state of things, before he sees the Duke of Bedford in his way to town.

I have seen and heard some other things in the same quarter, which I don't like, and shall be glad to explain to you, either this evening after 10 o'clock, or at any other hour to-morrow morning that you shall name.

I am, most sincerely yours,   Sandwich.

MR. WELBORE ELLIS TO MR. GRENVILLE.

Pope's, September 2, 1763.

Dear Sir,—I shall set out this day for Hampshire, where I shall be ready to receive and execute any commands you shall have for me. Having now pledged myself so fully and strongly to His Majesty and to you,

---

[1] Thomas Thynne, Viscount Weymouth, afterwards Marquess of Bath.

[2] The seat of Earl Gower.

[3] James, Earl of March, afterwards Duke of Queensberry. He was at this time one of the Lords of the King's Bedchamber. He died in 1810.

I will not do you or myself the injustice to think, that if I mention to you any wish or inclination with regard to myself, that you can consider it as making any conditions, which in truth I should think a very unworthy proceeding in me at this conjuncture: I persuade myself therefore that you will look upon it as a mark of my confidence in you, and an additional pledge of my sincerity when I testify an inclination to be obliged to you.

My opinion is that you design, if nothing should obstruct, to give the seals to Lord Sandwich, and shall be well pleased (if you should think it for your service) if you can gain by that opening Mr. T.[1] to support cordially His Majesty's affairs in your hands. If that should fail, I shall be truly glad if you can thereby, from any other quarter, add strength to Government; but if those views should be disappointed, I will own to you my ambition, that I should be very happy to serve His Majesty in that office, of the Admiralty, if that should not be thought too extravagant a wish; as I was many years conversant in that department, and took some pains to understand it.

I lay myself open to you with great frankness and confidence, and, let me add, with great cordiality and good humour, which I assure you, should His Majesty, or should you not think proper for me, will receive no alteration, but I shall be, as I am, with great truth and respect, &c., &c. W. ELLIS.

[1] Mr. Charles Townshend, who, it was expected, would be First Lord of the Admiralty, but the office was not offered to him upon *this* occasion.

MR. GRENVILLE TO LORD STRANGE[1].

Downing Street, September 3, 1763.

MY DEAR LORD,—You will probably have heard before this letter[2] can reach you, of the interview which Mr. Pitt had with His Majesty at the Queen's House, on Saturday and Monday last. Your situation and rank in the King's service, and the personal regard which is so justly due to you on every account, have induced me to write to you upon this extraordinary transaction, that I may mark that attention to you, which, both as a public and as a private man, I shall always be glad to pay you, and that I may be informed (as far as you shall judge proper to favour me with them) of your sentiments upon a subject so important to the King and to his Government [and upon which the advice and assistance of those who are attached to him and to their country is so necessary]. His Majesty's intention in sending for Mr. Pitt, and the proposition which he made, was to dispose of the office of Lord President, and of that of Secretary of State, vacant by the unhappy loss of my friend and brother, Lord Egremont, in any manner that might best contribute to the general satisfaction, and to take such farther arrangements as could be made agreeable to the parties concerned in

---

[1] James Lord Stanley, eldest son of Edward, the eleventh Earl of Derby. He usually called himself Lord Strange, though the title, which was a Barony in fee, had in fact descended to the Duke of Athol as heir-general of James, the seventh Earl of Derby. He was M.P. for the County of Lancaster, and Chancellor of the Duchy of Lancaster. He died in June, 1771, in the lifetime of his father.

[2] The same letter was also addressed to the Marquess of Granby, with the exception of the words placed between brackets, which were omitted in the letter sent to Lord Granby. It was read by Mr. Grenville to the King, and approved by His Majesty before it was sent.

them. At the same time the King declared that he would never consent to any proposal that was inconsistent with his honour in regard to the measures which he had followed, or to the protection of all those whose conduct towards him he had reason to approve. [I own I did not believe that this step thus made would be attended with good consequences to the King's service, and therefore when it was communicated to me I advised against it, for the reasons which I will explain to your Lordship when we meet, although I earnestly desired that no personal or private consideration of mine should be interposed to stop a measure which His Majesty was told would be for the public good. Lord Halifax joined with me in this advice, and we were sorry to see that the event answered our expectations.]

Mr. Pitt insisted upon excluding all that had had any hand in the Peace, which he represented as dishonourable, dangerous, and criminal, although he did not intend to break it, but to *ameliorate* it in the execution. With regard to persons, he proposed to turn out almost every civil officer of rank in the King's service, and to introduce all those who had engaged in the Opposition in their stead.

The great extent and the violence of these propositions, and of many others, the particulars of which cannot be comprised in this letter [and the consideration of His Majesty's honour in not abandoning those who had been called to his support, and of his conscience in not blaming a measure so salutary as he judged that of the Peace to be for his people], determined the King to reject such terms, and to put an entire end to this transaction.

He was then pleased to send for me, and to express

his desire that I should continue in the high post to which he had called me for carrying on his Government, and to declare in the most gracious terms his fixed and unalterable determination of supporting me to the utmost in the execution of it, and that he would upon no account submit to the force thus intended to be put upon him. I told His Majesty that I came into his service to preserve the constitution of my country, and to prevent any undue and unwarrantable force being put upon the Crown; that upon these principles I should continue to act, and would endeavour, as far as I was able, to assist the King in the difficulties he lay under; but that the success of these endeavours must depend upon the King himself, and upon the cordial union of all such as were attached to his service. As to the former, I have every possible reason to be fully convinced of His Majesty's firm resolution, and with regard to the latter, I cannot but believe that the necessity of it is too evident, and the reasons for it too cogent, to want any inforcement.

Lord Bute [out of regard to what he thinks will be most for His Majesty's interest] has declared that he is determined to retire, and to absent himself not only from the Councils, but from the presence and place of residence of His Majesty, until the suspicion of his influence on public business shall be entirely removed. I have now communicated to your Lordship the general state of things, as far as can be done by letter, reserving the particulars till I have the pleasure of seeing you here. I have done it that you may be apprized of it yourself, and that you may be able to obviate any wrong impressions that may be given to others. I shall always be most desirous to deserve your approbation, and I flatter myself, from the principles which I have acted upon, that in this instance I shall obtain it. I know your zealous attachment to the King and to the good of your country [and that from the approbation of men like you, the best and most solid support will be derived to the King's Government].

You will therefore allow me to express my wishes to hear from you on this critical situation, and to assure you of the most affectionate regard and perfect esteem with which I am ever, &c., &c.

GEORGE GRENVILLE.

Lord Granby is desired to come to town as soon as his health will permit.

MR. GRENVILLE TO THE DUKE OF LEEDS[1].

Downing Street, September 3, 1763.

MY LORD,—The audience which Mr. Pitt had of His Majesty at the Queen's House on Saturday and on Monday last, and the great extent of the demands then made, both with regard to men and measures, have made the King desirous that I should speak with the principal persons in his Government upon the subject of that extraordinary transaction, and the dispositions that will be necessary in consequence of His Majesty's refusal, and of his resolution never to comply with terms that he thinks inconsistent with his honour and his conscience. It is, therefore, by his command that I now trouble your Grace, to desire that you will come to town either to-day or to-morrow, at latest, if that is more convenient to you, and that you will appoint, by

[1] Thomas Osborne, fourth Duke of Leeds.

the messenger whom I shall dispatch with this letter, any time to-morrow, that I may have the honour of waiting upon your Grace. I am, with the highest respect, &c., &c. GEORGE GRENVILLE.

THE EARL OF SANDWICH TO MR. GRENVILLE.

Woburn, Saturday morning (September 3, 1763).

DEAR SIR,—I drop this letter in my way to Bushey (where I promised to dine with Lord Halifax, if I had done my business), to tell you that you may assure His Majesty that no one is more zealously devoted to him than the Duke of Bedford, who approves the present system in all its parts, and will give it every support in his power, both with his own activity and that of his friends.

I don't think he will choose an employment, but even that I am not quite certain of. I am, &c.

SANDWICH.

MR. GRENVILLE TO THE DUKE OF BEDFORD.

Downing Street, September 5, 1763.

MY LORD,—It was with infinite pleasure that I received from Lord Sandwich the account of your Grace's resolution to give every support in your power to the system which the King has been pleased to form for carrying on his Government in the present difficult conjuncture—a resolution worthy your Grace's character, and the attachment you have always shown to His Majesty and the Constitution of this kingdom.

The situation which this country was left in at the

happy close of the late ruinous war, and the spirit of licence and disorder which has attended it, and which has since been so industriously augmented, demand the strictest union in all who wish to put a stop to an evil that threatens equally the King and his people. This consideration, enforced by your Grace's example, and supported by your authority and abilities, will, I doubt not, open the eyes of many in an hour of so much public danger, not only to the honour and lawful rights of the Crown, but to the peace and happiness of the kingdom. I am confident that the King feels very sensibly this signal instance of your Grace's zeal and affection, at a time when the exertion of them is so necessary for the good of the whole. Allow me, however, my Lord, to express my earnest wishes that you would be prevailed upon to give your name as well as your weight and influence, to the support of the King's Government, at the head of his Council. The great and solid advantages that must be derived from it in every light are so evident, that it is unnecessary to enforce them. They will, I hope, be sufficient to excuse me for expressing my sentiments upon them in this manner, as they weigh so strongly with me, that though I think it extremely desirable to fill up that great office, if possible, without a moment's delay, yet I cannot advise any farther step to be taken in it, whilst I have any hopes of its being filled up so honourably and so beneficially to the King's service; and I own I cannot help flattering myself that, upon mature consideration, your Grace may still comply with it. It is impossible for me to put an end to this letter, without begging leave to return my sincerest acknowledgments and thanks for the favourable opinion which I had the pleasure of hearing from Lord Sandwich that your Grace entertained of me, and the obliging terms in which you expressed it. I shall always be ambitious to deserve it, and happy to maintain it, and consequently extremely desirous to obey your commands to the utmost of my power.

What Lord Sandwich mentioned to me about Mr. Vernon may, I hope, be brought to bear in some shape that may be agreeable to him. I understood, with the utmost satisfaction, from his Lordship, that your Grace would come to town as soon as ever these arrangements have taken place, and I hope it will be *before* they have taken place; but, whenever it shall be, I beg your Grace will allow me to have the honour of waiting upon you, as soon after as is convenient to you, at Bedford House, that I may receive your advice in person; and assure you that I am, with the highest respect, and most perfect regard, my Lord, &c., &c.

GEORGE GRENVILLE.

MR. GRENVILLE TO THE EARL OF EGMONT.

Downing Street, September 5, 1763.

MY LORD,—The audience which Mr. Pitt had of His Majesty at the Queen's House, and the great extent of the demands then insisted upon, both with regard to men and measures, have made the King very desirous that I should speak with the principal persons in his Government upon the subject of that extraordinary transaction, and the dispositions that will be necessary in consequence of His Majesty's refusal, and of his resolution never to comply with terms that he thinks so inconsistent with his honour, as well as with his opinions. It is, therefore, necessary for me, in pursuance of His Majesty's pleasure, to give your Lordship this trouble, and to desire that you will come to town as soon as ever you conveniently can. I shall be extremely happy to know the sentiments, and to receive the assistance of one whose abilities and knowledge will give so much weight to his advice, and whose attachment and fidelity will, I am sure, make him desirous to contribute all he can to the honour and happiness of His Majesty and of his country in this dangerous conjuncture. I enter into no particulars, as it is impossible to do it at length, and as I hope to hear from the messenger that I shall very soon have the pleasure of seeing your Lordship here, and of assuring you of the high regard and perfect esteem with which I have the honour to be, my Lord, &c., &c. GEORGE GRENVILLE.

P.S. I am this moment returned from His Majesty, who has ordered me to repeat to your Lordship his desire that you will come to town as expeditiously as possible; and as I have directed the messenger to be with your Lordship by to-morrow night, I hope to have the pleasure of seeing you by Thursday night, and that you will let me know, by the messenger, where I can have the honour of waiting upon you when you come to town.

THE DUKE OF BEDFORD TO MR. GRENVILLE.

Woburn Abbey, September 6, 1763.

SIR,—I was favoured yesterday evening with your letter by the Admiralty messenger, who at the same time brought me one from the Earl of Sandwich. I write to his Lordship that I wholly refer myself to the King's pleasure, determined to act in everything as he shall please to prescribe. I am much obliged to you, Sir, for the sentiments you express towards me, and I can assure you that no one will more zealously support than myself, whether in or out of employment, the Administration upon the plan His Majesty is now forming it.

Give me leave to return you my thanks for your good intentions towards Mr. Vernon, and to assure you that I am, with great truth and regard, &c., &c.

BEDFORD.

MR. WILKES TO EARL TEMPLE.

Paris, Tuesday, September 6 (1763),
Hotel de Saxe.

MY DEAR LORD,—I have now an opportunity of paying my respects to your Lordship without a chance of a Secretary of State's first reading it.

All the English in Paris are in high spirits from the agreeable news we have here of an entire change of the Ministry, and the restoration of your Lordship and the Whigs. I can only say, as to the small share I have in the political world, no news could give me such entire satisfaction, for I believe your Lordship's public virtue and love of my country to be superior to any man's. I do not presume to argue on the public prints, neither with respect to my own concerns, nor for the national business. I think that I am secure in your Lordship's approbation for everything.

I shall soon return to England, but it will be *by the way of Flanders*. I beg your Lordship to present my best respects Lady Temple, and to believe me, with unfeigned regard and the justest esteem, &c., &c.

JOHN WILKES.

THE HON. HORACE WALPOLE TO MR. GRENVILLE.

Strawberry Hill, September 7, 1763.

DEAR SIR,—Though I am sensible I have no pretensions for asking you a favour, and, indeed, should be very unwilling to trespass on your good nature, yet I flatter myself I shall not be thought quite impertinent in interceding for a person, who I can answer has neither been to blame, nor any way deserved punishment, and therefore I think you, Sir, will be ready to save him from great prejudice. The person is my deputy, Mr. Grosvenor Bedford, who, above five-and-twenty years ago, was appointed Collector of the Customs in Philadelphia by my father.

I hear he is threatened to be turned out. If the least fault can be laid to his charge I do not desire to have him protected. If there cannot, I am too well persuaded, Sir, of your justice not to be sure you will be pleased to protect him.

When I have appealed to your good nature and justice it would be impertinent to say more than that I am, &c., &c. HOR. WALPOLE.

MR. GRENVILLE TO THE HON. HORACE WALPOLE.

Downing Street, September 8, 1763.

DEAR SIR,—You certainly have the two best claims that can be made to every mark of regard and attention which is in my power to grant; I mean your own merit, and the friendship you have shown to me, joined to my warm sense of them, and my earnest desire to comply with any wish of yours.

I have never heard of any complaint against Mr. Grosvenor Bedford, or of any desire to turn him out.; but by the office which you tell me he holds in North America, I believe I know the state of the case, which I will inform you of, that you may be enabled to judge of it yourself. Heavy complaints were last year made in Parliament, of the state of our revenues in North America, which amount to between 1000*l.* and 2000*l.* a-year, the collecting of which cost upon the establishment of the Customs in Great Britain between 7000*l.* and 8000*l.* a year. This, it was urged, arose from the making all these offices sinecures in England. When I came to the Treasury I directed the Commissioners of the Customs to be written to, that they might inform us how that revenue might be improved, and to what causes they attributed the present diminished state of it. In their report, the principal cause which they assigned was the absence of the officers, who lived in England by leave from the Treasury, which they proposed should be recalled. This we complied with, and ordered them all to their duty, and the Commissioners of the Customs to present others in the room of such as should not obey. I take it for granted that this is Mr. Bedford's case. If it is, it will be attended with difficulty to make an exception, as they are every one of them applying to be excepted out of the order. You will see the nature of that difficulty by what I have stated. If it is not so, or if Mr. Bedford can suggest to me any proper means of obviating it without overturning the whole regulation, he will do me a sensible pleasure, as it will put it in my power to do an act of kindness to one you recommend, and to express in this instance, as I wish to do in every other, the sentiments of sincere regard and attachment, with which I am ever, &c., &c.   GEORGE GRENVILLE.

MR. GRENVILLE TO MR. WELBORE ELLIS.

Downing Street, September 8, 1763.

DEAR SIR,—I look upon the letter which you did me the favour to write to me on the 2nd of this month, as an additional mark of your friendship towards me, and of those dispositions which you so frankly and honourably expressed for the support of His Majesty's Government. The friendly manner, as well as the temper and moderation with which you explain yourself, gives me a very sensible pleasure, and will make me always desirous to promote every wish of yours where I can, and where I cannot, answer with the same openness and confidence with which you write.

Lord Sandwich, as you truly thought, will have the seals of the Secretary of State for the Northern Department, and the King has determined to appoint Lord Egmont to be first Commissioner of the Admiralty in his room, in order to avail himself of his character and abilities in the present conjuncture. This arrangement has made it impossible for me to carry into execution what you desire. I trust that you will be satisfied that the motives for it cannot be founded in the least disregard to you, or in an opinion that your wish is in the least extravagant or improper. I know nobody who could execute that office better than yourself, or who has more knowledge in that important department. The station you now serve the King in[1], is of very great consequence to his service, and the great approbation which His Majesty expresses of your behaviour in it, is the strongest proof of his good will, as well as of his good opinion. Indeed, I do not know how he could supply that situation, which you know is a very delicate one, so agreeably to himself, or so usefully to the public. I hope you will not think that I urge your merit as a plea against your pretensions, but merely as an argument to show you, that the appointment of Lord Egmont cannot be owing to the least disinclination to you, whom he retains in a department that gives you such constant access and employment with him, and which he must wish to have executed by one that is agreeable to him. I will tell you farther particulars about this when I see you, and explain to you the reasons for my not answering your letter sooner. In the mean time you will be glad to hear that the Duke of Bedford is to be Lord President, which he has agreed to in the handsomest manner. Lord Hyde is to succeed Lord Egmont as one of the Post Masters, and Lord Hillsborough to be First Lord of Trade, in the room of Lord Shelburne, who has resigned. All these appointments are to be declared, and all the parties, except Lord Hillsborough, who is coming from Ireland, are to kiss the King's hand to-morrow. Some part of this news was not finally settled till this evening, and I propose to send you a messenger with this account to-morrow morning, that you may be apprized of it as soon as is possible. I hope to have the pleasure of seeing you as soon as you return

---

[1] He was now Secretary at War.

to town, and shall always be glad of every opportunity to express the sincere regard and perfect esteem, with which I am, &c., &c. GEORGE GRENVILLE.

SIR JOHN PHILLIPS[1] TO MR. GRENVILLE.

Picton Castle, Sept. 8, 1763.

DEAR SIR,—I was honoured with your letter of the 2nd instant last night, and take the first opportunity of returning you my grateful thanks for the authentic account you are so kind to give me of the audience which Mr. Pitt had of His Majesty, and of the result of it; and I sincerely congratulate you, Sir, on His Majesty's fixed and unalterable determination of abiding by the system which he has formed for the preservation of the constitution of this country, and of supporting you in the execution of it, which I am sure must rejoice the hearts of all honest unprejudiced men. I was extremely concerned that His Majesty was advised to send to Mr. Pitt, because I fear it has in some degree given strength to a dangerous faction; but firmness in His Majesty, who must now be convinced of the evil tendency of Mr. Pitt's proposals, and a strict union among those who are attached to his person and government (who I have reason to believe are very numerous), must weaken it by degrees, and will I hope in the end entirely crush it.

It shall be my business, as I am sure it is my duty, to do everything in my power to promote that union, and to obviate all bad impressions, which at this time is

---

[1] M.P. for Pembrokeshire. He died in the following year, and his son was created an Irish Peer by the title of Lord Milford.

more particularly necessary, as the safety of His Majesty and the nation depend on it.

The sense of the gentlemen of this County you will see in an Address they cheerfully came into, which I have the honour to send by this post to Lord Halifax, who I am very glad to find joined with you, Sir, in your representation to His Majesty. Lord Bute's resolution of an absolute retirement is extremely prudent, though it must sensibly affect the King, who greatly loves, and is beloved by his Lordship.

As His Majesty did me the honour to call me to his Councils, and as I found myself growing old, and frequently visited with illness, I took the liberty before I left town of desiring a private audience of His Majesty, who was pleased to receive me with great cordiality, and as I saw a faction formed which appeared to me very formidable, I could not refrain from cautioning His Majesty (out of the great love I bear to him), from putting any confidence in them, as I knew their scheme was directly opposite to His Majesty's, which was to abolish all party distinctions, and to be King over all his people, whereas theirs was to take the throne by storm, to foment divisions, to proscribe all His Majesty's subjects from his service but themselves and their creatures, and to rule with an absolute sway, as they did in His Royal Grandfather's time; and I went so far as to say, that if His Majesty suffered that faction to prevail, he would be a King in shackles. His Majesty said he was sensible of the truth of what I told him, and that he was resolved never to take them into the Administration as a party, to the prejudice of any of those now in his service, but that he might possibly, if they returned to their duty, employ some of them. This it was impossible to object to, but I took the liberty of saying that I believed they were so cemented together, that it would be extremely difficult to separate them.

The truth of this observation is verified by Mr. Pitt's last proposals. His Majesty lamented Lord Bute's leaving him, saying he had lost a friend as well as a Minister, and spoke of you, Sir, with great regard; upon which I could not avoid giving my testimony of the rectitude of His Majesty's choice, and that as a man of virtue you could not deceive him, or the nation, concluding with my wishes that His Majesty would always employ men of character for religion and virtue, whose consciences would not suffer them to do any evil: this, the King said, it should be his constant endeavour to do, was pleased to thank me, and he said he had nothing so much at heart as the good of his people; and when I took my leave His Majesty said, Remember, Sir John, when you see me next, you will find me the same firm man you leave me.

I hope, Sir, you will excuse the length of this letter, as I thought it incumbent on me upon this occasion to let you know what passed between His Majesty and me, and I have the honour to be, with the greatest respect and regard, &c., &c.   JOHN PHILLIPS.

I forgot to tell you the address was sent to Sir William Owen, but he did not put his name to it, though all the other members now in the County have signed it.

MR. CHARLES TOWNSHEND TO EARL TEMPLE.

September 11, 1763.

MY VERY DEAR LORD,—I am sure you will be sorry to receive a letter from me upon a day when we were to have met, and I am sincerely concerned to find myself under the necessity of writing it, but Lady Dalkeith has a return of her ague, which alarms me and oppresses her very much; it comes at such a distance of time, and after so long a course of preventive medicines, that I am apprehensive of its effects upon a constitution naturally weak, and could not think of leaving her upon any consideration. In this distress, and under this disappointment, I can only say my heart travels with you, and my earnest affectionate wishes and zeal accompany you and our friends in every hour of council; and I hope, at your return, to be able to bring to Stowe a mind more at ease, and more worthy of your acceptance than mine is at this instant.

I must trouble you with my respects to the Duke of Devonshire, and I should be glad his Grace knew how unexpectedly and necessarily I am prevented waiting upon him.

My letters from town are received, and tell me little more than the lie of the hour; the pains taken to propagate the misrepresentation first made of Mr. Pitt's conduct are infinite, and the story of the Court turns chiefly upon the points and persons stated to me at Missenden. Wroxton[1], I am told, insinuates Mr. Legge

[1] Meaning Lord North, whose residence was Wroxton Abbey. Frederick Lord North was eldest son of Francis, first Earl of Guilford. He was a Commissioner of the Treasury in 1759, joint Paymaster of

is dissatisfied highly by his destination; it is there asserted that a general restitution was one indispensable condition: that almost every man at every board was by name marked out for sacrifice: and the general idea of Mr. Pitt's establishment is asserted to have been never accepted or approved in any one meeting. Thus the same party circulate their remonstrance in town and country, but I trust these arts will have no great influence, and I think there are circumstances undisputed by either, which must convince every impartial and free mind that the measure did not break upon a real objection, to the extent or nature of the terms and changes suggested by Mr. Pitt.

My brother tells me Lord Hillsborough succeeds Lord Shelburne; Lord Vere, Lord Sandwich; Lord Hyde to be Postmaster, if Lord Egmont should succeed to the Admiralty, and not Lord Vere; and the Duke of Bedford actually named President of the Council. They triumph much in this last promotion; but, in my opinion, his Grace means to try a second negociation, and that he accepts with that view, for he consents unwillingly, hates his colleagues, and despises the Cabinet. My brother himself writes calmly, and seems unhappy where he is. In my answer I have wrote fully and freely to him; I have touched every point that could animate, alarm, or satisfy him, and I should hope he will gradually return to a better way of thinking, and his own natural and wisest situation and party.

the Forces in 1766, Chancellor of the Exchequer in 1767, and First Lord of the Treasury in 1770, which latter office he continued to hold until 1782. He became Lord Guilford on the death of his father in 1790, and died in August, 1792.

They have made a story out of your visit to Calcraft[1], but I think it is frivolous.

I should be glad to hear from you if anything material has occurred in town; if not, I shall wait with some impatience for your return. I hope my friend, Mr. J. Grenville, is with you, and well. We should have laughed, as of old, upon the road, and I cannot bear the thought of being prevented. Adieu, my dearest Lord, and believe me to be, &c., &c.   C. TOWNSHEND.

My best compliments attend Lady Temple.

MR. GRENVILLE TO MR. STUART MACKENZIE.

Downing Street, Sept. 16, 1763.

DEAR SIR,—I received this morning the honour of your very obliging letter of the 10th of this month, and am thoroughly sensible of the kind expressions it contains towards me, and of that hearty and zealous attachment to His Majesty's Government and to the constitution of this kingdom which is at this time so necessary; and which, although I never doubted of it for a moment, cannot but give me the highest pleasure. The attempt which has been made, and the situation which has arisen in consequence of it, do certainly require the most cordial union and support from all those who have the same object in view for the public good, and for the honour and independence of the

---

[1] Lord Temple, accompanied by Mr. Pitt, had paid a visit of two hours to Mr. Calcraft on the 31st of August, much commented upon, because it was supposed to involve some new political movement.

Crown. You will have received, before this can reach you, the account of the several arrangements which the King has thought fit to make in his Government. They are such as I flatter myself will give strength and permanency to the system which His Majesty has formed, and that they will therefore meet with your approbation, which I shall always be extremely desirous to obtain. The impressions which the late extraordinary transaction has made in this part of the kingdom, seem to be much more favourable than they were even expected to be. I rejoice to hear of the perfect unanimity and good dispositions of that part where you are, and of the steps which you have already taken to promote an early attendance, which will certainly be of the utmost consequence in the present situation, as everything must depend upon the first appearance. The exact time of the meeting of the Parliament is not yet finally settled, but I think it very possible that it may be before Christmas; however, this is only a hint for yourself alone, and which many reasons at present will make it improper to declare. I understood, when I had last the honour of seeing you here, that you proposed to return hither about this time. I will not therefore attempt to enter into any detail upon the public business, which indeed it is not possible to do in the compass of a letter, but will refer myself to our meeting, which I hope will be soon; in the meanwhile allow me to assure you in this manner, that there is no man whose opinion and assistance I shall more gladly receive than yours, and whose favourable dispositions I more firmly rely upon, and more wish to cultivate. I have the honour to be, with the highest regard, &c., &c.

GEORGE GRENVILLE.

MR. WILKES TO EARL TEMPLE.

Paris, Friday, September 16 (1763).

My Lord,—As I have no opportunity but the common post, of transmitting this letter to England, I shall only add that I have not received any answer from Mr. Murray[1], who called once since at the Hotel de Saxe, while I was at Fontainebleau. I intend to set out for Menin, next Sunday the 18th, and perhaps shall be in England the end of the week. Wherever I am, while I have any sense or memory, I shall ever be most gratefully, &c., &c.
John Wilkes[2].

LE CHEVALIER D'EON[3] TO MR. GRENVILLE.

A Londres, le 19ᵉ Sept., 1763.

Monsieur,—J'ai l'honneur d'envoyer ci joint à votre Excellence, copie des deux billets qu'elle m'a fait

---

[1] The Honourable Alexander Murray, a brother of Lord Elibank. He was sent to Newgate by the House of Commons on account of his conduct at the Westminster Election in 1751. He concerned himself at this time in the affair between Wilkes and Captain Forbes, not, says Walpole, without suspicion of inflaming the quarrel. Wilkes enclosed to Lord Temple a long letter addressed to Murray upon the subject, which it is unnecessary to repeat here, as it has been printed by Almon in the *Memoirs and Correspondence of Wilkes*, vol. i. p. 220.

[2] This letter is *directed* in another hand.

[3] The Chevalier D'Eon came to England as Secretary to the Duc de Nivernois, the Ambassador Extraordinary for the negotiation of the Peace. He was then a Captain of Dragoons. Upon the departure of Nivernois, D'Eon was left Minister Plenipotentiary until the arrival of Comte de Guerchy, the new Ambassador, when he was ordered to resume his former post of Secretary, at which he was greatly mortified, and hence his animosity towards Guerchy. D'Eon having refused to present his letters of recall, he was forbid the Court, as having no longer any official character here. Until the Revolution deprived him of it, he enjoyed a pension from the French Government; and he spent the latter years of his life in England, passing for a woman, and always wearing the female costume. He died in 1810.

celui de m'écrire par rapport à la petite quantité de vin qui se trouve toujours à la Douane. Comme ces deux billets se trouvent absolument contradictoires, et que je présume que c'est uniquement une faute de Bureau, je supplié votre Excellence de me marquer au quel des deux billets je dois le plus m'en rapporter.

Si c'est au premier, j'ai l'honneur de faire mes sincères remercîmens à votre Excellence; si c'est au second, j'ai celui de la prévenir que le Ministre de France ne reconnoit pas plus les loix de l'Angleterre, que le Ministre d'Angleterre ne reconnoit celles de France. Tout ce que je sais et tout ce que je reconnois, c'est qu'il doit s'observer une réciprocité parfaite entre deux puissances telles que la France et l'Angleterre ; et comme j'ai eu l'honneur de remettre il y a peu dejours à my Lord Hertford les passeports du Roy mon maître les plus étendus, et les plus exempts de droits pour tout ce qu'il voudroit faire entrer en France, j'espère que votre Excellence voudra bien suivre un si bel exemple, surtout pour un article aussi foible que celui d'un tonneau de vin qui est pour la consommation de l'hôtel de France, autrement je serois forcé de prévenir my Lord Hertford de ne point compter sur la validité de ses passeports.

J'ai l'honneur d'être, avec un très sincère et très respectueux attachement, Monsieur, &c., &c.   D'Eon.

THE EARL OF HERTFORD TO MR. GRENVILLE.

Grosvenor Street, Sept. 20, 1763.

Lord Hertford has the honour of informing Mr. Grenville that he has conversed with Monsieur D'Eon since he was at the Cockpit this morning, and finds that the wine in dispute is now clearly his own, and not the Ambassador's.

Monsieur de Guerchy was little named, but such a stress laid upon reciprocity, that all the arguments taken from the laws of this country, evident inconvenience, and the acquiescence of the Ministers of his own Court could not remove. If any modification less than paying duty could satisfy Mr. Grenville, Monsieur D'Eon will plainly leave this delicate matter to his successor, and content himself by receiving something more than the limited quantity by favour and indulgence; but if the remaining quantity be judged, from the size of it, inexpedient to be passed duty free, the notes and letters which have passed upon it are to be sent to the French Ministry, in which case Mr. Grenville may probably be of opinion that it will be right to give Mr. Neville information of what has passed, to prevent disputes, and the necessity perhaps of future discussion and explanation, upon such a trifle, when partially and warmly stated.

MR. GRENVILLE TO THE EARL OF NORTHUMBERLAND.

Downing Street, Sept. 22, 1763.

MY DEAR LORD,—I most sincerely hope that this letter will find you perfectly well at Dublin, after a safe and prosperous voyage, and that every circumstance may contribute to make the beginning of your Government in Ireland as agreeable and honourable to you, as I am convinced the continuance of it will be beneficial to His Majesty's service and to the interests of that kingdom as well as this. I find that upon speaking to the King, His Majesty has himself explained to your

Lordship his resolution with regard to the grants, &c., in Ireland for lives or years, and, therefore, that it is unnecessary for me to trouble you any farther upon this subject, except with the assurances of my utmost endeavours at all times to confirm the King in such dispositions as may best tend to the ease and lustre of your Excellency's Government. Your constant attachment to His Majesty, and the very obliging expressions of your friendship and approbation towards me, flatters me with the hopes of your concurrence and assistance in everything that can facilitate the King's measures, and promote the success of the Administration which he has been pleased to form in this country. The situation of men and things, and the consideration of the business of the House of Commons, your Lordship will easily see must demand my utmost attention. Nothing must be omitted in that important scene that can unite or strengthen us, whatever reasons we may have to be confident of our success. The first thing essentially necessary is the earliest and most numerous attendance that can possibly be procured at the meeting of the Parliament. Upon the first division, which must happen immediately, everything will depend, as the opinion of our strength and stability will be formed in consequence of it. I would not, therefore, omit a single man whose presence with us might contribute to that great end.

This induces me to mention to your Lordship two gentlemen who I understand are gone over in your family to Ireland, whose dispositions I beg you will sound; and, if you find them favourable, that you will send them over to England to attend the meeting of the Parliament, which will probably be about the middle of November, though no time is yet finally settled, nor would it be proper to declare it, 'till about the time of the issuing the Proclamation, which in that case must, I believe, be in about a fortnight. The first gentleman I have to mention is Mr. Edmondstone, whom I have reason to believe as well inclined as possible. The second is Colonel Calcraft, whose relation to Mr. Calcraft[1], and whose other habitudes and attachments, may render his opinions and conduct more uncertain. If his present situation and obligation to you cannot determine him, perhaps his stay where he is may be desirable; but if it can, as I should hope, in that case I should be very glad you could send him over here as well as Mr. Edmondstone, and any other members of our House of Commons whom your Lordship can spare, and whose friendship you are convinced of. I cannot leave this in better hands than yours, and therefore there I leave it with pleasure. I have spoken to Lord Carysfort about Sir William Osborne, whom he has promised to write to, and of whose good dispositions he is confident. He will desire him to speak to your Lordship about his brother, Captain Osborne, in which case I told Lord Carysfort how kindly inclined you was to provide for him as Governor of some of the lesser garrisons in Ireland. Everything here continues to wear a very favourable aspect, and I shall be equally glad to hear they do so in Ireland, for every reason, and more particularly from the interest I take in what relates to your Lordship's satisfaction, and from the high respect and sincere attachment with which I have the honour to be, &c., &c.   GEORGE GRENVILLE.

---

[1] M.P. for Poole.

MR. WILKES TO EARL TEMPLE.

Great George Street, Friday, Sept. 27, 1763.

MY LORD,—I am just returned from Dunkirk, and beg leave to give your Lordship the very first assurances of the most entire regard, esteem, and devotion.

I am told that your Lordship disapproves of my conduct. If it is indeed so, I shall be truly unhappy, for I have ever looked upon your Lordship as the truest judge, and the most knowing, most accurate observer of men and things. I shall, besides, ever acknowledge the noblest proofs of your Lordship's partiality to me.

I am more impatient than words can express, to explain my whole conduct to your Lordship, and if your Lordship would give me leave, shall wait a very short time before I pay my duty at Stowe.

I trust that I have not passed my time unprofitably in France, but if I am returned to my own country, not under the auspices of Lord Temple, I am then unhappy, though amidst the applause of the rest of the world. I am ever, my Lord, &c., &c.   JOHN WILKES.

My respectful compliments ever attend Lady Temple.

EARL TEMPLE TO MR. WILKES.

Stowe, Sept. 28, 1763.

MY DEAR SIR,—I am very glad you are once again upon English ground, and that your usual spirit and fortitude have extricated you so far from another extraordinary situation. Your friends here began to be much alarmed at not hearing anything of you so late as Tuesday night. Were I to say that certain matters,

which have heretofore passed, met not with my disapprobation, I must contradict my own representations to you, which in some instances seemed to carry along with them your own conviction. When I have the pleasure of seeing you, I will, if you give me leave, with my usual freedom, go into some particulars of a later date. In the mean time I abominate writing by the post, or, indeed, at all, and it is not fit our good friends at that office should be apprized of more or less than that I am ever, &c., &c.
TEMPLE.

En attendant, shut up your ears. I am sensible to the many obliging expressions of all your letters.

EARL TEMPLE TO MR. WILKES.

"Iste tulit pretium jam nunc certaminis hujus;
Quo cum victus erit, *mecum* certasse feretur."

OVID. *Speech of Ajax.*

To John Wilkes, Esq.

WHAT Muse thy glory shall presume to sing?
So highly honoured by a mighty King!
The Minion, doubtless to exalt thy praise
Beyond the bounds of humble poet's lays,
Devised the contest, whence such triumphs rose
O'er lovely Freedom's most malicious foes.
What groveling Courts or influenced juries find,
Shakes not the tenor of thy manly mind.
Thy cause hath been by a whole nation tried;
For thee that mightier jury dares decide,
And from her ashes bids fair Truth revive,
In all her native charms of *forty-five.*

When Kings to measure with a subject deign,
The lustre of imperial state they stain.
For competition on a level brings
The meanest subject and the proudest Kings.
The truly great, pity, not vengeance take,
Most Royal when they reparation make
To the most helpless, whom the hand of power
Hath rashly injured in an angry hour,
Yielding to that high majesty of law,
Whose terrors keep a realm incensed in awe;
Whose breath could banish Stuart's tyrant race,
And on their throne, the milder Brunswicks place[1].

MR. WILKES TO EARL TEMPLE.

Great George Street, Saturday, Oct. 1 (1763.)

My Lord,—I am made extremely happy by your Lordship's kind letter from Stowe, of September 28th, and I hope to have the honour of paying my duty there on Tuesday noon, and after all my travels I mean to be a Buckinghamshire man the next week, and a Londoner the rest of the winter.

My fate has been, I find, very particular. The scribblers of my own country upbraided me with meanness and cowardice at the very time Grimaldi[2], at Versailles, sent his secretary to compliment me (and his Castilian pride into the bargain) that I had acted up even to the ideas of *Spanish* honour, and begged I would be assured of his high regard.

---

[1] The above verses, very much corrected and interlined, are in the handwriting of Lord Temple.
[2] The Spanish Ambassador at the Court of France.

At the Palais Royal I was diverted with the account I first read there, after dinner, that no gentleman would keep me company.

I am happy to find that my plain artless story has put down the scribblers of the day. I hope to be able to dedicate myself entirely to the noble cause I am concerned in, and to merit the approbation of every lover of the liberties and constitution of this country, of your Lordship above all. I am, my Lord, with the justest esteem and gratitude, &c., &c. JOHN WILKES.

MR. CHARLES TOWNSHEND TO EARL TEMPLE.

Adderbury, Monday, October 3 (1763).

MY DEAREST LORD,—I am much obliged to you for your kind inquiry after my health, which is now entirely restored. The bark has at last removed the ague, and I recover strength very fast.

We are concerned to find the weather has prevented us the pleasure of seeing your Lordship and Lady Temple, but we flatter ourselves that, though accidents may for a moment divide Stowe from Adderbury, nothing can separate them. If I continue as I am, and without any relapse, I shall be the next bird myself that goes over the waters. Whenever we meet it will make Lady Dalkeith very happy, as well as myself, and she desires me to tell you this.

I cannot learn with certainty when the Parliament meets, and I believe it is not absolutely determined. I wish it may not be 'till after Christmas. My letters are positive upon the subject of Lord Bute's dismission[1]

---

[1] It has been already stated that Lord Bute was not *dismissed*.

from the Privy Purse, but add that Lord Halifax is disappointed upon not having it. The creatures of Ministry, supported by the occasional declarations of Ministers themselves, continue to poison all ranks of men with their relations of the late negociation; and I hear, from authority, that they have inflamed Lord Granby by their invidious manner of representing Lord Albemarle as a rival set up by Mr. Pitt, and preferred to him. I can fix this falsehood upon Lord Sandwich.

I have not heard lately from my brother, but I know he left London in ill-humour. The Duke of Bedford's acceptance gave him some idea of the stability of the Administration, and I think Lord Granby and he are alarmed about Lord Albemarle.

I have seen a letter from Whately, the new Secretary to the Treasury, in which he says Lord Bute and the Ministry are *firmly united*. Lord North, on the other hand, assures me the Ministers are resolved *not to be duped*, and to resign if *Lord Bute* has any influence. Thus it is evident these rash and weak usurpers of power have no system; they have not plan enough to be able to give their followers a consistent story, and an enemy need only see two of their party to be convinced of their undecided, wretched situation.

The Stocks fell on Saturday to $90\frac{3}{4}$. This is no pleasant indication of discontent.

Beckford has made no bad speech upon the expiration of his Magistracy. It is composed upon good ideas of taste, and firm and explicit, without being indecent or warm.

Thus I have wrote you a long letter from not being able to restrain my mind when it is conversing with you. I will conclude here lest I fall into the same habit again, and the next subject I trust should run away with me in its turn.

Farewell! Lady Dalkeith desires her most respectful compliments to your Lordship and Lady Temple, to whom I beg my affectionate compliments also.

You told me in a former letter I was Secretary of State. I now tell you I am not Paymaster, and let me add that I shall be, my dear Lord, your sincere and invariable friend, C. TOWNSHEND.

MR. GRENVILLE TO LORD STRANGE.

Downing Street, October 15, 1763.

MY DEAR LORD,—I have this moment received the honour of your letter of the 12th of this month. I did not trouble you with a letter of thanks for the very obliging and kind expressions contained in your answer to my former letter; but I should be unworthy of them indeed if I did not feel most sensibly the impression which a conduct so full of attachment and duty to the King, and so friendly to myself, must make upon one who has long loved and esteemed you so highly as I have done. The meeting of the Parliament, which your Lordship will have seen is fixed for the 15th of next month, will, I flatter myself, give me the pleasure of seeing you soon in town. There are many things likely to come on at the very beginning of the ensuing session, in which I should most earnestly wish to have your opinion and advice, and which it is utterly impossible to enter into the detail of, and to explain sufficiently in a letter. Perhaps there never was a time when prudence, and firmness, and union, were more indispensably necessary to preserve the whole from ruin. Your own discernment must point this out to you; and your public spirit and affection to the King and to the constitution, will, I know, be the best incitement to you to give that assistance which will so much contribute to the support of both. There is one instance, however, in which I think the honour of the Crown, and of both Houses of Parliament, as well as the authority of the whole Legislature is so immediately concerned, that I cannot help expressing to you my earnest desire of communicating to you the measures that will be necessary to be taken in consequence of it, for your approbation and assistance. I mean, my dear Lord, the affair of Mr. Wilkes, which must be laid before the House the first day of the ensuing session. The propositions for the censure of that most extravagant libel ought to be made by one whose high rank and unspotted character, and whose experience and knowledge in Parliament, will give to it the utmost weight and authority; and where will that character, so necessary at this conjuncture, be so universally acknowledged as in Lord Strange? You cannot, therefore, wonder that, in a matter of so much moment, I should apply to you, who I am convinced see this in the same light that I do, and that I should beg the favour of you to come to town, if possible, by the end of this month at latest, that I may talk to you upon this very important subject, and settle a plan of proceeding upon it that I hope will be agreeable to you and induce you to comply with my request, and that of many of your friends, for your proposing it to the House.

I trust that you will believe me, when I assure you that, in making this request, I have wished to consult not only the King's service, and the honour of the House of Commons, which are so deeply interested in this

question, but your own reputation and character, which, from every public motive, and (after the kind and favourable opinion expressed in your last letter to me) you will allow me to say, from every private motive of friendship, and of gratitude, I shall always wish to advance to the utmost of my power. I am ever, my dear Lord, with the most affectionate regard and attachment, &c., &c.
GEORGE GRENVILLE.

MR. GRENVILLE TO THE BISHOP OF HEREFORD[1].

Downing Street, October 18, 1763.

MY LORD,—I have this moment received the honour of your Lordship's letter, desiring me to lay before His Majesty your request to be appointed to the Deanery of Windsor in case of its being vacant by the death of the present Dean. However desirous I may be to comply with any wish of yours, which I flatter myself that your Lordship is persuaded of, yet I am afraid that the King will not be disposed to give the Deanery of Windsor to be holden in commendam by any person in your Lordship's station. If it is to be given to any of the Bishops, I know of none whose rank and character, and long continuance without any removal, would give him fairer pretensions to it than your Lordship's, and very few whose claim I should be more glad to support if that were the case. I have the honour to be, &c., &c.
GEORGE GRENVILLE.

[1] Lord James Beauclerc. He died Bishop of Hereford in 1787.

MR. WILKES TO EARL TEMPLE.

Great George Street, Tuesday, Oct. 18, 1763.

My Lord,—I have seen Mr. Dunning twice since my return from the country, and have the satisfaction of finding him very sanguine in the law causes, both from the fulness of the evidence, and the general opinion of mankind, which is highly favourable.

Sergeant Glynn is not expected till the first week in November, but Mr. Dunning, who possesses his confidence, writes regularly to him. Mr. Beardmore says that I cannot fail of success, and that the action against Wood and Webb for the seizure of papers will be certainly tried on the 11th of November, and the actions against the messengers on the 16th. I feel the importance of one of these actions being tried before the Parliament meets, and as a privileged cause Webb's is already set down first, and I am told cannot be put off. I shall take care to distribute to the Jury, &c., copies of the *Letter on the Seizure of Papers*[1].

Governor Johnstone, the new Governor of West Florida, went last Friday to Mr. Brookes's lodgings, beat him very much, and made two passes with his sword at him, on a supposition of his writing the North Briton of Sept. 17th.

This *Brookes* is the *John Cæsar Wilkes*, and now writes the North Briton. Beardmore has drawn up his affidavit, and has sent to Lord Chief Justice Pratt to hold Johnstone to bail, before he can go out of the kingdom. The affair makes a great noise, and the people in general harangue on the mildness of the Government of West Florida.

[1] The Pamphlet written by Lord Temple.

The public is more irritated than ever against the Scots.

I have not yet received a single line nor message from Mr. Forbes, nor do I hear where he is. He is sunk very low in the opinion even of his own countrymen.

The report of Saturday was that Mr. George Grenville's heart failed him, and that fresh overtures would soon be made.

I take the liberty of enclosing to your Lordship all the foreign gazettes of Europe relative to my affair, and the state of the subscriptions to the *Proceedings*, the *North Britons*, &c., to last Saturday.

Your Lordship will see how little that same public, which bore me so triumphant, can be trusted to; or rather I am now to see it, for your Lordship saw it very clearly before: yet, though the public fail me, I will never be wanting to them, and shall have only to say at the end, *Il est grand, il est beau, de faire des ingrats.*

I am proud to have obligations to Lord Temple, yet they are so great, that I am uneasy under them, and such goodness overpowers me. Your Lordship gave me leave to submit my private affairs to you, I shall, therefore, take the liberty of going into them.

Independent of Mrs. Wilkes's jointure, of Aylesbury estate, of Leighton, &c., I have in possession in Bucks 135*l.* 13*s.* 4*d.* freehold, and in reversion in Lincolnshire 73*l.*, besides the advowson, manor, &c., which I can carry to market to-morrow, as your Lordship will see by Mr. Coxe's opinion, which I took some years ago. I wish to raise the sum of 3000*l.* to be entirely happy, and, therefore, I mean to dispose of these lands, both the possession and reversion; for it is no reflection on patriot Wilkes, in the cause of friendship and the public, to have 200*l.* a-year less, but it will hurt him to owe even to a tailor, though he makes his bill accordingly, and though the Duke of Newcastle, &c., have sinned ten times deeper than ever poor Wilkes did. To speak my sentiments fully, I wish to part with these lands to Lord Temple, only on the condition that his own lawyer finds my title full and good, and I should be glad your Lordship would make the enquiry as to their value; whatever that is, in your estimation, I agree to, and should infinitely prefer that, in your own county, they should be a trifling addition to a nobleman, who by every tie should command there. I am very far from wishing to put your Lordship to any inconvenience by the purchase: if it is not a suitable one to you, it will be very marketable.

As to my trustees they have nothing to do in the affair, nor is their consent at all necessary, because this is no part of the trust estate.

I mean to deduct what your Lordship has already advanced, for in a public concern no private purse ought to suffer, and still less from the nobleness of the owner. I ought to add that there is infinitely less reason in the present case, because the thing in general was against your Lordship's real opinion. I regret nothing that is past. I exult when I look back, and the testimony your Lordship has borne me is the glory of my life. I mean to lay the present age under a real obligation in the most darling cause to an Englishman; and, however I may suffer myself, the faithful historian's page and posterity will do me justice. There I keep my eye steadily fixed.

Your Lordship's goodness will not let me conceal anything from you. The 400*l*. I was bound for, on account of Mr. Stow (whose money it was, as I shall beg to show you under his hand), I must pay in a very few days, with the costs. I wish to settle that, and some other small things; but I know not what security I can give your Lordship, till I put you in possession of the estate, if your Lordship chooses the purchase.

I forgot to mention the *Defeazance of the Judgment,* which I enclose. It will convince your Lordship that it is not a money transaction, but turns entirely on suffering Mrs. Wilkes to live separate unmolested.

I have only in these money transactions the ambition of Horace:

> " Si neque majorem feci ratione mala rem,
> Nec sum facturus vitio culpaque minorem ;"

and I am superior to the having a shilling of any friend to gratify any passion or pleasure of my own.

As to politics, I have only to say that I have not printed a single line on the subject. I have lived here almost alone, and have even seen very few males, and but two females.

Mr. Mackintosh[1] is expected in town to-day. I am ready whenever the cause demands my poor abilities, and at all times when your Lordship wishes it, either openly or secretly, in any mode, and to any degree.

I enclose Beardmore's brief about Webb, as far as is yet finished.

I send so large a packet, as I have an opportunity of sending to, and hearing from, Stowe, without danger of post or coach.

---

[1] Robert Mackintosh, a barrister, intimately connected in politics with Lord Temple and Lord Lyttelton.

I beg your Lordship to present my most sincere respects to Lady Temple, and to believe me, with the justest esteem and gratitude, &c., &c. JOHN WILKES.

Mr. Churchill desires a postscript of his compliments at Stowe. His volume is not yet out.

SIR JOHN FIELDING[1] TO MR. GRENVILLE.

Bow Street, Oct. 19, 1763.

SIR JOHN FIELDING presents his most respectful compliments to the Right Honble. Mr. Grenville: it is with the greatest pleasure he acquaints him that the Horse Patrole established through his means gives infinite satisfaction to the public, especially those who inhabit in the neighbourhood of London, many of whom I have spoke with.

Sir John Fielding also thinks it his duty to give you the earliest notice, that the number of horsemen employed for this useful purpose, being only eight in number, appear on trial to be too few by two to cover the necessary ground, which would make the whole complete.

At present we shall be obliged to have one avenue unguarded every night, but as this will be a secret to every one but myself, it may not perhaps be attended with any ill consequence.

The additional expense of two horsemen for the time

---

[1] The well known Police Magistrate; he was half-brother to Henry Fielding the Novelist. Although blind from his youth, he was most active and sagacious in the performance of his duties. He died in 1780.

will be 150*l*., but you may be assured that I will use my utmost endeavours to make the eight already granted as useful as possible. Leaving, therefore, this matter to your consideration, I beg leave, with all due respect, to subscribe myself, hon^d. Sir, your sensibly obliged, and the public's humble Servant, JOHN FIELDING.

EARL TEMPLE TO MR. WILKES.

(October 20, 1763).

MY DEAR SIR,—As I intend to be in town at least a week, or possibly ten days before the Parliament meets, I will refer matters to be further talked over then, and as the trials are to come on so soon, the juries may perhaps, and I hope will, find a shorter way for you than you propose for yourself. Much, much depends on your trials, and more on the trial of you. I return you all your papers. I cannot, from the state of them, *greatly* applaud the generosity of the public, for though the expense of your law proceedings hath not hitherto been considerable, yet they seem not solicitous to make provision for what may happen.

I have not a sixpence in my banker's hands, having by Sunday's post replaced a sum of money for my brother Henry, but as you want to pay off the 400*l*., the expenses, and other small things, I send you a promissory note for five hundred pounds, which I will pay at three days' sight, having the money here, though not in town, and I take it for granted that will be deemed by any one as ready cash. Lady Temple desires her kind compliments.

As we shall meet so soon, I defer saying anything

more than that I am very much, my dear Sir, your affectionate and obedient TEMPLE.

I mention my brother's name instead of yours, as it prevents comments[1].

MR. CHARLES TOWNSHEND TO EARL TEMPLE.

Adderbury, October 21, 1763,

MY DEAR LORD,—I have had several violent returns since you heard from me, by which I am much reduced; but, being now a trunk of bark, I hope I shall be able to keep off the enemy, after having once expelled him. I escaped the fit yesterday, and am well this morning.

Morton[2] is returned from consultation: he was sent for to hear a manifesto read, in which every step and expression in the late negociation is represented: Mr. Grenville illustrated it with comments and anecdotes, and it was declared to have been prepared and communicated by the King's order. The enclosed letter[3] contains the matter of this manifesto, and I send it to you for that reason. I have heard indirectly a second time

[1] The back of the paper, on which this letter is written, is addressed in Mr. Wilkes's hand, "To Earl Temple, at Stowe." It seems probable, therefore, that Lord Temple exacted from Wilkes the return of all his letters (particularly after the celebrated *Seizure of Papers*), and this is an evident instance of his request being complied with. Besides, nearly all the letters in this collection from Lord Temple to Wilkes are the originals which had been sent to Wilkes, and in some cases the rough draughts in Lord Temple's hand have been also preserved.

[2] M.P. for Abingdon, and afterwards Chief Justice of Chester. He was in the intimate confidence of the Princess of Wales.

[3] It is very much to be regretted that this letter is not to be found; nor have I any clue to the *Manifesto* which it professes to describe.

from Lord B.[1], who seems to have had more audiences, and to have found in the Closet the same language, temper, and professions. Compare this with the proceeding I have related, and draw the melancholy inference[2].

I mean to have the pleasure of calling upon your Lordship, if I am permitted, but as yet, in my first hour almost of relief, I cannot assure myself so positively as I wish that I shall be able to do it.

I propose going from hence on the 28th, that I may look into some papers, and that I may see some people before the hurry comes on. We both think ourselves much obliged to your Lordship and Lady Temple for your continual kindness to us, and we earnestly wish every degree of prosperity and happiness to our friends at Stowe. I am, my dear Lord, &c. &c.

C. TOWNSHEND.

SIR FRANCIS BLAKE DELAVAL[3] TO MR. GRENVILLE.

Downing Street, October 24, 1763.

SIR,—I have received your letter, in which you are pleased to say that "many of my friends hope to see me in town." I should be very glad to know who my friends are, having never in this Administration been able to find one.

You persuade yourself that my zeal for the public

[1] If this means Lord Bute, the audiences must have been extremely secret, and the circumstances entirely unknown to Mr. Grenville.

[2] A *melancholy inference* indeed! if there were any truth in Mr. Townshend's insinuations.

[3] M.P. for Andover.

service will induce me to give my attendance in the House at this critical conjuncture.

My zeal for the public service has induced me to spend many thousand pounds in support of a parliamentary interest.

My zeal for the public service did induce me to go in person against the enemies of His Majesty.

My zeal for the public service did induce me to hazard and lose two brothers (very dear to their family) in the service of their country.

In consequence of this zeal I thought myself entitled, at this time last year, to ask a small favour of the Ministry, and easily obtained an absolute promise. My services were then desired in a stronger manner than by a mere form. They never more thought of me 'till now that they have occasion to apply to me again for fresh services.

It is for these reasons that I have taken the liberty to ask the favour of you to tell me whom, under these circumstances, you mean I should look upon as my friends. I am, Sir, &c., &c. FRANCIS BLAKE DELAVAL.

MR. GRENVILLE TO THE MARQUESS OF CARNARVAN[1].

Downing Street, Oct. 25, 1763.

MY DEAR LORD,—As the time approaches for the meeting of the Parliament, which is fixed by the King's Proclamation for the 15th of next month, it becomes necessary to consider of a proper person to move the

[1] James Brydges, afterwards third and last Duke of Chandos. His daughter and sole heir, Lady Anna Eliza, was the mother of the present Duke of Buckingham and Chandos. Lord Carnarvan was at this time M.P. for Radnorshire. He died in 1789.

Address in answer to His Majesty's Speech from the Throne.

Many reasons make me extremely desirous that in the present conjuncture this should now be moved by one whose high rank and character may give weight and credit to it. With this view it would be difficult for me not to turn my thoughts towards your Lordship, whose affection and zeal for the King and the constitution (and let me add with the highest pleasure), the friendly disposition you have expressed towards me, make me flatter myself that you will comply with my request upon this occasion; and if you approve of the Address, as I hope you will, that you will propose it to the House. For this purpose, and that you may receive all the information upon this subject that I am able to give, I beg the favour of you to come to town as soon as you conveniently can; and that in the mean time you will do me the honour to let me know your sentiments upon this subject, as it is necessary that the proper arrangements should be immediately taken upon it. I have the honour to be, &c., &c. GEORGE GRENVILLE.

MR. GRENVILLE TO THE EARL OF NORTHUMBERLAND.

Downing Street, Oct. 28, 1763.

MY DEAR LORD,—Your Lordship will have received from Lord Halifax an account of what are His Majesty's sentiments and directions upon the very delicate and important subject of the pensions and grants in Ireland, and you will see from thence that the King still remains in the same opinions as when you left us, both with regard to the expediency and fitness of not granting them for lives or years, except in extraordinary cases which His Majesty is the only judge of, and likewise with regard to the manner of communicating those intentions.

I am extremely concerned to find that upon a consideration of this matter with the servants of the Crown in that kingdom, your Excellency and they should be of opinion that the Declaration which His Majesty has allowed you to make of this resolution to the Members of both Houses of Parliament, would not sufficiently answer the good purpose of doing honour to the King's Government, and of giving that public satisfaction which was intended by it. I hope, my dear Lord, that you will feel the weight of the reasons which have induced the King to persist in thinking it not proper to proceed by an Address from the House of Commons, and an answer from the Lord-Lieutenant and from His Majesty.

This voluntary concession from the Crown should not have the appearance of the least force and constraint, which in these times might possibly be the case, if it is made in consequence of an Address of Parliament, and by this means the grace of it would be lost both to the King, who has approved, and to your Lordship, who proposed it. It would in that case be attributed to the weakness of Government and the inability of resisting this proposition, instead of the goodness of the Crown, and the disinterestedness of the Lord-Lieutenant, who, without the least compulsion, voluntarily promised, by the Declarations which you have been authorized to make, to restrain the exercise of this right, and to prevent for the future whatever may have been too much for the past. Your letter to me upon this occasion has,

I own, given me great uneasiness, as I see by it the full persuasion your Lordship is in, that it is both wise and honourable to give way to the wishes of the King's servants in Ireland; and I am convinced, on the other hand, that His Majesty is not disposed to change his sentiments in regard to it, or to go any farther than he has declared. I flatter myself, however, that your Lordship's wisdom and temper will enable you to get over this difficulty, and to show all reasonable people how unbecoming a return it would be, for this instance of His Majesty's condescension, to press the performance of it in any manner that would be disagreeable to him, and that may be thought to encroach upon the ancient and established rights of the Crown. This would at all times be dangerous, but more particularly at present, from the temper and spirit that has prevailed both in Great Britain and in Ireland. It is very much to have been wished that the two Houses of Parliament in Ireland had shown less difficulty to approve of the first great measure of His Majesty's reign, as their conduct on this occasion, and the influence they are supposed to have been under, will be an inducement to some of them to attempt to carry it farther in Ireland, and will encourage others in the same disposition here. The quiet and honour of your Lordship's Administration depend upon your checking the former, and I am fully persuaded it will be done by every act of prudence and moderation on the one hand, and of firmness on the other. With regard to the latter, though all possible endeavours are employed to spread discontent and uneasiness here, yet I flatter myself that these acts alone will not be successful if the real distresses which the kingdom is reduced to by the boundless expense of the late war, can be alleviated at least, if not removed. I hear that the Attorney General[1] has declared his intention to resign his office immediately, and I believe I may venture to tell your Lordship that this event will take effect in a few days. He assigns no reason for it whatever but the distance of his father, Lord Hardwicke, and his friends from the Government. I have expected this step for some time, and therefore am not at all surprised at it, though I am sorry that he thought himself obliged to take it. I am extremely obliged to your Lordship for your kind attention to what I desired in my former letter, and return you a thousand thanks for the friendly assurances of your assistance and good offices in our business here. I own I have very earnestly wished to avail myself of it still farther, if your Lordship will give me leave, by desiring the favour of Lord Warkworth[2] to move the Address, in answer to the King's Speech, if he returns to England time enough, and is not himself too unwilling to undertake it. Many reasons concur to make me wish this if possible, but the principal one with me is to show the world how happy I shall be to receive this public mark of the friendship and approbation of your Lordship and of your family.

I have seen Sir Francis Delaval, and hope that he is well disposed towards us, though at the beginning of his discourse it seemed to be otherwise. His brother, Sir John Delaval[3], does not, by what I could learn, think of leaving the North, and I should believe, from

[1] Mr. Charles Yorke.
[2] Eldest son of Lord Northumberland and M.P. for Westminster. The Address was moved by the Marquess of Carnarvan, and seconded by Lord Frederick Campbell.
[3] He was afterwards M.P. for Berwick.

what Sir Francis said, is not much disposed to engage in any election that is likely to be contested. He likewise talked to me about Lord Pollington[1], whose application will probably succeed, though not at present.

Our public business is coming on so fast, that it is with the greatest difficulty that I have been able to write this letter, in which I have been interrupted so often, that I scarce know what I have written. It is, however, of the less consequence, as your Lordship will see that this is a private letter, and as Lord Halifax's despatches have already given to you the King's answer upon the important but disagreeable subject of the pensions and grants, which I think cannot now be altered, and it is therefore of the utmost consequence to put a stop to any farther proceedings upon them. As this is the first act of your Government, in which, too, your Lordship has so much real merit to the people of Ireland, I hope you will be able to do it satisfactorily. I know the infinite importance it will be of in this conjuncture, that your Lordship's Administration may be as easy and honourable to you, as I am sure your good intentions towards the King and his people will deserve. For my part, it will be my utmost endeavour to contribute to it, both as a public and as a private man, from my duty to His Majesty's service, which is so immediately connected with it, and from the sincere attachment and high respect which I shall ever wish to show to you, and with which I am, &c., &c.

GEORGE GRENVILLE.

[1] John Savile Lord Pollington, afterwards Earl of Mexborough, in the Peerage of Ireland. He was M.P. for Shoreham.

LORD NORTH TO THE EARL OF HALIFAX.

Bird's Place, October 30, 1763.

My Lord,—I am very sorry to be obliged to excuse myself from waiting upon your Lordship to dinner on Wednesday next.

My brother Harris[1], at our last Board day, engaged us all to dine with him. I will, however, do myself the pleasure of paying my respects in George Street either that evening or Thursday morning.

The more I have thought upon the business which we talked upon the last time I had the honour of waiting upon your Lordship, the more I am convinced that the part I am desired to take in that affair will be attributed to your Lordship's particular reasons of dislike to the person principally affected. Support may certainly be expected from the office I hold, and that I should not fail to give, whether I had any connection with your Lordship or no. As the case stands at present, I have, personally, rather received civilities from Mr. ——[2], and the marks of favour received from His Majesty by my father and myself are not such as to make the world expect that we should be the first in this declaration of duty.

These reasons, added to the relation in which I have the honour to stand to your Lordship, and the kindness you have always showed me, will not fail to make every-

---

[1] James Harris, M.P. for Christchurch, and a Lord of the Treasury. He was the father of the first Earl of Malmesbury. Mr. Harris is remembered as the author of a Treatise entitled *Hermes*, which was praised by Bishop Lowth in the preface to his English Grammar, as the most beautiful and perfect example of analysis that has been exhibited since the days of Aristotle.

[2] Wilkes.

body turn their eyes towards you when they see me take the lead in this affair: especially if it should happen, as it has sometimes, that when the question is moved and seconded, and spoken to by the Minister, the rest of the company should sit as quiet as if they had no tongues in their heads.

In this case, notwithstanding the majority, nobody would appear to have the business much at heart, but Mr. Grenville and your humble servant. On all these accounts, I think my properer place will be to support the motion in debate than to make it. At least, I think the several questions should be put into several hands, and not all given to me, so that Government may be certain of more members than one or two putting themselves forward in the cause. I am, my Lord, with the greatest attachment, &c., &c. NORTH.

THE EARL OF HALIFAX TO MR. GRENVILLE.

Bushey Park, October 31, 1763.

DEAR SIR,—I have this moment received the inclosed from Lord North, which surprises me a good deal, as he left me with a full determination to take the part we wish he should in Wilkes's affair[1].

By the latter paragraph of his letter I think he still will, if the several parts are allotted to the several speakers on our side, which I take for granted will be the case.

His Lordship's uneasiness with respect to his father's

---

[1] Lord North subsequently consented to move the thanks of the House of Commons for the King's Message respecting Wilkes, and he also undertook to conduct the Parliamentary prosecution against him.

having been neglected is natural, but not to be imputed to us, who have wished for his preferment, and done our best to promote it, on the only opening we thought we saw.

Don't show Lord North this letter, nor take notice of your having seen it; but do what you can to fix him in the part he agreed to take in Wilkes's affair, and I will do the same. I am, &c., &c. DUNK HALIFAX.

MR. DE GREY[1] TO MR. GRENVILLE.

Lincoln's Inn Fields, November 1, 1763.

SIR,—The report of Mr. Yorke's intention to resign prevailing so strongly, makes me take the liberty of giving you this trouble. If, in the disposition His Majesty shall be pleased to make of the offices of Attorney and Solicitor General, I should be thought not unfit to supply one of the vacancies, I could wish to flatter myself with your favourable opinion, and that the appointment might not be found prejudicial to His Majesty's service.

It is difficult for me to say anything upon the subject, farther than that I am, &c., &c. WILLIAM DE GREY.

THE EARL OF SANDWICH TO MR. GRENVILLE.

November 5, 1763.

DEAR SIR,—I called at your house a little while ago, but knowing who you had with you, would not interrupt

[1] Upon the resignation of Charles Yorke, Sir Fletcher Norton was made Attorney General, and Mr. De Grey became Solicitor General, afterwards Attorney General and Chief Justice of the Common Pleas. He was created Lord Walsingham in 1780, and died in the following year.

you. My business was to tell you that I have set everything right with regard to what has passed between Lord C[1]. and me.

I was with him last night, and found him in very good humour, but still adhering to the impropriety of bringing the matter[2] before the House merely as a blasphemous and impious work; but said that if it was brought as a complaint on account of the improper mention of the name of a peer, he had no sort of objection to it, and that then the House would certainly take it up upon that and the other point likewise.

I asked him if Bishop W——[3] authorized me to complain in his behalf whether all his Lordship's objections would be removed, and that he would allow me to bring the thing on in that shape; he answered, by all means, and that he should entirely approve of it; in short, I think he was glad of this pretext to get off of the ground he had originally taken, and I thought it better to rest it there.

I have been this morning with the Bishop, and have showed him the papers. He comes heartily into the affair, says he will not only authorize me to complain in his name of this outrage, but will take any part in it himself that shall be judged proper by the King's Administration, and he seems much pleased with the scheme in general.

I shall apprize Lord C—— of the Bishop's language, and that in consequence of it, I mean to carry the affair into execution; so that I think we have now nothing to

---

[1] Lord Chancellor Henley, afterwards Earl of Northington.

[2] Respecting the Poem called *An Essay on Woman*, with notes, which had been attributed by Wilkes to the Bishop of Gloucester, because he had written the notes to Pope's *Essay on Man*.

[3] Warburton, Bishop of Gloucester.

do but to settle the mode of bringing it on, in which I shall hope for your advice and assistance.

You know that we have had Wilkes regularly watched ever since his return from France; I send you a note of his conduct upon the 2nd of November, where you will observe one very extraordinary visitor, who stayed with him half an hour. I am, &c., &c.

SANDWICH.

(*The following are specimens of the Reports made to the Secretaries of State, from the persons employed by them to watch the movements of Mr. Wilkes and his friends.*)

Monday, October 31st, 1763. Mr. Wilkes went out this morning at half an hour after ten o'clock to Mr. Belenger's in Hedge Lane, and stayed half an hour, from thence home to dinner. Mr. Leach, the printer, came at two o'clock, and stayed an hour and a half. We have not seen Mr. Wilkes since.

Tuesday, November 1st. Mr. Churchill came to Mr. Wilkes this morning at nine o'clock, and stayed an hour. Soon after, Mr. Beardmore, the attorney, came, but did not stay. We have not seen Mr. Wilkes this day.

Wednesday, November 2nd, 1763. Mr. Churchill came to Mr. Wilkes this morning at ten o'clock, and stayed an hour and a quarter. At one o'clock Mr. Walkub came, and stayed half an hour; he is a member of Parliament, and lives in Argyll Buildings. At half an hour after three o'clock Mr.

Thornton came, and at four o'clock Mr. Grendell, a surgeon, who lives in Austin Friars, in the city. They both dined with Mr. Wilkes, and stayed till six o'clock. Mr. Wilkes has not been out this day.

N.B. Mr. Wilkes's brother came this day, and stayed with him two hours.

Wednesday, November 2nd. Mr. Beardmore, the attorney, came to Mr. Wilkes this morning at eleven o'clock, and stayed an hour. At twelve o'clock, Mr. Walkub came in a hackney coach, and stayed half an hour. Mr. Wilkes dined at home, and have not seen him since.

Thursday, November 3rd. Mr. Wilkes went out this morning at half an hour after eight o'clock to Mr. Woodfall's, printer, Charing Cross; stayed ten minutes; from thence to Mr. Cotes's in St. Martin's Lane; stayed half an hour; from thence to Mr. Thornton's in Chapel Street, Westminster; stayed three quarters of an hour; from thence to Mr. Churchill's, stayed half an hour; from thence home. Mr. Beardmore, the attorney, came, and stayed an hour. At two o'clock Mr. Cotes came, and stayed an hour and a quarter. Mr. Wilkes dined at home, and have not seen him since.

Friday, November 4th. Mr. Beardmore, the attorney, came to Mr. Wilkes this morning at twelve o'clock, and stayed till past one. Soon after Mr. Cotes came, and stayed three hours. Mr. Wilkes dined at home, and have not seen him since.

Saturday, November 5th. Mr. Wilkes went out this morning at half an hour after ten o'clock, to one Mr. Karr's, at Vauxhall, where Mr. Churchill lodges, and stayed an hour and a half; from thence home. At three o'clock one of my Lord Temple's post-boys came to Mr. Wilkes on horseback, and delivered a parcel to Mr. Wilkes's footman; he stayed half an hour; whether he had any answer I know not. The boy went from thence to one Mr. Macey's, an attorney in St. Alban's Street, Saint James's Market, and delivered a packet there; from thence he went to Lord Temple's, where he got off his horse and went into the house, and stayed half an hour; from thence he went to Deptford, where he says my Lord Temple is: he says my Lord will be in town on Monday or Tuesday next. Mr. Wilkes dined at home, and have not seen him since.

N.B. Mr. Wilkes got out of the coach the other side of Westminster Bridge, and about the centre of the bridge he met Mr. Beardmore, the attorney, and talked with him a quarter of an hour.

Sunday, November 6th. Mr. Wilkes went out this morning at half after ten, to Saint Margaret's Church, and stayed till service was over; from thence he went home, and half an hour after one o'clock he went out in his chair to the Hon. Mr. Townshend's, in Grosvenor Square, but did not stay; from thence he went to Mr. Barnet's, in Bartlett's Square, but did not stay; from thence he went home, and have not seen him since.

N.B. The printers are very busy composing in the two-pair-of-stairs room, all this evening.

Monday, November 7th. Mr. Beardmore came to Mr. Wilkes this day at twelve o'clock, in a hackney-coach, and stayed ten minutes; soon after Mr. Balfe, the printer, came, and stayed an hour. At one o'clock Mr. Beardmore came a second time, and stayed near an hour; at two o'clock Mr. Cotes came, and stayed above an hour. Mr. Wilkes dined at home. At seven o'clock Mr.

Cotes came in a hackney-coach, and stayed half an hour.

The printers have been busy at work all this evening in the two-pair-of-stairs room.

Tuesday, November 8th. Mr. Wilkes went out this morning at half an hour after eight o'clock, in a hackney coach, to Mr. Beckford's, the present Lord Mayor, in Soho Square, and stayed three quarters of an hour; from thence he went to Mr. Onslow's, in Curzon Street, May Fair, and stayed an hour and a half. Mr. Wilkes brought Mr. Onslow in a hackney-coach to Spring Gardens, where Mr. Onslow got out, and said he had some business there, but would call on Mr. Wilkes presently; from thence he went home; soon after Mr. Cotes came. At half after two o'clock Mr. Wilkes, Mr. Onslow, and Mr. Cotes came out together, and parted at the top of George Street. Mr. Wilkes then went to Mr. Thornton's, in Chapel Street, but did not stay; from thence he went home. A little before seven o'clock he went out in his chair to my Lord Temple's, and left him there at nine o'clock.

Wednesday, November 9th. Mr. Wilkes went out this day in his chair at half an hour after twelve, to Sir John Cust's, Speaker of the House of Commons, stayed three quarters of an hour; from thence he went to Mr. Thornton's, stayed near an hour; from thence home. Soon after Mr. Cotes came; stayed half an hour. At half past two Mr. Wilkes went out in his chair to Mr. Woodfall's, the printer, at Charing Cross, stayed ten minutes; from thence he went to Mr. Legge's, St. James's Square, but did not stay; from thence he went to Lord Temple's, stayed three quarters of an hour; from thence home to dinner; we have not seen him since. At seven o'clock Mr. Blackman, the messenger, came to Mr. Wilkes, and stayed talking with the footman at the door ten minutes. The printers are very busy at work in the two-pair-of-stairs room.

Friday, November 11*th.* Mr. Wilkes went out this morning a quarter of an hour after nine o'clock, and walked once round the park, and then home; at half an hour after ten Mr. Cotes came to Mr. Wilkes's, and stayed near an hour. At a quarter before twelve o'clock Mr. Wilkes went out, when he went to Lord Harry Paulet's, in Albemarle Street, and stayed above an hour, and as Mr. Wilkes was turning the corner of the street to go towards Hyde Park Corner, my Lord Temple was crossing from St. James's Street into Albemarle Street; my Lord sent one of his servants after Mr. Wilkes, and told him my Lord would be glad to speak with him. Accordingly Mr. Wilkes went back, and got into the chariot, where he stayed talking with my Lord above a quarter of an hour, then parted; Mr. Wilkes went to 'Squire Walsh's, in Chesterfield Street, May Fair, and stayed half an hour; from thence he went home to dinner.

Saturday, November 12*th.* Mr. Wilkes went out this morning a quarter after eleven, with Lord Cornwallis[1], Lord Allen[2], and another gentleman, with him: they walked together till they came to Mr. Mackintosh's, where they parted. Mr. Wilkes went into Mr. Mackintosh's lodgings, but did not stay; from thence he went to Mr. Woodfall's, the printer, at Charing Cross, and

---

[1] Charles Lord Cornwallis, afterwards made a Marquess. He was Governor General of India, where he died in 1805.

[2] Joshua Viscount Allen, an Irish Peer.

stayed five minutes; from thence he went to Mr. Churchill's, in Parliament Street, but did not stay; from thence he went home to dinner. At half past five he went out in his chair to Lord Temple's, and left him there at eight o'clock.

Sunday, November 13th. Mr. Wilkes went to St. Margaret's Church this morning, and stayed till church was over; from thence he went home. At half after one o'clock he went out in his chair to the French Ambassador's, but did not stay; from thence he went to Mr. Onslow's, Curzon Street, but did not stay; from thence he went to Mr. Hopkins's; and from thence to Mr. Walsh's, but did not stay; they live in Chesterfield Street, and are both Members of Parliament; from thence he went to Lord Petre's, in Curzon Street, but did not stay; from thence he went to Lord Verney's, in the same street, and from thence to Sir William Stanhope's, in Dover Street, but did not stay; from thence he went to Lord Temple's, but did not stay; from thence he went home to dinner. At half an hour after five o'clock this evening he went out in his chair to Mr. Onslow's, in Curzon Street, and stayed till near eight o'clock; from thence he went home, and we have not seen him since.

LORD CLIVE TO MR. GRENVILLE.

Berkeley Square, November 7, 1763.

SIR,—As your friendship has induced you to be a mediator between me and the Court of Directors, in compliance with your desire I now send you the terms on which I am ready to make an absolute cession of all right and title to my Jaggeer[1], in favour of the East India Company.

That the East India Company shall pay to me or my heirs annually for twelve, or ten years at least, the amount of what they shall receive from my Jaggeer, provided that they hold those lands of which this Jaggeer (is) a quit-rent.

If these conditions are fulfilled, I do promise you, Sir, that I never will give any opposition to the present, or any other Court of Directors, and never will interfere in any of their affairs directly or indirectly. I am, with the greatest respect, Sir, your most obliged and devoted humble Servant, CLIVE.

THE KING TO MR. GRENVILLE.

12 minutes past 11 (Tuesday, Nov. 15, 1763).

MR. GREENVILLE[2].—Your account of the meeting last night gives me well-grounded hopes that everything in Parliament will go well; the continuation of Wilkes's impudence is amazing, when his ruin is so near; in reading over my Speech the following observation has occurred to me: in the paragraph to the H. of Com. it is said, *The heavy debts, &c., call for Our utmost attention, and the strictest frugality;* has not the Clerk mistaken? ought it not to be *Your utmost attention?* send me word how that stands in your Copy. G. R.

[1] A quit-rent upon certain territories in India, which was said to be worth from twenty-five thousand to thirty thousand pounds a year. The East India Company agreed to confirm Lord Clive's right to the Jaggeer for ten years, if he lived so long. and if they continued, during that period, in possession of the lands for which the revenue was paid.

[2] The King invariably adopted this mode of spelling Mr. Grenville's name; in future it will be corrected.

VOL. II. M

THE KING TO MR. GRENVILLE.

(Wednesday morning, Nov. 16, 1763).

Mr. Grenville,—Your very clear and methodical account of yesterday's debate gives me great pleasure as you will not escape a debate to-day, and I hope you will be the first with me at St. James's this day.　　G. R.

Gen. Conway's conduct is amazing. I am hurt for Lord Hertford; I shall propose to Mr. Grenville the dismissing instantly, for in this question I am personally concerned[1].

THE KING TO MR. GRENVILLE.

23 minutes past 11,
(Wednesday evening, Nov. 16, 1763).

Mr. Grenville.—These lines are only to thank you for your congratulations on the event of this day[2]; I cannot help expressing my approbation of your conduct, and make no doubt if those embarked with you act as fairly by you, as you do by them, that this session will be a very advantageous one, and be the source of order, and a due observance of the laws once again returning amongst us.

[1] The draught of Mr. Grenville's communication to the King has not been preserved; it may be supposed that he mentioned General Conway's adverse vote, but it seems that the *first* proposal for his dismissal came from the King.

[2] The Address had been voted without a negative; and Mr. Pitt's speech on the occasion had been much more moderate than was expected.

THE KING TO MR. GRENVILLE.

50 minutes past 10 (November 18, 1763).

LORD CH. SPENCER[1] brought me the message from the House of Commons as I was going to the Play. I mentioned one to-morrow; if that is too early for the House, the Speaker can easily keep the House back a little, or if Mr. Grenville will write a line to Lord Charles that I think half an hour past one the best time.

I think Ferronce's[2] request not improper.

THE KING TO MR. GRENVILLE.

35 minutes past 11, (November 18, 1763).

THE Speaker's illness is most unlucky; I hope it will not be of duration. The House not sitting this day is, perhaps, not quite disadvantageous, Mr. Yorke's attendance being not certain[3].

THE EARL OF SANDWICH TO MR. GRENVILLE.

November 19, 1763.

DEAR SIR,—I have positive intelligence that Mr. Pitt was between two and three hours on Thursday last at Lord Shelburne's, and Calcraft is at this instant at

---

[1] Brother of the Duke of Marlborough, and Comptroller of the King's household.

[2] Chief Secretary to the Hereditary Prince Charles of Brunswick, who soon after arrived in England to marry the Princess Augusta, the King's eldest sister.

[3] The House adjourned until the following Monday. Mr. Yorke had resigned the Attorney Generalship on the 2nd or 3rd instant. Lord Hardwicke was at this time supposed to be dying.

Mr. Pitt's, in Jermyn Street ; you will, therefore, judge whether there is anything on the *tapis* that may require explanations.

Should not the King know this immediately?

I am, &c. SANDWICH.

COUNTESS TEMPLE TO EARL TEMPLE.

Monday, November 20 (1763).

MY DEAREST LORD,—I have just received this note from Cunningham[1]; I suppose his friends have persuaded him from coming to you. Mr. Brand[2] has just parted from me. He says, as a looker on, he thinks you and Mr. Pitt have the finest game to play in the world, if you please; that you both may lead the Duke of Cumberland and Newcastle, and must be the head of any Opposition. He thinks Mr. Pitt's speech[3] has frightened many people that would return, and he can't imagine what he meant by it; that he was to be so candid, he was to praise everybody and everything, and then to add that he stood single; he thinks he might have crushed my Lord Bute if he had not been so ; but upon all accounts he need not have said it, for that was the reason the minority was so small. He thinks

[1] Colonel James Cunningham was an intimate friend of Lord George Sackville, and served in the same regiment. He was afterwards Adjutant General in Ireland, which office he was persuaded to resign, in order that Colonel Luttrell might be appointed, and the Governorship of Kinsale was given to Cunningham.—See *Junius's Letter XL.*, addressed to Lord North, August 22, 1770.

[2] Thomas Brand, of the Hoo, Herts. He married, in 1771, the Baroness Dacre.

[3] On the motion for the Address ; it was so satisfactory to the Ministers that Lord Barrington, in a letter to Mitchell, describes it as being worth 50,000*l.*, for it would secure them a quiet session.

there is a discontent everywhere, and that if there was an Opposition declared, people would flow in ; but this is his private opinion, for he does not give himself to be on either side. However, I plainly see to which side he is disposed, for I never heard him say so much, nor so eager in all my life. He says Wilkes is raised very high in people's opinion, and my Lord Talbot as low, and feels it so much that he has never lifted up his head since. I am most truly affectionate, A. T.

THE KING TO MR. GRENVILLE.

Eight o'clock (November 23, 1763).

THE Speaker's coming on Friday will be equally as well, as his attendance at the House is of the greatest importance. I am sorry so many acted inconsistently yesterday[1], that hurts us in some degree ; and the breaking the Orders of the House, which allow each Member to speak but once, and to make an explanation, is grown to be a constant evil, which, if not put a stop to, will cause long debate on matters that formerly an hour would have determined.

THE KING TO MR. GRENVILLE.

36 minutes past 9 (Thursday, Nov. 24, 1763).

THE great consequence of this day's debate[2] to the very being of this Constitution makes me most anxious for a line to make me acquainted of the colour things now bear; that Mr. Grenville may not be detained from his more necessary business I wish but for a line.

[1] The Minority had divided fifty more than on the previous debate.
[2] Upon the matter of Privilege in the case of a Libel.

THE KING TO MR. GRENVILLE.

40 min. past 7 (November 25, 1763).

BY your coming early, Mr. Grenville, the Speaker presenting the Address at half-past two will be very convenient. It rejoices me much that this great question should have been carried by so great a majority[1]. The Duke of Bedford and many others pressed much for the dismissing some of those that have gone against us; that if we defer it longer we shall lose more people.

I don't differ much with them in this, therefore should propose dismissing General Conway both from his civil and military commissions; also Mr. Fitzherbert[2], and any others who have equally with these gone steadily against us, and giving it out that the rest would have the same fate if they do not amend their conduct.

MR. GRENVILLE TO THE EARL OF NOTHUMBERLAND.

November 26, 1763.

MY DEAR LORD,—Your Excellency's letter of the 8th of this month gave me the highest concern, from the expressions which it contained of your uneasiness at the despatch which you had received from Lord Halifax upon the subject of the grants of pensions and places upon the Irish establishment. The difficulties and embarrassments of various kinds, which you have unavoidably met with from the difference of opinions which have arisen upon this occasion, have made me extremely

---

[1] The numbers were 258 to 133.
[2] William Fitzherbert of Tissington, M.P. for Derby, and a Lord of the Board of Trade, from which office he was soon after removed.

desirous to diminish them to the utmost of my power, and to do justice to your Excellency's zealous endeavours for the King's service, and the happiness and success of that Government with which you are entrusted. This is a duty that I owe, and you will allow me, my dear Lord, to assure you that I can never pay it more sincerely than I do to you, of whose public-spirited views I am so thoroughly convinced, and whose private friendship I so earnestly wish to cultivate. With these sentiments I have more than once represented to the King the difficult situation of his Government in that kingdom. This, I think, has been owing to the same causes which have produced the same effects, and have given so much trouble, here. The same firmness of conduct and good government will, I doubt not, get the better of them in both kingdoms; but in order to resist effectually the factious claims and unreasonable pretensions of individuals, the most steady support and encouragement is indispensably necessary; and I think there is not the least reason to doubt of His Majesty's determination to give it to those whom he has called to his Government, both here and in Ireland. The happy consequences of this resolution have been very visible in the success with which the public business has been carried on in this country, and will I hope be productive of more quiet and better dispositions than have yet appeared in the Irish Parliament. Some part of the transactions which your Excellency alludes to in your letter to me, and which has been confirmed by subsequent accounts, has very much surprised the King's servants here; but I flatter myself that your resolution, not to give way to any difficulties that may arise from it, will have entirely got the better of them before this time. I have read over the despatch which you desired me to consider, and trust that the letters which you have since received have fully convinced you of the opinion which His Majesty entertains of your abilities, as well as of your good intentions to carry on the Government of Ireland, notwithstanding the difficulties you have to struggle with, in such a manner as will be most honourable to yourself, and most advantageous to his service. The scene shifts so frequently where you are, that it is impossible to point out any particulars, and therefore the King's servants, at a meeting to consider of one of your Excellency's despatches, were unanimous in referring it to your judgment to determine on the spot, advising only to suspend any proceedings or engagements upon the sum of things, until the whole may be compared together, and the conduct of individuals shall be more settled than it yet appears to be. Such was the opinion of that meeting founded upon the confidence which they repose on your Excellency's discretion and wisdom, and upon their desire to give them free scope for the public benefit at this conjuncture. His Majesty's advice, which he was pleased to allow me to convey to you, with the most gracious expressions of his favour, was, that your Excellency would rather follow your own judgment than that of others, as he was convinced it would be free from passions and prejudice of every kind. The King, I believe, has repeated words to the same effect to Lord Warkworth, and I cannot, my dear Lord, give you a stronger proof that whatever has passed in your late transactions has been properly and fully explained. I cannot mention Lord Warkworth without wishing you joy, as I do most sincerely, of the very distinguished manner in which he has acquitted himself, upon a motion for a congratulatory message to the Queen, upon the birth of the young Prince. The reason you assigned in your letter made me decline the pressing his Lordship to take a part in the Address on the King's speech, and he was so obliging as to undertake that to the Queen without difficulty, and I hope you will think, considering the rank which your Lordship and Lady Northumberland held about Her Majesty, that there was no impropriety in my proposing it. The constant employment which we have had in the House ever since the session began will be my apology for having so long delayed to answer the honour of your letter. You will have heard of our success from others, and I will not, after so long a letter, trouble you with repeating the particulars. I will only observe that in the last division we had Lord Shelburne's three friends, his brother, Colonel Barré, and your Excellency's Aid-de-Camp, Lieut. Col. Calcraft, voted all against us. We have had some other extraordinary appearances of the same kind amongst the military gentlemen, notwithstanding which everything goes on as favourably as is possible, and in a manner that promises strength and stability to His Majesty's Government. I have the honour to be, &c., &c. GEORGE GRENVILLE.

THE EARL OF SANDWICH TO MR. GRENVILLE.

Whitehall, Sunday morning (Nov. 27, 1763).

DEAR SIR,—You may be perfectly easy about the Duke of Bedford's interfering about inserting the words in the Hessian Protocol. He says that Monsr. Alt[1] is a

[1] The Resident from Hesse Cassel.

lying fellow, and that he never mentioned a single word to him upon the subject, but thinks about it as you and I do.

I entirely agree with you about the question that has been discussed between our two law Lords. The best thing that could happen was their agreeing [q^y. arguing] the point together, nor was it, in my opinion, very material which idea prevailed. I am, &c. SANDWICH.

ADMIRAL RODNEY TO MR. GRENVILLE.

Hill Street, November 28, 1763.

DEAR SIR,—The friendship you have long honoured me with I have always regarded as one of the happiest incidents of my life; and as I have ever found you ready to promote my welfare, I shall, without further preface, acquaint you that in all probability a vacancy will soon happen in the sea department, which I aspire to, and for which I had much rather be indebted to your friendship than any other person's whatever.

I have this moment received a letter from Greenwich, acquainting me that Admiral Townshend has been struck with a palsy, and is in a dangerous way. Should he die, permit me to depend upon your friendship to succeed him.

I should not ask for it if it interfered with my duty as an Admiral. Sir John Jennings had it when he was only of my rank, and served afterwards; so did Sir John Balchen, and the present Governor was only Vice Admiral of the Blue when he was appointed. Give me leave to take notice to my friend that I am the only Commander-in-Chief who has returned from a successful expedition, and not (as yet) tasted of His Majesty's bounty.

I own I claim no other merit but that of doing my duty in the best manner I was able. If that in any degree contributed towards the Peace, I am happy; and whatever favours I may receive from the Crown, I had rather be indebted to your friendship for them than any other person's whatever.

A most violent cold, attended with some fever, prevents my applying in person to you, and I fear will prevent my obeying Mrs. Grenville's commands at cards to-morrow evening. Be assured that among your many friends you have not one more sincere than

Dear Sir, &c., &c.   G. B. RODNEY.

P.S. As I have not applied to Lord Egmont, be so obliging to take no notice of this letter to him.

LORD EGMONT[1] TO MR. GRENVILLE.

Admiralty Office, Saturday evening, Dec. 3, 1763.

DEAR MR. GRENVILLE,—I enclose a letter which I received two days ago from Commissioner Coleby, who is very lately returned to England. I desired him to put the account he gave me by word of mouth into writing, that you might see it before the naval money should be voted. The same account is likewise confirmed to me from another quarter.

You will see that the state of these twenty-six ships (as described in this letter referring to September last) puts the French more forward in the port of Toulon only

---

[1] First Lord of the Admiralty.

than we now are in all the ports of England together, for I wish that even our twenty intended guard-ships (five of which are not yet commissioned) may be equally ready for the sea in two months to come.

The true condition of the French naval force in the other ports, particularly Brest, is not clearly known, though I hope soon to be better informed. But in general we do know that they are not inferior in the port last mentioned, and will be probably soon as forward there; for they do now give, and mean to give, their greatest attention to the restoration of their marine, which will become formidable very soon.

They have a precedent for striking the first blow without warning, which they will not forget. Whenever they meditate that blow, for that very reason they must be quicker to strike than we to resist; and for another, that they can man a large squadron in half the time.

Twenty sail of the line, or less, would better strike this blow than a greater number, because it would give less previous alarm. And if struck either on the ports and docks of England, or by the landing a very few troops in Ireland (each of them the work but of a few days) it would be certainly decisive, and surely fatal at the outset of a war.

It has fallen in my way to receive informations from a very extraordinary person, whose name I must not communicate. This person has seen a confidential letter from one of the principal Ministers of France, expressly saying that their marine was resolved to be, and certainly should be, re-established in all events by the year 1764. That the moment this should be done, France was resolved to wipe off the stains of that most ignominious Peace to which, for a time, she was obliged to submit, but under which her glory could not suffer her to exist. *That Newfoundland should furnish the pretext for the intended rupture.* That in the mean time all the facilities should be given, and no dissatisfaction expressed, at the projects formed either by the English, or by the French, for the settlement of the Sugar Islands ceded by France. That, on the contrary, all encouragement underhand should be given, because whatever should be done in that kind would be done for the benefit of France, who was resolved to re-possess them soon.

This letter was wrote about four months since, and to a party by whom it was not suspected that it would be ever revealed; and I can almost venture to say, that I know what I have said of this letter to be absolutely true. Other dangerous hints, with respect to Ireland, have been dropped also from the same quarter.

From these and other reasons, I have long and constantly expressed (as you well know) my fears for what would pass upon the coast of Newfoundland: and we begin to see within these few days that these apprehensions were not groundless, as well by the complaints already made in form to Lord Halifax from the French Court, as by extracts of some letters lately received from our own officers on that station, which have been sent to him from this Board.

This scene, I fear, will still open more and more disagreeably, for M. de Guerchy was with me full two hours this morning, talking upon this subject in a strain which convinced me that these circumstances greatly merit your attention, and that this business, without great circumspection, may suddenly become very serious.

It is impossible for me, believing as I do, of the French intentions, and convinced as I am of their sufficient ability to put their navy into an alarming condition sooner than we generally suspect, not to wish heartily that you would shape the naval supplies in a way to afford as much as you possibly can towards the speedy repair of our fleet. The sum of 100,000*l*., which you told me some time since was all you could allow for the extra estimate, is actually less by 10,000*l*. than the money which we are bound by former contracts to pay before the end of next August for eight ships now building in the merchants' yards. Instead, therefore, of obtaining a large supply, which at the very first view must evidently appear necessary towards extraordinary repair of so vast a fleet, all returned or returning more or less from the severe service of the war, upon such a sum not a single shilling could be applied to that purpose. Nay, we must even cripple some other necessary service to pay the merchants for those eight ships only.

Yesterday, indeed, Mr. Stephens informed me that Mr. Jenkinson had told him you intended now to give 150,000*l*. to the extra Estimate. But even this will afford little more than 40,000*l*. for the rebuilding in the King's yards, and all the extraordinary repairs of the whole navy—a sum so trifling, as scarce to be of any use ; not to mention the warehouses, docks, &c., which will absolutely require soon a very great expense, only to be carried on in times of peace.

In a word, as by all I can learn, the ordinary Estimate has been made out with a strict view to economy, so much that considering that the tonnage of the navy is within ten years increased one-third, the number of our shipwrights is greatly less in proportion than in any former time. And as the extra Estimate sent you was certainly made with an earnest desire to conform as nearly as possible to your ideas, and to the difficulties which must attend your department at this time, even without admitting the supposition of any new disputes with France, I should hope that you would try to assist us with the full sum upon the head of the Extra, if not by increasing the quantum of the General Supply, at least by postponing a sufficient portion of the debt of the navy intended to be discharged this year, or by any other means which you may think more proper.

I am obliged in duty to lay these things before you, which I submit to your judgment, wishing earnestly not to give you the least embarrassment; but knowing that you, and the rest of the King's Ministers, are certainly as much concerned in any ill consequences that may arise from any sudden and untoward event, against which the navy of England should be unprepared, as I can possibly be myself, who have the honour to be, &c., &c. EGMONT.

GENERAL TOWNSHEND TO MR. GRENVILLE.

Audley Square, December 4 (1763).

DEAR SIR,—Having heard of the gambols of the City[1] upon the Order of the House of Commons, I suppose you will acquaint the House therewith to-morrow, and have at least some proper proceedings thereon. I must offer myself for this breach of public decency, government, and everything that ought to be and must be maintained.

[1] On the occasion of the burning of the *North Briton*, No. 45, by the common hangman.

I will not move without concert of Government, but I hope it will not be delayed or lowered. Yours affectionately,
GEO. TOWNSHEND.

GENERAL CONWAY TO MR. GRENVILLE.

Little Warwick Street, Sunday morning,
December 4, 1763.

GENERAL CONWAY presents his respects to Mr. Grenville, and having heard from Mr. Walpole that he is desirous to speak with him, begs leave to inform Mr. Grenville, that he will do himself the honour of waiting upon him at any time this morning, that is most convenient; and as the subject he is to speak on General Conway conceives to be one in which his honour and character are deeply concerned, he hopes Mr. Grenville will have no objection to his bringing with him a friend as witness to what he shall have the honour to say to Mr. Grenville; and for that purpose begs to propose the Duke of Richmond, a man of the strictest honour and partiality, whose personal connection with him, joined to his relation with some in high office under His Majesty, and his disposition to support the measures of Government, will, he doubts not, render him unexceptionable to Mr. Grenville.

If Mr. Grenville chooses to appoint an early hour, he humbly begs the favour of him to let the bearer be acquainted with the hour, that he may call on the Duke of Richmond, who will thereon be ready to attend him.

MR. GRENVILLE TO GENERAL CONWAY.

Downing Street, Sunday, December 4, 1763.

Mr. Grenville presents his compliments to General Conway. He desired Mr. Walpole last night to inform General Conway that Mr. Grenville would be glad to see him at nine o'clock this evening, which, as General Conway had lately done Mr. Grenville the honour to call upon him, he thought would not be disagreeable to General Conway, or put him under any difficulties; but if it is otherwise, as Mr. Grenville apprehends from General Conway's note, Mr. Grenville desires to decline it.

Mr. Grenville is engaged all this morning, and, therefore, could not appoint any part of it wherein he could have the pleasure of receiving or waiting upon General Conway.

Mr. Grenville thinks it right to inform General Conway that he has no proposition of any kind to make; that just before Lord Hertford left England his Lordship said a great deal in two or three different conversations with Mr. Grenville about General Conway's situation, and Mr. Grenville then desired his Lordship to assure General Conway of his personal regard, and of his sincere disposition to show it upon all occasions.

From what his Lordship then told him, Mr. Grenville flattered himself that those dispositions were mutual, and that General Conway would be equally desirous with himself to cultivate them; and to manifest the truth of what he then said to Lord Hertford, Mr. Grenville now proposed to have the pleasure of seeing General Conway; but if he is mistaken in it, he is sorry for the trouble he has given to General Conway and himself, and wishes not to increase it, as he does not see it can have any good effect whatever.

With regard to the Duke of Richmond's being present as a witness of what passes, if there were any conversation to be had that would make witnesses necessary, Mr. Grenville could not have the least objection to the Duke of Richmond, for whom he has the highest respect and regard, and whom he will at all times be extremely glad of the honour of seeing, but he would not give his Grace or General Conway any unnecessary trouble.

Mr. Grenville has been engaged upon business of consequence this whole morning, which has prevented him from answering General Conway's note sooner, and has obliged him to detain his servant longer than he intended.

GENERAL CONWAY TO MR. GRENVILLE.

Richmond House, Sunday, 2 o'clock (Dec. 4, 1763).

GENERAL CONWAY presents his compliments to Mr. Grenville, and begs to let him know that the only reason he had for troubling him with a note this morning was his having received a message last night by Mr. Walpole[1], by which Mr. Grenville acquainted General Conway he was desirous to see him; and, as he understood, this morning. If the evening is more agreeable, and Mr.

[1] *Memorandum, in the handwriting of Mrs. Grenville.*—"Mr. Walpole had far exceeded his commission, having told Mr. Conway much more fully than he was empowered to do, what had passed between Mr. Grenville and him upon this subject at Mr. Pitt's, particularly as Mr. Grenville, turning to Mr. Walpole, had said that no part of the conversation then passing was to go out of that room, and that he had no message to give to Mr. Conway, except Mr. Grenville's desire of seeing him in case Mr. Conway wished it."

Grenville is still desirous of it, he will then do himself the honour to wait upon him, and begs Mr. Grenville to believe it will be by no means disagreeable, but, on the contrary, very agreeable to him.

He, at the same time, begs Mr. Grenville to understand that he has not the least idea of receiving or making propositions, and that the only motive of his message, after that of obeying his commands sent by Mr. Walpole, was his desire of clearing up the matter of two different conversations Mr. T. Pitt has had with Mr. Walpole on this subject, by Mr. Grenville's desire, as also Mr. Grenville's with Mr. Walpole last night, in which he could not but think himself in a very particular manner interested.

General Conway does not doubt but that, in his situation, Mr. Grenville has very good reasons for making the Duke of Richmond and himself expect his answer so long, but hopes that, in regard to seeing him or not, to-night, Mr. Grenville will have the goodness to return yes or no by the servant, as well in regard to the Duke of Richmond as himself, who will both wait here for his commands.

General Conway, on recollection, begs further to put Mr. Grenville in mind that, by Mr. Walpole's report and message, he understood there was something which Mr. Grenville thought wanted to be immediately cleared up by him.

MR. GRENVILLE TO GENERAL CONWAY.

Downing Street, December 4, 1763,
Half an hour past 9 at night.

MR. GRENVILLE presents his compliments to General Conway, and informs him that his company has just left him, and that if General Conway has any commands for him, he will be very ready to see him and the Duke of Richmond, if his Grace will do him that honour.

LORD NORTH TO MR. GRENVILLE.

Grosvenor Street, December 13 (1763).

DEAR SIR,—I could not meet this morning in the House either Mr. Fitzherbert or Colonel Onslow, or any other person who confesses visiting Mr. Wilkes. I will send to Mr. Fitzherbert to-morrow if I do not find him in the House.

Dr. Brocklesby and Mr. Graves[1] are to be examined to-morrow in the House of Lords, so that I think we cannot fail of an opportunity of giving them timely notice to attend on Friday. I took the liberty to mention it as your desire to the Speaker, that the House might not adjourn to-morrow, farther than till Friday next. I am, Sir, with the greatest respect, your most obliged, &c., &c. NORTH.

LORD CLIVE TO MR. GRENVILLE.

Berkeley Square, December 13, 1763.

DEAR SIR,—The anxiety of mind under which I labour about the decision of a very important event, more essentially necessary towards establishing my peace of mind than the improvement of my fortune, has occasioned me giving you this trouble, which I know your friendship for me will excuse.

The ingratitude of the Court of Directors, if possible,

---

[1] The Physician and Surgeon in attendance on Mr. Wilkes, after he was wounded in the duel with Mr. Martin.

has affected me more than their injustice in withholding my fortune. Upon this occasion, I am under the necessity of saying that to our successes in Bengal is entirely owing the present great and flourishing state of our East India Company, without which they had been at this instant in that deplorable condition to which the French are now reduced; what the East India Company and Directors once thought of my services will appear by the enclosed papers.

The Directors, in their answer to my Bill, do not pretend that the Company have any right to what the Nabob's bounty bestowed upon me for particular services rendered unto him, and which they have suffered me to enjoy for four years; they only allege that my Jaggeer or Grant has not been confirmed by the Mogul, and that they may hereafter become answerable for what is paid to me on that account; they therefore desire that they may not be obliged to pay the money, or if they do, that I may give security; this is the principal plea of the Directors for withholding my right.

Give me leave, Sir, to inform you that the East India Company have acquired all their possessions by force of arms; by supporting one Nabob against another in the Carnatic, by deposing two Nabobs and setting up a third in Bengal, without the knowledge or consent of the Mogul; they have acquired in different parts of India a revenue of near one million sterling, unconfirmed to this day by the Great Mogul. Now, Sir, I submit it to your candour, whether you think the Court of Directors can have any apprehensions of being called to an account for my 30,000*l.* per annum, and not for their million.

It gives me pain, Sir, to put the Mogul in so ridiculous a light, but justice to myself obliges me to do it.

In the beginning of the year 1761, Major Carnac, at the head of the Company's troops, in conjunction with those of the Nabob, gave the Great Mogul himself battle, and defeated him in such manner that he was reduced to the necessity of surrendering himself up as a State prisoner, for which service Major Carnac received the public thanks of the present Court of Directors; and upon the Mogul's enlargement, Major Carnac presented the enclosed petition to His Majesty, desiring he would confirm to the Company all their possessions, and with them my Jaggeer: to this petition he consented upon receiving the usual present, which the Governor and Council of Bengal refused, not thinking the confirmation worth the expense. So much for the Great Mogul. I could write volumes of the insufficiency and inability of the Mogul ever to call the Company to an account, but that I think I have said enough to convince you, Sir, of the weakness of the Directors' plea for withholding my property.

No consideration on earth should induce me to desire the mediation of a person of your character and high station in life, in what is not strictly honourable. My request, Sir, is only to enjoy for a certain term of years, that which, according to the rules of equity and justice, *is my own*, and then to make over all my right to those who have the power to secure it to the Company for ever.

And now, Sir, I am come to the only part of your letter which gives me much uneasiness—" Whether I shall be able to succeed, it is (as you well know) impossible for me to answer."

I shall ever acknowledge, Sir, that you have behaved towards me with the greatest candour and sincerity; at the same time I must say that Lord Powis spoke with more confidence, and seemed not to entertain the least doubt of the success of your endeavours.

Discountenanced and hated by the party I have abandoned, as much as I was before respected and esteemed, if I should, through the obstinate injustice of the Directors (notwithstanding your powerful mediation), be disappointed, I must confess to you, Sir, that I have so much sensibility inherent in my nature, that my mind will be too much affected to recover so severe a shock for some time; but be the event what it will, I have taken my part, and you may be assured that my poor services, such as they are, shall be dedicated for the rest of my days to the King, and my obligations to you always acknowledged, whether in or out of power.

If you should find the Directors not disposed to accept of the terms proposed, I could wish they were not acquainted with the offer made in my letter not to oppose them in future; and if they should object to my heirs enjoying the Jaggeer for a number of years in case of accident to me, I am ready, if you think proper, to give up that point. I am, with the most sincere attachment, &c., &c.
CLIVE.

LORD CLIVE TO MR. GRENVILLE.

Berkeley Square, December 21, 1763.

DEAR SIR,—To-morrow morning I propose setting out for Bath; and if you should have any commands for me, you will be pleased to direct a line to me at that place.

There was nothing proposed at the Quarterly India Court this morning. All that I could learn was a determined resolution in the Court of Directors to distress me as much as possible; for which purpose they have within these few days drawn out a case of their own, and obtained an opinion in their favour by Thurlow[1]: this I take to be done with a design of preventing future solicitations. I propose very soon laying before the public a short sketch of my treatment by the Directors, and of the manner in which I obtained my Jaggeer grant from the Nabob; and if it should appear to you, Sir, that there is a determined resolution in the Court of Directors to overpower me by expense and delay, and to defraud me of my right, contrary to all equity and justice, I submit to your better judgment the possibility of seeking redress from Parliament. Some months ago I spoke to Mr. Pitt on this subject; and he admitted that such a thing was practicable, but advised me against it, saying, he could entertain little hopes of success from the violence of party. I should be glad to be favoured with your sentiments on this subject.

As Mr. Sullivan told you, Sir, that the person who in his own handwriting offered to confirm to me my Jaggeer grant was not the Mogul, I take the liberty to send you an extract from Mr. Vansittart's letter.

I am, &c., &c.   CLIVE.

Extract from Mr. Vansittart's Letter:—

"Abdully, before his departure from Delhi, proclaimed the Shahzadah, King, by the name of Shaw Allum, and left his son Jowan Buckt in the Regency during his father's absence. We have also acknowledged him as Sovereign of the Empire, and the Nabob

---

[1] Afterwards Lord Chancellor.

has ordered prayers to be read, and money to be coined in his name.

"Mr. Amphlett regularly makes you the remittances of your Jaggeer money, nor do I see what plea any one has to disturb you in the quiet possession.

"I am, &c., &c.   HENRY VANSITTART."

N.B. These letters were wrote after the instalment of the new Nabob.

MR. WILKES TO EARL TEMPLE.

Calais, Sunday, Dec. 25, 1763.

MY LORD,—I beg leave to pay my first compliments to your Lordship on leaving England even for so short a time.

I was chid not a little by my physician and surgeon for going out so soon. When I say my physician and surgeon, I desire to explain myself that I mean Dr. Brocklesby and Mr. Graves, and not Dr. Heberden and Mr. Hawkins [1].

I could not be satisfied without saying this, for even here I will breathe the free spirit of an Englishman. I suffered a good deal by the rude jolting of the chaise, through the cursed town of Rochester and through Dover, which the very handsome behaviour of the latter to me could not more than balance.

If I may now talk of myself half a moment like a true Frenchman, I should say that I am better than I feared for this poor carcase yesterday. The lips of my wound were much inflamed by the violent exercise, and I was

[1] The two latter had been appointed by the House of Commons to attend him.

so extremely sick in the passage that I have strained myself greatly. The passage was only of two hours, and three hours in the *Hanover* packet. We arrived here just at three.

I beg to wish your Lordship and Lady Temple all the compliments of this merry season.

I hope to be in Great George Street by the 14th of January, for at this season of the year I think two days are to be given extra for so fickle an element as Venus's own, the sea. I am, with the most just esteem and gratitude, &c., &c. JOHN WILKES.

MR. GRENVILLE TO THE EARL OF HERTFORD.

Downing Street, December 26, 1763.

MY DEAR LORD,—When I received the honour of your Lordship's letter about the information which you had received of Mr. Bunbury's[1] intentions to set out for Paris, as Secretary to the Embassy, my time was so wholly engrossed with the public business in the House of Commons, and the constant succession of engagements for every moment of the day when I was out of the House, that it has been utterly impossible for me to return an answer to it, or indeed to inquire into the state of it, until that scene was a little over. As soon as the recess came I took an occasion of speaking to the

---

[1] Thomas Charles Bunbury succeeded to the Baronetcy on the death of his father, in June, 1764. He had married in June, 1762, Lady Sarah Lenox, daughter of Charles, Duke of Richmond, which marriage was dissolved in 1776. Lady Sarah, by her second marriage with the Honourable George Napier, was the mother of the present Sir Charles James Napier and Sir William Napier. Sir *Charles* Bunbury (as he was usually called) represented the county of Suffolk in Parliament for 43 years. He died in 1821.

King, and represented, as I had often done before, the uneasiness which it gave to you, and your earnest desire that Mr. Bunbury should not come to you as Secretary of the Embassy at Paris. My representation had the effect I wished, for the present at least, as His Majesty was pleased to tell me that he would not send Mr. Bunbury to Paris during the present Session of Parliament, and I am convinced that if any other proper arrangement can be found for him before that time, the King will be disposed to come into it. I sincerely wish this account may be as agreeable to you, as it will always be to me to inform you of anything that frees you from the least degree of anxiety, and that may render your situation as easy and honourable to yourself, as I am persuaded it will be advantageous to the public. You will have heard the particulars of our transactions in both Houses of Parliament from others who, being less concerned in them than I have been, may speak of them more freely, and more properly than I can do. I will, therefore, only tell you that, in a general view of them, they have exceeded my most sanguine expectations hitherto, though I own I have felt great concern, as an individual, at differing in opinion so totally and upon such essential points, from some of those with whom I flattered myself I should have agreed, and particularly from General Conway, whose relation to you, as well as the sentiments which your Lordship knew, before you left England, I entertained of him, made me earnestly wish it could have been otherwise. I will still hope that this difference of opinion may go no farther, but however that may be, I shall certainly have the pleasure of knowing that I have endeavoured, by every means in my power, consistently with my duty, if possible to prevent it. This I owed to you and to myself, and I trust that you will be convinced that I have discharged it to the utmost. I have had great embarrassment and difficulty with M. de Guerchy upon the vexatious subject of his wine, which I inform your Lordship of, that if you hear any complaint about it, you may set it right. The quantity allowed here to ambassadors free from duty is only one tun, to which quantity I understood repeatedly that M. de Guerchy was willing to be restrained, if you would consent to the same restraint at Paris. For this purpose the letter was writ to your Lordship, and I was extremely surprised, upon the return of your answer, to find that M. de Guerchy understood that I had consented, if your Lordship had a right to enter any quantity you pleased free from duty at Paris, that he should have the same right here. This was the very reverse of what was proposed to your Lordship, and was certainly never in my intention, of which I need give no other proof than that it is by no means in my power. However, M. de Guerchy has been permitted to have eleven tun duty free, which is the same quantity as was allowed to M. de Nivernois, and is above double what any other ambassador ever has had, or ever will have for the future. Notwithstanding which, he seems to be displeased at my refusing to comply with the introduction of eighteen or nineteen tun more, making in the whole thirty tun free from duty, instead of the established allowance of one tun only.

I have troubled you with this tedious detail, that if it is pretended that any particular favour is shown to you with regard to your wine, beyond what is done to the French Ambassador here, you may know how far it is well founded. We are informed to-day that Mr. Wilkes embarked yesterday at Dover for Calais, in his way to Paris; whether with a view to stay there, or to return by the 19th, the day appointed for his hearing before the House of Commons, time must determine; and you will probably be sooner informed of it at Paris, than we shall be here, though I doubt whether he will now attempt to pay his respects to your Excellency as the King's Ambassador at the Court of France. I very sincerely wish you all happiness and success that the ensuing year can afford to you, and through you to this country; and I am, with the most perfect truth and attachment, my dear Lord, &c., &c. GEORGE GRENVILLE.

EARL AND COUNTESS TEMPLE TO MR. HORACE WALPOLE.

December —, 1763.

LADY TEMPLE is extremely obliged to Mr. Walpole for his verses[1], though they have occasioned a strange confusion amongst the winged kind at Stowe, who took their flight to Marble Hill some years ago; they think it very hard a parcel of chattering Magpies should be produced to sing so much better: the creatures can

---

[1] The Royal Letters Patent from Oberon, King of the Fairies, appointing Lady Temple his Poet Laureate, and in which she is addressed as—

"a noble dame
Whom mortals Countess Temple name:
To whom ourselves did erst impart
The choicest secrets of our art,
Taught her to tune the harmonious line
To our own melody divine,
Taught her the graceful negligence,
Which, scorning art and veiling sense,
Achieves that conquest o'er the heart,
Sense seldom gains, and never art."

See *Walpole Correspondence*, vol. iv. p. 345.

prate, say they, what business have they to sing; if Lady Suffolk listens to the inhabitants of Strawberry Hill, she will never be able to bear the music of anybody else.

(*The remainder is in the handwriting of Lord Temple.*)

Lord T. desires to thank you for your kind remembrance, and to assure you of his most affectionate respects.

Before the Parliament meets, thanks to the Prorogation, he will be quite recovered of his lameness. He already rides and walks very well.

MR. GRENVILLE'S DIARY:

ENTITLED, BY HIMSELF,

"SOME ACCOUNT

OF

THE MEMORABLE TRANSACTIONS

SINCE THE

DEATH OF LORD EGREMONT."[1]

Mr. Grenville went to Wotton, on *Wednesday the 3rd of August*, 1763.

The King had, about a fortnight before this, declared his intention of endeavouring to strengthen his government by proposing to Lord Hardwicke to make him President, and by giving an office to the Duke of Newcastle, contrary to the positive and repeated advice of Lord Halifax, Lord Egremont, and Mr. Grenville.

The King, however, gave his orders to Lord Egremont to speak to Lord Hardwicke, who at once rejected the offer, and said they would never come into office, but as a party and upon a plan concerted with Mr. Pitt and the great Whig Lords, as had been practised in the late King's time. That King William had been forced to a change of Ministry, so had King George the Second, who had thanked him, Lord Hardwicke, for advising him to it.

[1] This Narrative, or Diary, is chiefly in the handwriting of Mrs. Grenville, with occasional corrections and additions by Mr. Grenville.

When Lord Hardwicke's answer was reported to the King, he desired ten days to consider upon what he should think best to do, solemnly promising that if this did not take effect, he would lay aside all thoughts of it, and strengthen the hands of his three Ministers, and accordingly his two Secretaries of State spoke to him upon common business only, and Mr. Grenville went out of town.

On *Tuesday, the* 18*th of August,* he returned to London, saw the King, but spoke only upon official business.

Friday, 19*th.*—The King seemed by his conversation to the two Secretaries of State, and to Mr. Grenville, notwithstanding his former declaration, in the resolution of changing his government, notwithstanding Lord Hardwicke's refusal and the strong representations made by the three Ministers against it. Mr. Grenville went in after the two Secretaries of State, remonstrated strongly against the measure, went into a long deduction of the inconveniences arising from it, the King's abandonment of the Peace, and those who made it, which, such as it is (lower in terms as His Majesty knew than he wished it, and had urged for it), was what he, Mr. Grenville, must ever vindicate; the sacrificing his servants in Mr. Wilkes's affair, though acting by His Majesty's commands; the repeal of the Cyder Tax; all which he must expect would be the terms upon which alone the Opposition would treat.

Saturday, 20*th.*—The King saw the two Secretaries of State, seemed more inclined to abide by his then present Ministers, spoke to them with great praise of Mr. Grenville, and said he could never have anybody at the head of his Treasury who would fill that Office so much to his satisfaction as he did.

Sunday, 21st.—The King sent to Mr. Grenville at nine o'clock, to order him to come to him immediately; he went directly, and the King told him that he had fully considered upon the long discourse Mr. Grenville had held to him on the Friday; that he had no desire to change his Ministers; on the contrary he liked them all, he approved of their conduct, and meant to strengthen them by every means in his power; that he had sent for Mr. Grenville to talk with him about it, to enter fully into the matter, and to desire him to bring him his thoughts in writing upon such measures as he should think expedient, in order that he might talk with him about it before he saw the two Secretaries of State, for that by his advice he meant to conduct himself; that it was necessary to restrain the licentiousness of the times; that even in the carrying a criminal to justice (the coachman condemned for a rape), the people had interposed and endeavoured to prevent his execution[1]; that it was time a remedy should be found to these evils, for that if he suffered force to be put upon him by the Opposition, the mob would try to govern him next.

Mr. Grenville left His Majesty at a little before twelve, and went to Lord Egremont's to give him an account of what had passed; he met Doctor Duncan at the door of his dressing-room, who told him that Lord Egremont was struck with an apoplexy, and was past all hopes of recovery. Mr. Grenville was severely shocked with this great and unexpected misfortune, and passed the rest of the day with his unhappy family.

---

[1] Matthew Dodd, coachman to the celebrated courtesan, Kitty Fisher: in consequence of the interference of the mob, the military were sent for, and the execution was not effected until eight o'clock in the evening, upon Kennington Common.

The King sent many times in the day to inquire after Lord Egremont; at eight o'clock he expired, and Mr. Grenville went with Lord Halifax to the King to give him notice of it. His Majesty lamented the loss of his servant, and spoke in very high commendation of him.

Monday, 22nd. The King spoke of nothing but Lord Egremont and his family to Mr. Grenville, and told him his thoughts must be too much disturbed by this misfortune to allow him to turn them to business, that therefore he did not expect it from him.

Tuesday, 23rd. The King again talked of nothing but Lord Egremont, made Mr. Grenville give him a very particular account of his will, and inquired much after all the family.

Lord Halifax and Mr. Grenville had agreed upon the three options necessary to state to the King, and Lord Halifax mentioned them to him on Monday, when His Majesty said he never would consent to the last, and on Tuesday said the same to Mr. Grenville.

Lord Halifax went in after Mr. Grenville came out, and in discourse told the King it became necessary for His Majesty to come to a resolution as to the carrying on of his Government, particularly after this heavy blow; that His Majesty had three options, either to strengthen the hands of his present Ministers, or to mingle them with a coalition from the other party, or to throw the Government entirely into the hands of Mr. Pitt and his friends.

The King said the last was what he never could consent to.

Wednesday, 24th. Mr. Grenville did not see the King: Lord Halifax did: he told his Lordship that he had seen the Duke of Bedford, who had told him that his Government could not stand; that His Majesty must send to Mr. Pitt and his friends; that he, the Duke of Bedford, had no view of his own in this advice; that all that party hated him, but that he desired no office; he would live chiefly in the country, but meant to support His Majesty's measures when he did come to town. The King, in repeating this to Lord Halifax, said again that he had told the Duke of Bedford that he would not put himself into the hands of Mr. Pitt.

Lord Bute, this same day, *Wednesday, 24th* (or Thursday morning), sent to my Lord Mayor (Mr. Wm. Beckford), to procure through his means an interview between his Lordship and Mr. Pitt, who came to town the next day and saw Lord Bute for a long time, and, as Mr. Pitt's friends say, settled with him the terms upon which he and his party would come in (Lord Bute and his friends deny this, but Mr. Pitt as positively affirms it), saying that from those terms he would not depart, and therefore if the King could not consent to them, he had better not see him.

Thursday, the 25th, the King saw Lord Halifax and Mr. Grenville, but nothing passed.

Friday, 26th. The King opened to Mr. Grenville his intention of calling in Mr. Pitt to the management of his affairs, declaring that he meant to do it as cheap as he could, and to make as few changes as was possible. Mr. Grenville expressed his surprise and concern at this step, declared strongly that it was absolutely contrary to his advice and opinion; put the King in mind of His Majesty's late declarations to him upon this subject, viz., "that he never would consent to it, but would rather submit to any extremities;" that he,

Mr. Grenville, saw no necessity in the King's affairs which could urge such a surrender, and that he could never be a party to it, it being impossible for him to act with people whose every principle was so diametrically opposite to his own; that no private consideration of his own should ever have weight with him where his duty was concerned, but that he never could in any shape be a party to this; but upon the King's insisting upon his giving him his opinion, he recapitulated all he said before upon this subject, but left the King still in the resolution of carrying it into execution.

Saturday, 27th. Mr. Grenville went to the King, saw Mr. Pitt's servants waiting in the Court at the Queen's House, and was near two hours before the King called him in. Mr. Grenville found His Majesty a good deal confused and flustered; he resumed the conversation of the former day, entered fully into his own situation from the time he had been first called upon by His Majesty to the management of his affairs, stated the declarations that were made to him of support to be given to him then, and of the usage he had met with, at all which the King seemed much disturbed; reminded His Majesty of Lord Bute's letter to him in October, 1761, in which his Lordship told him that the King would never abandon him, that his honour was the King's honour, his disgrace the King's disgrace. The King held pretty near the same language as before, took no notice of Mr. Pitt's having been with him, and in less than twenty minutes bowed to Mr. Grenville, told him it was late, and, as he was going out of the room, said with emotion, " *Good morrow, Mr. Grenville,*" and repeated it again a second time, which was a phrase he never had used to him before.

Sunday, 28th. Lord Bute went in the morning to Kew, where he saw Mr. Elliot and Mr. Jenkinson, where they had a long discourse with him, in which they terrified him so much upon the consequences of the step he had persuaded the King to take, that he determined to depart from it, and to advise His Majesty to send to Mr. Grenville.

Mr. Grenville received a message in the afternoon from the King, to come to him at eight o'clock in the evening. When he came he found the King in the greatest agitation. His Majesty told him he had seen Mr. Pitt[1], that he had acquainted him he sent for him, not for any apprehensions he was under from Parliament, but as a general strengthening to his Government at the close of the Peace, by which he meant to abide; that this period, and the heavy burdens his people lay under from the heavy taxes in consequence of the war, made him wish to turn all his thoughts to the easing them, and at the same time restraining the general licence which prevailed; that he therefore wished to take all the assistance that could give the most general satisfaction, saving both his honour and conscience towards those already in his service, whose conduct he approved, and whom he meant to protect; that he was willing, upon the vacancy made by Lord Egremont's death, to give him the office of Secretary of State, to fill up any other vacancies in such manner as should give the most satisfaction, and to call the Duke of New-

---

[1] This was told in general terms on Sunday, and the King asked Mr. Grenville if the terms were not too hard, and if he, Mr. Grenville, would abandon him, and oblige him to submit to them, rather than which he would die in the room he then stood in. The particulars were not told Mr. Grenville till the next day.—*Note by Mr. Grenville.*

castle to some office of State, continuing his protection to those who had served him well, and whose conduct he approved. Mr. Pitt told him that he was a poor infirm man, declining in years as well as in health, unable to go through a constant parliamentary attendance; that such little strength as he could bring to His Majesty was derived from the good opinion of his friends, and of such people as attributed part of the former successes to his poor endeavours, but that if His Majesty thought fit to make use of such a little knife he must not blunt the edge; that he and his friends could never come into Government but as a party; that Lord Temple must be First Lord of the Treasury (that he was not sure Lord Temple would take that office or any other, but that he knew he would never forgive him if he did not name him for it to His Majesty), with Mr. James Grenville Chancellor of the Exchequer, if Lord Temple wished it, if not, it might be Mr. Legge; that the Board must be entirely changed; that Lord Rockingham must be First Lord of the Admiralty, with an entire new Board, excepting one, viz., his nephew, Mr. Thomas Pitt, whom he hoped would long live to serve His Majesty (N.B. Mr. Thomas Pitt was placed in the Admiralty by Mr. Grenville, and does not acknowledge the obligation of this exception, as he would not have availed himself of it); that Lord Besborough[1] must be at the head of the Board of Trade, with a new Board, or else to be restored to the Post Office, in the place of Mr. Hampden. The Duke of Devonshire to be Chamberlain; Mr. Charles Townshend to be Secretary of State in the room of Lord Halifax, and to carry on the King's business in the House of Commons when he himself could not

[1] William, second Earl of Besborough. He died 1793.

attend, which, broke as his health is, could never be above two or three times in a session. The Duke of Bolton[1] to have the Garter, and the Duke of Grafton[2] to be called to the Cabinet Council, the Duke of Newcastle to be Privy Seal, and such of his friends provided for as he should wish. These were his terms in respect of offices, with an entire removal of such others as should be necessary to fulfil what other demands were necessary. Lord Hardwicke was to be President, Lord Chief Justice Pratt made a Peer, and brought forward. Lord Holland and Lord Mansfield, on no account whatever, to have any share in Government. The King combated each of these demands. Mr. Pitt said he could not abandon those friends who had stood by him. The King asked him, then, how he thought it possible for him to give up those who had served him faithfully, and devoted themselves to him? Mr. Pitt said that reproach would 'light on his Ministers, and not on himself. As to public measures, he strongly arraigned the Peace, but said he did not mean to break it, but to have it *ameliorated*. He asked for some insight into foreign measures. The King told him of the Treaty with Russia, which he said was right, but that it ought to have been made through the King of Prussia. The King shrunk at the unreasonableness of the terms he demanded. Mr. Pitt said he saw the boat was sinking, that what he proposed was merely to keep it afloat, and that in order for so doing it was fit to break this Government, which was not founded on true Revolution principles; that it was a Tory Administration.

---

[1] Charles, fifth Duke of Bolton. He died suddenly, by his own hand, in 1765.

[2] Augustus Henry, third Duke of Grafton.

The King said he would consider on what he had said, and Mr. Pitt withdrew. The King told Mr. Grenville that this was pretty near the sum of what passed; that Mr. Pitt had said it was necessary to take some great and distinguished person through whom the recommendations for the Army promotions should come; the King said I suppose you mean Lord Granby, he answered, " or Lord Albemarle." Mr. Pitt had excepted Mr. Elliot and Mr. Oswald[1] out of the general removal.

The King said to Mr. Grenville that these terms were too hard, that he could not think of complying with them; he had therefore once more sent to Mr. Grenville, to tell him that he wished to put his affairs into his hands; that he gave him the fullest assurances of every support and every strength that he could give him towards the carrying his business into execution; that he meant to take his advice, and his alone, in everything: that it was necessary the direction should be in one man's hands only, and he meant it should be in his; that he had no right, after what had passed, to expect a compliance with this proposal, but that he hoped for it, from the zeal, attachment, and love with which he had hitherto served him. Mr. Grenville answered, that those sentiments which had before prompted him to sacrifice every private consideration to devote himself to His Majesty's service would make him again engage in the performance of his duty in such manner as His Majesty should please to direct; but that to enable him to make

---

[1] The former was now Treasurer of the King's Chambers, and the latter one of the Vice Treasurers of Ireland; both were in the intimate confidence of Lord Bute, which renders the circumstance of their exception the more remarkable.

that duty and zeal of real service to His Majesty, he must arm him with such powers as were necessary, and suffer no secret influence[1] whatever to prevail against the advice of those to whom he trusted the management of his affairs. The King told Mr. Grenville that Lord Bute desired to retire absolutely from all business whatsoever, that he would absent himself from the King for a time, 'till an Administration, firmly established, should leave no room for jealousy against him.

Monday, 29th of August.—Mr. Grenville went to the Queen's House between two and three o'clock. The King sent him word he was much fatigued, and desired not to see him till the evening. Mr. Grenville went at eight o'clock. The King told him that Mr. Pitt had again been with him, and had again rose in his demands; that the King told him they were such as he could by no means comply with, upon which, with some general expressions of duty and respect, and a long encomium upon Lord Temple, he withdrew. His Majesty repeated his desire to Mr. Grenville, that he should take the management of his affairs, with the fullest assurance of his thorough support. He read part of a letter to him from Lord Bute, in which his Lordship speaks with the greatest regard imaginable of Mr. Grenville, advising the King to give his whole confidence to him; showing the necessity of his own retreat, from the reasons of nationality, unpopularity, &c., &c.

Mr. Grenville, in discourse with Mr. Elliot at Shene, on Sunday, the 16*th of October*, 1763, was told by him, that Lord Bute had sent to Mr. Beckford on

---

[1] The King, by his reply, seems to have understood that Mr. Grenville here alluded to Lord Bute.

Monday, *the 29th of August* (the morning after Mr. Grenville's interview with the King), to express how sorry he was the negociation with Mr. Pitt had failed by the high terms he had demanded; that it still might do, if he would be contented with the filling up the two Secretaries of State, and putting a neutral person at the head of the Treasury instead of Lord Temple (which person was thought to be Lord Northumberland), promising that in six months' time it should be open to Lord Temple, and that other offices might immediately be disposed of; but that His Majesty could not consent to have his measures arraigned, and must give rewards to his servants who had stood by him. Mr. Beckford ran with all haste to make this offer to Mr. Pitt, before Mr. Pitt went the second time to the King, but could not prevail with him to listen to it.

Observe that this extraordinary offer was made by Lord Bute after the King had told Mr. Grenville that he looked upon the negociation with Mr. Pitt as over.

Tuesday, August 30th. Mr. Grenville saw the King, and had much confidential discourse with him.

Wednesday, 31st. Mr. Grenville went to the King's Levée, saw Lord Temple and Mr. Pitt there. The King spoke one sentence to Lord Temple, and two to Mr. Pitt. After the Levée they went to visit Mr. Calcraft in Parliament Street, and dined at Lord Lincoln's, where the Duke of Newcastle and others met them. Circular letters were dispatched by Mr. Pitt on his first message to most of the Opposition, who all came to town immediately.

Thursday, 1st of September. The King whispered to Mr. Grenville in the Drawing Room, to come in before the Secretary of State; he talked very confidentially to him, and approved of the arrangements he mentioned to him.

Friday, the 2nd. The King told Mr. Grenville that Lord Shelburne had been in his closet, to desire leave to resign his office of First Lord of Trade: he says he means to support the King's Government, and has no dislike to the present Administration, but finds the business of the Board disagreeable to him, and attended with too many difficulties, and subjecting him to too close an attendance. He came in the evening to repeat the same to Mr. Grenville.

Saturday, the 3rd. Mr. Grenville went to the King in the evening, to tell him that Lord Sandwich had brought strong assurances from the Duke of Bedford, of his intention to support his Government, with expressions of great personal civility to Mr. Grenville.

Mr. Grenville read the letter to the King, which he had written to Lord Strange[1], and to many others, stating the late transaction with Mr. Pitt, His Majesty's commands to Mr. Grenville, his (Mr. Grenville's) motives for the execution of them, and Lord Bute's declaration of an utter retreat from business.

Sunday, the 4th. Mr. Grenville went to dine at Shene; made an opening to the Duke of Leeds for President, declined by his Grace from motives of health and retirement, but assurances of duty and regard to the King and the Government.

Monday, September 5th. Mr. Grenville reported to His Majesty the conversation with the Duke of Leeds. Lord Egmont sent for out of Somersetshire. The King in discourse said that Lord Bute's retreat was his own

[1] See *ante*, page 104.

act; that His Majesty did not see the necessity of his going into the country; that when he had told it to Lord Powis, his Lordship said he was sorry for it. Mr. Grenville told His Majesty he must know how great a ferment there was against him; the King said it is true. Mr. Townshend saw his brother Charles at Missenden on Sunday; he seems to determine to continue in opposition, did not wish for the Admiralty, after having been put in nomination by Mr. Pitt for Secretary of State. (N.B. The Admiralty was not offered to him.)

Tuesday, 6th. Mr. Grenville received intelligence in the evening that the negociation with Mr. Pitt was begun by Lord Bute, through Lord Shelburne to Mr. Calcraft[1], and through him the Duke of Bedford was interested in it. It had been on foot since the 12th of August.

Wednesday, 7th. Mr. Grenville had the strongest confirmation of the above-mentioned intelligence, which was begun on the 8th of August, by Lord Shelburne going to Mr. Calcraft, and engaging him to make an opening to Mr. Pitt, at the same time desiring him to write to the Duke of Bedford, Lord Gower[2], and others of that party, telling them that the then present Ministry could not stand, that Mr. Pitt was applied to, and desiring to know how they should stand affected in such a change, Lord Shelburne bidding him add that they might easily believe he would not begin such a transaction without being authorized.

Mr. Pitt accepted the proposal as far as treating,

---

[1] See letter to Lord Temple, *ante* page 90.

[2] Lord Shelburne wrote himself to Lord Gower. This party declared themselves willing to act with Mr. Pitt.—*Note by Mr. Grenville.*

but declined engaging if the Duke of Bedford was to have an office in the Government. Mr. Grenville wrote yesterday to the Duke of Bedford, offering him the office of President, which, by a letter to Mr. Grenville to-day, he means to accept.

Thursday, 8th. Mr. Grenville talked with the King upon the subject of Lord Shelburne's transaction; said it was publicly known. The King said, it is true, Mr. Grenville, but let us not look back, let us only look forward; nothing of that sort shall ever happen again. Mr. Grenville said he hoped not; that he put himself entirely upon His Majesty's protection; that he had advised him to call to his Government, not such as were his friends, viz., the Duke of Bedford and Lord Sandwich, but such as he thought could best strengthen it; that these might prove too strong for him, his only reliance was upon His Majesty's truth and honour, and on that he trusted he might depend. The King assured him he might; that he would never fail him, nor forget his services. His Majesty again dropped something of Lord Bute's retreat not being necessary, or at least might be shortened.

Mr. Grenville dissented, and spoke again of the great uneasiness and ferment there was against him.

Lord Mansfield saw the King yesterday, said he came to take his leave of him; that he desired no more to be called to council, but should look upon himself as an independent man, and take such a part in business as was consistent with his opinions, wishing all success to the King's affairs, but saying that none of the present Administration were agreeable to him except Mr. Grenville, whom he had ever known and loved, who would serve the King faithfully and ably.

Friday, 9th. Lord Sandwich kissed hands as Secretary of State; Duke of Bedford, President; Lord Egmont, First Commissioner of the Admiralty; Lord Hyde, Joint Postmaster; and Lord Hillsborough, then in Ireland, was appointed First Lord of Trade. The new Ministry all dined together at Lord Sandwich's, and the Duke of Bedford made the strongest professions of support to the King's affairs to Mr. Grenville, spoke to him earnestly about Lord Bute's retreat, saying it must be immediately carried into execution; all the Ministry agree in the same, and press for some means to effect it. Mr. Grenville agrees strongly in the necessity of the measure, but wishes it could be brought about without force. Lord Bute holds the most flattering language imaginable upon Mr. Grenville's subject, to all who see him, with the most ardent wishes for his success.

Saturday, 10th. Mr. Grenville saw the King—nothing remarkable passed.

Sunday, 11th. Mr. Grenville did not go out.

Monday, 12th. Mr. Grenville saw the King. Mr. Grenville received a letter from Lord Strange full of the most cordial approbation of his conduct, and promise of support, and a full disapprobation of the application made to Mr. Pitt, and of his behaviour.

Mr. Grenville received letters from Lord Oxford[1] and Sir John Phillips to the same effect.

Tuesday, 13th. Mr. Grenville did not see the King. Went to the Drawing Room at Leicester House.

Wednesday, 14th. Mr. Grenville came too late to see the King. Went to see the Duke of Bedford, who told him in discourse that he thought something should

---

[1] Edward, fourth Earl of Oxford. He died in 1790.

be settled as to the distribution of offices; that he hoped there would be no catching at offices among the King's servants; that all belonging to the House of Commons must and ought to be disposed of by Mr. Grenville; that, as to others, the rest of the King's Ministers should also recommend. Mr. Grenville made general answers to this, saying that he never meant to catch at offices, and was desirous of everything that could promote union in the Ministry.

Tuesday, 15th. Mr. Grenville saw the King after the Drawing Room: he told him the Duke of Bedford had held the same language to him in regard to the disposal of offices, saying that himself and the two Secretaries of State, he supposed, were alternately to recommend. The King told Mr. Grenville he had given a general answer to this, but that in reality he meant to take Mr. Grenville's recommendations, and his alone; that he would not put the difficult task upon him of contending this point with these Lords, but that he himself should always pause upon any recommendation of theirs, which pause would be till he knew Mr. Grenville's sentiments upon it, for that he meant that all graces should be done through Mr. Grenville alone, but that this conversation was to be only between His Majesty and Mr. G., as it would not be prudent to tell it to the other Ministers. Mr. Grenville assured His Majesty of the full sense he had of his goodness to him; that he should be very willing to forward any wish of the Duke of Bedford's, or the two other Lords, as it would ever be his purpose to promote union among His Majesty's servants.

Friday, 23rd. Lord Sandwich showed a letter to Mr. Grenville from Lord Holland, in which he declares very strongly his surprise at, and disapprobation of, the late transaction with Mr. Pitt; says he means to give every support in his power to the new Ministry. Mr. Ellis[1] came to Mr. Grenville, by Lord Holland's desire, to assure him of his Lordship's concurrence and support in all the measures of Government.

He mentions, in one part of his letter, that he knew Lord Bute looked upon Lord Halifax, Lord Egremont, and Mr. Grenville as his enemies, for that at the time *that* ministry was formed, Lord Bute told him (Lord Holland) that he knew they had vowed his (Lord Bute's) ruin.

Lord Granby, upon his return from Scarborough, made the most affectionate and warm declaration to Mr. Grenville of his thorough approbation of his conduct, and his determination to support him to the utmost. He said the Duke of Newcastle was his old friend, but that he should never lead him into measures which he totally disapproved and condemned; that in regard to the present Ministry, his attachment was to Mr. Grenville singly; that he did not love the Duke of Bedford, nor Lord Sandwich, and was not much acquainted with Lord Halifax. He held pretty near the same language to the King, with very high commendation of Mr. Grenville, which the King repeated to Mr. Grenville.

Monday, 26th. The King told Mr. Grenville, that Lord Bute being to go soon out of town, he had resigned the only remaining office which he held, viz., the Privy Purse, which the King said he meant to give to Sir William Breton[2]. Mr. Grenville told His Majesty he

---

[1] Welbore Ellis, Secretary at War.

[2] He had been long employed in the Household of the King, when Prince of Wales.

hoped he meant to strengthen his government by the disposal of that office to a Peer, and named Lord Guilford to him. The King said, it was not of rank sufficient for him. Mr. Grenville then quoted the Peers to His Majesty, who, under different reigns, had held it; but, finding the King not disposed to give it in that manner, after some pause he proposed to His Majesty that he himself should hold the office without salary, as Lord Bute had done, and bring him the money himself. To this the King consented, saying, he could afterwards give the money to Sir William to pay the robes, &c.

Mr. Grenville, at the beginning of the conversation, desired to lay the state of the Civil List before His Majesty, and asked if he meant to continue the allowance for his Privy Purse the same as it had been under Lord Bute; the King said, "yes, yes, exactly the same;" and stopped that part of the conversation hastily.

Wednesday, 28th. The King gave many assurances to Mr. Grenville of his support of him against the Duke of Bedford, or any other who should strive against him.

Thursday, 29th. Mr. Grenville was told by Mr. Hotham, in the Drawing Room, that he heard Sir Wm. Breton was appointed Privy Purse.

Friday, September 30th. Mr. Grenville desired the King's leave to speak to him once more upon the subject of the Privy Purse before any step was taken in it. He represented to His Majesty how much umbrage would be taken at Sir Wm. Breton's executing that office; that he was so nearly connected with Lord Bute, that it would stand as strong to the public, as if it was Lord Bute's Private Secretary; that he, Mr. Grenville, had no view in desiring to hold it himself, except His Majesty's service; that he meant neither pleasure nor profit by it. The King heard it with impatience and emotion; claimed the right of disposing of an office so immediately about his own person; said that it had never belonged to the First Commissioner of the Treasury; that Lord Bute had held it as his immediate friend, and as a person to whom he had long been accustomed; that in the last of these lights he meant to employ Sir William, who had been known to him since his childhood. Mr. Grenville still urged the reasons above mentioned; said the large sum of money appropriated to it would become matter of talk and comment; that Sir William Breton's appointment would still serve to increase the jealousy and the reports industriously spread about the short duration of the present Government.

The King upon that grew warm, and said, "Good God! Mr. Grenville, am I to be suspected after all I have done?" he said, not by me, Sir, I cannot doubt your intentions; after all you have said to me, it would not become me to do so; but such is the present language and suspicion of the world.

The King told him Lord Bute had been with him on Wednesday, to take his leave of him; that His Majesty had seen him with great uneasiness, had advised him to read no newspapers, nor hearken to any of the lies that were spread; that he had felt the ingratitude of mankind, and so would he (Mr. Grenville), for Lord Bute had neither obliged people by forwarding their requests, nor by rejecting them; he said Lord Bute had spoken in the highest terms of commendation of Mr. Grenville.

Saturday, 1st of October. Mr. Grenville told the King that, finding His Majesty was fixed in his resolution in regard to Sir Wm. Breton, and that he did not choose to adopt the proposition he had laid before His Majesty, Mr. Grenville saw no benefit arising from his having the nominal office of Privy Purse, but thought it had better go on in the usual manner.

The King seemed pleased to have got rid of this matter according to his wishes.

Wednesday, October 5th. Lord Bute went out of town to Luton, in Bedfordshire.

Tuesday, 11*th.* Lord Sandwich came to Mr. Grenville, and said that he understood from Lord Halifax, and hoped to find from Mr. Grenville, that he was to stand exactly in the same situation as Lord Egremont had done.

Mr. Grenville told him that no man could stand to him in the degree of nearness and dearness of friendship that Lord Egremont had, but that he had every degree of regard and good will to his Lordship. Lord Sandwich said he supposed the disposition of offices was to be in partition between them three, Lord Halifax, himself, and Mr. Grenville, and that Lord Halifax intended to mention it to the King. Mr. Grenville said that as to that he could say nothing, the King must take such determination upon it as he pleased, but that he must observe to his Lordship that the Duke of Bedford was not likely to be pleased with that partition, and that for his own part he would never consent that any of the House of Commons' offices should go through any channel but his own; that he would be glad to receive the recommendations of his friends, and to forward them when it was in his power, but that people must speak to him himself; that he did not do this from the

P 2

thirst of power or patronage, but from knowing it to be essentially necessary whilst he held that station in Government. When Mr. Grenville went the same morning to the King, His Majesty told him that Lord Halifax had been with him, forwarding the pretensions of Lord Sandwich, whom he supposed His Majesty meant should stand precisely as Lord Egremont did, and that the patronage was to be jointly among the three. The King said he had told him that he could make no stipulation upon that head; that when the former Ministry was formed he had told Lord Egremont, Mr. Grenville, and his Lordship, that he should be glad to have his servants agree in their opinions and recommendations, and, where they did not, should endeavour to reconcile them the best he could; that he kept very much to general terms in his answer, which he told Mr. Grenville was because he meant to put his Government solely into his hands, and that he could not forbear expressing his surprise to Lord Halifax at his being so eager to forward Lord Sandwich's pretensions, who had already left him twice for the Duke of Bedford, and bid his Lordship take care that it did not happen a third time. Lord Halifax acquainted him that Lord Sandwich was to wait upon His Majesty the next day to make this demand. Lord Halifax took this extraordinary step without ever mentioning one word of it to Mr. Grenville.

The day before this Mr. Grenville had mentioned to His Majesty Lord Thomond's desire of being appointed Lord Lieutenant of Somersetshire, whenever a vacancy should happen there. The King consented to it very graciously, and said he supposed he meant to hold it for the young Lord Egremont, and that His Majesty was glad to do anything to show his good wish to the family.

Thursday, 13th. Mr. Grenville went to Lord Halifax in the evening, and had a long conversation with him, both in respect to his demands for Lord Sandwich and his own desire of the disposal of all employments that became vacant. Mr. Grenville showed his Lordship in how very few instances he himself had had the power of obliging a friend of his own; that Dr. Lloyd's[1] Prebendary had been promised ever since the time when Mr. Grenville had declined the Speaker's chair; that Dr. Barton was appointed to the Deanery of Bristol at his desire, but that these were the only two instances in which he had disposed of anything to his own friends; that Lord Sandwich he had named, knowing Lord Halifax wished it; that Lord Hyde was out of regard to Lord Egremont's memory; and that as to inferior offices, his Lordship knew how many he had ceded to his wishes, but that he must freely tell his Lordship, that in the situation he stands in the House of Commons, he must be known to have the patronage, or the whole must break; that in regard to Lord Sandwich standing exactly in the same situation as Lord Egremont had done, his Lordship knew very well no such thing was intended at the first appointment, nor could he see why his Lordship should wish it, as it would only be a means of strengthening the Duke of Bedford's hands, who, together with Lord Holland and Lord Sandwich, had been forming a party to themselves for these twenty years; that he, Mr. Grenville, had none, and therefore it was

---

[1] Philip Lloyd, afterwards Dean of Norwich. He was brother to Mr. Charles Lloyd, Private Secretary to Mr. Grenville.

the more necesary that he should reap what aid he could from patronage, which, however, he by no means thought of engrossing ; that the Duke of Bedford would expect a share, and it was fit he should have it. Lord Halifax answered all this with great friendship and temper, said he saw the force of what he said, and that he did own Lord Sandwich's equal share was not intended at the time of this nomination; he professed great good will to Mr. Grenville, and said he should ever find him facile and ready to yield.

Friday, 14*th.* As Mr. Grenville was going into the King's Closet, he met Lord Halifax and Lord Sandwich coming out, who beckoned to him, and desired to speak to him before he went in ; when he came to them, Lord Halifax told him that a man upon whose veracity he could rely, and who had the means of knowing, had desired to speak to him upon urgent business; that when he came he told his Lordship that Mr. Beckford had bought an estate near Luton, from whence he had been to visit Lord Bute, to whom he had lamented the strong terms Mr. Pitt had insisted upon with the King; that Lord Bute had said it was that alone which had broke off the treaty ; that he was sorry for it, and that if Mr. Pitt could bring himself to be more reasonable, it was not yet too late ; that Mr. Beckford went immediately to Hayes to report this conversation, and to endeavour to bring Mr. Pitt to milder terms, but that he returned to Lord Bute, complaining heavily of Mr. Pitt, who, he said, could not be persuaded to disengage himself from "that old rogue the Duke of Newcastle," though he thought he had made some impression upon his mind, and softened it a little. Lord Halifax said he and Lord Sandwich had just related this to the King, who denied it, said he did not believe that Lord Bute had seen Mr. Beckford, that he believed it was all a falsehood, and that he had not the least idea of changing his Government, and that he did insist with both their Lordships, that they should upon no account mention this thing to any human being except Mr. Grenville, because nothing could be more detrimental to the present Government than such a report. When Mr. Grenville went in, the King mentioned it to him with great surprise, said he did not believe it, and he was persuaded that Mr. Grenville did not believe it; that Lord Bute had told His Majesty that he did not intend to see anybody whatever in the country, not even his friends, and that he knew Mr. Elliot had complained of his not letting him go down with him; that, as to himself, he had not the most distant thought of a change in his Government; that when he had called Mr. Grenville to undertake it, he had told him that he put his affairs into his hands never to take them out again, 'till he, Mr. Grenville, should tell His Majesty that he could not carry on the Government; and that such was his firm resolution, he never would break his word with him, and thought it hard that after such assurances he should be suspected of changing them with the next breath; that Lord Halifax was too eager, and believed reports too easily; that he had enjoined strict secrecy to him upon it, and had told him that if Lord Sandwich had not been by at the narration, he should have forbid his even telling it to him; and said to Mr. Grenville that if this piece of information had happened to have come first to Mr. Grenville, he was sure none but himself would have known it; that he would have trusted it to no third person. Mr. Grenville assured His Majesty he did not believe the report, and greatly commended His Majesty's prudence and wisdom in endeavouring to stifle it, for that any degree of belief of such a transaction getting abroad would be utter destruction to his present Government, and awaken a hundred jealousies, and that Lord Bute ought not upon any account whatever, no not as a common visitor, to suffer Mr. Beckford to come near him, for that a visit alone might give grounds to such a suspicion. The King afterwards told Mr. Grenville the general terms with which he had answered Lord Sandwich's demands upon the subject of patronage, told his Lordship that he hoped his servants would agree together in their recommendations; that where they differed, he must decide between them the best he could; that by this he meant to take the person whom Mr. Grenville should recommend, though he did not tell Lord Sandwich so, but that he told him, Mr. Grenville, of it because such was his determination.

Mr. Grenville was informed that Lord Shelburne went about telling his friends that he had two letters from Lord Bute in the space of a week. Mr. Grenville mentioned this to Lord Le Despenser, who went to Luton on Monday; and from thence wrote to Mr. Grenville to assure him of the falsehood of this assertion, and to tell him at the same time that Lord Bute's sense of his (Mr. Grenville's) honour and truth was equal to that he Lord Le Despenser had of it.

Mr. Mackenzie came to Mr. Grenville October 19th; made very full declarations of his support to the present Ministry, which he made no doubt was strong enough to get through all difficulties, if all would heartily set themselves to the task. He told Mr. Grenville he had seen Lord Bute, and that the political line was finally drawn for ever between him and Lord Shelburne.

Thursday, October 20th. The King talked again to Mr. Grenville upon the report of Mr. Beckford's having been with Lord Bute to negociate between him and Mr. Pitt, and asked him his advice whether he did not think it right that Lord Bute should be apprized of the report; that he looked upon it as an absolute falsehood, and could not think Lord Bute could do so base a thing, nor a thing that would so much disgrace him; that if it was possible to be true, what a figure must he (the King) make in it after all he had repeatedly said to Mr. Grenville. His Majesty dwelt long upon the great regard and good opinion Lord Bute had of Mr. Grenville; that he had only withdrawn for the present to facilitate his carrying on of the Government, seeing how necessary Mr. Grenville was to the King's affairs.

In this conversation the King several times told Mr. Grenville (as he had done in several others) that His Majesty spoke to him with an openness and confidence with which he spoke to no other of his servants.

Saturday, October 29th. Mr. Jenkinson went to Lord Bute at Luton, and on Monday 31st he came to acquaint Mr. Grenville that he had told Lord Bute of the report concerning his Lordship and Mr. Beckford; that Lord Bute told him it was true that he had seen Mr. Beckford, who as a neighbour at Luton had sent him a card to say he would come and dine with him; that he did so, but never in the whole time was alone with Lord Bute, nor no conversation passed but upon indifferent subjects, except that when he got up to go away, Mr. Beckford said aloud, and before the company, that, though he loved his friend Mr. Pitt, he could not but say that in the last negociation he had been in the wrong and Lord Bute in the right, to which his Lordship made him no answer. Lord Bute farther told Mr. Jenkinson that he most earnestly and sincerely wished success to Mr. Grenville's Administration, thinking it the only safety for the King's affairs; that he told every friend he had in the world that such was his opinion and his wish, in order that every friend of his might contribute every degree of strength and support they could give to it; but bid Mr. Jenkinson to tell Mr. Grenville to be aware of his colleagues in Government, wishing that they might not one day or other betray him.

Mr. Grenville reported to the King Lord Bute's disavowal of Beckford's negociation; the King said he was glad to hear it; that he never doubted the falsehood of it, knowing that Lord Bute could not do so base a thing.

Wednesday, 2nd of November. Mr. Yorke had an audience of the King, to resign his office of Attorney General. He was above half an hour in his closet, expressed himself with the greatest duty and affection to the King, put the step he had taken entirely upon his father, under the Duke of Newcastle's influence, lamented the extremities to which this had drove him in this final step, showed great reluctance in the doing it, and burst out into tears. The King answered him firmly, and said his future conduct must be the rule by which he must judge of what he had said to him.

The King reported the whole conversation to Mr. Grenville, said that Mr. Yorke had described Mr. Grenville to him, in talking of his Ministry, as a man whose integrity, ability, and firmness must do honour to any Administration; that he had long known him, and had ever found him the same, both as to his private conduct towards him, and his public one. The rest of the Ministers, he seemed to say, he had never had much connection with. The King told Mr. Grenville one circumstance, which he said he would tell to no other person whatever—viz., that Mr. Yorke had dropped the word, "*If any circumstance should ever bring him back to His Majesty's service,*" to which His Majesty returned no answer.

The King said he had seen Lord Halifax that morning, "*and between you and I, Mr. Grenville, he knows no more of money affairs than Mr. Pitt does.*"[1]

Thursday, November 3rd. Lord Halifax came to Mr. Grenville, and, after talking of many other things, complained with warmth of Lord Hillsborough in regard to some transactions at the Board of Trade; said that Board had quite abandoned him; that everybody saw the difficulties the Ministry was under, and took advantage of it; that they must gulp at it now, but if the time should come that they were better established, and upon a firmer footing, it was fit to make them feel the consequences of their conduct.

Thursday, November 10th. When Mr. Grenville went to the King, His Majesty began to open a plan to him of sending Mr. Stanley to the Hague in the room of Sir Joseph Yorke, of which he supposed him to have been apprized by Lord Halifax and Lord Sandwich, who had proposed it to His Majesty. Mr. Grenville assured His Majesty it was the first word he had ever heard of it, at which the King expressed great blame and surprise against them both.

The King gave Mr. Grenville an account of what had passed between His Majesty and Lord Holland, at the audience Lord Holland had the day before. He had made great professions to the King of his giving

---

[1] His sister, Mrs. Anne Pitt, is reported to have often said that he knew nothing accurately except Spenser's "Faerie Queene."

the strongest and most thorough support to his Government. Naming Lord Shelburne, he said he would certainly be with the Government as long as he thought the Ministry likely to continue. He told the King, amongst other things, that when the Duke of Bedford was in France, he had declared to the Duc de Choiseul, in confidence, that his favourite object in government was the being at the head of the Treasury, to which the King made no other answer than to observe, how very extraordinary a secret it was to trust to the French Minister, who acted in full as extraordinary a manner, in revealing this secret to Lord Holland, whom he saw but twice[1].

Mr. Grenville saw Lord Holland the same day; the visit passed civilly, but with no professions on either side, further than general words from Lord Holland of his intentions to support Government. He told Mr. Grenville, in the course of talking, that when Mr. Wilkes went over to France in the summer, Mr. Rigby had recommended him very strongly to the Duke of Bedford, with whom he had in consequence of it dined three times, and had been received by him with distinction. Mr. Grenville received a letter from Lord Halifax in the evening, naming the destination of Mr. Stanley, and earnestly pressing, in consequence of it,

[1] Walpole mentions (*Memoirs of George the Third*, vol. i. p. 89) another indiscretion of which the Duke of Bedford was accused, in having told M. de Bussy, the French Minister, in 1761, " that he was sorry for his departure, as we were no longer in a situation to make war." This was reported upon the authority of several persons, to whom Bussy told it, but particularly Lady Hervey, who has also related the circumstance in one of her letters (See *Letters of Mary Lepel, Lady Hervey*, pp. 279 and 284); and Lord Temple, alluding to it in the House of Lords, " complained of those who had betrayed the secrets of our situation to Bussy." The Duke of Bedford, however, declared in reply, " upon his honour, that he had told no such thing as had been hinted at to Bussy."

such arrangements as should immediately bring Mr. Frederick Mountague[1] into the Board of Trade, although Mr. Grenville had not had the disposal of one single House of Commons office since those he named when he was First Commissioner of the Treasury, and consequently could not yet have provided for any friend of his own.

Mr. Stanley came to Mr. Grenville the same evening; Mr. Grenville explained very fully to him the urgent necessity of his bringing forward such people as were personally attached to him, and would stand by him in this critical juncture; that in the situation he stood in the House of Commons, he could never consent that any of the offices held by members of that House should go through any channel but his own. Mr. Stanley acknowledged the force of his argument, but was not very strong in his professions; said he should vote with the Government in Mr. Wilkes's affair, but seemed to disapprove the proceeding.

Friday, November 11*th.* When Mr. Grenville came to St. James's, he found Lord Halifax and Lord Sandwich in the King's apartment; they stopped him before he went into the Closet, to press him to advise the King to Sir Joseph Yorke's recall, in order for Mr. Stanley's appointment. Mr. Grenville was cold as to the proposition in general, and particularly so to the calling home of Sir Joseph Yorke at this moment, when Lord Hardwicke's life was despaired of, and when lenity to Sir Joseph might be the means of his being a bond of union and conciliation for the rest of the family, after Lord Hardwicke's death; the Duke of Bedford, who joined the three Ministers, yielded to Mr. Grenville's reasons, but the others looked disappointed.

[1] At this time M.P. for Northampton.

The King, as soon as he saw Mr. Grenville, asked him if the two Secretaries had talked with him upon this subject, saying they had been pressing it upon him, but that he had given no determinate answer, nor would 'till he knew Mr. Grenville's opinion. Mr. Grenville urged the same reasons to His Majesty against the precipitating this measure, as he had done to the three Lords. The King entirely approved of them, and said he would take no step in it for the present, and that he thought Mr. Grenville perfectly right in his reasons for delaying it. The King used many gracious expressions to Mr. Grenville, both as to the confidence he placed in him and the support he meant to give him, and seemed displeased at the over hasty decision of his two other servants.

Saturday, November 12th. Mr. Stanley came to Mr. Grenville in the evening, had a long conversation with him. Mr. Grenville again repeated to him his determined resolution to have the sole disposal of the offices belonging to the House of Commons, and of giving them to such persons only as would shew themselves to be his friends; that though he had great regard for Lord Halifax and Lord Sandwich, he could not, in this instance, look upon them as his colleagues, because, whilst he was understood to manage the King's business in the House of Commons, he could acknowledge no colleague there.

Mr. Stanley was much more explicit than in the former conversation, and declared fully that he meant to support the King's Government, and to show his personal regard to Mr. Grenville.

Monday, November 14th. The King mentioned with great indignation to Mr. Grenville the abusive *North Briton*, published the Saturday before; expressed great abhorrence of the scandalous manner in which Lord Egremont was treated in it, but said he could not help making one observation—viz., that the abuse was entirely levelled at Lord Egremont, Lord Northumberland, and Mr. Grenville, with scarce a word against Lord Halifax. The King ordered Mr. Grenville to write him an account of what should pass in the House of Commons the next day, be it up ever so late, in order that if things went well he might have the pleasure of knowing it before he saw Mr. Grenville the next morning. Mr. Grenville offered to wait upon His Majesty, but he said he would not have him, because the fatigue would be too great after sitting so long in the House.

Tuesday, November 15*th*. The House of Commons sat 'till between one and two o'clock in the morning. There were two divisions relating to Mr. Wilkes's affair; the majority on the side of Government was about two hundred; personal altercation passed between Mr. Pitt and Mr. Grenville, the former extremely warm; he made a very abusive attack upon the late Attorney General and the Solicitor, but the day was very triumphant on the Court side. Mr. Grenville sent the King an account of it in writing, to which His Majesty returned an answer in writing, expressing his approbation of Mr. Grenville, and great surprise at Mr. Conway's vote both times with the minority, and declaring his intention to remove him[1].

Wednesday, November 16*th*. Mr. Grenville went to the Levée, where His Majesty enquired how he did, after the fatigue of the House of Commons, and bid him come in to him before the other Ministers (as His Majesty had already done in his note). When Mr.

[1] See the King's letter, *ante*, page 162.

Grenville went in, the King marked extreme approbation of his conduct, and great satisfaction at the success of the day. He wished to have dismissed Mr. Conway directly, but Mr. Grenville advised His Majesty to defer it 'till the whole affair was concluded relating to Mr. Wilkes, and Mr. Conway's conduct thoroughly known upon it. The King said Mr. Grenville was right in his opinion, and he would follow it. Whilst this conversation was passing, somebody scratched at the Closet door, and Lord Halifax and Lord Sandwich came in to acquaint His Majesty that Mr. Wilkes and Mr. Martin had fought a duel upon words which had passed in the House of Commons; that Mr. Wilkes was wounded, but not dangerously. The King immediately desired Mr. Grenville would go down to the House of Commons and do what he thought best in regard to the proceedings against him. When Mr. Grenville came down, he proposed that as gentlemen had wished for time to consider precedents, the matter of privilege should be deferred till the Friday following, upon which Mr. Charles Townshend got up and said that there was so much humanity, temper, and candour, in that motion, that he seconded it with all his heart, and the House went upon the King's Speech and the Address. Mr. Pitt made a very long speech and a very fine one, said the King's Speech was the best he ever heard from the throne, and the Address the properest and the most temperate; that there was not a word in it to which he could not set his hand: he afterwards went into great variety of matter, but with the utmost temper and decency, which was totally different from the tone of the preceding debate. Mr. Grenville answered him, went through all the business of the summer (avoiding to name the negociation with Mr. Pitt), laid before the House his plans of economy, and various other matters. He was excessively applauded during the whole course of his speech, and afterwards complimented and congratulated by numbers of people upon the firmness of his conduct, and the establishment of the King's Government, which now seemed thoroughly settled.

He sent the King an account of what had passed, to which he again returned an answer still more flattering to Mr. Grenville than the former. Mr. Grenville received a letter that same day from Lord Northumberland, complaining bitterly of the severe and harsh terms of a late despatch which he had received from Lord Halifax, professing great regard to Mr. Grenville, and asking his assistance to have his conduct properly stated to the King.

Thursday, November 17th. The King spoke to Mr. Grenville in the Drawing Room to come first into his Closet. When he came in he told him that he had heard from everybody with what superiority of talents and judgment he had spoke the preceding day in the House of Commons; that he had put his Government upon so firm and good a footing as must give great strength to it.

Mr. Grenville spoke to him about Lord Northumberland. His Majesty said his mind must be soothed and softened, and no hard terms used to him.

In the evening Mr. Harris came to Mr. Grenville, told him he had just seen Mr. John Yorke, who, with tears in his eyes, came to tell him that Lord Hardwicke was dying, or at least so ill that he feared he would not recover; that in this situation his brother, Mr. Charles Yorke, was apprehensive he could not go down to the House of Commons to follow up with spirit, as he meant to do, the great question of Privilege which was to come on the next day; that he wished to support and maintain with strength the opinion he had given; that he was most highly offended with the unworthy usage he had met with from Mr. Pitt; that his treatment of him the first day of the session, with an intent to ruin him with the Parliament, after having done him all the mischief he could with the King, by urging his father upon the subject of his resignation; that, for these reasons Mr. Charles Yorke wished, if possible, that Mr. Grenville would put off the question of Privilege 'till another day. Mr. Grenville seems to think he cannot do it, as Lord Hardwicke's illness, or perhaps his death, may delay Mr. Yorke's attendance beyond the time proper to bring on this question, especially as men's minds are animated and warm with the prospect of success.

Friday, November 18*th.* The Speaker[1] of the House of Commons was taken ill, which obliged the House to adjourn 'till Monday.

Mr. Grenville went to the King, who told him Lord Mansfield had been with him for a long time, declaring his zeal for his service, and expressing great satisfaction at the happy prospect of His Majesty's affairs. Mr. Grenville met him at dinner, at Lord Sandwich's, where he held the same language, with many compliments to Mr. Grenville upon the great performance he had made in the House on Wednesday.

Sunday, 20*th.* Mr. Grenville told the King the intelligence he had received of Mr. Pitt's having been an hour and a half, the Friday before, at Lord Shelburne's. His Majesty said he was glad of it; he desired no better than to see Lord Shelburne in the Opposition.

[1] Sir John Cust.

Mr. Grenville took occasion, upon Lord Effingham's[1] death, which again diminished the number of the Queen's Ladies of the Bedchamber, to mention Lady Aylesford. His Majesty said the Queen had no thoughts of enlarging her family, but that the very first that was appointed should be Lady Aylesford.

Tuesday, November 22nd. The King told Mr. Grenville that Lord Sandwich had been with him to ask his approbation for his being a candidate for Steward of the University of Cambridge, in case it should be vacant by Lord Hardwicke's death; that he had told His Majesty that Lord Halifax and Mr. Grenville concurred in this nomination. Mr. Grenville told His Majesty that the two Secretaries had mentioned it to him; that he had not opposed it, and thought it very proper that one of His Majesty's Secretaries of State should be named; that the other people talked of were Lord Tavistock, Lord Granby, and Lord Royston; but he thought it his duty to acquaint His Majesty, that upon talking with many of the Cambridge people, particularly the Bishop of Chester, he had told him that the nomination might probably do for Lord Halifax, but that it would be very difficult for Lord Sandwich, and Mr. Grenville said to His Majesty, that his Government and recommendation must not be disgraced.

The King seemed displeased at Lord Sandwich for coming in that manner to steal his approbation from him; that he was trying to take the lead in everything, and that under pretence to Lord Halifax of following

---

[1] Lord Effingham died on the 19th instant; he married a sister of Alderman Beckford. I do not understand this passage, unless it means that Lady Effingham would resign her office upon the death of her husband.

his opinions, he was getting the start of him, and governing him absolutely. Mr. Grenville said that he could not say much to that, he believed it was so, but that as long as His Majesty thought fit to employ him in his service he should go on straightforward, not looking much to right hand or to left, at his colleagues.

The King said he was perfectly in the right; that though they took these precipitate steps, he would never decide anything without speaking to Mr. Grenville about it, and that he spoke to him from the bottom of his heart, and with a confidence and trust, with which he spoke to nobody else.

In the evening Mr. Grenville mentioned to Lord Halifax, under the seal of secrecy, the difficulties Lord Sandwich would meet with at Cambridge, that the nomination would be much easier for his Lordship. He told Mr. Grenville that Lord Sandwich and he had agreed between themselves, that the first should be Steward, and the last Chancellor. Lord Halifax thanked him for his advice, and seemed pleased with him for giving it.

Memorandum.—Lord Sandwich is trying in the same manner to steal the nomination of the Knight of the Shire for Cambridge when the vacancy happens.

Wednesday, November 23rd. The House of Commons was to have gone upon the question of Privilege, but the debate was solely upon the previous question, viz., whether they should postpone the main question 'till Mr. Wilkes should be able to attend. They divided upon it at nine o'clock at night. The minority were fifty more than they had been on the first day's debate. Mr. Grenville sent the King an account of the numbers, at which he seemed a good deal disappointed. Mr. Yorke and all his brothers were in the minority.

Thursday, November 24th. The House of Commons went upon the matter of Privilege in the case of a libel. The debate lasted till two o'clock the next morning. The minority lost about thirty of the number they had gained the preceding day. The three people supposed to be influenced by Lord Shelburne, viz., Mr. Fitz-Maurice, Colonel Barré, and Mr. Calcraft, were in the minority, and Mr. Conway, in all the three questions. The King sent a note to Mr. Grenville at nine o'clock at night, to order him to send him word how things went. He went out of the House of Commons and wrote three lines, to tell His Majesty how well Mr. Yorke had acquitted himself, and that Mr. Pitt had spoke, but had made no impression on the House, and that the appearance seemed to promise success. He wrote His Majesty an account of the debate after he came home, to which he received an answer, expressing his satisfaction, and desiring him to come to him early.

Friday, November 25th. The King, greatly pleased with the success of the day, showed great resentment at Mr. Conway's conduct, and was inclined immediately to have dismissed him; but Mr. Grenville advised His Majesty to wait 'till the recess at Christmas, as a more usual time, and not so obnoxious, and then to extend it to Colonel Barré and some others; to which the King consented.

His Majesty told Mr. Grenville he had been impatient for his coming to talk over the debate with him, that Lord Sandwich and two or three other people had already been with him wanting to give him an account of what had passed, but that he had waived that, as he meant always to receive the account of what passed in that House from Mr. Grenville himself.

Sunday, November 27th. Mr. Grenville went to the King, he thought his countenance a little more gloomy than usual; and when Mr. Grenville named the removing Colonel Barré, he did not seem to answer so readily or decisively to it as Mr. Grenville expected.

Monday, 28th. Mr. Grenville found the King much more easy and cheerful than the day before.

Tuesday, 29th. Mr. Grenville did not see the King. He went to the House of Lords to hear the debate upon the Resolution of the House of Commons. Lord Chancellor and Lord Mansfield distinguished themselves extremely for the question. Lord Temple was the best speaker against it. Lord Lyttelton made a speech for the question, Lord Shelburne against it, making a compliment to Lord Bute (absent), and flattering the Crown. When the question was put, the minority consisted only of 27 against 90 odd, exclusive of proxies. (The Duke of Cumberland voted in the minority.) Lord Bute had given his proxy to Lord Le Despenser. The day was triumphant, like that in the House of Commons.

Wednesday, November 30th. Mr. Grenville found the King in great spirits, and greatly pleased with the success of the preceding day. He desired Mr. Grenville to give him an account of that part of the debate in the House of Lords which he heard, telling him that he could rely more on his report than on that of any other man whatsoever.

The King consented to remove Colonel Barré from his employment, and Mr. Calcraft from his, but said he could dismiss nobody except General Conway was to be of the number, reckoning the offence in him who was in his Bedchamber greater than the others. Mr. Grenville was a good deal averse to this, considering his alliances, and particularly for Lord Hertford's sake. The King said he was sorry upon account of the latter, but that it must be. The two Secretaries of State are eager for the measure. The Duke of Bedford adopts Mr. Grenville's opinion.

Friday, December 2nd. When the King again resumed the conversation about Mr. Conway, Mr. Grenville still combated His Majesty's opinion about removing him. The King told him he would do what he (Mr. Grenville) should think best, but still inclined strongly to dismiss him, and at last proposed that Mr. Grenville should send to speak to Mr. Conway, and endeavour to make him explicit upon the occasion, viz., whether he did actually mean to join the Opposition, or that the votes he had given upon the late questions were merely from opinion, and that in other measures he would fairly and roundly support the King's Government. Mr. Grenville approved of this expedient, and sent to desire a meeting with Mr. Conway, through the means of Mr. Thomas Pitt, who was to mention it to Mr. Walpole.

Mr. Calcraft was dismissed from the office of Deputy Muster-Master yesterday.

The King waits to determine upon Colonel Barré 'till Mr. Conway has seen Mr. Grenville.

Saturday, December 3rd. Mr. Jenkinson sent Mr. Grenville a letter he had received from Lord Bute, in which he thanked Mr. Jenkinson for the accounts he had sent him of the Parliamentary proceedings, with which he seemed much pleased, and on the other page bid him tell Mr. Grenville how happy he was at this successful beginning of his Administration, both from his attachment to the King, and his love of his country, to both of which Mr. Grenville, by his firmness and conduct, had rendered essential service; that it gave him the utmost pleasure, and not less on the accounts already mentioned than for the esteem and regard he had for him personally. Mr. Grenville wrote to desire Mr. Jenkinson to express his warmest thanks to Lord Bute for this.

Mr. Grenville was in great haste, going to some appointments, and, amongst others, to meet Mr. Walpole at Mr. Thomas Pitt's, where he had a long conversation with him relating to Mr. Conway, extremely unsatisfactory, as it only tended to desire Mr. Grenville to have patience, but always letting him see that Mr. Conway would not come to any explicit delaration in regard to his future conduct, but saying at the same time that he (Mr. Walpole) did not believe he meant to go into Opposition. Mr. Grenville always wished to hear that declaration from himself, and Mr. Walpole always said his delicacy would not allow of it. Mr. Grenville said that he himself had his difficulties and delicacies too, and if the one had nothing to say, he had nothing to say neither, but that he would see Mr. Conway, if he wished it, at nine o'clock the following evening.

The *North Briton, No. 45*, was ordered to be burnt this day at the Royal Exchange: the mob gathered to incredible numbers and opposed it; took the faggots away from the pile, and beat the constables and the Sheriff (Mr. Harley[1]), with them, who was the only person of the City Magistracy who attended.

---

[1] Alderman Thomas Harley, a younger son of Edward, third Earl of Oxford. He represented the City of London, and subsequently the County of Hereford. He died in 1804.

Sunday, December 4th. Mr. Grenville received a letter from Mr. Conway, desiring the Duke of Richmond might be present as a witness of the conversation he was to have with Mr. Grenville, to which Mr. Grenville returned an answer tending to decline a conference from which it now became plain no good was to be expected.

Mr. Conway and the Duke of Richmond came to Mr. Grenville between nine and ten in the evening. They had a very long conversation, the result of which was, Mr. Grenville telling Mr. Conway that he had nothing to propose to him; that he had no right to question him upon the past, nor did not do it; that he had desired to see him, to manifest the truth of what, in former conversations with Lord Hertford concerning him, he had said to the latter of the good will he bore to Mr. Conway, and his desire of showing his regard to Mr. Conway upon any occasion in his power; that he should be very glad to hear that his dispositions were to support Government, but had neither proposal to make to him for the future, nor question to ask him of the past, nor had he empowered Mr. Walpole to give him any other message than merely to desire to see him to talk upon the general state of his situation and dispositions.

Mr. Conway's answer tended to say that he had taken no engagement whatever with anybody in Opposition, nor did not intend it; but could make no declaration of supporting the Government, as he looked upon it as drawing the line between himself and many of his friends now in Opposition, to whom he had obligations, and with whom he lived. He never departed from this, nor Mr. Grenville from the general terms within which he confined himself. Mr. Conway deprecated a good deal against what he supposed to be the King's intention of dismissing him, trying to make a difference between his military and civil office, and showing how many people in the former capacity still held their employments, though they had been for two years in Opposition, viz., Lord Albemarle, Lord Frederick Cavendish, &c., &c.

Mr. Grenville always waived entering into what might be the King's intention, and never would admit the distinction between the civil and military, quoting many examples to the contrary in former reigns.

Mr. Conway spoke very respectfully of the King, and made a compliment to Mr. Grenville upon the fairness and candour with which he had spoke to him.

Mr. Walpole had far exceeded his commission, having told Mr. Conway much more fully than he was empowered to do, what had passed between Mr. Grenville and him upon this subject, particularly as Mr. Grenville turning to Mr. Walpole had said, that no part of the conversation then passing was to go out of that room, and that he had no message to give to Mr. Conway, except Mr. Grenville's desire of seeing him in case Mr. Conway wished it.

Mr. Grenville went to the King in the morning; he found him much disturbed and exasperated at the outrage committed the day before in the City; he told Mr. Grenville that he had had a long conversation with the Chancellor and Lord Mansfield upon it; that the latter was very clear and warm in his professions to him, that his opinion in this instance seemed to be not to make too great a stir upon it, but to endeavour to trace it up to its source; the King thought so too, and asked Mr. Grenville if he was not of the same opinion. He differed totally from them, said the affront to the whole Legislature was too great to be submitted to, and that means must be taken to show it was so. The King readily adopted this opinion, and approved of what Mr. Grenville said. The Duke of Bedford came to Mr. Grenville in the evening, outrageous at the conduct of the mob, and full of desire that resentment might be shown upon it: his discourse was full of regard and personal civility to Mr. Grenville, and they both concurred in opinion that notice ought to be taken of it. When the Duke of Bedford opened this subject in the House of Lords, he inclined strongly to throw the blame upon the Lord Mayor[1] and the Magistracy of the City. The Chancellor took it up upon more general terms, and with more moderation towards the City of London. Lord Mansfield's opinion was still more moderate than the Chancellor's. This occasioned some difference of opinion amongst the friends of Government. Mr. Grenville was not for urging the blame upon the Mayor, and the King was strongly against the doing anything that might exasperate the City. The House of Commons pretty much followed this idea. Mr. Grenville fears this may offend the Duke of Bedford, who was very warm in the contrary opinion. One of the people, in their examination before the House of Lords, said he heard the mob say " we have nothing to fear, the Duke of Cumberland and Lord Temple are with us."

Monday, 5th December. Mr. Grenville related the

---

[1] Alderman Bridgen had succeeded Beckford in the Mayoralty.

conversation between Mr. Conway and him to the King, in the most favourable manner he could, still advising the King not to dismiss him; the King entered into Mr. Grenville's reasons, said they were right, and that he would follow his advice in the affair. He used many expressions of kindness and approbation to Mr. Grenville, and said they two always agreed, but that observing his countenance as he went through his antichamber to receive the Address, he was afraid the Duke of Bedford had been urging him about the removal of Mr. Conway; the King told him no, for that His Grace perfectly agreed in his opinion. Mr. Grenville reminded His Majesty that Lord Shelburne was still in his service as Aid-de-Camp, and asked him if he thought it right to continue him; the King paused a moment and then said, no, I will remove him, he has acted like a worthless man, and has broke his word with me.

Colonel Barré and he are both to be dismissed on Wednesday.

Lord Sandwich still continues canvassing for the Stewardship of Cambridge, though Lord Hardwicke is much better: the King would be glad if he would give up the pursuit, but he says he meets with great encouragement to persevere, though the opinion of people in general is that he will not succeed. The King seems to dislike his activity, and often tells Mr. Grenville he does not approve of the factions of great Lords who are making parties for themselves. It is said that Lord Royston actually canvasses for the same object as Lord Sandwich.

Tuesday, December 6th. Mr. Grenville went to the Duke of Cumberland's levée, but came too late; they told him the levée had been over a quarter of an hour.

There was a council of the Opposition then holding. The Duke of Devonshire's chariot, Lord Temple's, &c., &c., were waiting.

Friday, December 9th. A Common Council was held in the City, to consider whether thanks should not be returned to the Sheriffs, for the zeal and activity they had shown in the execution of their duty on the Saturday preceding; the numbers were even, and the Mayor gave the casting vote in the negative, and in his speech alleged, amongst other reasons against the returning thanks, that he should look upon it as prejudging Mr. Wilkes's cause.

The King seemed much hurt and offended when he heard of this.

Saturday, 11th. Mr. Grenville received a note from the Chancellor, desiring to see him the next day upon something relating to the King's affairs, and of great importance to his Lordship. When Mr. Grenville came to him he found him in a good deal of heat, saying he had sent to him to acquaint him that he was determined no longer to hold the Seals, complaining that the King had withdrawn his confidence from him ever since the summer, when he had declared his disapprobation of Lord Bute's conduct; that when he sees the King he never speaks confidentially to him, though he does to Lord Mansfield, and that he would no longer continue in his service, since that was the case.

Mr. Grenville endeavoured to soothe him as well as he could, and to make him depart from his resolution. His Lordship declared the warmest personal attachment to Mr. Grenville, and, after a great deal of talk, consented to take no hasty step that could distress the King.

Tuesday, 13th. Mr. Grenville acquainted the King with what had passed between him and the Chancellor, at which His Majesty was much surprised. He did it in the most favourable terms he could, and advised His Majesty to show him such regard as should induce him to continue in employment, which the King promised to do, and ordered Mr. Grenville to acquaint his Lordship of his good will towards him, and how greatly he was satisfied with the spirit and good sense with which he had supported his Government in the late questions, and desired to see him himself the next day.

Mr. Grenville went to him in the evening, to let him know the King's pleasure. His Lordship seemed exceedingly pleased with what Mr. Grenville told him from the King as a message, as well as with the conversation which had passed upon the subject. He talked with great friendship and frankness to Mr. Grenville, and in the discourse told him that the King had told his Lordship in the summer, that upon occasion of some disputes between Lord Egremont and Lord Shelburne, relating to the Board of Trade, Lord Mansfield had given it as his advice to His Majesty to show favour to Lord Shelburne, in order to play them one against another, and by that means to keep the power in his own hands. Lord Chancellor made some complaints to Mr. Grenville about the Duke of Bedford, which rather surprised him, as he thought those two Lords had been particularly well together.

Wednesday, December 14th. Lord Shelburne was at the Levée, and the King told Mr. Grenville he took no notice of him, but spoke to the two people on each side of him, which, he thought, was the treatment he deserved, for having broke his word and honour with him, having pledged both upon his not going into Opposition, and then taking the first opportunity to oppose a measure which personally regarded the King. His Majesty talked with great ease and kindness to Mr. Grenville, told him he had seen the Chancellor, who went away from him perfectly well satisfied.

Saturday, 17th. The King told Mr. Grenville that Lord Mansfield had been with him, speaking with the warmest zeal for his service; that he had told His Majesty that he should not declare it in public, but that he should tell His Majesty that, according to his opinion, no man had ever behaved so shamefully as Lord Chief Justice Pratt had done; that Lord Chief Justice Jefferies had not acted with greater violence than him, for that he had denied to His Majesty that justice which every petty justice of the peace would have granted to a highwayman.

Mr. Yorke came in the evening to see Mr. Grenville, and had a long conversation with him, the sum of which was to advise him to enlarge the bottom, by taking in aids from the Opposition. Mr. Grenville always represented that this could not be done without changing the Government, which he by no means thought expedient, but should always be ready to receive individuals as occasion should offer. Mr. Yorke laid great stress upon the clamour of the people, which Mr. Grenville showed him could not be appeased by any change of Ministers, since it was no longer a cry for the Duke of Newcastle, Lord Hardwicke, or even Mr. Pitt, but for Pratt and Wilkes. Mr. Yorke spoke rather discontentedly of the exigency of the times, which has (as he called it) *whirled* him out of so eminent and advantageous a post in the law.

Mr. Grenville received notice at this time that Count Woronzow[1] was in correspondence with Mr. Pitt, and had private interviews with him; that he made very unfavourable reports of the Ministry to his own Court, and that he complained particularly of Mr. Grenville, whose economy would not suffer him to give any subsidy towards the election of the King of Poland.

Monday, 19*th*. The King sent to Mr. Grenville to come to him early. He talked to him very confidentially upon all his business, and particularly upon foreign affairs, in which he said he was persuaded Mr. Grenville and he were of a mind. Mr. Grenville's advice to him was to take no first part in regard to the Polish Election, but to remain in such a state as should make him be courted as a neutral power by all the contending parties.

There was a meeting in the evening at the Chancellor's of the King's principal servants, among whom there was great unanimity and good humour.

December 24th, Saturday. When Mr. Grenville went to the King he spoke to him upon the subject of the exorbitant demands made by the King of Prussia for indemnification for his subjects during the war, and which, if not complied with, seem to threaten danger to the Electorate of Hanover. He found the King greatly offended at the King of Prussia, and rather inclined to stand the consequences than to submit to so insolent a demand; and in the course of the conversation His Majesty told him that Lord Sandwich had reported to him a conversation which his Lordship had had with Count de Seilern (the Imperial Minister), in which he expressed himself, both on his own part and on that

---
[1] The Russian Ambassador.

of his Court, with the most cordial dispositions towards the Court of Great Britain, and an eager desire to have the old friendship between them renewed, but he desired the strictest secrecy upon this head, as everything depended upon that. The King seemed highly pleased at this declaration.

Dr. Duncan told Mr. Grenville that Lord Hardwicke had written a card of thanks to the Duke and Duchess of Newcastle for their inquiries after him, adding that he had not so far drank the waters of Lethe as to make him forgetful of them; that could he, indeed, have forgotten modern politics, it would have been without regret.

Sunday, December 25th. Lord Sandwich came to Mr. Grenville to acquaint him with the conversation already mentioned with M. de Seilern, who had said that it was strongly his opinion that if the King of Prussia should attack the Electorate, the Court of Vienna would not see it with temper, and that they wished nothing so much as to return to the old system of friendship with England. Mr. Grenville advised Lord Sandwich to communicate this to the Duke of Bedford.

Tuesday, 27th. Mr. Grenville saw Lord Holland at the Cockpit: he had a great deal of conversation with him. He talked with great zeal in support of the Government, and desired Mr. Grenville to tell him which he should choose for him to do, either to go back directly to France and return again in spring, or to stay now and go in the spring, and return in the summer. Mr. Grenville chose the latter, as thinking he might be of use here to those he could influence.

He said the last summer's negotiation with Mr. Pitt had done the King great prejudice in the minds of foreigners; that many had said to him, in France, " Il faut avouer que c'est une démarche *misérable* qu'a fait votre Roi."

Sunday, December 31st, 1763. Mr. Grenville went to Woburn. The Duke of Bedford was very cordial and friendly.

The Duchess expressed great admiration of the Queen, and as great averseness to the Princess Dowager, who, she said, had once told Princess Amelia that the King was of a terrible temper, that she had had great difficulties with him, and that she should pity his wife. Princess Amelia repeated this to Lady Waldegrave, who told it to the Duchess.

[The following, in the handwriting of Mrs. Grenville, is her own Narrative of events from November, 1763, to January, 1764.]

November 14th, 1763. Whenever I see Mrs. Murray she presses me strongly upon the necessity of Mr. Grenville's uniting with Lord Bute for the good of the whole, and availing himself of his Lordship's favour with the King.

Lord Bute sent strong professions to Mr. Grenville, by Mr. Jenkinson, Mr. Mackenzie, and Mr. Elliot. She presses for a return of kind expressions from Mr. Grenville. This may be the reason of Mr. Elliot's coldness. He went from the meeting upon the King's Speech last night, to Mr. Whately's, where he stayed till between twelve and one. All Lord Bute's friends hold this language.

The Queen ordered me to tell Lady Egremont, on

Sunday, the 13*th of November*, to come to her on the Tuesday following at twelve o'clock, when the King would be at the House of Lords. She received her with great kindness, mentioned every part of the family with great regard, and said the King could never forget the obligations he had to Lord Egremont for his services. She took notice how very ill Lord Thomond and I looked, spoke friendly of us both, and told Lady Egremont she heard the speech that Mr. Grenville had made for the King was a very fine one.

Mr. Elliot came to Mr. Grenville on *Thursday,* 17*th of November,* made him a great many compliments upon his performance in the House of Commons the day before, and the fullest declaration imaginable of his own hearty concurrence and support of his measures.

Mr. Elliot came to see me *Saturday, the* 19*th,* held the same language to me, wished me joy of the Government being so well established in Mr. Grenville's hands, said it was scarce in the power of anything to shake it; that for his part he should support it to the utmost; that he could do it without any breach of friendship to Lord Bute, being authorized by his Lordship to say that he wished every friend of his to give their thorough assistance to Mr. Grenville's Administration. He talked of Mr. Pitt's conduct, adopted the general idea of his intention to endeavour to work his way into Government again by means of Lord Bute, and told me that Mr. Dundas had just told him that Mr. Pitt was yesterday an hour and a half with Lord Shelburne, but Mr. Elliot fears no danger in the present hour.

Mrs. Murray went with me to Court upon the Princess of Wales's birthday; she exclaimed against Lord Shelburne's conduct, and said that the night before Lady Jane Stuart[1] had asked her if she had heard of the part Lord Shelburne had taken in the House of Lords, wondering what he could mean by it, and saying she knew of no friend he had, and seemed to disclaim all intercourse between him and her father, which all Lord Bute's friends in general do. I told Mrs. Murray I hoped there was none, and did believe it in the present hour, but with so fluctuating a mind as Lord Bute's, nobody could answer what would be the case in the next; but that for my own part I was ready to meet any change in Mr. Grenville's situation; that I was content in having seen him touch the summit with the applause and approbation of all mankind, and if by the caprice of anybody whatsoever a change should happen, those who had either mistrusted his abilities or weight in the House of Commons, were proved to have judged ill, and he would stand to the world in the high and approved light in which his conduct had placed him.

Lord Denbigh[2] told me, some days before the debate in the House of Lords upon Privilege, that he had wrote to Lord Bute for his proxy, believing that if he gave it, it would be to him. Lord Bute gave it to Lord Le Despencer.

During the two or three days' suspense upon Mr. Pitt's being at the head of the Administration in August last, Lord Northumberland went immediately to see

---

[1] Second daughter of Lord Bute: she was married in 1768 to Sir George, afterwards Earl Macartney; and died, aged 86, in 1828.

[2] Basil Feilding, sixth Earl of Denbigh. In 1761 he was made Master of the Harriers and Foxhounds. He died in 1800.

him. Princess Amelia heard this, and having invited Lord and Lady Hertford, and Lord and Lady Northumberland to dine with her at Gunnersbury, after dinner Her Royal Highness began talking of the late negociation with Mr. Pitt, and turning to Lord Northumberland, said that, short as that transaction had been, she did not doubt but that some people had been to call upon him for fear of being too late; he looked very much confounded, and after the company was upstairs she asked some of them if she had not roasted him well. Mr. Walpole told me this, who had it from Lord Hertford.

Thursday, December 15th. I went to see Madame Welderen[1], who told me the Hereditary Prince had overheated himself at Potsdam by dancing, and afterwards taking too hasty a journey to Brunswick, which made it be feared his wound would break out again, which must retard the marriage. It is supposed he has an affaire de cœur with the King of Prussia's sister.

Sunday, December 18th. Lady C. Edwin came to see me; we had a great deal of conversation; she told me she heard the Queen looked very dejected and melancholy, that it had been particularly observed Thursday night at the play, and that all those who went to her observed her dejection; the Princess of Wales had mentioned it to Lady Charlotte.

Monday, December 19th. Lady Egremont saw the Queen. I had no opportunity to tell her what passed on Sunday, but her own observation exactly tallied with

[1] The wife of Count de Welderen, Minister from the States of Holland.

the former account; she said Her Majesty had almost tears in her eyes, and that by words dropped, she understood that they told her nothing about the Princess Augusta's marriage, neither when nor in what manner it was to be. The Princess of Wales is cheerfuller, and in better spirits than she has been for some time.

Sunday, January 8th, 1764. I met Lord Hillsborough at the drawing-room, who told me that some event was expected after the holidays. I pressed him to tell me what he meant; he told me he grounded his suspicions upon something that passed in a company where Mr. Hume[1] (the *Home*) had been present; he enjoined secrecy to me, and then told me that it was said that Lord Bute's friends would hold back upon some of the most material points when the Parliament met again, and upon my pressing him to tell me who was meant, he named Mr. Elliot and Mr. Oswald, and that all this had been said and the parties named before Mr. Hume, who did not contradict it. Mem. This is directly contrary to Mr. Elliot's language, both to Mr. Grenville and me.

Friday, January 13th. The Hereditary Prince[2] arrived at Somerset House. He waited upon the King

---

[1] David Hume the Historian. He was private Secretary to Lord Hertford, and afterwards Secretary of Embassy at Paris; or perhaps the allusion here may be to the Rev. John Home, the author of the Tragedy of "Douglas."

[2] The Hereditary Prince Charles of Brunswick succeeded to the Dukedom in 1780, and after long military services was mortally wounded at Auerstadt, and died in November, 1806. After his decease, the Princess, his wife, returned to England, and died in 1810. The late unhappy Queen Caroline was their daughter, and one of their sons the well-remembered Duke who fell at Waterloo.

and Queen, Princess Dowager, &c., the next day, having before had a levée. He had another levée Sunday, and on Monday the marriage was celebrated, at seven o'clock, in the council chamber at St. James's :—present, Peers, Peeresses, their eldest sons and all their daughters, Privy Councillors and their wives. The King came in first, then the Queen, the Princess Dowager, the two youngest Princesses, and the two youngest Princes, then the Prince of Brunswick. Lord Chamberlain went to bring in the Princess Augusta, who came led in by Prince William. After the ceremony was over, the King went and saluted the Princess, the Queen did the same, and then the Princess kneeled down, and took the Princess Dowager's hand and kissed it.

The King went out, the Queen followed, and the Prince of Brunswick led the Princess Dowager, and Prince William led the Hereditary Princess.

The next day there was a drawing-room at St. James's, to which the Prince and Princess came, but nobody was presented to them; there was a ball at night.

THE EARL OF HERTFORD TO MR. GRENVILLE.

Paris, January 4, 1764.

DEAR SIR,—I think myself obliged to you for the part you have at different times taken about Mr. Bunbury[1]; I know your candour, and therefore shall make

[1] Lord Hertford was desirous of appointing his own private Secretary, Mr. Hume, to be Secretary of the Embassy, instead of Mr. Bunbury, who had been intended for that office by the King.

the less excuse; my credit in this country, as well as in my own, being so much affected by it, will, I am assured, justify me for pleading against a disgrace which never fell upon any of my predecessors in this place.

I can assure you, Sir, I have been much concerned at the part my brother took in the opening of this session of Parliament, and particularly as I differ widely with him in opinion. But it is still a satisfaction to me to know he acted entirely from principle, and not with any design of giving opposition to His Majesty's Government.

He has likewise, to my knowledge, great respect for you and your character, and I am very sure you will feel for him, that explanations upon Parliamentary conduct are matters of a very delicate nature to a man who thinks nicely, and holds from the Crown after he may be supposed to have offended it.

I know he is very sensible of your candid and obliging behaviour upon the late occasion, and I hope that the joint respect which you have for each other will mutually produce that good understanding which has my best wishes and endeavours to promote it.

My brother, I owe it to him to say it on this occasion, has every good quality which is necessary to form a good subject and an honest man. He may, therefore, be sometimes, perhaps, too delicate; but you have too much candour, and too just a judgment, to form your opinion of such a man upon the ordinary principles which govern mankind.

That he has been hurt I will confess: he thought himself neglected upon his return from Germany, when he was most anxious to receive some mark of His Majesty's favour in approbation of his military conduct there; but this, I can venture to assure you, has had no influence upon his behaviour in Parliament.

My affection must naturally lead me to interest myself very essentially in everything that concerns a brother whom I love so well; and it was from this motive, and from the respect I have for you, that I was anxious, when I had the honour of talking to you upon this subject in London, to remove every uneasy sensation of this sort from him, knowing how deep an impression His Majesty's favour must make upon a mind thus delicately formed.

I congratulate you upon the success you have had in Parliament, and heartily wish that His Majesty's business may go on quietly and to his satisfaction, through the remaining part of the session.

Mr. Wilkes is now at Paris: he came here, I believe, pretty early in the last week, and was, soon after his arrival, at my door; I did not think it proper to admit him, and he left his name. He was afterwards, as my chaplain tells me, here on Sunday at the Chapel, when there is a general freedom for Divine service, but I did not see him, being then at Versailles.

Upon my return from thence, I made inquiry what my immediate predecessors at Paris had done in relation to this gentleman, and I was informed that the Duke of Bedford had visited him and invited him twice to dinner, and that Mr. Neville had had his name wrote at his door. I have, therefore, in compliance with these examples, which I had never heard condemned, gone so far as to have my name wrote at his door by one of my servants, but I shall think it my duty, in the situation I am now placed here, not to show this gentleman any further countenance, except His Majesty should think fit to prescribe me a different conduct. I hear from a person who has seen him here that his wound is still open, though he has the spirits which usually attend him, and that he proposes being again in London by the 16th instant.

If I can be of any use to you or Mrs. Grenville in this country, I hope you will give me an opportunity of testifying the truth and respect with which I am, &c., &c. HERTFORD.

THE REV. DR. FRANCIS[1] TO MR. GRENVILLE.

Saturday morning (January, 1764).

SIR,—Mr. Jenkinson last night informed me that you proposed doing me the honour of recommending me to

---

[1] The translator of Horace and Demosthenes, the author of some forgotten tragedies, and a political writer of little note. He was domestic Chaplain to Lord Holland, by whose patronage he had been appointed to the Chaplainship of Chelsea Hospital, and through whose influence also his son, afterwards the well-known Sir Philip Francis, obtained a small place in the Secretary of State's office, which was the foundation of his future fortunes. The claims of Sir Philip to the authorship of *Junius* have been very ingeniously advocated, but not successfully established. I have found nothing in Mr. Grenville's papers which can explain the reason why Dr. Francis was recommended by him to the King for a pension of three hundred pounds per annum. His literary talents were scarcely sufficient to justify such a reward, and his political writings, however serviceable they may have been to his patrons, are almost unknown to, and entirely unappreciated by, the present generation. Horace Walpole relates, in the *Memoirs of the Reign of George the Third*, vol. ii. p. 36, that "Among Churchill's papers was found a collection of letters from Lord Holland to Francis,

the King for three hundred pounds a year on the establishment. I know, Sir, that in the usual forms of gratitude, I should tell you how sensibly I feel this great obligation. Yet I have ever thought that all over-earnest professions seem to suspect their own sincerity. Permit me, therefore, only to say that, in my zeal, affection, and duty to His Majesty, I wish to deserve his bounty; that I love and revere the Constitution, and feel an honest indignation against those who, either for interest or ambition, would betray or destroy it.

These, I am persuaded, Sir, are your own sentiments in the service of His Majesty and your country. If I maintain them firmly and inviolably, I promise myself your future patronage and protection. At present I shall only beg leave to assure you that I am, with all possible respect, &c., &c. PHIL. FRANCIS.

MR. STUART MACKENZIE TO MR. GRENVILLE.

Burlington Street, Tuesday evening, Jan. 10, 1764.

SIR,—I happened to hear this day that the Opposition intend to make a great bustle with the Hereditary Prince[1], when he arrives; that they purpose to invite him to their houses, and to make the most splendid entertainments for him; my intelligence was from a low

---

who had furnished them to the satirist against his late patron. In one of those epistles, Francis complained of Lord Holland for not making him an Irish Bishop, and threatened to publish something that would prove Lord Holland a still greater villain than the world believed him. To silence that wretch, Lord Holland sent him 500*l*., and gave him a place in Chelsea College."

[1] Walpole, writing to Lord Hertford at this time, says, "Such

person, who very accidentally dropped to me that there were great doings already preparing at Lord Rockingham's for the Prince's reception. You may possibly know more of this matter than I do, if so, you will forgive my troubling you with this, which can only proceed from a good motive in me, as I take it for granted you would not wish that the Prince should (for want of being put upon his guard) fall into the company of those who, under pretence of opposing the Ministry, are thwarting every measure which His Majesty may judge proper to pursue. I am, with great respect, &c., &c.

J. S. MACKENZIE.

MR. HORACE WALPOLE TO COUNTESS TEMPLE.

(January, 1764.)

MR. WALPOLE cannot express how much he is obliged and honoured by the trust Lady Temple is so good as to put in him, nor will her Ladyship's modesty let her be a proper judge how great that is. He will say no more but that more than slight corrections in measure would destroy the chief merit of the poems, which consists in the beautiful ease and negligence of the composition—a merit which correction may take away, but can never bestow. To do real justice to these poems, they should be compared with the first thoughts and sketches of

pains were taken to keep the Prince from any intercourse with any of the Opposition, that he has done nothing but take notice of them. He not only wrote to the Duke of Newcastle and Mr Pitt, but has been at Hayes to see the latter, and has dined *twice* with the Duke of Cumberland."

other great poets. Mr. Addison, with infinite labour, accomplished a few fine poems; but what does your Ladyship think were his rough draughts [1]?

MR. WILKES TO EARL TEMPLE.

Paris, Hotel de Saxe, Monday, Jan. 16, 1764.

MY LORD,—A gentleman who is just returned from Italy, and embarking for England, gives me five minutes to pay my compliments to your Lordship. I shall only venture, by a conveyance of which I am not quite certain, to assure your Lordship of the deepest gratitude and the highest esteem, and to mention an anecdote or two relating to the Chevalier D'Eon, which I have from the best authority. When this Court demanded him to be given up, Lord Halifax said, *il est aussi méprisable qu' inviolable.*

The Duc de Choiseul offered a gentleman I know here, ten men and any sum of money he should de-

---

[1] Lady Temple had sent Walpole a fair copy of her Poems for his approval and correction, and to be printed at the Strawberry Hill press. The manuscript was returned with scarcely any alteration, but with the addition of some lines by himself addressed to Lady Temple, which are prefixed to the volume of Poems printed under his own superintendence. Walpole's verses commence thus:—

> "Long had been lost enchanting Sappho's lyre,
> Its graceful warblings, and its tender fire," &c. &c.

Sappho's lyre was of course supposed to have been *found* by Lady Temple. In the *Royal and Noble Authors*, it is stated that "Lady Temple was forty years of age, before she discovered in herself a turn for genteel versification, which she executed with facility, and decked with the amiable graces of her own benevolent mind." With regard to the compliments contained in the letter above, it may be imagined that he was pretty well assured of their favourable reception before he ventured to administer such inordinate flattery.

mand, to go over to England and to kidnap D'Eon, as Fratieaux was. The gentleman refused, from the improbability of success, D'Eon's nephew and three others constantly attending him [1].

I take the liberty of sending to your Lordship the *Anti-Financier*, the author of which is now in the Bastile, and almost the whole impression at the Duke of Choiseul's; and some excellent maps of the theatre of the late war.

I have not been out of my room for some days, and am attended every day by the celebrated Dufouart, who now gives me hopes of the wound closing this week.

Miss Wilkes joins with me in the most respectful compliments to Lady Temple. I am, my Lord, with infinite regard and attachment, &c., &c.

JOHN WILKES.

THE REV. DR. FRANCIS TO MR. GRENVILLE.

January 19, 1764.

SIR,—It is not the least among the many obligations I have had the honour of receiving from Mr. Grenville, that he permits me to thank him for his last favour. There was a time, Sir, when I presumed to talk of gratitude, and make professions of service. But one im-

---

[1] D'Eon was supposed to have been formerly employed by Louis the Fifteenth in some secret affairs, and the French Ministers were desirous of obtaining possession of him, to prevent his disclosure of circumstances connected with them. Horace Walpole, mentioning D'Eon soon after, says, "that poor lunatic was at the Opera on Saturday, looking like Bedlam. He goes armed, and threatens, what I dare say he would perform, to kill or be killed, if any attempt is made to seize him."

prudent paper¹—I dare not even claim the little merit of that zeal to serve, that earnestness to be grateful, with which it was written. No, Sir. Let me rather ask pardon for the disquietude which it has too probably given to your good nature. Or if I may ever ask one favour more, permit me to hope you will believe me, when I assure you that I am, Sir, with perfect integrity of heart, your most obliged, &c.   PHIL. FRANCIS.

THE KING TO MR. GRENVILLE.

January 20, 1764.

MR. GRENVILLE, the Debate of yesterday² has given me great satisfaction; I hope to see you as soon as my Levée is over, that I may know the whole previous to the City's Address³.

---

[1] Probably an anonymous publication in some of the journals or periodicals, and therefore it may not now be possible to ascertain its purport. In Debrett's *Collection of Scarce Tracts*, from 1763 to 1770, he ascribes to Dr. Francis, a short tract of seven or eight pages, entitled a *Letter from the Cocoa Tree to the Country Gentlemen*. There is nothing in it, however, which displays "that zeal to serve," or "that earnestness to be grateful," with which he comforts himself. The "last favour" was the Pension of 300*l*.; but the expression implies former favours, and consequently former services. It may be assumed that Francis had long been a writer in support of Mr. Grenville's political views. In a list of Pensioners on the Irish Establishment, printed in the *London Museum* for 1770, I find the following, "John Stear, Esq., assignee of Philip Francis, Esq., 600*l*., for 31 years, from September 16th, 1762." So this valuable politician cost the country 900*l*. per annum!

[2] On Wilkes's complaint of Breach of Privilege.

[3] On the marriage of the Princess Augusta with the Hereditary Prince of Brunswick.

THE EARL OF SANDWICH TO MR. GRENVILLE.

Whitehall, January 27, 1764.

Dear Sir,—The Duke of Bedford most thoroughly approves of the idea of our meeting once a week; I shall therefore hope for the pleasure of seeing you for the first meeting, at dinner, at my house, on Tuesday next[1]. I am, &c.   Sandwich.

MR. HORACE WALPOLE TO COUNTESS TEMPLE.

January 28, 1764.

I have now, Madam, very carefully studied your Ladyship's poems, in which, as I told you, I can find no faults but in the longer metre. This I have tried to supply here and there by a syllable, or by little inversions which mend the cadence; and these I submit to your Ladyship's judgment as mere mechanic corrections, and not at all as improving the ease and natural grace of the original, much less the poetry, which perhaps suffers by my dull criticisms.

Your Ladyship will probably improve on my hints, for your own genteel pen is much more likely to strike out proper alterations, than I, who work by dull rules, can do. One thing I am sure of, that larger changes than I have ventured to make, would entirely prejudice the agreeable air of your verses, which is so much and so peculiarly your own.

When I have the honour of seeing you, I will hope for further orders as to the impression, which I trust

---

[1] This arrangement was probably the origin of the "Cabinet Dinners," which subsequently became an established custom.

will not be so rigidly confined as you first proposed[1]. I am, Madam, your most obedient and most sensibly obliged humble Servant,   HOR. WALPOLE.

MR. GRENVILLE TO THE EARL OF HERTFORD.

Downing Street, January 28, 1764.

MY DEAR LORD,—My best endeavours will always be employed with pleasure to prevent anything that may be disagreeable to you, or that may in the least contribute to render your situation less pleasing or honourable to you. I flatter myself that there are no thoughts of Mr.

---

[1] It was limited to one hundred copies. See *Walpole Correspondence*, vol. iv. p. 431. As the volume is now extremely rare, it may be as well to mention that it contains the following poems, in addition to Horace Walpole's Address to Lady Temple:—
1. Verses written in 1756, on Lady Elizabeth Keppel.
2. Apollo's rout.
3. The Mice: a fable.
4. Marble Hill.
5. The City Mouse and Country Mouse: a fable.
6. To the Duke of Dorset, on his birthday.
7. To Lady Elizabeth Germaine, on her birthday.
8. The Lady and the Spider: a fable.
9. To the Duchess of Leeds.
10. The Lion in love: a fable.
11. The Ant and Fly: a fable.
12. Verses sent to Lady Charles Spencer.

It has been well observed (if I mistake not, by Mr. Croker, in a note to the *Suffolk Correspondence*), that "a want of delicacy was so common a deficiency among even people who boasted of the best breeding, that Maids of Honour of the last century, in their epistolary communications, are sometimes found making use of expressions which in the present day would rarely fall from the lowest of their sex." So it is unfortunately with some of Lady Temple's poems which still remain in Manuscript. Some of them I cannot venture to quote, but there are others which I may perhaps have occasion to notice hereafter.

Bunbury's going to Paris at present, and I should be sincerely glad if any other arrangement could be found for him, to put that matter out of doubt; in which case, though I know there will be competitors here to succeed him, yet I believe the King will avoid any further difficulty upon the subject by not appointing any other Secretary to the Embassy, in like manner as has been done both at St. Petersburgh and the Hague.

I shall be extremely happy to find that your Lordship's wishes and mine with regard to General Conway may be well founded, and that what has happened hitherto may not be the effect of any permanent indisposition to those that compose His Majesty's government, or of an unbounded attachment to those that oppose it.

I perfectly agree with you in thinking that in such a situation, with a man of delicate feelings, explanations are not likely to be productive of any good. All that can be said upon it on either side, must be known and felt, and therefore to that I will leave it, with my sincere desire that it may take that turn which I am confident will be most honourable to him and agreeable to you, and which no proper endeavours of mine, however unsuccessful, shall be wanting to promote. A little time must necessarily show upon what footing this matter stands, and must determine the opinion of mankind with regard to it; in the meanwhile your Lordship does me justice in thinking that I will, as long as I possibly can, avoid forming any judgment upon a subject which has already given me a great deal of concern.

Our Parliamentary business continues hitherto to go on with the greatest success. We have got rid of Mr. Wilkes, who was expelled with only one negative voice, and who will find, too late, how much too far he has gone.

I told your Lordship, in my last letter, that I had had a dispute with M. de Guerchy about his wine being admitted to enter without duty and without any limitation of quantity, as it is allowed to your Excellency at Paris. I was informed from the Custom House that he had entered eleven tuns free from duty, which was the quantity that M. de Nivernois had; but in that they were mistaken, for M. de Guerchy had had between eight and nine tuns only. However, so many applications were made from the other Foreign Ministers in consequence of it, and so many complaints from our own people at the introduction of French goods of every kind, that I could go no farther than I had gone, and I was forced to tell M. de Guerchy that the allowance made to M. de Nivernois could be no precedent, because, as the two kingdoms were at war, he could not be admitted to an entry paying the duty, and therefore that he could not have any wine at all, unless it was without duty. This was the only reason for making that allowance to M. de Nivernois, which never had been made in any former instance to an Ambassador of France, or of any other Power, and which neither had been, nor would be, followed hereafter on any other occasion. I added, that in order to do what was agreeable to M. de Guerchy, I had already greatly exceeded the bounds to which this privilege had been carried out; that I had given directions to prevent this being quoted as a precedent for the future, which I desired that he might be fully apprized of, and that the regard shown in going so far was merely personal to himself. In consequence of this, M. de Guerchy sent back a large quantity of wine to France, rather than pay the duty for what remained, and seemed very much dissatisfied that the privilege was not allowed for any quantity he might enter.

THE EARL OF HERTFORD TO MR. GRENVILLE.

Paris, February 11, 1764.

SIR,—You must give me leave to trouble you with a complaint, and to desire your orders for the immediate release of some few things of mine, which have been taken from Lawson, one of His Majesty's messengers, by the Custom House officers at Dover.

An account of the whole is enclosed herewith, by which you will see how trifling the value is: they are chiefly small presents of Lady Hertford's to her friends.

The grievance I chiefly complain of is, stopping any packet where there are letters, and to which my own seal is affixed. It is not probable that the person whom the King thinks proper to trust with his orders at this court, is likely to abuse the favour which may be shown him on that account, and become a smuggler.

The loss or delay given to letters of business may, by such an unexpected event, be very prejudicial to private affairs. I shall submit to any, the most severe rules which have been imposed upon my predecessors here, though I might not agree in the propriety of a very strict execution of them in such an instance.

But if it has been usual, or is thought right, to pay any respect to an Ambassador's seal, whilst he is employed in that character here, I shall hope, from your candour, that some distinctions will be allowed, and some reprimand given, for the very severe and arbitrary manner in which the Custom House officers at Dover have, in this instance, thought proper to stop everything. I have the honour to be, &c., &c.

HERTFORD.

THE KING TO MR. GRENVILLE.

Tuesday night, 40 min. past 10 (Feb. 14, 1764).

MR. GRENVILLE, this is merely to desire you not to forget to send me, early to-morrow morning, a line with the sketch of this day's debate[1].

MR. GRENVILLE TO THE KING.

Wednesday morning, 35 min. past 9,
February 15, 1764.

I HAVE the honour to inform your Majesty that the House is but this moment up[2]; the examination of the evidence was not over 'till near one o'clock in the morning, at which time Sir William Meredith[3] opened what

---

[1] On Breach of Privilege, and the cases of Webb, the Solicitor to the Treasury, and Wood, the Under Secretary of State, and upon Sir William Meredith's motion to declare the granting of General Warrants illegal.

[2] Walpole states that the House rose at half-past seven in the morning: "the longest sitting on record, exceeding that on the Westminster Election in 1741, and the last sitting on the Militia Bill in 1755."

[3] A very active member of the Whig party: he was at this time M.P. for Liverpool, and was subsequently a Lord of the Admiralty, and in 1774 Comptroller of the King's Household. He is said to have been the author of a pamphlet, entitled "*A Reply to the Defence of the Majority, on the question relating to General Warrants.*" Sir William died in 1790.

he proposed, which consisted of two motions. The first was, that the practice of granting warrants by the Secretaries of State for taking up persons without specifying their names, and for seizing their papers, is not warranted by law. The purport of the second was that the granting such warrants against Members of Parliament was a breach of the privileges of Parliament. Mr. Frederick Vane[1] seconded the motion. Lord Frederick Campbell[2] spoke with great spirit, and extremely well, for determining the cause of the persons charged by the complaint of the breach of privilege before the House proceeded upon the general matter.

Mr. Wood[3] then spoke for having his charge decided, and this seemed to make a good deal of impression.

Mr. Yorke then proposed to adjourn the debate to Friday upon Sir William Meredith's question, from the great importance of it, and the lateness of the night. This, after some conversation upon it, the Attorney-General agreed to, and I concurred with him; but we both told the House that we did not intend, by this means, to restrain ourselves from moving a question, immediately after the adjournment of this debate, for discharging the complaint of breach of privilege against

---

[1] M.P. for Durham.

[2] M.P. for Glasgow. He was the fourth son of John, Duke of Argyll, by Mary Bellenden. He married Mary, Dowager Countess Ferrers, and sister to Sir William Meredith. She was burnt to death at Combe Bank in 1807. Lord William died in 1816, in his 87th year.

[3] Robert Wood, M.P. for Brackley. He had been for some years Under Secretary of State, and in that capacity was concerned in the issue of the General Warrants. He was the author of a Dissertation on the Genius and Writings of Homer, and also of a well-known work on the ruins of Balbec and Palmyra, the result of his travels in the East in 1750 and 1751. He died in 1771.

Mr. Wood, Mr. Webb[1], and the three Messengers. To this Mr. Pitt objected, at first temperately, but afterwards more warmly, and in this he was followed by all the other speakers in the Opposition: Mr. Charles Townshend, General Conway, Lord George Sackville, and many others.

At the beginning they said they meant nothing against the persons charged; but in the course of the debate they insisted that they were legally guilty, though not intentionally so, and therefore desired that the question with regard to them likewise should be adjourned. This was refused, and Mr. Yorke then declared his intention was to adjourn the whole.

To this, after so many good friends had spoken for bringing the cause of those who were charged to a decision either of acquittal or censure, it was impossible to consent. This question was debated a great while, and about four o'clock the question was put upon an amendment to the motion for adjourning the former debate, by inserting the words, together with the complaint of the breach of privilege. The division for the amendment was 197, and against it 207. The occasion of this small majority was owing partly to the time when the question of adjournment was put, and partly to the defection of several gentlemen who have hitherto voted with the Government.

After this was over the motion was made by Dr. Hay[2] for discharging the complaint against Mr. Wood. Mr. Pitt opposed this with great vehemence in a long

---

[1] Philip Carteret Webb, Solicitor to the Treasury, M.P. for Haslemere.

[2] At this time a Lord of the Admiralty.

speech, to which, notwithstanding it was so late, I found myself obliged to reply, though neither the speech nor the reply was confined to the question, but went upon the general measures and state of the Government. This lasted 'till about six o'clock, and was prolonged by other speakers 'till a little after seven, when we came to a second division, upon another motion for adjournment, the numbers upon which were 184 for adjourning, and 208 against it. This ended the whole, for the questions were immediately put for discharging the complaint against each of the persons charged, and were carried without any division; and it being then eight o'clock, the House adjourned 'till to-morrow morning. As the debate was not at all a regular one, I beg your Majesty will forgive my not being able at present to send a list of the speakers, or of the chief persons that voted upon this occasion, of which I should have been extremely happy to have transmitted to your Majesty a more perfect and a more satisfactory account.

THE EARL OF BATH TO MR. GRENVILLE.

Piccadilly, February 16, 1764.

Sir,—I had something to communicate to you that I apprehended to be of importance, but it will be too late to do it to-morrow; perhaps I had better never mention it to anybody, nor take upon me to be answerable for any public measure, but my inclination to serve you made me desirous of communicating to you a scheme[1] I had

[1] Probably one of the latest schemes of a man who had been scheming through a long life. What was the nature of it, or whether it was ever communicated to Mr. Grenville, are points upon which there is no information. Lord Bath died in July following, in his 83rd year.

in my head to disappoint those who flatter themselves of carrying their question on Friday next. I have the honour to be, &c., &c. BATH.

MR. GLOVER TO MR. GRENVILLE.

Exchange Alley, February 16, 1764.

DEAR SIR,—I shall certainly attend the House tomorrow. Give me leave to say with some confidence that Sir William Meredith's motion will pass, unless you snatch that occasion out of the hands of Opposition by an amendment, and secure to yourself all the credit which else will remain with them.

I will not trouble with arguments, either political or personal, one whose own consummate knowledge and sagacity is more a master of the subject, and of his own situation, than I can pretend to be. I shall, therefore, conclude with my conception of an amendment stated below, and remain, &c., &c. R. GLOVER[1].

"That the issuing of General Warrants for the apprehending printers, publishers, and authors of seditious libels, together with their papers, or of any other person or persons whatsoever without a charge of some crime, hath been a practice erroneous and oppressive from the year 1662 down to the present times, and not warranted by law."

[1] Richard Glover, a Merchant in the City, and M.P. for Weymouth. He is now chiefly remembered for his Poem of *Leonidas*, and a ballad always popular, called *Hosier's Ghost*. The proposed amendment was not adopted. The Opposition, on the occasion of this question of General Warrants, had great expectations of victory. When the Speaker called the *ayes* and *noes*, says Horace Walpole, "*they* went forth, and when I heard one side counted to the amount of 218, I did conclude we were victorious, but they returned 232. It is true we were beaten by 14, but we were increased by 21."

MR. GRENVILLE TO THE KING.

Downing Street, Saturday, February 18, 1764,
30 min. past 7, in the morning.

I HAVE the honour to inform your Majesty that the House continued sitting till ¾ past 5 this morning[1].

The Division was made at 5 o'clock, upon a question for adjourning the debate upon the former motion for four months, which was carried for adjourning it by 232 against 218, as appears by the enclosed minute.

Mr. Yorke and his family and friends voted with the minority, as did likewise some few of the Tory country gentlemen; Colonel Howe[2], Mr. Cocks[3], Mr. Staunton[4], Mr. Elliot of the Board of Trade, and many other individuals, which made up the large number of 218.

Mr. Bacon, of the Board of Trade, I believe voted with the majority.

Mr. Pitt spoke very late in the debate, and appeared to be very faint and languid.

Lord George Sackville, General Conway, and Mr. Charles Townshend, all spoke with the minority, and the latter the best of the three.

Dr. Hay, Mr. Stanley, Lord Barrington, Mr. Elliot, Lord North, Mr. Nugent, the Attorney General, Mr. Wedderburn[5], Mr. Richmond Webb[6], Mr. Fazakerly[7], and Mr. Wilbraham[8] spoke with the majority, and some of them very well, but the debate in general was but an indifferent one.

---

[1] The debate was upon the question of General Warrants.
[2] M.P. for Nottingham.   [3] M.P. for Reigate.   [4] M.P. for Ipswich.
[5] At this time he represented the Ayr District of Burghs.
[6] M.P. for Bossiney. He was afterwards made a Welsh Judge.
[7] Nicholas Fazakerly, M.P. for Preston.
[8] Randle Wilbraham, M.P. for Preston.

Sir John Phillips spoke after me just before the division, promising the House that he would move for the Bill to correct what was amiss in these warrants.

I will endeavour as soon as possible to get a list of the speakers, and an account of any extraordinary persons who voted on either side, in order to transmit them to your Majesty.

THE KING TO MR. GRENVILLE.

10 min. past 10, February 18, 1764.

MR. GRENVILLE, if you should be up in time, I should be glad if you could be at St. James's by twelve; the defection last night is undoubtedly very great, but my nature ever inclines me to be acquainted with who are my true, and who false friends; the latter I think worse than open enemies. Firmness and resolution must now be shown, and no one's friend saved who has dared to fly off; this alone can restore order, and save this country from anarchy; by dismissing, I mean not till the question is decided, but I hope in a fortnight that those who have deserted may feel that I am not to be neglected unpunished[1].

MR. WILKES TO EARL TEMPLE.

Paris, Rue St. Nicaise, February 25, 1764.

MY LORD,—Mr. Shirley's return to England gives me an opportunity of paying my compliments to your Lordship before the important productions of this mischievous pen can be read by either of the Secretaries of State,

[1] The King evidently remained firm in his determination of dismissing General Conway.

or the Post Masters General. Yet I could almost wish that this might fall into their hands, for I am sure it must be no small anguish to a bad mind to know that virtue and honour are always the objects of veneration, and that the just esteem I have long conceived for your Lordship's superior talents and goodness follows me everywhere, and inviolably attaches me to you. I only lament that I am so unprofitable a servant, and my first wish is to have it in my power to demonstrate the sense I have of the many and great obligations I have received.

I am not disposed to lose myself in womanish complaints on the hardness of my fate, and the variety of persecutions I have suffered even from those I had most obliged. Nature has given me some philosophy; books and observation have added greatly to the stock. I am resigned to my fate, and I have only to reproach myself with a neglect of the most wise and salutary advice which was ever given; yet if I was disposed to justify myself in any manner, which I am not, I would plead some of the natural causes which operate always so strongly, the rashness of my time of life, and the contempt of difficulties and dangers which has ever attended me. Fidelity and disinterestedness I trust that I shared in no small degree.

I believe that I have not lost my time here, yet I will wait a little longer that I may not obtrude on your Lordship ideas and facts in a crude and slovenly manner, as I should now be forced to do. Besides the business of the day, which I do not neglect, I wish to give posterity an useful book, in which I would *first* at large examine our ideas of political liberty; in the *second* part, treat of the English constitution and government; and in the *last,* relate my own story, with all the vouchers, &c. Perhaps I should be able to obtain the notes of the Chief Justice, which would make the work still more interesting.

Since I wrote the above, and have waited Captain Shirley's return to England, I have been informed of the verdicts of the 21st[1]. I will only say in the anguish of my heart, that I owe what I suffer to the neglect of your Lordship's advice, that I foresee all the consequences of being so entirely at the mercy of an abandoned Administration and vindictive judge, and intend never to put myself in their power, though I leave my dear native country, and all the charms it ever had for me. I will add one thing more, that I will never make the most distant kind even of what might be interpreted a submission, but will endeavour to act, wherever I am, a great, an honest, and disinterested part, to continue to me, as I hope, the good opinion of your Lordship and of all men of honour.

May I mention that I find Miss Wilkes exceeds my most flattering hopes, and that she is an absolute favourite here in every place, where I wish her to be so. My most sincere respects ever attend Lady Temple.

I beg your Lordship to add to your Library the folio of Louis XIV.'s medals, which I have met with here, quite perfect and fine impressions. I am ever, &c.

JOHN WILKES.

---

[1] He had been found guilty of republishing the *North Briton*, No. 45, and of printing the *Essay on Woman*. It was contrary to Lord Temple's advice that he reprinted the *North Briton* in his own house, for in so doing he furnished the Government with that evidence against him which had not previously existed upon the original publication.

MEMORIAL TO MR. GRENVILLE IN FAVOUR OF DR. SHEBBEARE[1].

February 29, 1764.

Sir,—Dr. Shebbeare, whose circumstances are much reduced, having for above two years past, taken every opportunity of serving His Majesty and his Administration by his writings, and particularly those mentioned on he other side, and being desirous of continuing his services, the necessity of which we apprehend appears by the constant malevolent publications of the enemies of the Government, we make it our request that you will be pleased to obtain from His Majesty an annual pension for him, that he may be enabled to pursue that laudable inclination which he has of manifesting his zeal for the service of His Majesty and his Government.

We should not have taken this liberty if we had not been informed that the late Dr. Thomson, Pemberton, Johnson, Smollett, Hume, Hill, Mallet, and others

---

[1] John Shebbeare, commonly called Doctor Shebbeare, was the son of an Attorney at Bideford in Devonshire, where he was apprenticed to a Surgeon. He became a very voluminous and notorious political and satirical writer: his most celebrated performances were a series of *Letters to the People of England, on the progress of National ruin, &c.* For the sixth letter of this series he was prosecuted, and sentenced in December, 1758, to stand in the Pillory, and be imprisoned for three years, both of which he suffered. In consequence of this Memorial, and with the assistance of Sir John Phillips, he is said to have obtained from Mr. Grenville's Administration a pension of 200*l.* per annum. He died in 1788. It will be observed, that the above list of Dr. Shebbeare's writings is confined to the three years previous to its date.

have had either pensions or places granted them as Men of Letters[1]. We have the honour to be, &c., &c.

> J. Hynde Cotton[2]. Richd. Bamfylde[9].
> Thos. Willoughby[3]. Thos. Stapleton[10].
> Dudley and Ward[4]. Ri. Lowndes[11].
> John Phillips[5]. J. Glynne[12].
> J. Walter[6]. C. K. Tynte[13].
> A. Wodehouse[7]. Ed. Kynaston[14].
> St. John[8]. W. W. Bagot[15].

A List of what has been Published within these Three Years by Dr. Shebbeare.

A letter to the Right Honourable Author of a Letter to a Citizen, &c.

The History of Sumatra, in 2 vols. 8vo.

Invincible Reasons for the Earl of Bute's immediate Resignation of the Ministry.

A Letter to the Right Honourable the Earl Temple on the 45th No. of the *North Briton*.

Another Answer to the Letters of the Right Honourable William Pitt to Ralph Allen, &c.

---

[1] See Note [1], next page.
[2] M.P. for Cambridgeshire. [3] M.P. for Nottinghamshire.
[4] John Ward, sixth Baron Ward, created Viscount Dudley and Ward, April, 1763. He died in 1774.
[5] M.P. for Pembrokeshire. [6] M.P. for Exeter. [7] M.P. for Norfolk.
[8] M.P. for Wotton Basset. [9] M.P. for Devonshire.
[10] Sir Thomas Stapleton, M.P. for Oxford City.
[11] M.P. for Buckinghamshire. [12] M.P. for Flint.
[13] Fifth Baronet, M.P. for Somersetshire.
[14] M.P. for Montgomeryshire. [15] M.P. for Oxford University.

The Expediency of a Peace deduced from Candid Considerations of the respective states of Great Britain and her Enemies.

An Epistle to the irreverend Mr. C. C——ll.

Many Papers in the Gazetteer.

[1] The following is a copy of the Pension List, as it existed for the Michaelmas quarter 1763, from the original in the handwriting of Mr. Charles Jenkinson (at that time Secretary to the Treasury), with his receipt attached for the total amount, 2655*l.*, paid into his hands by Mr. Grenville. Of the names mentioned in the above Memorial, I only find that of Dr. Johnson, but in a similar list for the Midsummer quarter following, David Hume's name appears for 200*l.* per annum.

	£	s.		£	s
Mr. Tyrrel, *half a year*	100	0	Brought forward	1680	0
Querré, the French Pilot, *one year*	100	0	Dr. Campbell, *half a year*	200	0
Springer, the Swedish Merchant, *half a year*	50	0	Mr. Ross Fleming, *one quarter*	25	0
Lady Warwick, *one quarter*	75	0	Mr. Anderson, *one quarter*	37	10
Lady Charlotte Rich, *one quarter*	50	0	Mr. Samuel Johnson, *one quarter*	75	0
Sir John Fielding, *half a year*	300	0	Mr. Allen, Gentleman Usher, *one quarter*	12	10
Mr. Gordon, *one quarter*	30	0	Mr. Osterman, Wards' Chymist, *one quarter*	50	0
Mr. Hamilton, *half a year*	100	0	Mr. Wight, Wards' Chymist, *one quarter*	75	0
Mrs. Krahé, *half a year*	25	0	Mr. Allen, Mr. Onslow's nephew, *one quarter*	50	0
Mrs. Boons, *half a year*	200	0	Rev. Mr. Lloyd, *one quarter*	50	0
Mr. Hewet, *half a year*	200	0	Mrs. Ker, *one quarter*	25	0
Mr. Guthrie, *one quarter*	50	0	Mr. Francis, *one quarter*	75	0
Mr. Sheridan, *half a year*	100	0	Harwich Expenses, *half a year*	50	0
Colonel Mordaunt, *one quarter*	300	0	Mr. Keith, *one quarter*	250	0
Carried forward	1680	0		2655	0

LORD CLIVE TO MR. GRENVILLE.

February 29, 1764.

Dear Sir,—Enclosed I send you General Colland's defence. I must request that you will give this extraordinary defence a reading, and then return it to me again, as I would not have it known I have such a paper in my possession.

I shall only observe that, in consequence of the Directors' letter, General Colland was dismissed the Company's service, and, upon his arrival in England, laid before the Directors the accompanying defence; he was not only acquitted by those gentlemen, but had their public thanks for his services abroad.

This gentleman was the person who, by Mr. Vansittart's order, surrounded and made prisoner the Nabob, Jaffeir Ally Cawn, in his palace.

The Directors have obtained His Majesty's Brévet of Brigadier-General for Mr. Colland, and he is now going out to that country Commander-in-Chief. I leave you to judge, Sir, what must be the consequence when the Nabob hears the news of his arrival; in all probability it will occasion another Revolution, and be the cause of the death of many young gentlemen, who will fall a sacrifice to the Nabob's resentment, at the subordinate settlements.

I cannot help thinking that when the General Court have made this, as well as many other very extraordinary transactions, public, but the Parliament may be induced to take these matters into their most serious consideration, as the honour of the nation, the salvation of the lives of so many British subjects, and the existence of the Company, depend upon an inquiry, and if the Proprietors are biassed by party or splitting of votes, to do themselves justice, I hope you, Sir, will approve of my making a motion to that purpose.

The General Court will be over to-morrow, and if you will appoint me any time to lay our proceedings before you, and to discourse with you upon the foregoing subject, I will attend you with great pleasure.

I am, &c., &c. CLIVE.

THE EARL OF NORTHUMBERLAND TO MR. GRENVILLE.

Dublin Castle, March 2, 1764.

DEAR SIR,—I received yesterday, by the messenger, the honour of your letter, dated the 25th of last month, and without loss of time I communicated your wishes to Lord Farnham[1] and Lord Malpas[2], the only English Members now here (except Mr. Hamilton)[3], and strongly represented how agreeable I knew it would be to His Majesty, and how advisable I thought it for them to attend immediately the business of Parliament in England; the former assured me that he had been preparing for his journey for some time past, and only waited for the yacht, which is now ready, and will sail the first fair wind; the latter will also set forward at

---

[1] Robert, second Baron Farnham, created Viscount in 1761, and Earl of Farnham in 1763. He was now M.P. for Taunton; he died in 1779.

[2] George Viscount Malpas, son of the third Earl Cholmondeley, by Mary, daughter of Sir Robert Walpole. He was at this time M.P. for Corfe Castle. He came to London from his regiment in Ireland, and died of inflammation a few days after his arrival.

[3] William Gerard Hamilton, M.P. for Pontefract.

the same time, but desires that His Majesty may be made acquainted with the difficulties under which he undertakes this journey, not only on account of leaving his own private affairs in a very unsettled state, but his regiment, which is lately come from America in great confusion, as his Lieut.-Colonel is now actually in arrest, in order to be tried by a Court Martial on many complaints that are lodged against him.

I esteem myself very happy to have successfully executed your commands in this instance, as I shall wish to do in every other wherein I can give you any proof of my friendship and zeal for your service. The late divisions in the House of Commons do not appear to me to be in any degree alarming, as I am very sensible how easily people are led away by ideas of popularity and upon questions of privilege. I experienced this at the beginning of the session here, where all difficulties are now happily subsided; and I do not in the least doubt but by the wisdom and prudence of your measures, by the uprightness of your intentions, and by the firmness of your conduct, that the same will happen in England, and that clamour and opposition will soon be reduced to the same weak and despicable situation in which they appeared some time ago. My best wishes and my most earnest endeavours shall be employed to promote that end, as I have nothing so much at heart, as the steady, honourable, and effectual support of His Majesty's Government, and of your Administration.

I am extremely sensible of your obliging conduct and friendly attention to the ease and honour of mine here, and I therefore cannot entertain the least doubt but that you will, upon this occasion, contribute towards it by preventing any confusion that may arise upon what you mention concerning the disposal of the late Lord Charleville's[1] employments.

My private letter to the Earl of Halifax, of the 24th of February, to which I beg leave to refer, as I hope his Lordship has been so good as to lay the same before His Majesty, will fully convince you of my situation and engagement upon that subject, and I flatter myself that the reasons I have there stated, and which I need not repeat, will induce you to resist and discountenance all other applications, and to join with me in interceding with His Majesty, in favour of my humble request that the employment lately held by Lord Charleville may be granted to the Earl of Belvidere[2] during His Majesty's pleasure.

My great regard and esteem for Mr. Luttrell would have made me very happy, if I had not been thus circumstanced, to have concurred with his wishes on this occasion, and I sincerely hope that you will easily find some other arrangement that will equally answer his expectations; but I should esteem myself deficient in my duty to His Majesty, and inattentive to his service, and my own honour, if I did not represent in the strongest and most explicit manner, as I beg leave to do, the insurmountable difficulties and the general dissatisfaction that would arise in this country, and how impossible it will be for me to carry on His Majesty's Government here with any degree of credit, satisfaction, or success, if this employment, the only one that has fallen

---

[1] Charles, second Baron Charleville, in Ireland, created Earl of Charleville in 1758. He was Muster-Master General of Ireland, and died on the 17th of February in this year.

[2] Robert Rochfort, first Earl of Belvidere, in Ireland. He succeeded Lord Charleville as Muster-Master General, and died in 1772.

in this kingdom since my appointment, should be disposed of (directly contrary to my recommendation and to the plan which I had with so much difficulty successfully adjusted) in favour of a person who is not in either House of Parliament here, and who has no interest nor connection in this kingdom, that can in any degree contribute to assist Government.

I could urge many other reasons in support of these sentiments and declarations, but I am persuaded they are unnecessary, and that I may depend upon your friendship fully to represent to His Majesty, whose gracious acceptance of my zealous and unwearied endeavours for his service I have always experienced, and who I hope will put the same favourable construction upon the subject which I now beg leave to submit to his royal consideration. I am, with the utmost attachment, &c. NORTHUMBERLAND.

GENERAL TOWNSHEND TO MR. GRENVILLE.

Audley Square, Sunday, March 4, 1764.

DEAR SIR,—I have heard so much observed upon the transaction relating to the letter to prevent two gentlemen summoned to Mr. Wilkes's jury, that I cannot help now communicating to you what first occurred to me upon the hearing of this.

Everybody seems to be surprised that the Government does not take this up, by publishing a reward for the discovery of the person who sent that false notice.

The notice came to a relation of mine, a very worthy gentleman of considerable property. He told me he was convinced that the thing came not from any agent of the Government.

He shall wait upon you whenever you please, but, my dear Sir, the enemies of the Government are at this moment taking advantage of its inaction to cast a suspicion upon it, which distant and uninformed minds in this kingdom may be greatly misled by. I own, for one, I am too much concerned at the impression this makes, and the difficulties it lays upon those who wish well to the credit of Government, to avoid inquiring of you why the Secretary of State can allow this matter, as well as the reflections upon the insult of the Morocco Ambassador, to remain unanswered, and the subject of every man's censure. A proclamation in the Gazette of the King's reward will probably lead you to the rascal who forged this, with certainty to the justification of the honour of Government, and will tend to show the multitude the poison which is every day prepared for it. Excuse this from a zealous friend[1], &c.

Geo. Townshend.

COMTE DE GUERCHY TO MR. GRENVILLE.

A Londres, 6 Mars, 1764.

Monsieur,—J'ai l'honneur de supplier votre Excellence de vouloir bien m'envoyer un ordre pour Messieurs les Barons de la Cour de l'Echiquier, contenant la permission de visiter les anciens titres qui y sont en depôt, et qui peuvent interesser la France, ainsi que votre Excellence a eu la bonté de me le promettre avant hier.

---

[1] General Townshend had been for some time very ardent in his support of Mr. Grenville's Administration. A few days after the date of this letter he became Viscount Townshend by the death of his father, on the 12th instant.

Je la supplie d'être bien persuadée de tous les sentimens distingués avec lesquels j'ai l'honneur d'être, Monsieur, de votre Excellence, &c., &c.   GUERCHY.

MR. GRENVILLE TO THE EARL OF MANSFIELD.

Downing Street, March 7, 1764.

MY DEAR LORD,—I am informed that Lord Hardwicke died yesterday, by whose death there is another vacancy of a Governor of the Charterhouse. You are fully apprized, my dear Lord, of the reasons which induced me to offer myself a candidate upon the last election, and will easily see of how much consequence it is that I should succeed upon the present occasion. I flatter myself that I shall meet with no difficulty, but whether I do or no, I shall feel the highest pleasure in knowing that I shall have your assistance and friendship, and therefore take the earliest opportunity of applying to you for them upon this occasion, and at the same time of assuring you of the sincere attachment and regard with which I am ever, &c., &c.   GEORGE GRENVILLE.

THE EARL OF MANSFIELD TO MR. GRENVILLE.

Wednesday, March 7, 1764.

MY DEAR SIR,—I am not engaged, except by my inclination to serve you upon every occasion in my power, and I think the Governors cannot make a better choice.

If you have a majority I dare say there will be no opposition, and that depends upon so few it may very easily be soon known. Let me intreat and advise you not to let anything precipitate or indecent be done.

There is always a reasonable time given, and there is a respect to the deceased, as well as the Governors, not to be too hasty. If the Archbishop is confined, the meeting may be held at Lambeth. It should be called as usual by the Archbishop. Something dropped from your Secretary which makes me give you this hint, and indeed opinion. I am most affectionately yours, &c.

MANSFIELD.

THE LORD CHANCELLOR TO MR. GRENVILLE.

March 31, 1764.

DEAR SIR,—The friendship I bear you, not from acquaintance, but from my opinion of your abilities and service to the King in your great office, oblige me in honour to write this letter.

The very extraordinary meeting we had last night at my house, gives me a despair of public business, since persons are friends to the Administration that disavow supporting even the King's measures, founded on their own advice.

The futility, the confusion, the embarrassments arising from thence, seemed not to make the impression I expected on the King's servants, and therefore I shall henceforward never do more than give my opinion at a meeting on the question proposed.

Having stated this by way of Proeme, I think I can't, without deserting the affection I bear you, but suggest that I see a thousand difficulties on the short B. proposed by the G^t. D——[1].

---

[1] The Duke of Bedford. The Cabinet was much embarrassed at this time by the proceedings of a very insignificant but very troublesome personage—the Chevalier D'Eon. He had recently published a quarto

I may be in all this, impolitic, but I think I am right, and that I suggest material matter for Government interest, incapable of being thoroughly discussed in a meeting too large for the Arcana Imperii. This I write only in honour and confidence to you personally, and no other, except a liberty to speak of it, if necessary, to my King and Master, whose interest, and that of the Constitution, are my only concerns. I have the honour to be upon the most honourable principles your most sincere friend, &c. HENLEY.

MR. GRENVILLE TO THE LORD CHANCELLOR.

Downing Street, March 31, 1764.

MY DEAR LORD,—I should be very unworthy of your friendship, aud the favourable opinion which you so kindly entertain of me, if I did not feel and value them

volume of *Lettres, Mémoires, et Négociations*, containing very scandalous libels on M. de Guerchy, the French Ambassador, and the Ducs de Nivernois and de Praslin, and some confidential letters of which he had surreptitiously obtained copies when he was Secretary to the Duc de Nivernois. The Law Officers were divided in their opinion as to the power of the Crown to send D'Eon out of the kingdom. Lord Halifax had said that he was *aussi méprisable qu'inviolable*. The Duke of Bedford had proposed a short Act of Parliament to supply the defect in the existing laws, and to enable the King at once to accede to the wishes of the whole Corps Diplomatique, who considered the publication of these libels as insulting to their order. The book caused a very great sensation as well at Paris as in London, and the Attorney General was ordered to prosecute M. D'Eon for the libel on M. de Guerchy. Walpole says that " D'Eon, even by his own account, is as culpable as possible, mad with pride, insolent, abusive, ungrateful, and dishonest, in short a complication of abominations, yet originally ill-used by his court, afterwards too well ; above all, he has great malice and great parts to put that malice in play." The state of the question respecting D'Eon is very amply explained in the following letter from Mr. Grenville to the Lord Chancellor.

as I ought, and endeavour to express the grateful sense I have of them.

They must indeed be doubly felt at this conjuncture, when the embarrassment arising from the circumstances which your Lordship so justly describes and laments must make them, if possible, still more welcome, from the support which not only I, but, what is much more material, the King's Government, has derived from the firmness and wisdom which, in this and many other instances, you have so honourably exerted.

I am extremely happy that my sentiments agree so perfectly with your Lordship's, concerning the short Bill that was proposed, and the difficulties to which it is liable. I see no other proper method of proceeding but that which was proposed by your Lordship last night, and which I then approved, and understood to be to take the opinion of the King's Advocate, and of the Attorney and Solicitor General, upon the question of the libel, and of the power of the King to send M. D'Eon out of the kingdom; to prosecute the printer and publisher as far as the law will allow; and if the opinion of the King's lawyers is, that M. D'Eon may lawfully be sent out of the kingdom, to do it immediately; but if they doubt, or give an uncertain opinion upon that point, then to send it by the King's order to the Judges for their opinion, who I cannot think will, in such a case as this, refuse to give it; but if they should, still I should think it right, as the King's Ministers would then have done all they could, and they are not answerable for so great a defect in the law and constitution as this seems to be, in many particulars that might be enumerated.

In these sentiments I have talked to the Duke of Bedford, who came to see me this evening, and I found him very ready to give up the plan of an Act of Parliament, from the objections that were made to it, and which I enforced again to-night more fully than yesterday.

After we had conversed a good while upon this subject, on which it was a great pleasure to me to find that we did not disagree, the Attorney General, whom I had desired to see before I knew of the Duke of Bedford's visit to me, came in, and declared his opinion, upon the matter being opened to him, to be, that the King had the power to order M. D'Eon out of the kingdom, and if he refused to go, then to send him away by force; and in this opinion he seemed to be extremely clear himself, and did not apprehend any doubt in the Advocate or Solicitor General. If they all join in a full and positive opinion of the legality, I imagine that the Secretaries of State will probably proceed and act in consequence of it, which will be the properest end to this embarrassing and vexatious transaction; but if it should be otherwise, I am still of the opinion I have mentioned above, and will tell the Secretaries of State so, when I see them, unless you disapprove of it, to whose judgment I shall most willingly submit my own, being perfectly satisfied that, in doing so, I shall act for the good of the King and of the Constitution. I write to you, my dear Lord, with the same confidence and freedom, and to you personally, with the same reserve to the King our Master only, whose sentiments I believe you will find comformable to what I have mentioned.

I have now informed you of all that I know concerning the present state of this business, which I hope is in a fair way to be brought to the best issue that can be given to it.

After this long letter I will trouble you no more, except to assure you that I am, with the truest respect and attachment, &c., &c. GEORGE GRENVILLE.

THE KING TO MR. GRENVILLE.

32 min. past 10 P.M. (April 2, 1764).

MR. GRENVILLE, fix Thursday, at one o'clock, with the Chancellor, for the passing the Bills.

MR. GRENVILLE TO THE KING.

10 min. past 12, Monday night, April 2, 1764.

I WILL take care to obey your Majesty's orders by informing the Lord Chancellor that your Majesty has been pleased to fix upon Thursday, at one o'clock, for coming to the House of Lords and passing the Bills. The warrants prepared by the Secretary at War, directing the agents to repay to the Paymaster General the monies remaining in their hands, are necessary to be signed by your Majesty before that money can be repaid, without which the Committee cannot be closed time enough for the Parliament to be up before Easter. I beg your Majesty's pardon for mentioning this necessity, that if it is not inconvenient to your Majesty, they may be signed and returned to the War Office to-morrow morning, as Mr. Ellis says they have been laid before your Majesty, and left to be signed for some days.

LORD HYDE[1] TO MR. GRENVILLE.

April 3, 1764.

MY DEAR SIR,—I have had too long a conversation with Lord Middlesex[2] for the compass of a letter: I will deliver the particulars by word of mouth at any time from this moment, that you please to appoint, excepting from about ten 'till two to-morrow, which I propose to give to the Post Office. The substance is honest, moderate, and sensible.

He has never been in a system of opposition, but wishes to have such a declaration of a favourable intention from His Majesty as will justify to himself his adherence to the friends of Government. He is not impatient of place or employment, yet intimated that he should duly weigh what might be offered now or to D. of Dorset; and some other thing, as I said at first, not of a nature to be delivered in this way. I am, with true devotion, &c., &c. HYDE.

MR. GRENVILLE TO THE KING.

10 min. past 11 P.M.,
Downing Street, Wednesday, April 4, 1764.

I HAVE but this moment received the honour of your Majesty's note on my return home from the House of Commons.

The Duke of Bedford had called here, but being told

[1] Thomas Villiers, second son of William, second Earl of Jersey; created Baron Hyde in 1756, obtained the Earldom of Clarendon in 1776, and died in 1786. Lord Hyde was at this time one of the Postmasters General.

[2] Eldest son of the Duke of Dorset.

that I was still at the House, he went away and left word that he would appoint some other time for our meeting. I am most truly sensible of your Majesty's goodness in apprizing me of the measure intended to be proposed, which seems to me not to be sufficiently considered for a question of this delicacy and importance, in which the least mistake would be attended with very unhappy consequences. The seizing M. D'Eon's papers by Sir John Fielding's warrant, would, I fear, in the present situation, contribute very little to put a stop to what is complained of, and would, if the legality of the proceedings should be even questionable, be the subject of much clamour and uneasiness.

I am happy beyond the power of expressing it, in your Majesty's resolution not to encourage any man to act against law, and I am fully satisfied that the wisdom and propriety of that resolution, as well as the goodness and justice of it, will upon mature consideration be evident to all.

It was intended yesterday that there should be a meeting this evening at Lord Halifax's, between the two Secretaries of State and the Attorney and Solicitor General, to consult together, and to settle agreeably to Law, every step, which shall be judged proper to be taken, in this transaction. I do not know whether this meeting has taken place, but I hope it has, as I think it the likeliest means of getting through this difficulty with safety, and with honour to your Majesty's Government.

I have informed my Lord Chancellor, and the Speaker of the House of Commons, of your intention to be at the House of Lords to-morrow at one o'clock to pass the Bills, and I will punctually obey your Majesty's orders with regard to burning the note, with which you have been pleased to honour me[1].

LORD HYDE TO MR. GRENVILLE.

April 8, 1764.

My dear Sir,—Lord Middlesex seems well pleased with the opening of his business; his plan is to mention to the Duke of Dorset what is in agitation, then to meet you in the House of Commons and appoint a day for him to wait on you and explain himself.

He proposes, likewise, to attend at Court pretty soon, and pretty often.

I am very happy in thinking and in acquainting you that my relation and friend Weymouth intends, if an opportunity properly occurs, to support your Supply Bill, and to apply to serious, and the principal business that comes before the House of Lords.

If you have as many friends as I wish you, you will be the strongest, and I verily believe you will be the best Minister this country ever had in similar circumstances. I am, &c. Hyde.

Sir John Rushout[2] has been at my door. I have not seen him, but I fancy he is impatient, dreading uncertainty during a long vacation.

---

[1] A memorandum in Mr. Grenville's hand prefixed to this draught of his letter to the King, states that he *burned the King's note accordingly.*

[2] M.P. for Evesham.

LE CHEVALIER D'EON TO MR. GRENVILLE.

A Londres, le 9 Avril, 1764.

Monsieur,—Si je n'eusse pas craint de déplaire à votre Excellence ou de la compromettre, j'aurois surement eu l'honneur de lui aller faire ma Cour, depuis mes premières sorties, pour la remercier, dans toute la sincérité de mon cœur, de l'humanité, et de la justice de votre Excellence, auxquelles seules je dois l'air que je respire, et la liberté dont je jouis; les deux seules choses que mes ennemis ne m'ont pas ravies—ennemis qui auroient été mes amis s'ils l'eussent voulu, et s'ils n'eussent pas violé, à mon égard, toutes les loix de l'honneur et de l'équité. Ils en veulent plus à mon ancien général qu'à moi. Mon attachement opiniâtre, et qui ne finira qu'avec ma vie, a fait et fait encore aujourd'hui tout mon crime. Je ne puis le regretter, quoi qu'on fasse. Vous êtes éclairé, vous êtes juste, vous êtes le Ministre d'un grand Roi, et d'un Roi vertueux, que ne puis-je, Monsieur, avoir le bonheur de vous entretenir un instant, pour vous faire sentir au doigt et à l'œil l'injuste et cruelle persécution que j'éprouve. Mes mémoires peuvent vous la faire assez appercevoir, et vous devez y reconnoître que je ne vous ai jamais trompé, lorsque j'ai eu l'honneur de traiter avec votre Excellence. Ma conduite est assez connue dans ma patrie et dans les différentes Cours où j'ai été. Je n'ai jamais fait un pas ici sans les sages conseils de M. le Comte de Viry, qui a bien voulu être mon Mentor.

Tous mes parens ont toujours joui de la réputation de la plus exacte probité, aussi ont-ils toujours été pauvres; et mon intention n'est pas aujourd'hui de dégénérer de leurs vertus pour m'enrichir. Je ne ferai valoir que ces dispositions, et elles suffisent auprès d'un Ministre aussi équitable que votre Excellence pour m'assurer la continuation de sa bienveillance et de sa protection. Je suis, avec respect, &c., &c.   Le Chev. D'Eon.

LORD HYDE TO MR. GRENVILLE.

April 9, 1764.

My Dear Sir,—I can't forbear congratulating you on a most public-spirited letter we have received from Mr. Allen[1], in consequence of one we writ intimating that the increase of revenue from the Bye and Cross Roads Postage restrictions that Parliament is going to enact on Franking, should belong to the public. He renounces it all, and will carry every farthing into the Treasury. I will order the letter to be sent to you.

The more I reflect on D'Eon's case, the more delicate and difficult I think the subject. The instances you took the trouble to give me are not in point. The Emperor's Resident abused the King personally, and, if I recollect right, the nation. The affront was such that the legality of the resentment was never considered.

Gillenbourg was conspiring against the Crown, and to bring in a Pretender, consequently was under the protection of no laws whatever.

Schutz's impertinence, if I recollect right, was about a writ for the Duke of Cambridge. He obeyed the order, without being obliged by law, and his dismission was not forgiven by his Sovereign. I have not looked into these things, but I doubt whether you will find a precedent for the intended exit, as I do, whether the

[1] Ralph Allen, of Prior Park, near Bath.

proceedings against Andrada and St. Germain can be justified.

But my concern is on your account personally, as I value you from my soul, and for my country more than I ever did any Minister in your situation, both on private and public considerations.

I hope, if we meet at Court or anywhere to-morrow, you will enable me to say something authentic to Lord Middlesex. He is nothing to me, but, as I think, he may be something to you. I know you will be cautious on D'Eon's affair, but I must be anxious, as I am so perfectly and affectionately yours. HYDE.

LORD EGMONT[1] TO MR. GRENVILLE.

Admiralty, April 16, 1764.

DEAR MR. GRENVILLE,—I return your draught of the King's Speech as you desired. Do not take it ill that I have scored a part of it which relates to the Fleet. I hope you will give another turn to the words inserted there. The circumflex about the word *ample*, and that about *other words* which follow, will point out the kind of alteration which would approach nearer to my ideas. And why should an assertion be so strongly enforced at the end of this sessions, which will certainly be reflected upon at the beginning of the next? You will thank me next year for suggesting this to you at present.

Let who will inform you otherwise, I will maintain and prove that you have not now (guardships included) in Great Britain seventeen ships of the line complete. The vast ordinary of the ships returned since the Peace

[1] Now First Lord of the Admiralty.

to Plymouth, Portsmouth, Chatham, &c., have hardly yet had a shilling laid out upon them.

Nothing worth mentioning can be saved out of the 4*l.* per man per month towards *extraordinary repair.* The wear and tear, &c., will consume it all. The extra estimate goes only to the building of new ships, or (what is nearly the same thing) to the large repair of four or five old ones, not to mention other services superadded since, to be incurred, and not provided for.

Few or none of the new ships are proportionably followed as they ought to be, by their rigging, sails, or cables. I question whether any one of the ships of the whole ordinary have any of their stores provided (which they ought all to have) in proportion to the state they are in, and to that degree of repair they appear to want, according to their respective surveys.

I am told that we have a tolerable quantity of hemp, and of sail-cloth, and are getting forward with anchors. But this is not sufficient. The stores are very empty of sails, rigging, and cordage, and these are necessary to keep pace with the condition of the hulks of all the ships, if we mean to maintain the fleet in a proper and respectable state. The hulls themselves (upon the whole fleet) may be computed to want little less than half their original cost, for rebuilding or repair. A very great sum, since the value of the present Navy, if complete, is above six millions.

Though the money and number of seamen voted is larger this year than heretofore, so is the tonnage of the fleet by the addition of one-half greater than it was in the year 1753; the services greatly more extensive, and the work in the yards, from the nature of those services, exceedingly increased.

The artificers in the yards with all this are reduced almost as low as they were in the year 1748, and are still unavoidably decreasing every day. Yet that reduction (though the fleet was then but two-thirds of what it is now) brought on such a decay in five or six years that, when the last war broke out, the danger of this country was extreme from this cause, and two years more of the like economy in this branch must have irretrievably ruined the whole Navy of this kingdom; which ought never to be forgot. You will judge, therefore, what will be the real case of the fleet, from these general and great outlines, without entering into any plausible detail, which would only tend to amuse and to deceive.

It is my duty in the place I hold to tell you this, and I am confident you will take it (as I mean it) a friendly intimation given, not with a light, a vain, or an unkind intention. And if you think it deserves regard, it will induce you to modify the expressions in the King's Speech with respect to this matter, in a different manner, which is at present all I mean to suggest in giving you this trouble. I am, &c., &c. EGMONT.

THE EARL OF MANSFIELD TO MR. GRENVILLE.

Monday, 3 o'clock, April 16, 1764.

MY DEAR SIR,—I have fully considered the inclosed draught[1], and I think of it now, as I did upon the first reading yesterday. It cannot be mended either in matter or form. I am most affectionately yours.

MANSFIELD.

[1] Of the King's Speech for the close of the session.

MR. GRENVILLE TO THE EARL OF EGMONT.

Downing Street, April 16, 1764.

My dear Lord,—Your letter, which I have this moment received, has given me very great concern, not from any uneasiness to any particular expressions in that part of the draft of the King's Speech which you object to, but from the nature of the objection itself, and of the principle upon which it is founded. I will not enter at present into the detail of the particular arguments you use, though with respect to many of them I can by no means agree, because the discussion of them, as they ought to be discussed, would exceed the bounds of this letter; but I must observe to your Lordship, as a general and great outline, that if 1,450,000*l.*, which is near double the sum which used to be allowed in times of peace, is not now a sufficient establishment to justify the words that are proposed to be inserted in the King's Speech, of provision being made " for maintaining the Fleet in a respectable state," I am, indeed, quite at a loss to say what will, or how to prevent that reflection which you are apprehensive will be made upon it at the beginning of next sessions. I am confident that the adoption of an opinion that this great sum is not sufficient to maintain the Fleet in a respectable state in times of peace would occasion great and universal uneasiness, and will be attended with many evil and dangerous consequences both at home and abroad. The inquiry which I have always recommended, and rejoice to hear that your Lordship is determined to make, into the expenditure of this vast sum, will, I hope, convince your Lordship that money may be spared out of the wear and tear for 16,000 seamen, and the great increase of the ordinary estimate of the Navy towards the repair of the Fleet. The most reasonable and knowing part of the world have long been persuaded that all the naval money is by no means applied in the most frugal manner, and, as I have thought so myself, I did resolve, when I had the honour to be in that office, to make the strictest and most careful examination into a matter of this great moment, and had taken some steps towards it, but my short continuance in that station prevented me from carrying it into execution. I am fully satisfied that the representation which you have made upon this occasion arises from no other motive but a sense of what you think your duty to the King, and to the public service; and I certainly feel it as you mean it, without any unkind intention towards me. You will allow me with the same freedom and friendly dispositions, and with that regard which everything that comes from your Lordship deserves, and will meet with from me, to say that it is impossible for me to think or admit, as I am at present informed, "that provision is not made for maintaining the Fleet in a respectable state." No other good reason but such an admission can be assigned to His Majesty, and the rest of his servants, for leaving them out, and such an admission I am by no means warranted at present to make. These are the reasons which make me think it advisable not to alter the King's Speech, in the manner which your letter, and the marks you have made in the draft, seem to point out. As to the word *ample*, if the omission of that epithet could be sufficient to answer your Lordship's intention, I should have less objection to that alteration than the other, though I think it of some consequence to have it thought abroad that ample provision has been made for maintaining the Fleet in a respectable state, agreeable to what was recommended to us so particularly, and which I think we have complied with. I am, &c., &c.

GEORGE GRENVILLE.

COUNTESS TEMPLE TO EARL TEMPLE.

April 17 (1764).

WINTER is come back again in town, I don't know how it may be in the country, but I hope you will take care not to be too late out in the evening, for it is very rheumatic weather, and many people are ill of that distemper. Sir James Lowther[1] keeps his bed with a fever, and her assembly for to-morrow is put off: Lord Pomfret[2] is to be married the first week in next month, and Miss Draycot is learning astronomy that she may figure a countess well; she says, as she never thought of aiming to that high station in life, she is not accomplished enough, and that she must study how to behave against the time happens, so she has began by astronomy. Lady Dalkeith[3] has bought all her weddingclothes, is very great with her, and laughs at her, as her Ladyship's usual behaviour is to everybody.

Mr. Wm. Hamilton[4] is going to Naples in the room

[1] M.P. for Cumberland. He married the eldest daughter of Lord Bute, and was created Earl of Lonsdale in 1784. He died in 1802.

[2] George Fermor, second Earl Pomfret, was married to Miss Draycot, with a large fortune, on the 30th instant.

[3] Eldest daughter of John, Duke of Argyll, widow of Francis, Earl of Dalkeith, and now the wife of Mr. Charles Townshend: she was afterwards created Baroness Greenwich, in her own right.

[4] Son of Lord Archibald Hamilton, and at this time M.P. for Midhurst. He had been one of the King's Equerries and Aide-de-Camp to General Conway. He was afterwards better known as Sir William Hamilton, the British Minister at the Court of Naples, and for his fine collection of Etruscan Antiquities, now in the British Museum.

of Sir James Grey. Mr. Grenville has done it for him at his own request, in the most handsome manner in the world, as he says; his wife has a terrible state of health, and he thinks the climate will do her good. This is all the news I can pick up, and so adieu! my dearest Long man [1]. A. T.

MR. GRENVILLE TO THE EARL OF HERTFORD.

Downing Street, April 18, 1764.

MY DEAR LORD,—It is with a very real concern that I write to your Lordship upon a subject of a very delicate nature, which must necessarily give you great uneasiness, as it had long done to me, and which I have therefore for some time past avoided, and would still avoid, if it were possible; but the regard I truly bear to you will not suffer me to be totally silent, and to let you hear from other hands what I heartily wish there was no occasion for me to inform you of. You cannot, I think, be surprised at hearing that the King has, for some time past, been much displeased with General Conway. That displeasure has at length determined His Majesty, however unwillingly, to part with him from the employment he held in the King's Bedchamber, and from the command of his regiment of Dragoons.

I have so often expressed to you my anxiety for his situation, and my grief for what was likely to be the consequence of it, that I hope it is quite unnecessary for me to repeat it. I should have been extremely

[1] Lord Temple was a very tall man, and probably somewhat awkward in his gait, as in the satirical publications of the day he was often styled "Lord Gawky." Lady Temple was very short, and therefore her Lord would appear to her a very *long* man.

happy if your Lordship's wishes and mine with regard to him could have prevailed, and that what had happened might be the effect of a mind, to use your Lordship's own expression, perhaps sometimes too delicate, and not of any permanent indisposition, or unbounded attachment to others. I agreed perfectly with you in thinking that in such a situation with a man of delicate feelings explanations were not likely to be of any good, and therefore I did not seek any.

All that could be said upon it must be known and felt, and to that I left it with a most sincere desire that it should take that turn which, I am confident, would have been most honourable to him and agreeable to you, and which no proper endeavours of mine, however unsuccessful, have been wanting to promote. Of the truth of this I believe General Conway himself is convinced, and I earnestly wish, from many considerations, that they could have been more effectual; but, as they could not, I can only lament what it was not in my power to remedy[1]. I feel most sincerely for you this unpleasing

[1] There can be no doubt of Mr. Grenville's sincerity in this declaration. It is true he had acquiesced in the dismissal of General Conway, but he had not recommended it, nay, he had in some degree endeavoured to prevent it. It may almost be said, that had he exercised his own judgment, and consulted his own wishes upon the subject, the measure would not have been adopted. The proposal came in the first instance from the King to Mr. Grenville, immediately upon His Majesty being made acquainted with Conway's adverse vote, and before he could have had any opportunity of communicating with Lord Bute, who was not then in London. General Conway, being of the King's Bedchamber, His Majesty considered it as an affair in which he was personally concerned, and although the dismissal was delayed at the recommendation of Mr. Grenville, yet the King seems never to have swerved from his determination of carrying it into execution at the first convenient opportunity; and therefore in any future consideration of this measure the policy of it should be attributed to the authority of the King alone. General Conway, writing to his brother upon the

situation, and how unhappy it is in every light, but I flatter myself that you have too much candour, and too just a judgment, not to see it as it is, or to suffer that affection which you must naturally feel for a brother to carry you beyond the bounds of reason and justice, and of what you owe to yourself, your King, and your country.

They are all deeply concerned upon this occasion, and I am persuaded, from your character and temper, will have their due weight with you, and that you will never permit the inclination of a private man to get the better of a public duty, which you have exercised with so much reputation to yourself, so much approbation from His Majesty, and with so much benefit to his kingdom.

These, my Lord, are my earnest wishes, and, I will truly add, the wishes and expectations of many who honour and respect you as I do, who shall always think

subject, says, "I don't exactly know from what particular quarter the blow comes; but I must think Lord Bute has, at least, a share in it, as, since his return, the countenance of the King, who used to speak to me *after all my votes*, is visibly altered, and of late he has not spoke to me at all." And Horace Walpole's gossip upon it adds, that "after long search and much information, I cannot fix the deed on any single man. There was but one man among the suspected that ever solemnly denied having a share in it; and he constantly did—I mean Lord Bute. All the rest have charged it on others, though still without disavowing having had a hand in it themselves. The King often afterwards protested to Lord Hertford that his Ministers forced him to it. Grenville declared that His Majesty was more eager for it than any of them. The Duke of Bedford alone was frank, and avowed that, though he had not recommended the measure, he had told his colleagues, when they proposed to remove Mr. Conway from the Bedchamber only, that it was foolish to provoke him by halves; and that to leave him his regiment, and take away the Bedchamber, would be telling other officers that they might oppose the Court with impunity."
—*Memoirs of George the Third*, vol. i. p. 403.

my best endeavours well employed whenever they can prevent anything that may be disagreeable to you, or that may in the least contribute to render your situation less pleasing and honourable. I am, &c., &c.

GEORGE GRENVILLE.

COUNTESS TEMPLE TO EARL TEMPLE.

April 19, 1764.

MY DEAR LONG MAN,—I received your note, and have paid it away this morning. I can send you no news for certain, but it is confidently reported that the Queen's brother and my Lord Halifax are to have the Ribbons[1].

They have served a writ upon M. D'Eon to make his appearance upon account of what he has said of Guerchy in his book; he did not at all understand what it meant, nor what he was to do, so went to Wedderburn, whom he knew abroad, and he explained it to him, but I don't find intends to have anything farther to do in the cause—I mean on his side. I hear he persists in saying he will print on; if he does I must read, though I do not approve of the man.

I am, &c. A. TEMPLE.

MR. JENKINSON TO MR. GRENVILLE.

London, April 21, 1764.

DEAR SIR,—I troubled you in my letter of last night, by Mr. Lloyd, of all that had passed 'till that time. The

---

[1] The Duke of Mecklenburg Strelitz and Lord Halifax were soon after invested with the order of the Garter.

talk concerning General Conway's dismission begins to be great.

The factious give out that other sacrifices are to be made, and try to make a common cause of it among the gentlemen of the Army, but without any prospect of success. Mr. Conway went out of town yesterday to Park Place, and the Duke of Devonshire went with him.

Great application is making for the office of Inspector of the River. The Commissioners of the Customs have presented and recommended Mr. Nicholas Ridley, who is at present a surveyor. Lady Harrington has sent to recommend him, and I have also received the enclosed letter of Mr. Amyand, and his own memorial on that subject.

There is vacant, by the death of Mr. Westwood, the office of Inspector of the Ale and Wine Licence Duties. The salary of this is 50*l.* per annum. There are, I believe, no perquisites. If you are not otherwise engaged for this, it might do for Craddock, Col. Hervey's friend, and for whom he has been applying very long.

I have seen this morning M. de Feronce[1], and have finished all that remained to be settled with him concerning the Princess's portion. Mr. Magens is approved of by him as a proper person to purchase the stock, and as Magens was so ill that he could not come to me, I thought it necessary to write to him the enclosed letter, which I hope you will approve of.

I talked to Mr. Worsley[2] this morning about what Lord Fife desires; I could not get him to say that even the small addition proposed by Lord Fife would

[1] Chief Secretary to the Hereditary Prince of Brunswick.
[2] M.P. for Orford and Surveyor General of the Board of Works.

not be a nuisance, and incommode the other inhabitants of Whitehall. He said, however, that it would be greatly less so than what had been proposed by Mr. Steele, and that if the King thought it a proper mark of favour to be conferred on Lord Fife, he should have nothing further to say against it. He was, however, very angry with Lord Fife for having written a letter to his clerk, attempting to influence him with a bribe. The clerk had brought the letter to Worsley, and he had shown it to the King, who approved of his rewarding the clerk's honesty by promoting him upon the first vacancy that happened. I intend to see Lord Fife to-morrow, and tell him what I have said to Mr. Worsley by your order.

I have had a letter from M. de Guerchy, who has had some silks seized upon one of his couriers. I have written him an answer in very general terms, and, as there has been so much clamour of late concerning the importation of French silks, you may depend upon my acting with the greatest caution on this occasion. I have, &c., &c. C. JENKINSON.

THE EARL OF SANDWICH TO MR. GRENVILLE.

Whitehall, April 23, 1764.

DEAR SIR,—From some conversation I had to-day with the Duke of Bedford, I fear he is a little uneasy at the disposal of the Red Ribbon without your having mentioned a word to him upon the subject, more especially as he says the King promised him that Colonel Draper[1] should have the first that was vacant.

[1] Afterwards Sir William Draper, who was the correspondent of "Junius."

I told him that I was persuaded your having said nothing to him was owing to your hurry to go to Bath, and to your taking it for granted that you could persuade Col. Draper to acquiesce upon the present occasion, which, however, as Mr. Jenkinson informs me, is not the case.

I think a letter from you to the Duke of Bedford in consequence of this hint will set everything right, which consideration must plead my excuse for the trouble I am giving you. I am, &c. SANDWICH.

MR. JENKINSON TO MR. GRENVILLE.

London, April 23, 1764.

DEAR SIR,—Lord Sandwich told me on Saturday morning that he had heard the King had promised Colonel Draper, upon the Duke of Bedford's application, should have the first Red Ribbon that was vacant, but that he thought it reasonable he should give way to Lord Clive on this occasion. I paid no attention to it then, but Lord Halifax said the same thing to me to-day at Court, and that he recollected it was as the Duke of Bedford represented; that Colonel Draper was very angry, but that he thought he ought to let Lord Clive have it, but advised me to talk to the Duke of Bedford, and get him to satisfy Draper. I saw his Grace immediately afterwards, who said that the King had certainly promised him the Ribbon for Colonel Draper; that he had also told you of it, but did not wonder you should forget it among your multiplicity of business. He added that he could not see why Lord Clive could not be satisfied with having it sent after him[1], but upon my showing

[1] Lord Clive was about to proceed to India as Governor General.

him the importance of his being clothed with that honour upon his first arrival in that country; and having observed to him how very good a friend Lord Clive was, he appeared sensible that the greatest attention should be shown him, but said that he wished I would write what he had said to you, and that he had a doubt whether there was at present any vacancy at all of a Red Ribbon. I have thus obeyed, therefore, his orders, and I send this letter by a messenger, as the contents of it are not fit for the perusal of a country Post Master, if they should have the curiosity of which Tommy Townshend[2] and the Opposition accuse them.

You expose me to great temptation by being out of town. I have resisted not only bribes, but the charms of the French Ambassadress, who sent for me this morning, and endeavoured to show me the propriety of her having her silks duty free. I refused, and left her very dissatisfied with me, but in hopes that you would be more kind when you came to town.

You have, I doubt not, already heard of the death of Madame Pompadour. She died last Sunday was se'ennight. I hope that this will not produce any alteration in the politics of the French Court. I have, &c., &c.

C. JENKINSON.

THE DUKE OF BEDFORD TO MR. GRENVILLE.

Bedford House, April 25, 1764.

DEAR SIR,— . . . . There has an affair of a much more serious nature, with regard to myself, considered as a part of the Administration, come

[1] M.P. for Whitchurch, afterwards Secretary of State and Viscount Sydney. He died in 1800.

to my knowledge since your going out of town, and which has given me infinite concern, as not only my own weight and reputation as a Minister, but even the King's honour seems essentially interested therein, and this is the superseding Colonel Draper's promise of the next Red Ribband to his detriment in favour of Lord Clive. You must very well remember, Sir, that I told you and the Earl of Halifax, some time ago, of the gracious promise His Majesty had made, on my recommendation, to Colonel Draper, of the first stall that should be vacant, in case there was none then actually vacant. Lord Halifax told me that he was sure there was none vacant, as Sir Charles Cook completed the whole number. This mistake was the sole cause of Colonel Draper's not having it then, and you yourself, as well as the Secretaries of State, seemed to approve the step I had taken. I will now leave you to judge how much it must have surprised me to have heard on Friday last, at Court, after the King's return from Chapel, that Lord Clive was to have immediately a vacant Red Ribband. I insisted upon it (and I had good reason to do so), that this could not be, as there neither was an actual vacancy, or had there been one, was it disengaged. But on my return to town on Easter Monday I not only found this report well grounded, but that it was done through your means, and that it was to take effect this day. Mr. Jenkinson will have informed you what I there said to him, and I was in hopes it would have been postponed 'till your return to town; but as I had never been consulted by any one, I did not chuse to interfere myself in the putting it off.

I must freely confess to you, that on my coming to Court to-day, after Lord Clive's investiture, I did remonstrate to the King that I thought Colonel Draper and myself had met with hard treatment. Mr. Draper being disappointed of that he had a right to expect, and which he actually might have had, had it not been for the misinformation Lord Halifax had received, and myself for being disavowed in what I had reported to an officer by His Majesty's permission.

The King, in return, said that he thought everything had been made easy by you towards Colonel Draper, and as I was willing to think that what has happened disagreeable with regard to myself had been occasioned solely by the multiplicity of the different businesses you have been engaged in at the close of this session, I did not press the King any stronger with regard to the disgrace that is thrown upon me. I am sorry to have been obliged to take up so much of your time in your short recess from business, but I was willing to let you know my feelings upon this subject before we talk it over at your return to town, where I hope to see you on Monday or Tuesday next. I am, &c., &c. BEDFORD.

THE EARL OF SANDWICH TO MR. GRENVILLE.
Whitehall, April 25, 1764.

DEAR SIR,—I find the Duke of Bedford so uneasy at the disposal of the Red Ribband that I cannot avoid sending this by express to tell you how much he is hurt, and how much it is to be wished we may find some means of rectifying this mistake. He told me to-day, upon seeing Lord Clive go into the Closet to receive the Order, that he was quite struck with astonishment, as the King had authorized him, some time since, to tell Colonel Draper he should have the first vacancy, which he had accordingly done, and that to see an arrangement contradictory to that promise carried into execution, without so much as its being mentioned to him, could not but give him the utmost concern.

I endeavoured to soften him by every means in my power, and repeated what I had told him before, that your not having communicated this matter to him was, I took for granted, owing to the hurry in which you left London, and to your not having doubted that you should have been able to persuade Colonel Draper to be satisfied to wait for another vacancy. He said he hoped and believed that I attributed it to the real cause; but still I cannot conceal from you that I think he feels a great deal, and considers himself as slighted both by his master and his friends. You will receive a letter from him by this night's post, I therefore thought it might not be amiss to prepare you for it before it comes to your hand.

In all cases of this sort, whenever any mischief is done, my whole attention is employed to find the remedy, and I can think of but one, which, if it has your approbation, may, I believe, be carried into execution.

The number of the Knights of the Bath is limited in the statutes of the Order (which I have examined) to 38, but there is a saving clause at the end which gives the King a power of adding to, altering, or amending any of those statutes by his Sign Manual. Why, therefore, should not the number be increased to 40? It would give you the means of obliging two other persons without a shilling of expense, and entirely remove all uneasiness from the mind of a very considerable and valuable man, who, I am well assured, you would not wish should have any just cause of complaint.

When Lord Halifax and I were in the Closet to-day

we told the King of the Duke of Bedford's uneasiness, and I suggested the idea of adding two to the Order as a very practicable and advisable scheme. His Majesty said he was afraid of drawing too many applications from other quarters, and added that he would consider of it; but from his manner of receiving the proposal it did not appear to me that he showed any averseness to it, and I have no doubt but that if you join in recommending the measure that he will easily be brought to agree to it, and this, I am positive, would set everything right; nay, if possible, would add to the Duke of Bedford's good disposition to the general system, and to yourself in particular.

My earnest desire to prevent everything that may prejudice our cause, and give the least advantage to our enemies (which any idea of discontent in a man of the Duke of Bedford's consequence must do), occasions my laying this before you. I shall therefore make no apologies for troubling you a second time upon this disagreeable affair. I am, &c., &c. SANDWICH.

THE EARL OF HERTFORD TO MR. GRENVILLE.

Paris, April 26, 1764.

DEAR SIR,—I shall freely acknowledge that I have seldom felt a more sensible uneasiness than I received from the perusal of your letter, though wrote with the utmost delicacy and regard. The disagreeableness of the subject could not be overcome by your friendly manner of treating it.

My brother's conduct in Parliament this winter I never approved of; I have represented to him strongly my sentiments on that head; I foresaw that he would incur His Majesty's displeasure, but I own to you that I did not foresee or imagine that the offence would be followed with such consequences, or that the merits of his military character could ever be obliterated by his Parliamentary conduct; civil offices are supposed to be conferred from favour or purchased by civil services, and it is natural to imagine that they may be forfeited by opposite causes; but employments in the army have commonly been thought to be out of the reach of Ministerial influence; very few instances to the contrary have occurred in our time, and those have always been considered as violent and extraordinary. It is particularly grievous to me that my brother, for an offence so usual in our Government, should be treated with such unusual severity, and I may add that the weight of this punishment falls the heavier, on account of the public employment with which His Majesty has at present been pleased to honour me.

Nothing could possibly have given me greater consolation than your assurances that my conduct at this Court has been so happy as to obtain His Majesty's approbation; and your assurances on this head were the more agreeable, as I should have been inclined from this and other incidents to have entertained very melancholy apprehensions to the contrary.

But though no personal displeasure shall ever relax my zeal in His Majesty's service, yet I am afraid that I may henceforth have less influence in promoting it, and that the French Court, seeing my family at home distinguished by such particular marks of resentment, may, on occasion, pay less regard to my sentiments and remonstrances.

This frankness of mine in declaring my different

reasons of complaint will, I hope, be regarded with indulgence; I have already made you my confidant with respect to some of them. It must be contrary to His Majesty's interest to lessen in any degree my credit with the Court where I reside, and if my situation contains any disagreeable circumstance which is of a public nature, and cannot be concealed, it ought, in my humble opinion, in sound policy, to be corrected.

I have, &c., &c.   HERTFORD.

MR. JENKINSON TO MR. GRENVILLE.

London, May 1, 1764.

DEAR SIR,—I have this day had the honour of your kind letter of the 20th ultimo. I have solicited such of our friends who are proprietors of East India Stock, in the manner you have desired, and I have acquainted Lord Clive of the directions you have given in this respect. I have tried to see his Lordship, that I might mention to him the advice you give him, that he should take no definitive step but in concert with his friends. I have not yet been able to see him, and I think it more prudent not to write it, lest it should be supposed to imply more than was intended.

The enclosed note from Mons. de Marmora[1] came to-day, desiring that I would open it, if you was not in town; I have done what is desired in it with respect to Mons. de la Perrier's baggage, and I sent word that you would not be returned 'till to-morrow evening.

There is no news but what is lately arrived from the East Indies; I know no more of that than what I read

---

[1] Envoy Extraordinary from Sardinia.

in the public papers; it is affirmed that Monson has been defeated by one whom we have learnt the art of war, when he commanded the sepoys in our service, but who is now become a Prince of the country, and turned against us.

Lord Clive's friends think that this event will be of use to them at the General Court to-morrow, as it makes Lord Clive's presence more necessary in India.

I rejoice to hear of the kind and polite reception you met with at Bristol. It will have a good effect; the fame of it has reached here already. I have, &c.

C. JENKINSON.

I hope that Colonel Draper called on you at the Bath, and made suitable apologies. He assured Mr. Drummond that he would do so, and that he was in perfect good humour.

LORD CLIVE TO MR. GRENVILLE.

Berkeley Square, May, 1764.

DEAR SIR,—The great troubles of body and anxiety of mind which I have experienced for these three months past, must convince every impartial person how much I have sacrificed for the good of the East India Company; indeed, the inclinations which you were pleased to testify for my going abroad had more weight with me than the persuasions of all my other friends put together; at last, when all difficulties seem to have been surmounted, and I had prevailed upon myself to undertake a voyage, much against my own inclination, and the interest of my family, and under restrictions very disagreeable in many respects, the Directors, from timidity and want of capacity, refuse to give me those powers which they have already given and sent to Mr. Vansittart, and without which it would be entirely out of my power to render the Company the least service, and would at the same time cover me with shame and disgrace among the natives and Europeans, who by this time are acquainted with the extent of those powers given to another.

Whatever proofs I may have shown of my disinterestedness, in giving way upon every point where that question hath been agitated, I cannot recede an inch where my own honour and reputation are at stake, and I am determined never to appear in India with less authority (when I ought, if possible, to have much more) than my predecessor, Mr. Vansittart.

As far as concerns myself, I am very happy in the reflection of disengaging myself from a service which, from the opposition which has been given, must at all events make it very disagreeable. I am, &c., &c. CLIVE.

LORD VERE TO MR. GRENVILLE.

St. James's Square, May 3, 1764.

SIR,—I would have attempted to have paid my respects to you, but conclude your absence will have occasioned you visitors enough, and variety of applications and business; it is, therefore, with the greatest regret that I even trouble you with this; but as I am informed that the Bishop of London can't possibly recover, and my brother is at his diocese, and nobody here to solicit for him but myself, I hope you will forgive me.

He was the senior bishop to the present Bishop of

London when it was given him, and is now the senior of any who would accept of it, and I think has been near eighteen years Bishop of Hereford[1]. I therefore hope so glaring a slight will not a second time be put upon him, and, indeed, upon the family.

I will venture to say his character and conduct does not deserve it, and I shall hope his being a gentleman may not be an objection; I must, therefore, entreat the favour of you to represent his case properly to His Majesty, who all the world knows is always disposed to do justice to all his subjects, in whatever station they may be; for, to speak freely to you, I must own it is in that light I see it. I am, &c., &c. VERE.

THE BISHOP OF PETERBOROUGH TO MR. GRENVILLE.

Clarges Street, May 5, 1764.

SIR,—I think myself very unfortunate in being prevented from waiting upon you at this time, when I have so much reason to wish for the earliest opportunity of expressing my acknowledgments for the very kind part you have taken in promoting my application to His Majesty.

Mr. Ryder has given me particular pleasure by assuring me, from you, that I am happy in having His Majesty's gracious disposition so entirely approved by you, and the rest of his Ministers. I shall consider this as the strongest call to such a conduct on my part, as may not discredit the honour of your patronage, nor disap-

---

[1] Lord James Beauclerc, seventh son of the first Duke of St. Albans, and grandson of King Charles the Second. He continued Bishop of Hereford until his death in 1787.

point His Majesty's expectations in placing me in so important a station as the See of London [1].

The Bishopric of Peterborough, when given to me, was estimated at 1000 guineas per annum clear of deductions. By some little improvements, which have been made by me, it may perhaps be now set at eleven hundred pounds clear.

My vicarage at Twickenham, at the extended value, is 200*l.*, clear about 140*l.*

I have ventured to take the air this morning, and hope in a few days to be able to pay my respects to you. I have the honour to be, &c., &c.

RIC. PETERBOROUGH.

THE BISHOP OF GLOUCESTER [2] TO MR. GRENVILLE.

Prior Park, May 5, 1764.

HONOURED SIR,—The goodness which His Majesty has been graciously pleased, on occasion, to express towards me to some of my friends has emboldened me in the liberty I now take.

We have a report here of the Bishop of London's death; and that unaffected consciousness of the real want of subjects adequate to such a station, which should naturally discourage my pretensions, is, I do not know how, by the delusion of comparison, the very thing that stimulates them; being almost persuaded of this, that my concurrents, whoever they may be, are likely to keep me in countenance.

I am sure it was necessary, however, to make some

---

[1] Dr. Terrick was translated from the See of Peterborough to that of London, on the death of Dr. Osbaldiston.
[2] Dr. Warburton.

apology for my presumption before I ventured to solicit your good offices, on this occasion, with His Majesty; I who have nothing to support my pretensions but an unfeigned zeal for the service of Religion and of my Royal Master; and the honour of being allowed to subscribe myself, Sir, your most faithfully attached servant,

W. GLOUCESTER.

MR. GRENVILLE TO THE BISHOP OF GLOUCESTER.

Downing Street, May 8, 1764.

MY LORD,—The honour of your Lordship's letter of the 5th of this month came to my hands too late last night for me to be able to acknowledge it, which I would not omit the first opportunity of doing.

The report of the Bishop of London's death, at the time it reached you was not true, but he is so dangerously ill that it is hourly expected, and in this situation your Lordship will easily believe that some consideration must necessarily have been given to the appointment of a successor to that See, in case the event shall happen, which was thought to be probable before my arrival in town from Bath.

When I spoke to the King upon this subject, I found that His Majesty had destined the Bishop of Peterborough to the bishopric of London, even so early as when the present Bishop of London was appointed to it, and the King considered himself as too strongly engaged to depart from it upon the present occasion.

This destination will, I believe, certainly take effect, and has prevented any farther application with regard to it, but you will allow me to assure you, my Lord, that

His Majesty, before I received your letter, was pleased to express himself in the most gracious and favourable manner towards you, and consequently there was not the least necessity for any apology from you, especially to me, who entertain a very just opinion of your Lordship's learning and character, and shall embrace with pleasure any proper opportunity of expressing the sincere regard and esteem with which I am, &c., &c.

GEORGE GRENVILLE.

THE PRINCESS AMELIA TO COUNTESS TEMPLE.

Gunnersbury, May 10, 1764.

I AM most sincerely obliged to you, my dear Lady Temple for your Poems[1]; I am no connoisseur, which I am more sorry for now, than I have ever yet been, for what I shall say to you in their praise, can give you no pleasure, coming from me, but that I feel obliged to Mr. Walpole to have waked them into life. The Lady and the Spider is charming, and the moral so good and so right, that I wish everybody would practise it.

Dear Lady Temple, you are so well-bred, and humane to everybody, that I almost suspect you of having been so indulgent to your friends to have these works printed to reform them, by amusing them. My letter would be too long, if I was to commend all I admire: here I stop, with assuring you that your kind friendship to me, is returned sincerely by your friend, AMELIA.

---

[1] The volume recently printed at Strawberry Hill.

THE BISHOP OF GLOUCESTER TO MR. GRENVILLE.

Prior Park, May 11, 1764.

HONOURED SIR,—I have your obliging favour of the 8th.

I entirely agree with you, that "His Majesty's destination, once known, ought to prevent any further application." And I readily believe, that before I wrote my letter, "some consideration must necessarily have been given to the appointment of a successor to the See of London."

My mistake lay in not conceiving that the consideration had taken place so early. However, I have presumption enough in His Majesty's goodness, to hope that now the same early consideration of a future event will be had in *my* favour.

The King's gracious disposition towards me is my felicity. It is all that a faithful subject has any pretence to: and in the service of so good a Master I shall be still content with my fortune, *Bene facere, et male audire.* I have the honour to be, &c., &c.

W. GLOUCESTER.

COUNTESS TEMPLE TO THE PRINCESS AMELIA.

May 11, 1764.

MADAM,—I cannot help intruding upon your Royal Highness's time so much as to return ten thousand thanks for your gracious acceptance of my—I am ashamed to call them Poems; there are not many books printed, but those that are I dispose of to my best friends and most intimate acquaintance, knowing their partiality to me; amongst the former your Royal Highness's goodness encourages me to presume to place you.

But now, Madam, give me leave to divest you of your Royalty—only for a few minutes—and imagine you of a lower class; a *Poetess* is nothing without imagination—a Poetess, ha! ha! ha! I say, Madam, let me take away your Royalty, and I may, without presumption, value myself upon having a sincere friendship and esteem for the most sensible, most amiable, and best of women; but that I may not let you remain too long in this diminished state, I beg leave to subscribe myself, with much sincerity and due form, Madam, your Royal Highness's most devoted, most obliged, and most respectful humble Servant, ANNA TEMPLE.

LADY HYDE[1] TO MR. GRENVILLE.

The Grove, May 14, 1764.

SIR,—Encouraged by a thorough sense of your friendship, I venture to lay before you a case that shall not be a request till you think it practicable. I feel neither vanity, ambition, or an improper impatience, but reverence to my ancestors, justice to my situation and posterity, and a grateful conformity to the late Lord Hyde's testamentary disposition, make it a duty in me to offer it.

By his will, which his father approved, I became the

[1] Charlotte, wife of Thomas Villiers Lord Hyde, and eldest daughter of William third Earl of Essex, and his Countess Jane, eldest surviving daughter of Henry Hyde, the last Earl of Clarendon and Rochester, grandson of the Lord Chancellor Clarendon. The Earldom solicited by Lady Hyde was not granted until 1776.

heiress of their family; it behoves me to endeavour to obtain the honours, and to support the dignity of it. My Lord applied to the Ministers in the late reign, for me to obtain one of the principal titles that lapsed by the death of my grandfather, the Earl of Clarendon and Rochester. Mr. Pelham told me that might or would be granted, but advised to be at first contented with the Barony, which ceased with my uncle, and which we might both enjoy; (and was certainly, for that reason, most pleasing to me ;) our memorial, from compliance, went then no farther. The late King, however cautious in augmenting the Peerage, no sooner saw it than he graciously declared, as Lord Granville often assured us, that he should have a pleasure in granting the request.

His Majesty listened to the argument, that it bore rather the appearance of a revival than of a creation : he condescended to recollect the station and services of my great-great-grandfather, and that the Hyde family had, ever since the Restoration, been distinguished and supported by the Crown. Such has been Royal goodness to that faithful servant, Minister, and Patriot, and his descendants: even his youngest son was made an Earl, and both his sons enjoyed the chief honours and employments of this country.

His grandson, my grandfather, had 4000*l*. a year from the Post Office till his death, besides former bounties, which circumstances I only mention that my petition may not appear ill-founded, I being lineally from that Chancellor, and being the first representative of his family who has not been higher in rank than I am, and who has not been favoured with emoluments: I omit some relating to his posterity, too great for a subject to mention[1]; but I cannot omit indulging in one, and I think you will join with me in it; it is the known stand he made, when first in credit with his King, against the unconstitutional forwardness for monarchical power, by which virtuous spirit, though he was a sacrifice then the third time for his adherence to his principles, that liberty was preserved which enabled the nation to call in the Prince of Orange and the House of Hanover.

Without saying more, I can but flatter myself that the title of Clarendon, so considered by the Crown, so dear to the Constitution, so known and respected in history, may be delivered down, as others have been, through the same blood to later posterity, without detriment to Peerage, or a fear of a precedent from similar reasons.

My Lord don't wish for it to descend to his, by any future marriage, neither would it be coveted by either, but from the injunctions and considerations above mentioned. The same rank already exists in his, and in my father's family: actuated by strong motives, powerful on me, I may seem to urge the like arguments; without them I should not presume to ask such an honour; but whatever pretensions I may imagine, we should accept the dignity as the highest mark of goodness, and acknowledge it with constant gratitude: no neglect and ill usage affected that we felt for the title conferred by the late King: a greater, if possible, we should consistently for ever retain on the completion of all we desire.

---

[1] Alluding to the marriage of Anne Hyde, the Lord Chancellor Clarendon's daughter, with James, Duke of York, afterwards King James the Second.

I heartily wish, out of regard to your time, that I could have shortened this application, but certainly I should have been blameable not to have made it, having such a friend and a relation to represent it to the most benevolent of Kings.

The time for the importunity, I, with entire confidence, leave to your judgment and goodness. I am, with great regard, Sir, &c., &c. C. HYDE.

MR. GRENVILLE TO MR. THOMAS PITT[1].

Downing Street, May 15, 1764.

MY DEAR SIR,—I did not think, when we parted, that I should have any occasion of troubling you with a letter before I should have the pleasure of seeing you again, and, indeed, I give so little credit to the report about which I now write to you, that it scarcely seems worth the while to take notice of it, though my desire to recall to your mind and my own what has passed in any way relative to that subject, has prevailed upon me to do it. It has been reported industriously, that when I met Mr. Horace Walpole at your house I told him that if General Conway voted in Parliament according to his conscience he was unfit to have any command in the King's army, and it has been said that this absurd and monstrous falsehood has not been discouraged by Mr. Walpole himself. I know, as you must, who was present at all which passed, that the first part is void of all foundation, and I am persuaded that the latter is so likewise, as the

---

[1] M.P. for Old Sarum: only son of Thomas Pitt, of Boconnoc, elder brother of William Pitt, afterwards Earl of Chatham. Thomas Pitt was created Lord Camelford in 1784, and died at Florence in 1793.

belief of it would be as great an injustice to him as the former would be to me.

You must remember that upon your informing me of the constant expressions of friendship and good opinion which Mr. Walpole did me the honour to profess to you with regard to me, and of his firm persuasion that General Conway was in no plan or system of opposition, which I even then apprehended to be the case, and I understood Mr. Walpole wished I should be satisfied was not so. I told you that I had no objection to hear anything which he would say to me upon that subject. In consequence of which I met him in the most friendly manner at your house, where nobody else but yourself was present. Our conversation was of the most open and confidential kind; but so far was I from making use of the expression which I have mentioned above, or anything like it, that I am quite sure, and when you come to state it you cannot but recollect, that the very reverse of it was the truth. I begun with saying to Mr. Walpole what I had often before said to you, that I hoped no officer, either civil or military, would be dismissed from the King's service for giving his opinion upon this or that particular measure agreeable to his conscience; but that if any gentleman of high rank in either capacity should engage in an open, regular, and systematical opposition, it seemed to me very difficult, and unlikely for him to continue long in that situation; and that I was so far from seeing any exception in such a case in favour of the army, that I thought a military command, in factious hands, would be more dangerous to the public safety than most civil offices could possibly be, which I exemplified in the case of tumults and insurrections against the Government.

This brought on the discussion of the difference which has been endeavoured to be established in favour of military offices, and of the several instances of the contrary practice. The result of this conversation was Mr. Walpole's repeating frequently to me what he had before said to you, that he was fully convinced that General Conway had no thoughts of engaging in any system or plan of opposition, and that he believed Mr. Conway would have no difficulty whatever in saying so, though Mr. Walpole could not take upon him to make that declaration for a man who had such delicate feelings upon matters of this kind, to whom, therefore, after having declared his own conviction upon it, he desired to refer himself upon this subject. I told Mr. Walpole that General Conway had called upon me a few days before, and that I had missed him by being abroad when he came, but that I should be very glad to see him whenever it was agreeable to him. The next evening was mentioned for that purpose, and Mr. Walpole undertook to let General Conway know it, which he did accordingly, and the next day, after two or three notes had been exchanged between us (in which General Conway desired that the Duke of Richmond might be present to hear what passed), the Duke of Richmond and he came to me. General Conway had understood from Mr. Walpole that I had something to say to him, or there was something which I wished to be satisfied in, and to have explained by him. I assured him that was a mistake; that I had no proposition whatever to make, nor any explanation to ask, but that I was ready to hear anything which he should think proper to say to me. The conversation soon fell upon the same subject, and was to the same effect with that which passed the night before at your house. The same distinction laid down by me between a conscientious opinion relative to this or that particular measure and a regular systematical opposition, and the same sentiments expressed by me with regard to each of them. The same observations about the army and the civil offices, and the several instances which had happened in the former. The conclusion was that General Conway declared that he had taken no engagements, nor had then any intention of entering into a regular and systematical plan of opposition; but that he did not understand that by this any line should be drawn between him and some in the Opposition, to whom he owed both friendship and obligation, and mentioned, for this purpose, the Dukes of Grafton and of Devonshire. This was the account which was agreed to be given, where any should be necessary, of that conversation, and I have not the least reason to think that any other has been given. This was the account which I gave to you and to Mr. Walpole in the House of Lords, below the Bar. I have never spoken to Mr. Walpole nor writ to him since. What happened in consequence of it at that time, and what has since happened, you and all the world are no strangers to. My long tale is told, which I have done to recall to your memory the state of facts, that if they are true, as I am sure they are in all the essential parts, you may recollect such as passed before you, and through you, and by your recollection confirm me in them, or set me right if in any particular of less moment I have erred, which I certainly have not done knowingly. If in every conversation with you, if in that with Mr. Walpole before you, if in that with General Conway, and with everybody else with whom I have spoken at all upon the subject, I have invariably made the distinction between a conscientious opinion and a systematical opposition, you will know how true it is that I told Mr. Walpole, that if General Conway voted in Parliament according to his conscience, he was unfit to have any command in the King's army; a declaration which, I may venture to say, those who know me will not believe me capable of making to any one, and which, in this instance, appears, from what I have before stated, not only not to be true, but to be the very reverse of the truth.

I know not how to credit what has been said of Mr. Walpole's not having discouraged this scandalous falsehood. Write me word whether you have heard anything of this honourable report, what part of this transaction you remember, and what you think of the whole of it. If it were not for the circumstance of Mr. Walpole's name being mentioned in it, and for the pains which I am told have been taken to propagate it, I should have let it pass unnoticed in the bundle of lies of the day, and have saved you the trouble of this long letter upon this tiresome subject.

I wish you all the health and happiness which you can propose to yourself from your excursion into the country, and I am ever, with the truest affection and regard, &c., &c.   GEORGE GRENVILLE.

MR. THOMAS PITT TO MR. GRENVILLE.

Boconnoc, May 25, 1764.

MY DEAR SIR,—I am as much surprised as you can be at the report you mention, and the misrepresentation of what passed at my house, and will venture to answer for it, that Mr. Walpole is so far from being capable of having silently acquiesced in it, that I am sure he will make it his business to state the direct contrary when he knows of the report, which I shall not fail to acquaint him with by letter. The facts are, I believe, precisely as you represent them.

The meeting at my house did take its rise from expressions of friendship and good opinion towards you, which Mr. Walpole had used in conversation with me, and from a firm persuasion that he had expressed to me that General Conway was not engaged in any *plan* or *system* of opposition.

It was in consequence of this, for the mutual satisfaction of yourself and Mr. Walpole, that I was very desirous of that meeting to which you both consented. I am ready to testify that in that conversation there appeared in you every mark of kindness and friendly disposition to General Conway; that you did frequently distinguish (what I have heard from you so often, not only upon this, but upon many other occasions) the difference between a *conscientious vote* upon a *particular measure*, and a regular *system* of opposition to Government, which by many arguments you proved must render any one equally unfit for a high rank in military command, as for civil employment, and in some instances, as in cases of tumults and insurrections, more dangerous to the safety of the King and Commonwealth.

It was upon this distinction between a *conscientious vote* and a *system* of *opposition*, that far the greatest part of the conversation turned, nor did you in the least demand any explanation with regard to the votes which General Conway had given, but wished only to know whether he was in a declared *system* of *opposition* to *Government*.

Mr. Walpole again repeated, what he had before professed to me, his firm belief that he had taken no such engagement, but would not by any means take upon himself to answer for it, and referred you to any certainty upon that head to General Conway himself, as the only person capable of giving it to you. You mentioned on this occasion that Mr. Conway had been at your door, when you had not been at home, but that you were ignorant whether or no anything more was intended by it than a mark of mere common civility, and expressed a readiness if not a desire to see him; upon which the meeting with Mr. Conway was agreed upon for the next evening, which Mr. Walpole undertook to apprize him of.

I must not omit to take notice that through the whole course of this conversation, Mr. Walpole principally insisted upon the high point of honour and delicacy of sentiment of his friend; that he thought him incapable in any situation of doing anything but from mere motives of conscience and honour, and did not at all doubt but that time would make the purity and integrity of his sentiments free from any bias of party consideration whatever.

When you communicated to Mr. Walpole and me below the Bar the result of your conversation with Mr. Conway, you told us, to the best of my recollection, that Mr. Conway had declared that he was not then engaged, nor did at that time intend to engage, in any system of opposition; but that at the same time he desired not to be understood to intend to separate himself from persons to whom he had friendships and obligations, or something to that purpose, and I believe you said he named the Dukes of Grafton and Devonshire.

This, Sir, is the state of the whole transaction, as far as I have any knowledge in it, and which I am ready to testify. It is impossible for me from memory to recall the particular terms and expressions which were made use of, but I am very well satisfied I have given the true purport and meaning of them.

After this I do not wonder it is mortifying to you to have so gross and palpable an absurdity put into your mouth as that "if Mr. Conway voted in Parliament according to his conscience, he was unfit to have any command in the King's army." Whoever knows you will easily see how little it is *probable*—I who know and was witness to the transaction declare it *to be false;* unless indeed that General Conway's conscience inclining him to a *systematical opposition* to the King's Government, that in that case you may have been construed to have said, what in my poor judgment you may have said wisely, that *such a conscience* must render it very difficult and unlikely for him long to continue in his situation.   I am, &c., &c.   THOS. PITT.

MR. CADOGAN[1] TO MR. GRENVILLE.

May 25, 1764.

SIR,—I am informed by letters from the Duke of York, that his Royal Highness, by experience, finds his income inadequate to the expenses of his foreign expe-

[1] Charles Sloane Cadogan, son of Lord Cadogan, and M.P. for Cambridge. He was Treasurer to the Duke of York, Surveyor of the King's Gardens, &c.

dition, and in consequence of that has commanded me to desire that you will, in his name, lay this circumstance in the most respectful manner before the King, and add his request that His Majesty will be graciously pleased to take into his consideration the impossibility he must be under in his present situation of ascertaining and exactly regulating his expenses, and consequently judging with precision what the exceeding may be; but, if it should not appear an unreasonable one, hopes it will be made up to him. His Royal Highness will receive any mark of the King's kindness to him on this occasion with gratitude, in proportion to the great concern he feels at troubling him with this application, which nothing but the necessity of it could make him do.

After his Royal Highness's officers, other servants, stable expenses, and what remains here of his establishment are paid, I am not certain of being able to remit to him abroad above 1500*l.* a quarter; what the exceeding on the whole will be I am not in a situation to make any conjecture about, but the Duke seems to think about 4000*l.*; the only power I have of judging is from the money already drawn for, which inclines me to fear it will be more rather than less.

I have, &c., &c. W. CADOGAN.

MR. GRENVILLE TO THE DUKE OF YORK.

Downing Street, May 25, 1764.

SIR,—I received this morning the honour of a letter from Mr. Cadogan communicating to me your Royal Highness's commands, that I should lay before the King in the most respectful manner, for His Majesty's consideration, the impossibility which you must be under in your present situation of ascertaining and exactly regulating your expenses, and your hopes that the exceeding, which Mr. Cadogan says in his letter, your Royal Highness seems to think about 4000*l.*, may be made up.

I immediately laid the contents of Mr. Cadogan's letter before His Majesty, who has ordered me to inform your Royal Highness, that he has been pleased to give me directions to pay to Mr. Cadogan the above-mentioned sum of 4000*l.*, or such part of it as Mr. Cadogan shall find it necessary to apply for. I have the honour to be, &c., &c. GEORGE GRENVILLE.

LORD VERE TO MR. GRENVILLE.

Hanworth House, May 26, 1764.

SIR,—I am extremely sorry to trouble you again so soon, but since I had the honour of waiting on you the other day, I have been informed by those who have the care of the Duke of St. Albans' affairs during his absence, that, amongst many other inconsiderate parts of his very imprudent conduct, he has neglected since his father's death to apply for another life's being added in his Patent of Hereditary Registrar of the High Court of Chancery; it is, indeed, only a matter of form, but, however, should have been mentioned to the King before, and not have been omitted so long. May I therefore request of you to lay the case properly before His Majesty, and obtain his directions for the adding another life, as has always been done upon such application, ever since the grant by King Charles the Second.

I am, &c., &c. VERE.

ANONYMOUS[1] TO MR. GRENVILLE.

(May 27, 1764.)

SIR,—His Majesty having determined to give the Bishopric of London to Dr. Terrick, a man in himself most unexceptionable, it is hoped by those who regard His Majesty's honour, that care will be taken to prevent the Bishop's taking into his patronage Dr. Butler[2], a particular friend of the infamous Wilkes, with whom he lived in the closest connexion two summers at Winchester, whilst he was engaged in the *North Briton*. It is feared the Bishop may make him his Chaplain, or show distinguished marks of his favour to this man, from his intimacy with him in Bishop Hayter's time; to whom he was a tool, and had a great hand in blowing the flame betwixt the said Bishop and Lord Harcourt on one side, and those on the other side, in the family at Leicester House, where he acted as Hayter's spy; and has since distinguished himself by writing two pamphlets against the present Ministry; who has often vindicated in conversation that infamous *North Briton*, No. 45; who at first shammed *Orders;* then was preferred, when he got real *Orders*, by Sir J. Astley, a true Blue, and who is *now* acting the part of a Whig, so he calls himself; but he is much nearer to the character of a Jesuit. Despise not this intimation from a real friend to His Majesty and yourself.

---

[1] In a disguised handwriting.
[2] The author of *Some Account of the Character of the late Right Honourable Henry Bilson Legge*, and of several political tracts. He was made Bishop of Oxford in 1777, and translated to Hereford in 1788.

THE EARL OF HERTFORD TO MR. GRENVILLE.

Paris, May 29, 1764.

Sir,—Upon being informed from England that His Majesty has thoughts of making a promotion from the Earls' bench, give me leave by your means to throw myself at His Majesty's feet, and to implore his favour, in case such a promotion should take place, to advance me to the title of Marquess, which was long enjoyed by my family[1].

I need not enter into any detail upon this subject to a Minister who is so well informed of every advantage I can pretend to derive from my birth: I shall only say they are such as will, I flatter myself, make my title to that honour as little liable to objection from the world as any person whom His Majesty may have in his view.

If my poor services at this Court have any kind of merit, as you have been pleased to say, it would make me particularly happy to receive this mark of His Majesty's approbation of them at a time when I must be anxious to convince the Ministers at Versailles, where the King thinks proper to employ me, that I am so happy as to enjoy his favour.

You, Sir, are the only one of His Majesty's Ministers to whom I write upon this occasion, and I shall be grateful if you are pleased to undertake my cause. I do not mean to be deficient in any proper application, and particularly to the noble Lord in whose department I serve, if you give me encouragement; 'till then, I hope you will treat my petition with as much secrecy as your judgment shall think necessary to my present circumstances. I have, &c., &c. Hertford.

[1] Lord Hertford did not obtain the promotion until 1793.

LORD VERE TO MR. GRENVILLE.

Hanworth House, May 29, 1764.

Sir,—I return you many thanks for the honour of your letter, but as ignorant people always wonder, I must own it surprised me; my inexperience of Grants, either hereditary or reversionary, is certainly very great, and how this particular one in question is worded, I can't know, for I never read it, but I conclude nobody can doubt of King Charles's having meant and designed it as a part of the small provision he made for my father, and that therefore in equity it belongs to the family. I remember to have heard, after my father died, for I was then abroad at sea, that as he died without a will, there was some doubt whether this office was not personal estate, and therefore ought to have been divided amongst the younger children; but upon advising with the best counsel then in England, my Lord Chief Justice Reeves, it was said no; it was so far freehold as it was tied to go with the title, and I verily believe that great and good man would have thought any king very ill advised who should refuse to fulfil his predecessor's affectionate intentions to his natural son's family, and indeed no one of his successors hitherto have ever thought of it, and yet my father's conduct to Queen Anne was very different from that my family has invariably shown to the present Royal family, ever since their accession to the throne.

I therefore hope less favour will not be shown us in this reign than has been in times past, when we had much less reason to expect it.

I beg pardon, Sir, for detaining you so long: I do it with the greatest regret, as I am, &c., &c.   VERE.

COUNTESS TEMPLE TO LADY HARRIET CAMPBELL.

June —, 1764.

MY DEAR LADY HARRIET,—I am always extremely happy to hear from you, but doubly so, when you convey any commands from Her Royal Highness. I beg you will tell the Princess I shall ever think myself highly honoured whenever she has any for me; and shall feel the greatest pleasure in obeying them: I hope Her Royal Highness will excuse the blue paper cover to my Verses. Not foreseeing the great honour they were to have, they were all bound alike, except that I presented to Her Royal Highness by your Ladyship's hand. Had I been in town they should have been put into golden attire, but as it is, I hope she will do me the honour to look down upon them in their country garb. Besides, thus, inside and out perfectly agree, neither the one nor the other being of any value.

I am sensible that nothing but *our Princess's* goodness and kind partiality to me could make the Princess of Hesse wish for them[1].

The weather is vastly cold from the absence of the sun, who hides himself that he may shine out with the brightest lustre when Her Royal Highness honours this mansion, proud to lend his assistance upon this occasion to the grateful master and mistress of Stowe. I am truly glad of the marriage you mention, as it is very likely to turn out happy for both: what a joy to Lady Albemarle[2]!

---

[1] The Princess of Hesse had desired to have a copy of Lady Temple's Poems.

[2] The marriage of her daughter, Lady Elizabeth Keppel, with the Marquess of Tavistock.

COMTE DE GUERCHY TO THE DUC DE PRASLIN.

Londres, 5ᵉ Juin, 1764.

[This is a copy, to which Mr. Grenville has added in a note "*Private, in his own hand.*"]

J'ai essuyé depuis quelque tems des difficultés de la part de la Douane de Londres d'après l'ordre de Monsʳ. Grenville, entre autres celles de m'avoir retenu à la Douane un habit de gala[1] que j'avais fait venir pour mettre hier, jour de la naissance du Roy, et dont j'avois annoncé l'arrivée, comptant qu'il me seroit remis comme cela s'est pratiqué pour M. de Mirepoix, ainsi que pour M. de Nivernois. *Tout le reste du Ministère Britannique m'a marqué son étonnement d'un pareil procédé ; cependant, quoique my Lord Halifax soit du nombre de ceux qui m'ont dit que c'étoit une chose étrange, il n'a pas pu se dispenser* de me répondre à une lettre que je lui avois écrit à ce sujet, comme si c'étoit par l'ordre du Roi son maitre que cette retenue d'habit avoit été faite.

Je lui avois demandé de me faire savoir précisément en quoi consistoit la franchise des ambassadeurs, pour qu'on établit sur cela une reciprocité parfaite en France. Il m'a envoyé une lettre de la Trésorerie à ce sujet, à qui il n'avoit pu se dispenser de communiquer la mienne ; comme c'est en Anglois, et que je n'ai pas le tems d'en faire faire traduction, je ne la joins pas ici ; le Duc de Bedford a aussi parlé très fortement, mais inutilement, pour me faire rendre mon habit.

---

[1] The Comte de Guerchy was not the only Ambassador who had been disappointed about his Court dress: it will appear from a subsequent letter that the Count de Haslang was in a like dilemma respecting his *habit d'été brodé en argent*.

MR. HORACE WALPOLE TO MR. THOMAS PITT.

Strawberry Hill, June 5, 1764.

DEAR SIR,—You tell me a report has been maliciously raised and propagated by Mr. Grenville's enemies, that in the conversation which passed at your house, Mr. Grenville said, that if Mr. Conway voted in Parliament according to his conscience, he was unfit to have any command in the King's army. You add, that what makes this report more painful to Mr. Grenville, is, that I am said not to have discouraged it: and you conclude with desiring, if I agree with your state of that conversation (which you send me to refresh my memory) that I would use my endeavours to put a stop to a groundless report.

I will begin with telling you that I am far from having forgot the conversation you mention. At the very time it passed I thought it so extraordinary, that the next day I wrote down an account of it; as I did also of what I heard passed at Mr. Grenville's on the same subject. I have it at this moment lying before me, and therefore can speak very accurately on that topic.

If, therefore, you ask me whether Mr. Grenville said totidem verbis, that if Mr. Conway voted in Parliament according to his conscience, he was unfit to have any command in the army? I answer directly and truly, no: I never heard him say those words, nor have I certainly ever said he did. Yet I think the report may easily have arisen from what he assuredly did say, and which I avow I have said, he said.

Mr. Grenville said twice, *the King cannot trust his army in the hands of those that are against his measures.* Now give me leave to put you a little in mind.

The expression of *the King not trusting his army in such hands,* you first dropped yourself in my room. You cannot forget the surprise it occasioned in me, and the answer I made you. Did I not, I ask you upon your honour, reply, " Good God! Mr. Pitt, what are you going to do with the army? or what do you think Mr. Conway is going to do? Do you think he is going into rebellion? If the tenour of Mr. Conway's services and character do not entitle him to be trusted with a regiment, I do not know what can entitle any man to one. Is he factious? what do you think he is going to do?" Mr. Grenville at night, in your room, *twice* used the same expression *of not trusting the army in such hands.*

I did then, and still think them the most extraordinary words ever used by English Minister. I repeated the same answer that I made to you. I appeal to yourself whether this is not strictly true? When I saw Mr. Conway, I told him of these words before Lady Ailesbury; I mentioned them to the Duke of Devonshire; I believe when it was agreed the Duke of Richmond should be present at the conversation between Mr. Grenville and Mr. Conway, I told them to his Grace, but of this I will not be positive. I do know that, to prevent any mistakes thereafter, I set down the very words; and I am glad I did so. That paper has been seen by those who will bear me witness that it is no new account, nor do you or Mr. Grenville I dare to say suspect me capable of having written it now, and calling it an old account; nor could it be necessary: I desired to have you for witness to my conversation with Mr. Grenville, being so much convinced of the rigid strictness of your honour, that, though much more Mr. Grenville's friend than mine, I was sure you would do me justice, if it should be necessary to appeal to you. I do appeal to you in the most solemn manner; nay, I appeal to Mr. Grenville himself, whether every syllable that I have here stated to you be not most scrupulously and conscientiously true, not only in syllables, but in sense and purport; for I would scorn to report words, however true, which yet, by adding to or taking from, I should set in a different light from that in which they were intended by the speaker.

I now come to the case as you state it, which in general agrees very much with my own paper; but we differ widely in the conclusions we draw from what passed. You allow I insisted principally upon the high point of honour and delicacy of sentiment in Mr. Conway, and that I thought him incapable, *in any situation*, of doing anything but from mere motives of conscience and honour. Has he not acted invariably as I foretold? Has he not sacrificed his fortune to his conscience? and do you not ipsissimis verbis own, that it would have been an absurdity in Mr. Grenville to say Mr. Conway was unfit to have any command in the King's army, if he voted according to his conscience; UNLESS, INDEED, *his conscience* leading him to a systematical opposition to the King's Government, *in that case Mr. Grenville may be construed to have said that such a conscience* must render it very difficult and unlikely for him to continue long in his situation? Without dwelling on the words, *such a conscience* (though a man acting uniformly in opposition, against his interest, may be supposed as conscientious as a man acting uniformly with his interest for Government), it is evident from your words and opinions, that if Mr. Conway's conscience led him to opposition, he probably would be removed. If, therefore, Mr. Conway's conscience led him not to systematical opposition, but to opposition to one single measure, and yet he has been dismissed, will not the world say with reason—indeed, can it say otherwise? than that Mr. Grenville's declared opinion led him to remove officers for systematical opposition from conscience, and that the practice has been to remove them for one single conscientious vote? And unless Mr. Grenville declares (which I, if authorized, will publish with pleasure) that he had no hand in the removal of Mr. Conway, I do not see how anybody can help thinking that Mr. Grenville's opinion and practice went together. You approve the wisdom of removing men in the former case; I wonder you did, even in speculation; surely the execution has not convinced you of the wisdom of this measure, which has so much offended mankind, and has intimidated nobody. From all this you must see clearly, that if I contradicted the essence of the report, I must contradict you and the truth, who agree together.

You allow I was positive in opinion, that Mr. Conway neither was, nor intended to be in opposition; I was most assuredly of that opinion, and am now convinced that I was in the right, as in every question that did not relate to the warrants he voted with the Administration. In the next point, which is matter of opinion, you think Mr. Grenville showed every mark of kindness and friendly disposition to Mr. Conway. Give me leave to say it did not strike me in that light. Mr. Grenville, with great warmth and eagerness, persisted in thinking Mr. Conway rooted in opposition, which occasioned, what you own, my repeated declarations of believing the contrary. This did not strike me as any great mark of kindness or confidence to either Mr. Conway or me. Less did I think it kind to insist with the vehemence Mr. Grenville used, on positive declarations from Mr. Conway. Such demands appear to me highly unconstitutional, and therefore I do not see how they can be made with friendship to the party. Those demands of positive declaration were, I believe, made before the Duke of Richmond, as well as to me.

You know I went so far as to tell you that Mr. Conway was, I firmly believed, not only not in opposition, but should he be ever so ill-used, and the Ministry should propose a question which he thought right for this country, he would vote for it. I remain exactly of the same opinion. He has been as ill, as hardly, and as unjustly used, as ever man was; and yet he will do what he thinks right, though his behaviour may serve his bitterest enemies; for he will never suffer his personal resentments to carry him to do a wrong thing, even to his foes, much less towards his country.

When I say he has been ill-used, I repeat with great sincerity—and you who have known, and are so good as to allow my real regard to Mr. Grenville, will believe me—that few things would give me more pleasure than to be assured that the dismission of Mr. Conway was without Mr. Grenville's consent or approbation.

You say that below the Bar of the House of Lords, Mr. Grenville told you and me that Mr. Conway had declared that he was not then engaged, nor did at that time intend to engage in any system of opposition; but at the same time desired not to be understood to intend to separate himself from the Dukes of Grafton and Devonshire, to whom he was obliged. This agrees with the message I myself delivered to Mr. Grenville from

Mr. Conway, that he was in no opposition, nor thought of being in any; but in answer to Mr. Grenville's question, whether there was anything he would like, he declared he would accept nothing while those Dukes were dissatisfied with the Administration. Both your state of the case and mine, which agree together, do not at all coincide with Mr. Grenville's letter to Lord Hertford, that he had found Mr. Conway's connections with his friends *unbounded*.

I have omitted, for the last, one passage, which I had forgotten in my own memorandums, which yet, from your own assertion—who I am sure will adhere, in every point, to the strict matter of fact, let it affect whom it will—I am not only persuaded passed, but I think I recollect it myself, from the circumstance of the particular day on which it passed. You say Mr. Grenville told me that a regular system of opposition to Government would render any one unfit for a high rank in military command; and that in some instances, as in cases of tumults and insurrections, such a man would be more dangerous to the King and Commonwealth. I am sure I do not remember the word *Commonwealth* being used; though, if you assert it, I cannot take upon me to say it was not used, for I remember this salvo but imperfectly. I know the day of the conversation was after the tumult on the burning of the *North Briton;* Mr. Grenville was much flustered, and very likely applied the case of the day to the subject we were discussing; and if he did, it probably made the less impression on me, because my mind had been already struck with the same singular words from you *before* the tumult happened; and therefore, when I heard them repeated by a Minister, it was natural for me to conclude you had heard them from his mouth, as you came to me with a message from him; and I am bold to declare, such words in the mouth of a Minister are to me exceedingly alarming. As such I have repeated them, and I leave you, who know me, to judge whether I will retract anything I have said, which I am particularly authorized, by having taken down the words, to affirm are true, and to the very substance of which you agree, as I am sure you will to the precise words, being thus put in mind of them, especially as you own you are not exact in the very words.

I love and honour Mr. Conway above any man in the world; I would lay down my life for him; and shall I see him every day basely and falsely traduced in newspapers and libels, and not say what I know is true, when it sets his character in so fair and noble a light? I am asked to discourage reports. I am ready to discourage such as are *not* true, and do *not* come from me.

Mr. Grenville is welcome to publish this letter; it will be the fullest answer to anything that is said against him without foundation. Let Mr. Grenville, in his turn, discourage and disavow the infamous calumnies published against Mr. Conway, the authors of which, I dare say, are unknown to Mr. Grenville, but who, not content with seeing Mr. Conway's fortune ruined, would stab his reputation likewise. Thank God! they cannot fix a blemish upon it. I will certainly bear witness to it as much as lies in me. Fear or favour will not intimidate or warp my friendship. Yet I wish Mr. Grenville so well, that I will take the liberty of giving him through you this piece of advice.

It is high time for the Administration to discountenance and disclaim the language held by all the writers on their side, particularly by the author of the Address to the Public, *that officers are to be dismissed for their behaviour in Parliament.* Such doctrines are new, and never were *avowed* before. They clash with all parliamentary freedom; they render the condition of officers in Parliament most abject, slavish, and dishonourable; they alarm all thinking men, and, I will do them the justice to say, do not seem universally the sentiments of Ministers themselves, as so many generals and officers in Parliament, who are avowedly in opposition, retain their commissions; a circumstance that makes the singling out of Mr. Conway, who was not in opposition, look more like the effect of private pique and resentment somewhere or other, I don't know where, than a settled determination to make officers in general the absolute tools of the Ministry.

I will now conclude this tedious letter, with adding, by your leave, a few words on myself.

It has more than once been insinuated to me, that I might ruin myself if I took Mr. Conway's part. I do Mr. Grenville the justice to declare, that I believe him incapable of countenancing such insinuations. Come they from whom they will, I despise them. My place[1] is a patent for life, and as much my property, by law, as your estate is yours. Oh! but I have been told the payments may be delayed or stopped: they may, by violence or injustice, and that insinuation I despise likewise.

Mr. Grenville's civilities and regularity on these occasions I acknowledge with gratitude, though I disclaim all dependence, all paying of court; I would fling up my

---

[1] He was Usher of the Exchequer, and held besides one or two other sinecure places.

patent to-morrow, if it was capable of making me do one servile act, if it deterred me one moment from following the dictates of conscience and friendship. Both in Parliament, and out of it, I will say and do what I think right and honest. I was born free, and will live and die so, in spite of patents and places. I may be ruined as Mr. Conway has been, but I will preserve my honour inviolate. If I did not, I might receive you here with more magnificence, but I had rather receive you, as I hope to do, without a blush. You know the passion I have for Strawberry Hill; but trust me, at this moment I know I could with pleasure see it sold, if reduced to it by suffering for my country and my principles. Remember this, my dear Sir, you, who are much younger, and have longer to live than me. It is this satisfaction of conscience which sweetens every evil, and makes Mr. Conway at this instant the happiest man in England. I am your sincere and affectionate humble servant,

HORACE WALPOLE.

P.S. I am so desirous of not saying a syllable that is not strictly true, that I choose to contradict in a postscript, rather than erase, one passage in which I had said what I *believed* had passed. On showing this letter to the Duke of Richmond, his Grace says he cannot say that before him Mr. Grenville made a demand of a positive declaration, though he expressed a strong desire that Mr. Conway would declare what his general system was.

If I have, therefore, stated the argument too strongly, I willingly retract so much as is overcharged; though I must own I see little difference between a Minister demanding a positive declaration of a Member of Parliament, and expressing a strong desire of a declaration; because, if a Minister will take upon himself to catechise Members of Parliament, he must know that either the gentler or rougher method will be effectual, or both will be resisted. The Duke says he remembers very well my telling him the words *cannot trust his army*, &c., *before* his Grace saw Mr. Grenville.

THE EARL OF SANDWICH TO MR. GRENVILLE.

Whitehall, June 6, 1764.

DEAR SIR,—I had this morning a long conversation with the French Ambassador, and really think I have made an impression upon him that will have good consequences.

I began by telling him that I thought the public tranquillity depended upon a mutual confidence and friendly concurrence between our two Courts; that as we were the two great Powers of Europe, peace or war depended upon our measures, and that when the French Administration threw difficulties upon us, they acted equally against their own public and private interest; that civilities shown on one part, would claim civilities from the other side, but unless we helped each other reciprocally, a very few sinister events would throw things into confusion; that upon the confidence we had in their sincerity the Parliament had been told more than once that the Powers with which we had been at war would faithfully execute the engagements they had contracted with us; and that unless we could make good those promises, the next session of Parliament would be an unpleasant one. He seemed much struck, and most thoroughly to enter into my reasoning; he repeated several times that I had absolutely convinced him about the money to be paid for the maintenance of the French prisoners, and that he now saw we could not accept it as a round sum to wipe off all scores, but must receive it on account; and that it was necessary we should receive it on account before the Houses met. He promised me, in the most serious and solemn terms, that he would support this language with all the credit and ability he was master of, on his return to France; and, indeed, I have no doubt of his being in earnest in this point; I think, when you come to converse with him, you will find that what I say is well founded: in short, I think he will go to France thoroughly well disposed to support the measures of the present Administration of this kingdom. You may imagine that he laid in his pretensions to civilities from us, in order, as he said, to prevent his being taxed at his return with being too much an Englishman, and thereby rendered incapable of carrying his good intentions, as far as he could wish to do, into execution; but he insisted on no express conditions, and aimed at nothing which I think is a capital object, so as to interfere with the immediate points that we may wish to be in possession of at the opening of the Parliament.

I shall see you so soon that I will not enter into any farther detail upon this subject before we meet; but I thought it necessary to tell you thus much, as there is a possibility of your seeing Monsieur de Guerchy sooner than I shall have the pleasure of seeing you, and as it may be material that you should know the summary of what passed between us, and use all possible gentleness and management with him, to keep him in his present good disposition.

I think the idea of a change of Administration seems to decline, and I see no symptom that gives me any apprehension on that head. I believe, however, it is certain that Mr. Pitt has put off his journey to Lord Lyttelton's, and remains at Hayes, as he says, by the advice of his physicians, who think that so much motion might endanger his health; though, by the bye, I thought he was better, to appearance, when he was at Court last week, than I have seen him for some years. I am also told that Lord Rockingham and the Duke of Devonshire are come or coming to town; you will best know whether these phenomena portend any stormy weather.

Lord Halifax and I were with Lord Chancellor the night before last. He is in perfect good humour, and I think will recommend Dr. Marriott[1] to be the King's Advocate. Indeed, as matters stand at present among the professors of the Civil Law, I believe he is the fittest person in point of ability, exclusive of other considerations, which altogether gives him a better claim than any who can be in competition with him.

I go to-morrow to Woburn: whether I shall return on Monday night or Tuesday morning is uncertain; but be assured, wherever I am, &c. SANDWICH.

MR. THOMAS PITT TO MR. HORACE WALPOLE.

Boconnoc, June 10, 1764.

DEAR SIR,—I have just received your answer to my letter of the 25th ultimo, which contains matter of

[1] Afterwards Sir James Marriott, and Judge of the High Court of Admiralty, in 1778. He was Master of Trinity College, Cambridge.

various kinds. The matter of fact is what I am principally concerned in, and is therefore what I shall first begin with. I must still, as I did before, declare that I am totally unable to charge my memory with particular words in a long conversation, which I had not the precaution at the time to write down, but which is fresh enough in my mind not to suffer any material circumstance to escape me: and this I think it necessary to premise, I am sure you will do me the justice to believe, not with an intention to misrepresent, disguise, or conceal, but from that regard for truth which I ever have, and I hope ever shall esteem above all ties and obligations whatsoever, and which, as it should make me most scrupulously testify against myself, so it should against my father, my brother, or my friend.

Having said thus much, I proceed to the circumstance about which you appeal to me. I do perfectly well remember, in conversation with you, justifying the removal of Mr. Conway, from the danger there appeared to me at this time, supposing him to be in a systematical opposition to Government, in trusting in his hands an important military command.

I remember you took me up eagerly, and replied, I verily believe the words you mention:—" Good God! Mr. Pitt, what do you intend to do with the army? or what do you think Mr. Conway is going to do with the army?" &c. I do very well remember the same sort of expression falling from Mr. Grenville, of apprehension from the army being in the hands of persons in systematical opposition to the King's measures, I dare say in the terms you make use of, as you remember them so distinctly, " that the King cannot trust his army in the hands of·those that are against his measures," and I very well remember he applied the instance of the tumult in the City, to show how dangerous it would be for the safety of the King (I will not swear he added the word *Commonwealth*, though I hope I know him well enough to be persuaded that he never disunited their interests in his thoughts), to trust the defence of the King against a tumult raised upon account of burning the *North Briton* to a person who was known publicly to have defended the cause of the author of that paper; to which you replied to this effect, " that you thought, from Mr. Conway's character, that defence might nevertheless be trusted to him with safety."

This was, Sir, indeed the whole scope of Mr. Grenville's conversation, as it appeared to me, upon my honour, viz., that Mr. Conway seemed to be in a systematical opposition; that he wished to be enabled to say it was otherwise; that if it was so, he could not see there was that difference between a military and a civil employment that could render it possible for Mr. Conway long to continue in his situation. He did frequently explain his sentiments with regard to the injustice of removing any man from his employment for a single vote, or conscientious opposition to a particular measure; and though I declare myself ignorant of what part he may have taken in Mr. Conway's affair, yet I will take upon me to say, had he seen that gentleman's conduct in the light you represent it in, perhaps, with great truth and justice, he would not have been a party to what has happened.

The report which Mr. Grenville resents, and for the falsehood of which he appeals to me, and for which I likewise appeal to you, is this, " that if Mr. Conway voted in Parliament according to his conscience he was unfit to have any command in the King's army." This report is false. Mr. Grenville did, on the contrary, repeatedly declare—what I have heard him say a hundred times upon other occasions—that from difference of opinion a man might give his vote against the Government, in particular instances, without being in opposition to Government, and consequently would not render himself *unfit* for any trust from Government, civil or military.

If, on the other hand, the report had been that Mr. Grenville had declared what you mention, " that the King cannot trust his army in the hands of those that are against his measures," I protest—though I do not recollect the particular words, which I dare say you have set down with truth and exactness—I do remember the sense of them well enough to declare that I understood that to be his opinion then delivered at my house; but give me leave to say it widely differs, not only in *terms*, but in *essence*, from the other proposition.

An opposition to the King's measures, his motives for which he is the only judge of, would, in the latter case, be the reason to render him unfit for a high rank in military command, and not his having voted according to his conscience.

Alarming would it be, indeed, to every friend to liberty if we could conceive an English Minister uniting the two propositions, " that an officer voting in Parliament according to his conscience was *therefore* unfit to serve," and " that the King did not dare to trust his army in any hands but of such as were ready at any time to vote in Parliament against their consciences." But, Sir, there are different opinions and different convictions. A Minister who means honestly by his King and country, and is conscious of the integrity of his own intentions, will make use of every constitutional method to carry his purposes into effect. He will be apt to suspect those of sinister views who oppose his measures, which he knows are well intentioned; at least he will endeavour to prevent the means that are taken to oppose and render them abortive, even though he should not suspect the principles of those who oppose.

On the other hand, those who from principle and conscience condemn the measures of the Minister, will be apt to suspect the Minister of bad intentions towards the public, and will, in consequence of that conviction, endeavour to discredit and diminish his influence, and to oppose his measures.

I do not find, my dear Sir, that we differ about matters of fact, though we, indeed, differ widely in our conclusions.

Perhaps we may be both of us warped in our reasonings by our partialities; but as *matters of fact* are the immediate objects of our consideration, to the truth of which I am appealed to on both sides, and which are not the objects of partiality, I am glad to be able, with the strictest adherence to truth, to join issue with both parties.

The report raised against Mr. Grenville is, by your own concession, not true, viz., "that if Mr. Conway voted in Parliament according to his conscience he was unfit to have any command in the King's army."

What you assert *I believe* to be true, in the *very words* in which you repeat them; I am ready to *attest* the truth of the *sense* of them, as delivered in that conversation which passed at my house, viz., "that the King cannot trust his army in the hands of those who are against his measures."

The first of these propositions is, I hope, on both sides confuted. The second is a text which may bear a comment according to the different conceptions, prejudices, and passions of mankind, though, in the sense in which I understand it, it is neither new or unconstitutional. I, for one, do from my heart believe the contrary doctrine of the absolute immunity and independence of the army to be much more new and dangerous to the constitution. However, I avoid entering further than is necessary upon this subject, as I know I have not the happiness to agree with you in it, and as I am not called upon to give my opinion and sentiments concerning it.

With regard to your unshaken and disinterested friendship for Mr. Conway, it is such as well becomes the generosity and disinterestedness of your character, and those persons, whoever they were, who have endeavoured to throw unworthy insinuations into your mind by menaces of oppression and injustice, must have known as little of Mr. Grenville, if they thought he could countenance such an idea, as they did of you if they thought you could be affected by it. No, Sir, I have the honour to live in friendship with Mr. Grenville; I love and esteem him much. I will freely own he is the only attachment I have to any public or political situation; but could I once suppose him capable of taking so base and unjust an advantage over a man to punish him for a conduct which does him honour, I should renounce all connection with him, from that hour, as the lowest and most unworthy of men.

In the meantime you will do me the justice to believe

that, whether he is Minister or no Minister, as long as I continue to think of him as you know I do at present, I shall never fail to give him every mark of comfort, support, and feeble assistance in my power, under the great load of calumny and misrepresentation which, from quarters you have no dealings with, are every day heaped upon him. In short, I shall endeavour to imitate your own virtues, which will, I doubt not, give me that cheerfulness and self-satisfaction which you promise as the reward of an unblemished conduct. I am, &c., &c.

THOS. PITT.

MR. GRENVILLE TO THE EARL OF HERTFORD.

Downing Street, June 12, 1764.

MY DEAR LORD,—As soon as I had received the honour of your Lordship's letter of the 29th of last month, I took the earliest opportunity of laying the contents of it before His Majesty, who ordered me to inform your Lordship that he had not the least thought at present of making any promotion from the Earls' Bench.

I was not at all surprised at this declaration, as I know that the King has frequently expressed the greatest unwillingness, when applications have been made to him upon this subject.

I thought, however, that I should better answer your intentions, and the friendly confidence you repose in me, by communicating your wishes, and the grounds upon which they are founded, to His Majesty, than by giving you my opinion only, which could not be equally satisfactory.

I was the rather induced to execute your commands

in this manner, as I was fully persuaded that the application (whatever the success might be) would be graciously received.

In this persuasion I was not mistaken, the King having been pleased to express himself in the most favourable terms towards your Lordship in every other respect, though he could not comply with what you wished upon this occasion.

He directed me to assure you of his favour and approbation, and to take particular care that no person whatsoever should be informed of what you had writ to me: your Lordship may therefore depend upon it that the matter will be an absolute secret from every body except His Majesty, and those to whom you have communicated it.

MR. GRENVILLE TO MR. THOMAS PITT.

Downing Street, June 19, 1764.

DEAR SIR,—I have read over Mr. Walpole's letter to you which you did me the favour to send to me in yours of the 10th of this month. You will not now, I believe, venture to answer, as you did in your former letter, that Mr. Walpole is so far from being capable of having silently acquiesced in the report which I had writ to you about, that he would make it his business to state the direct contrary. His letter and conduct upon this occasion will best speak for themselves, and need no comment to a gentleman and a man of honour like you, who was present at, and know this whole transaction, the motives from which it proceeded, and the consequences which did actually attend it. I should, therefore, not have thought it necessary to make any observation upon them;

but as he has appealed, not only to you, but to me, "whether every syllable that he has there stated to you be not most scrupulously and conscientiously true, not only in syllables, but in sense and purport," I do most solemnly declare to you, that the account which I gave you in my first letter upon this subject—and which you tell me in yours of the 25th of May last, you believe to be precisely as I represent it—is, to the best of my knowledge and belief, an exact state of the substance, sense, and purport, and, as near as possible, of the expressions which were made use of in that conversation.

I think the representation of what passed, as it stands in Mr. Walpole's letter, differs widely from that account in substance, sense, and purport, as well as in the expressions; and in as much as it does, it is absolutely and entirely ill-founded.

With regard to the words quoted in it, and which are said to have been twice repeated by me—though, as you truly observe, it is very difficult to recall the particular terms and expressions—yet I am confident that I did not make use of those words to Mr. Walpole, which, if I had done it twice I should not have totally forgotten, neither did I send you with a message to him, and desire or authorize you to make use of those words in any manner from me, or as containing my opinion, the truth of which you know, though Mr. Walpole concludes the contrary to be true.

He tells you in his letter, "that in answer to those words, he repeated to me the same thing which he had said to you—'Good God! what are you going to do with the army?'" and in another part, "that the day of the conversation was after the tumult on the burning of the *North Briton*; that I was much flustered, and very likely applied the case of the day to the subject we were discussing."

His expression that I was much flustered at a tumult, seems to me a singular one, but it is not so singular as his having quite forgotten in his memorandums, and scarcely recollecting from the circumstances, so material a part of what passed in this conversation at the very time when he insists so strongly upon his correctness, and says that he can speak very accurately upon that topic.

I am extremely glad to be able to supply, in some measure, so great a defect, by recalling to your memory some of those material circumstances which, if you remember them, may explain the grounds, and enable you to judge of the exactness from whence he thinks this report may easily have arisen. In doing this, I will not state a syllable which I have not the fullest conviction passed at that meeting. I trust that those who know me believe that I am incapable, upon any consideration, of disavowing, much less of falsifying, what I have said; and in this instance I have no temptation to do it, for though I am very confident that I did not use those words, yet I am far from seeing them in the same light that he does.

It is certain that my thoughts at that meeting were full of the dangerous tumult which I had just received an account of, and that I expressed my sentiments upon it strongly, being very much surprised to find Mr. Walpole, so far from being flustered, much more indifferent about it than I expected.

I asked him repeatedly whether he thought that an officer who approved in any degree of the doctrines contained in that paper, and who disapproved of the censure of it, or of the punishment of the author, would be a proper person to be trusted at the head of a regiment of guards to quell a tumult and insurrection occasioned by the burning of it. This was pressed by me more than once, and at last produced the following answer, with some heat and peevishness: "Good God! what do you intend to do with the army?" to which I replied, to defend the King and the Commonwealth, and to carry the laws into execution. The first part being repeated more than once was, I suppose, the foundation upon which the mistake in that expression which he says I twice used was built, especially as I am very sure that Mr. Walpole's above-mentioned answer to it was made upon this occasion, to which my reply was as I have stated it. Nor is this capital instance the only mistake in his letter; there are other particulars which are either mistaken, like that of the demands of a positive declaration which he mentions in his postscript, or else are utterly void of any foundation whatever, such as the supposition that in answer to my question whether there was anything General Conway would like (which question was never asked by me), he declared he would accept nothing while the Dukes of Grafton and Devonshire were dissatisfied with the Administration (which answer was never made by him to me). After having thus mentioned some parts of this extraordinary narrative, which I entirely differ from, I will mention what I must suppose Mr. Walpole has quite forgotten, but which I trust you will remember. Before we parted at your house I told Mr. Walpole that no part of that conversation which had then passed was to go out of that room, and that I had no other message to send to General Conway but that I should be glad to see him if it was agreeable to him, which I imagined might be the case, by his having called upon me.

Of this I am very sure, as I had occasion the next morning to take notice of this message in my answer to a note of General Conway's, wherein he appeared to me to have totally misunderstood it, and in that answer (a copy of which I have now before me), I informed General Conway of the message I had sent to him, and that I had no proposition of any kind to make to him; that I flattered myself from what I had heard that our dispositions of personal regard to each other were mutual, and that General Conway would be equally desirous with me to explain and cultivate them; that if I was mistaken in it, I was sorry for the trouble I had given to General Conway and to myself, and wished not to increase it, as I did not see it could have any good effect whatever.

When I saw General Conway and the Duke of Richmond in the evening, I began by telling them that Mr. Walpole had mistaken me extremely; that I had nothing to say, but that if Mr. Conway wished to say anything to me, I was ready to hear it. I believe, but I am not quite certain, that I told you afterwards, that Mr. Walpole had mistaken me, and had said to General Conway much more than he was empowered to do; and I am persuaded that the Duke of Richmond and General Conway must both remember my telling them that Mr. Walpole had much mistaken me. I could then have no interest in saying this if it had been otherwise; and surely if I had reason to know that he had been very inaccurate in the delivery of the only message with which he was charged, and in the report which he made of this conversation within an hour after it happened, I have no cause to think him less so in what he may afterwards have said to others upon this subject, and in the account which he now thinks fit to give of it. What passed further in my interview with General Conway and the Duke of Richmond I do not think myself at liberty to repeat, because it was agreed that no part of it should be reported, except what I afterwards told to Mr. Walpole and to you, below the Bar of the House of Lords, which it was settled just before they left me was the only report to be made of it, wherever it should be necessary to make any.

To this I have strictly adhered, as you know, having never given you any other account of it; and I am persuaded that both General Conway and the Duke of Richmond have adhered to it likewise. I should have thought I had done an injustice to Mr. Walpole, if I had not believed the same of him with respect to what passed at your house; you will now be able to judge from his letter how far that is the case; but after all I have said to you, let me assure you that nothing passed at either of those meetings which would give me the least uneasiness, if truly stated. The precaution taken that nothing should be reported but what was agreed upon, arose from the knowledge I had that in conversations of this kind the alteration of an expression, or even of a single word, may be made use of by any of the parties to change the sense of the whole, and from thence be productive, as in the present instance, of altercations and appeals, which are seldom cleared up to the satisfaction of those who are concerned. If I had thought it possible, after what you told me of Mr. Walpole's sentiments towards me, and what you know of mine towards him, that such a use as has been made of it was then intended, I should never have consented to the meeting which you desired between us, as I should not have thought myself at liberty to have put down in writing what part I pleased of that conversation, and to have produced it as the sense of what passed there, without the consent or even the knowledge of the parties.

I avoid entering into the various reasonings, reflections, and opinions, contained in Mr. Walpole's letter; I neither make panegyrics nor encourage abuse. My opinions will be best known from my actions; by them my public character ought to be, and I trust will be, judged; upon them I am sure the satisfaction of my own conscience, which I have frequently shown to be full as dear to me as that of his can be to Mr. Walpole, must depend. I have, therefore, endeavoured to confine myself to facts; these I have writ to you, without heat or passion, for your satisfaction and for my own; for after what I have met with, you will not wonder at my telling you that I will have no farther intercourse with Mr. Walpole upon this subject, neither directly nor through the channel of any one else, and consequently I shall have no copies[1] of the kind you mention to transmit to you.

I am now come to an end of this tedious letter, which has grown under my pen much beyond my intentions; but I cannot close it without taking notice of the only pleasing circumstance which has attended this disagreeable, and, I must say, very unexpected dispute.

Let me, therefore, my dear Sir, return you my sincerest thanks for the very kind expressions of your good

[1] Mr. Pitt had requested that he might be furnished with copies of any communication Mr. Grenville might think necessary to make to Mr. Walpole, in consequence of his (Mr. Walpole's) letter to Mr. Pitt.

opinion and friendship towards me, in your letter to Mr. Walpole; I feel them very sensibly, and I flatter myself that I shall never forfeit either the one or the other.

The same behaviour which hath, in any degree, acquired the former, will, I hope, enable me to preserve it; and my best claim to the latter will be that true affection and regard which I bear to you, and with which I am, ever, &c., &c. GEORGE GRENVILLE.

MR. GRENVILLE TO THE LORD CHANCELLOR.

Wotton, June 20, 1764.

MY DEAR LORD,—I proposed to wait upon your Lordship by nine o'clock on Monday evening, but was detained at Bedford House till half an hour past ten, when I came to leave my excuse, and not to trouble you at so late an hour.

I wished, if it had been possible, to have come to you on Tuesday evening last, but the variety of business which I was obliged to despatch before I went out of town the next morning prevented me.

I was very sorry to find, from Lord Halifax, whom I saw the night before I left London, that the arrest of M. de Guerchy's servant, and his imprisonment of the constables—all of which, I hoped, was in a fair way of being settled—was subject to more difficulties than I had expected. Your Lordship has probably heard of them from the Secretaries of State before this time. For my part, I shall think that, if the imprisonment of the constables in this case was irregular, as I have apprehended it was, that the best way would be to convince M. de Guerchy of that irregularity, and to put an end to the complaint on both sides, which can be productive of no honour or advantage to either. And if M. de Guerchy continues too warm to hear reason, then to transmit an authentic account of it to Lord Hertford, that he may make an end of it at Paris. These are my sentiments upon this business, which belongs immediately to Lord Halifax's department; but I have communicated them to you, that I may be confirmed in them if you approve them, and that if they are wrong your opinion may set me right. With regard to the office of King's Advocate, I perfectly agree with your Lordship in thinking it very undesirable to purchase the acceptance of an office of that rank by an additional salary, and shall certainly take no farther steps towards the disposal of that office till I am able to talk with you upon the subject of it. The King has been graciously pleased to give me leave to stay here a week longer, and if nothing particular shall call me to town sooner, I intend to make use of that permission. I shall endeavour to wait upon you the first evening that I am at liberty after my return. I am, &c., &c. GEORGE GRENVILLE.

COUNT HASLANG[1] TO MR. GRENVILLE.

Londres, le 22 Juin, 1764.

MONSIEUR,—Il y a plus de trois semaines qu'on me retient un habit d'été brodé en argent à la Douane, sous prétexte qu'il étoit neuf: cependant après y avoir bien regardé, l'homme même qui en a fait la visite, a confessé lui-même après, qu'il s'avoit mépris, et qu'il croyoit bien qu'il a été porté bien de fois: après cette confession

[1] Envoy Extraordinary from Bavaria.

j'avois cru qu'il n'y auroit plus de difficulté à me le rendre : comme je vois cependant, qu'ils s'obstinent sur cela, je suis contraint de m'adresser á vous, et de vous prier de me rendre justice : je me suis offert dès le commencement d'envoyer mon valet-de-chambre, et de le faire prêter un serment que cet habit a été porté, mais on ne l'a pas accepté : vous pouvez cependant être assuré, Monsieur, que je ne permetterois pas pour un million, qu'un de mes gens fassent un faux serment : s'il est neuf, il faut le bouler (?) certainement : s'il a été porté, il faut me le rendre. Je ne demande point de graces, mais la justice : c'est pourquoi, Monsieur, je me flatte que vous donnerez ordre, qu'au premier jour on me porte mon habit. En attendant j'ai l'honneur de me dire très parfaitement, &c., &c.

Le Comte de Haslang le fils.

LADY HARRIET CAMPBELL TO COUNTESS TEMPLE.

Gunnersbury House, June 23, 1764.

Your Works, dear Lady Temple, arrived safe, and have since travelled. Her Royal Highness[1] ordered me to give you early notice of her intended visit to Stowe, that if the time the Princess names should happen not to be convenient either to your Ladyship or Lord Temple, it might be adjusted to make it so. Her Royal Highness's present intention stands for Monday, July 23rd : the distance of time renders it now impossible to name the particular time of that day : I understand that will depend upon the weather; if hot, to be at Stowe by dinner-time, or sooner; but as the time

---

[1] The Princess Amelia.

approaches, you shall have intelligence of her Royal Highness's motions. The Princess is in perfect health; no complaint but heat, which we all partake with her Royal Highness in; that has been most excessive this last week, nor does the storm we have had as yet cool the air. I hope the variety of weather we have had from heat to very cold, now great heat again, has had no disagreeable effects upon your constitution. I don't fear any other changes in Lady Temple, any more than in her most sincere and faithful humble Servant,

H. CAMPBELL.

Her Royal Highness brings Lady Barrymore with her. I beg my compliments to Lord Temple.

SIR JOHN FIELDING [1] TO MR. JENKINSON.

Bow Street, June 26, 1764.

SIR JOHN FIELDING presents his most respectful compliments to Mr. Jenkinson, and in consequence of what has passed with him this morning, begs he will do him the honour to acquaint Mr. Grenville that his application for the continuation of the horse patrole for a short time longer was as a temporary but necessary step, in order to complete that which had been so happily begun by said patrole; but if, at the end of three months, it should then appear absolutely necessary that this or some such plan should be continued, Sir John Fielding will in the fullest manner state the reasons for such continuance, and lay them before Mr. Grenville; but flatters himself that from the amazing good effects this patrole has already had by bringing so many old offenders to justice,

[1] The celebrated Police Magistrate.

that a little farther assistance of this kind may be sufficient to prevent these outrages from arising to any great height for a considerable time, and is his sincere friend and obedient humble Servant, JOHN FIELDING.

COUNTESS TEMPLE TO LADY HARRIET CAMPBELL.

June 26, 1764.

MY DEAR LADY HARRIET,—I am obliged to you for your intelligence of *my Works*. I think they are come to very great honour. I wish they could improve by travelling; but alas! like most young gentlemen, they will arrive at their journey's end without being one jot the better for it; however, as they have a letter of recommendation from so great a personage, I don't doubt their being well received. Her Royal Highness is always very gracious and good, but as her time is of so much more importance than our's, it ought to be first considered; it is happily fixed for us, as it gives full time for my Lord Temple to recover a very bad sprained ankle; he has been obliged to be carried about in a chair, but is able now to walk a little, and does not doubt but by the time the Princess names he shall be able to have the honour of attending her Royal Highness anywhere. We could not bring ourselves to name this misfortune without an absolute necessity, for fear of putting a bar to our pleasure, at least for some time, so little philosophy have we. My most respectful duty waits upon her Royal Highness. I am always happy to hear her named, but much more so when you tell me she is in perfect health. I hope for my own sake your Ladyship will never find any alteration in me with regard to my friendship, for it never can be planted in a better soil, and therefore must lose by removing. I am, &c., &c.

A. TEMPLE.

THE KING TO MR. GRENVILLE.

(Tuesday evening, June 26, 1764).

MR. GRENVILLE,—In answer to the question I put on the cover of the draught to Lord Hertford, I received the enclosed note from Lord Halifax, which I own I don't comprehend entirely; the only solution to it that I can think of is, M. de Guerchy's having told Lord Halifax that he had brought the Attorney General to his opinion. I beg you would enquire into this, and send me an answer.

MR. GRENVILLE TO THE KING.

Tuesday, June 26, 1764,
Ten minutes past 12 at night.

THE moment I received the honour of your Majesty's commands, I went to Lord Halifax to enquire into the present situation of this business, and am just now returned from thence, after a very long discussion of it with his Lordship and the Attorney General, whom I found there.

Lord Halifax had seen Lord Mansfield this morning, whose opinion with regard to the apprehension of the Ambassador's servant, and to the imprisonment and detention of the constables, seemed more favourable to M. de Guerchy than the Attorney General would declare his to be.

In this state Lord Halifax declines taking any step,

or writing any letter upon it till he has the Attorney General's opinion; and the Attorney General seems determined, after hearing what has passed, to give no positive opinion, but to refer himself to the Court of King's Bench to decide how the law stands upon this question.

If M. de Guerchy's heat will allow of it, the wisest way for him, and the least troublesome to your Majesty, would surely be to make an end of this matter, and for that purpose to convince M. de Guerchy (if possible) of the irregularity of his own behaviour in imprisoning and ill-using the officers of justice, which appears to be the likeliest means of making him less pertinacious upon the question of his servant's apprehension.

I took no notice to Lord Halifax that I had seen his note to your Majesty, nor of your orders to me to endeavour to explain it, which he himself will have the honour of doing to-morrow morning, more satisfactorily.

I hope that this business will take the turn which it ought to do; but if your Majesty has any commands to honour me with in consequence of it, notwithstanding your gracious permission to me to go into the country, I shall be happy to do my duty by staying in town to obey them, and have therefore directed the messenger to wait that I may receive your Majesty's pleasure upon this subject.

SIR JOHN FIELDING TO MR. JENKINSON.

Bow Street, June 28, 1764.

SIR JOHN FIELDING presents his respectful compliments to Mr. Jenkinson; thought it his indispensable duty to his country to transmit to him the enclosed account of robberies committed since Monday night last, and to acquaint him that in consequence of these repeated informations, he last night sent a foot patrole consisting of a peace officer and three assistants, into the fields near Tyburn and Tottenham Court Roads, to search the ditches where footpads have lately infested, that before they got out of the coach which carried them to the spot, they narrowly escaped being murdered, by three footpads, who without giving them the least notice fired two pistols immediately into the coach, but thank God without effect; two of them were afterwards taken, though not before one of them was dangerously wounded; all which circumstances might, I am convinced, have been prevented. There is nothing I so sincerely lament as the want of an opportunity of convincing Mr. Grenville of the amazing importance of the police to Government; for notwithstanding his most laudable resolution not to lay any permanent expense on the Crown that can be avoided, yet I am sure that he will never spare any necessary expense where public good is the object. For my part I can only propose and inform, which I shall always do most faithfully; but, in justice to myself, cannot conclude this letter without assuring you that your manner of behaviour to me the other morning gave me much real concern, it being totally different from any that I have ever received from any person, in any department whatever, on whom I have been obliged to attend, in consequence of my miserable employ. However, I still hope, that time will convince you how little I deserve the most distant diffidence. Your sincere friend and the public's faithful servant,

JOHN FIELDING.

Account of Robberies committed—

1. Christopher Pratt, driver of Mr. Stanton's waggon of Market Harborough, with the Bedford and Huntingdon waggoners robbed on Finchley Common on Friday night by two footpads, who beat and wounded them much.

2. Francis Walker, master coachman, of Nag's Head Yard, Oxford Road, drives No. 325, robbed on Tuesday night by two or three footpads near Paddington, of his own watch and money; and two ladies of their purses.

3. Mr. Taylor of King Street, Golden Square, brewer, in company with another gentleman, robbed the same night near Gunnersbury House, by a single highwayman.

4. The Honourable Mrs. Grey, robbed the same night near Sion House, by a highwayman.

5. Mr. Kearr, whipmaker of the Mews, with three other gentlemen in post-chaises, all robbed the same night near Turnham Green, by a highwayman.

6. Mr. Jackson, of Great Queen Street, robbed in one of the Hampstead stages, near Kentish Town, by a single highwayman, on Monday night.

7. The Bath and Bristol coaches on Hounslow Heath, Tuesday night.

8. Mr. Rosser, near Islington, last night, of his gold watch, by two footpads.

MR. JENKINSON TO MR. GRENVILLE.

London, June 28, 1764.

DEAR SIR,—I hope that you and Mrs. Grenville are safely arrived at Wotton.

I suppose you will receive the Government accounts of the disaster that has happened at Lisbon; I know nothing of it but what I read in the newspapers, or hear from common report, but the loss of the merchants who trade there is said to be very great.

I hear that Mr. Allen of Bath is very ill, and likely to die.

I send you enclosed two notes I have received from Sir John Fielding concerning the horse patrole, and beg your orders on that subject. I had some conversation with him, and tried to make him more explicit on the time that the patrole should be continued; but he would give no answer but the enclosed, and, as you will see by one of his letters, I made him very angry by not putting what he calls *confidence* in him. I am, &c., &c.

C. JENKINSON.

MR. WHATELY[1] TO MR. GRENVILLE.

Parliament Street, June 29, 1764.

SIR,—The devastation of the fire at Lisbon is reckoned to amount to 600,000*l.*, of which about 60,000*l.* is supposed to have been British property; a larger proportion to have belonged to Hamburghers; but the greatest share of all to the Portuguese, as the goods were principally the cargoes of the Brazil fleet, and very small quantities of European commodities were in the warehouses that were burned.

Mr. Pitt's going to the Levée has occasioned a report

---

[1] At this time M.P. for Ludgershall, and Secretary to the Treasury. He was for many years in the very intimate confidence of Mr. Grenville, as his future correspondence in these volumes will testify.

of his coming in immediately; but though warmly propagated and firmly believed in the City, it is observed that it is received with great indifference, and stocks do not rise upon it.

I have given to an attorney the draught you approved of to be laid before Mr. Yorke; but he gives me such an account of Mr. Yorke's dilatoriness in answering cases, that I doubt whether you will get his opinion so immediately as you wish, though I have in the case itself desired him to despatch it, and the attorney will use his most pressing instances to forward it.

I have the honour to be, &c. THOMAS WHATELY.

THE EARL OF HALIFAX TO THE COMTE DE GUERCHY.

A St. James le 29 Juin, 1764.

MONSIEUR,—Ayant mis sous les yeux du Roi la lettre dont votre Excellence m'a honoré du 21, au sujet des gens qui ont eu la hardiesse de tacher d'arrêter son Ecuyer dans la basse cour de son hôtel, Sa Majesté, qui a tous les égards et attentions possibles aux priviléges des Ambassadeurs et Ministres étrangers, et qui souhaite, en toute occasion, de donner des preuves de son amitié pour le Roi votre maître, et du cas que Sa Majesté fait du mérite personnel de V. E., m'a commandé de lui témoigner le grand regret avec lequel Sa Majesté a vu la plainte portée par votre Excellence.

Je dois aussi vous assurer Monsr. combien je suis faché de ce qui s'est passé sur ce sujet. Les gens qui ont commis cette offense sont prêts a vous faire leurs soumissions, quand il plaira à votre Excellence de les recevoir; et j'espere qu'elle en sera contente puis qu'ils ont agi par ignorance sans aucune intention de lui donner offense. J'ai l'honneur d'être, &c., &c.

DUNK HALIFAX.

THE EARL OF SANDWICH TO MR. GRENVILLE.

Belvidere, June 30, 1764.

DEAR SIR,—I had a letter from Dr. Marriott last night, informing me that Dr. Smallbrooke refused the office of King's Advocate, unless he had a salary annexed to it, and earnestly requesting to have it upon the usual conditions. I prevented his being in question for it while it was likely to be sought after by any person of consequence in the profession; but as it now absolutely goes a-begging, I cannot help wishing you would give him your support, as I know of no competitor he can have but Dr. Wynne, whose demerits in our late Cambridge contests are so great that it would be absolute destruction to our cause if it was given to him. I shall be in town to-morrow, or on Monday, and will see Dr. Hay, whose authority in favour of Dr. Marriott, or against him, ought in my opinion to have weight; and if it appears that he is as well qualified as any of those who can put in for it, I hope his late behaviour and assurances for the time to come will incline you to think he deserves the preference on this occasion. I am ever, &c., &c. SANDWICH.

I believe Lord Halifax sent a letter last night to the French Ambassador with the approbation of Lord Chancellor and Lord Mansfield, which, if he is not very unreasonable indeed, will put an end to any farther altercation about the arrest of the Ecuyer; the reason, I only say *I believe*, is, because the letter was sent to His Majesty for his approbation, to Richmond, just as I set out from London last night.

MR. JENKINSON TO MR. GRENVILLE.

London, July 2, 1764.

DEAR SIR,—Since I wrote to you last, Lord Bath has been very ill of a fever, and there was for some time thought to be no hopes of his life; but on Saturday noon he began to mend, and I heard last night that he continued to do so. There is great reason still, however, to doubt whether, at his age, he will have strength enough to struggle through such a disorder as this.

I send you enclosed an account of two very important resolutions which the French Government have thought proper to come to; the one concerning the exportation of their corn, the other on the re-establishment of their East India Company. As far as I can understand them, they neither of them are likely to produce effects at which this country need be alarmed.

As they only allow their corn to be exported without granting any bounty, I should hope that they will not be able to beat us out of the foreign market. I am anxious to know whether they have taken off their provincial taxes upon corn.

As to the re-establishment of their East India Company, as the possession of the Islands of Mauritius and Bourbon is taken from the Company, I infer from thence that they mean to give up the idea of settlements anywhere else; and if this should be the case, it is the most fortunate event that ever happened to our commerce in those parts, and particularly to our possession of Bengal.

There are two or three points of Treasury business which I wish you would turn in your thoughts against your return, that I may then receive your commands upon them.

In the last session of Parliament you assigned as a reason for not going on with the Stamp Act, that you waited only for further information on that subject. This having been said, should not Government appear to take some step for that purpose? I mentioned this to you soon after the Parliament was up. I remember your objections to it; but I think the information may be procured in a manner to obviate those objections, and without it we may perhaps be accused of neglect [1].

---

[1] On the 10th of March, in this year, a series of Resolutions had been moved by Mr. Grenville in the House of Commons, of which the 14th was to the following effect, viz., " That towards further defraying the said expenses, it may be proper to charge certain stamp duties in the said colonies and plantations." This Resolution, intended to produce a comparatively small addition to the revenue of Great Britain, for the protection and support of her colonies, was the cause of one of the greatest revolutions which has been recorded in the history of the world. It was in the following year subdivided into fifty-five resolutions, and these were afterwards formed into a Bill, and the Bill passed into a law, under the name of the Stamp Act 5th George III. c. 12. Mr. Grenville's name has been always associated with the American Stamp Act, because he is generally believed to have been the author or inventor of it, and the zeal with which he invariably defended it has strengthened that opinion. Mr. Jenkinson, however, in his place in the House of Commons in May, 1777, directly asserted the contrary; and who so likely to be well informed on the subject as Mr. Jenkinson, who held the office of Secretary of the Treasury, and was in Mr. Grenville's most intimate confidence? He said, " that the measure of the Stamp Act was not Mr. Grenville's: if the Act was a good one, the merit of it was not due to Mr. Grenville: if it was a bad one, the errors or the ill policy of it did not belong to

Another point worthy of consideration is the situation of Mr. Fawcett, now at Hanover, which you mentioned to me one day at the Board. It is certain that he is now there at a great charge, and yet doing very little for it. On the other hand, it is absolutely necessary that there should be somebody there, first to meet Monsieur de la Salle, the French Commissary, to settle the account of the prisoners of war. This negociation proceeds very slowly, and the French will certainly continue to do all they can to delay it; but if we should recall our Commissary, while the French continue to keep one there,

him." This declaration from Mr. Jenkinson has led me to infer that it was he himself who first suggested the idea to Mr. Grenville, by whom it was warmly adopted, and they mutually exerted themselves in bringing the measure to perfection. But there is also reason to believe that the idea did not originate with Mr. Jenkinson. I have found among Mr. Grenville's papers a letter addressed to Mr. Jenkinson, by one Henry McCulloh, dated "*Turnham Green*, July 5, 1763." It contains "a brief state of such taxes as are usually raised in His Majesty's old settled Colonies on the Continent of America, viz., North and South Carolina, Virginia, and Pennsylvania;" and afterwards informs him, that "a stamp duty on vellum and paper in America, at sixpence, twelvepence, and eighteenpence per sheet, would, at a moderate computation, amount to upwards of sixty thousand sterling per annum; or, if extended to the West Indies, would produce double that sum." This letter was accompanied by the draughts of two Bills, "most humbly addressed to the consideration of the Right Honourable George Grenville, Esq.;" one of them entitled *Proposals with respect to a Stamp Duty on America, &c.*, and the other *For creating and issuing bills of credit, under the denomination of Exchequer Bills of Union, for the general use of His Majesty's Colonies in America*," &c. The latter is stated to have been "submitted to the Right Honourable the Earl of Halifax, in 1755, and with some alterations will answer the end proposed at this time." It has also been occasionally said that Lord Halifax was the originator of the Stamp Act, and his knowledge of and connection with McCulloh may have afforded some grounds for the supposition. I have not succeeded in ascertaining any particulars respecting McCulloh. His letter is written in a clerk's hand, signed only by himself; and, to judge from the tremulous mode of writing his name, he must have been a man very far advanced in years.

we shall appear to break up a negociation for the settlement of an account from whence we have hoped to reap great advantages; and you may recollect that Mr. Mildmay was employed, at the end of last war, upon a commission similar to this. There is also another business in which Fawcett is employed; I mean the receiving the magazines and stores that were seized, and the disposing of them. It is true that these two commissions might be executed by a person who would cost Government less; but as he now is there, and really does his business well, you will judge whether you would recall him, and send another who will cost less, to supply his place, which in such case I think you must do; for there is no one else, I believe, on the spot, in the service of the Crown, who could be employed in this business.

The last point is the revenue of Quebec. Some resolution should be taken on this subject before the Board of Trade breaks up, so that proper instructions may be sent to the Governor in the course of this summer. You know that we have long done all that we could to put this affair forward, and that it rests, like many other questions, with the Attorney General. I will call on him, however, before your return to town, and endeavour to get this done.

I ask pardon for troubling you with so long a letter on these subjects; but I imagined you might like best to turn them in your thoughts while you was in the country. I have, &c., &c. C. JENKINSON.

THE EARL OF SANDWICH TO MR. GRENVILLE.

Whitehall, July 3, 1764.

DEAR SIR,—I will see the Lord Chancellor, and try to get him to speak in favour of Dr. Marriott; I am perfectly satisfied with this reference to him, and agree with you that his sanction is necessary to this measure.

The reports of a change of Administration are in the mouths of many people, but I see no symptom of their being founded either from His Majesty's behaviour in the Closet, or from any observations I can make elsewhere. Mr. Pitt was certainly most coldly received when he made his appearance at the Levée last week; the King talked to every body near him before he took notice of him, and then asked him a single question, and scarce waited for an answer: of this I was an eyewitness. I am, however, inclined to think Mr. Pitt has hopes of coming into employment from some division among ourselves; and I understand, from those who talk his language, that they lay great stress upon differences they believe have happened between the Duke of Bedford and Lord Bute. To what this report can owe its rise I am at a loss to guess, as I am convinced it is utterly void of foundation. The Duke of Bedford, when he was in town the other day, was in the utmost good humour, and nothing fell from him, in several conversations I had with him, that shewed the least uneasiness: he just dropped that he imagined the making the Irish Peers[1] was Lord Bute's doing, but without any

---

[1] The additions to the Irish Peerage were; Sir Edward King, to be Baron Kingston; Mr. Stephen Moore, Baron Kilworth; and Sir Ralph Gore, Baron Gore: the latter was afterwards Viscount Belleisle and Earl of Ross.

animadversions upon it, or urging the impropriety of the measure. I have this morning asked Lord Gower whether he has observed any symptoms, in the Duke of Bedford's language, of his being inclined to show any discontent in consequence of his dislike to Lord Bute; he assures me that he thinks he is quite easy and pleased with the present situation of things, and that though he is jealous of Lord Bute, and naturally adverse to him, he does not believe he is at all disposed to show any discontent upon that subject, and is of opinion that the report is utterly groundless.

I think of passing a day at Woburn the latter end of this week, and hope to find you in town at my return. If I pick up anything there worthy your notice, you shall see me as soon as I come back.

I am, &c., &c.   SANDWICH.

THE EARL OF HALIFAX TO MR. GRENVILLE.

Great George Street, July 3, 1764.

DEAR SIR,—With this I send you the letter which I wrote to the French Ambassador on Friday night. Justice Kynaston waited on him on Sunday, and made his submissions; since which M. de Guerchy's courier has arrived from Paris. He was with me this morning, and showed me a letter he had received from the Duc de Praslin, in which that Minister expresses his surprise at the violation of the Ambassador's privilege, and says that in case reparation be not made, the English Ambassadors will not be any longer allowed the privileges they now enjoy in Foreign Courts. He said he would send me a letter, informing me officially of the contents of that he has received from the Duc de

Praslin. He likewise said he could not tell me whether he should be satisfied with Mr. Kynaston's submission 'till he should hear again from his Court, which he did not imagine he should do before to-morrow se'nnight.

I have wrote a strong letter to my Lord Rochfort[1] upon the interruption given to our logwood-cutters, which I thought proper and necessary.

I am, &c., &c.   DUNK HALIFAX.

THE LORD CHANCELLOR TO MR. GRENVILLE.

London, July 3, 1764.

DEAR SIR,—I had the honour of yours by the last post, and readily admit your excuse for not giving me the pleasure of seeing you before you left London, being perfectly sensible of the multiplicity of your engagements.

I have seen, as you suppose, Lord Halifax on the business of Guerchy's last complaint, and I informed him of my idea, how I thought that matter might be quieted, without committing himself, viz., by the magistrates apologizing for the consequence in the execution of their warrant; and if that did not satisfy, to desire to know with more precision than yet, what they insisted upon as the accepted law of nations in their own Court, by a State Act, that he might give an answer upon so serious, political, and delicate a question. All their memorials, that I have seen, are general, loose, and vague; and I am persuaded the Corps Diplomatique will hesitate on a Précis on this occasion.

My Lord seemed in general to adopt my way of rea-

[1] British Ambassador at Madrid

soning, and wrote a very civil letter to Guerchy in consequence of it, a draft of which I saw; and I think, if the Minister hath any prudence, he will close his complaints. I have on this subject to add, I think our tone is too low in conversing with these exalted foreigners.

The papers have informed you of the death of Mr. Allen, of Bath.

I wish you would suspend any engagements of a political nature *there* 'till I have the honour of speaking with you.

I concur with you that the King's Advocate will keep cool.

I sit daily, and were you a private person, could, therefore, but write after the newspapers.

I have only to add that I am, with great respect and sincerity, &c. NORTHINGTON.

MR. GRENVILLE TO THE EARL OF HALIFAX.

Wotton, July 4, 1764.

MY DEAR LORD,—Your Lordship knows my sentiments upon the arrest of M. de Guerchy's servant, and the imprisonment of the constables, by what passed when I had the honour of seeing you last. I will not take upon me to say whether the privilege of a foreign Minister can protect a servant charged upon oath with a design to commit a murder, and to set fire to a house, and prevent his being taken up in his court-yard, because I question whether that protection, in case of crimes, is throughly settled and established by the law of nations; but it has always seemed clear to me that no foreign Minister can have a right to imprison and to abuse the officers of justice acting under the legal and judicial authority of the country where he resides. I agree, therefore, in opinion with the Attorney General, that in this respect the Ambassador's conduct, as it has been represented to me, is highly improper and irregular. I think, too, that in the disposition in which M. de Guerchy is, the likeliest way to put a proper end to this troublesome business was to have convinced M. de Guerchy and the Court of France of that irregularity; and the answer which you have received from him since your letter, and the submissions in consequence of it, confirm me in that opinion, in which I sincerely wish the event may shew I am mistaken. I am glad that you have writ to Lord Rochford upon the subject of the interruption given to our logwood-cutters, contrary to the express article of the last Treaty; and I think it necessary that orders should be immediately given to the Commanding Officer of His Majesty's ships at Jamaica to send a Captain of a man-of-war, whom he can rely upon, to visit that coast and our settlers there, and to report a true state of the facts, which, we may depend upon it, will be stated very differently by the Spanish Governor and by our people; and a great deal of time will be lost by the Court of Spain in making the inquiries into it, whilst the complaints of this infraction of the Treaty will augment, and the neglect of the only proper means be attributed to those whose duty it is to put as speedy a stop as is possible to such proceedings, as will otherwise, in a few years, rise to a height not to be stopped, and occasion fresh disturbances between the two kingdoms. To prevent this it seems to me necessary that one of the King's vessels should be sent to that coast every year at least, to examine and to report to his superior officer, and to the Governor of Jamaica, for your information, and that of the Board of Trade, the state which our logwood-cutters are in. I propose to be in town on Monday next; in the meantime I would not omit sending you my thoughts upon matters of this great moment. I am, &c., &c. GEORGE GRENVILLE.

MR. GRENVILLE TO THE BISHOP OF GLOUCESTER.

Wotton, July 5, 1764.

MY LORD,—I received with great concern yesterday, the account of the death of that virtuous and good man, Mr. Allen[1], together with the memorial and papers which your Lordship transmitted to me in consequence of his direction. I have sent them to town to be laid before the Treasury, that we may consider them agreeably to Mr. Allen's desire, and may afterwards consult with the Postmaster General of the most effectual means for putting that branch of the public revenue which he had so greatly improved upon the properest footing. I sincerely lament and condole with your Lordship upon the melancholy event of Mr. Allen's death, from the loss which the public sustains of such an example, and from the grief which it must occasion to all those who had the happiness of seeing him more nearly. I am, &c., &c.

GEORGE GRENVILLE.

---

[1] Mr. Allen distributed a very large fortune in most munificent charities, and liberal legacies to his friends; among others, he bequeathed one thousand pounds to Mr. Pitt. His niece was married to Dr. Warburton, Bishop of Gloucester, and they constantly resided with him at Prior Park. He is said to have been the original *Squire Allworthy* of Fielding's novel of *Tom Jones*, in which is given a description of the beautiful situation of Mr. Allen's house at Prior Park, near Bath, the scene of the early years of Tom Jones.

MR. JENKINSON TO MR. GRENVILLE.

North End, July 5, 1764.

DEAR SIR,—I am sorry to find that you are so uneasy at what has passed with respect to the Sheriff of Banff.

I hope you will consider the point well before you take any step upon it.

I shall feel the same uneasiness on this account, if I could see any reason to impute it to a motive of hostility to you; but I should hardly give credit to this upon the suggestion of any man breathing. I will tell you all the facts I know upon this subject when you come to town, and, if you please, the authorities on which they are grounded. Without a true state of the case, it is as impossible for me to write to Mr. Mackenzie as for you. I shall be ready, when you are properly informed, to convey to him your sentiments as from yourself; I always execute your commands with zeal and with pleasure; and I have more than once, as you may well know, spoke my sentiments with freedom against measures which I did not approve; but I cannot, from myself, charge any man with an offence of which I have not reason to think him guilty; and you would not, I am sure, wish that I should disoblige a friend by doing what could be of no use to you.

I took an opportunity of seeing Lord and Lady Bute this morning; and I delivered, in your's and Mrs. Grenville's name, the message of congratulation you desired me, to which they desired me to return you and Mrs. Grenville their thanks.

Mons. D'Eon endeavoured yesterday to get his trial put off. His Counsel urged that M. de Guerchy had sent several persons away that were necessary witnesses for his defence, but the Attorney General proved that these had been out of the kingdom more than three months before the fact was committed on which M. D'Eon is accused.

The Court upon this would not allow of any delay, and ordered the trial for the sittings after term.

It is now thought that Lord Bath will not recover. Mr. Legge is said to be wonderfully better, in consequence of his drinking some waters upon Blackheath; but I pay little credit to this, which seems to be an old woman's story.

Since writing the above, I have seen Lord Sandwich. He desired me to say that he had followed Mr. Mackenzie's recommendation implicitly, and that he understood from you, at the beginning of the session, that this was what you approved; but that if he had suspected that what has been done with respect to the Sheriff of Banff could have been disagreeable to you, he should certainly have preferred your recommendation to that of any one else.

He says he knows nothing of what passed between the King and Sir James Lowther; but that Sir James desired him to take the King's orders, informing him of what was to be done, and begging that he, and not Lord Halifax, might carry the King's orders into execution.

I have seen also Mr. Robinson, who talked much of the gracious manner in which the King treated Sir James Lowther; but he did not seem to know what had passed, and I, on the other hand, did not think it proper to appear either inquisitive or ignorant.

I forgot to mention that Lord Sandwich, in consequence of a conversation he had with Lord Gower, has dropped all his gloomy apprehensions. I have, &c.

C. JENKINSON.

THE DUKE OF YORK TO MR. GRENVILLE.

Milan, July 7, 1764.

MR. GRENVILLE,—On my arrival here, I had the pleasure of finding a letter from you among those returned from Florence, in which you inform me that the King had been pleased to order me 4000*l*.

I desire you will convey my thanks to His Majesty in the most respectful manner, and assure him that every mark of his favour will ever be received by me with the most grateful acknowledgments. Remaining your very affectionate friend, EDWARD.

MR. JENKINSON TO MR. GRENVILLE.

North End, July 9, 1764.

DEAR SIR,—As soon as I received your letter of the 2nd, I went immediately to Lord Sandwich, who, as Secretary for the Northern Department, has the disposal of the Sheriffs Depute of Scotland.

He told me that a new Sheriff Depute for the county of Banff had been appointed more than ten days ago, and that it was now impossible to recall the appointment. I believe that all the steps he took in this affair were at the recommendation of Mr. Mackenzie; but I was told this morning that the contest on this occasion lay between Lord Fife and Lord Findlater, who is the Hereditary Sheriff of that county, and has much the largest estate in it, and urged on that account his pretensions to recommend the Deputy.

These and many other reasons I heard this morning in defence of the propriety of Mr. Mackenzie's recommendation, from a man whose faith I think I can rely on; but I would not have you take this state of the case from my representation, as I know that Lord Fife thinks me, for some reason or other, his enemy, which I assure you is not true. On the other hand it would be improper to make Mr. Mackenzie uneasy on a point which is irretrievable, and where it is possible he may be found upon enquiry to be right, especially as I find of late that he is said to have expressed great dissatisfaction; but all this I submit to you.

I find, by Lord Sandwich, the King has given orders for the appointment of Sir James Lowther's friend to the Deanery of Carlisle[1]. Lord Sandwich, who took the King's orders, and who writes to you by this convenience, will inform you of what passed on this occasion; I suspect that Sir James stays in town to wait on you, for I find that he has put off his journey to the Spa for a few days.

Lord Warkworth and Lady Anne[2] were married yesterday, and the young couple are at present at Sion.

I urged very much to Sir John Fielding that the expense of the horse patrole, if it was to be permanent, should be a county charge: he did not make any objection to the propriety of such a proposal, but said that the members of the county would never hear of it.

If you have no objection, I should think that as

[1] Dr. Thomas Wilson.
[2] Lady Anne Stuart, daughter of Lord Bute.

robberies are very frequent, it might as well be tried for three months more.

Lord Bath is much better. I am told his fever has totally left him.

I have reserved to the last the information you desire concerning Mr. Pitt's reception. I thought you would have received a full account of this from other hands; I should otherwise have sent it to you sooner. I was told by those that were present that the King took great pains to make it appear, that he did not mean him any particular civility; that he passed him at first, speaking to those on each side of him, but not to him; that he said something of little importance to him; and went to some one else, and then returned again and shortly said something else to him. As to the paragraphs in the papers on this subject, they are to be slighted. If the enemy finds that they give any uneasiness, there will be ten thousand times more, for they are easily invented, and Lord Bute suffered much by being known to be sensible to them. On the other hand, Lord Sandwich thinks that Mr. Pitt has something in view. He will write to you on this subject. I think his information proves only that Mr. Pitt has lowered his pretensions, and would be content to come in on less terms, and to separate himself from the Duke of Newcastle, and that part of the Opposition. What he has heard differs from what Sir Richard Lyttelton told you only in this, that he is supposed to have said that he did not mean to touch the Boards; that he wanted no more than a majority in the Cabinet; and it is also said that some of his friends have been in spirits of late. I cannot, however, discover that he has had any expectations or hopes given him from any quarter whatsoever. There is every appearance to the contrary; and yet as a politican I cannot but have apprehensions, and should think it wise in you to prepare remedies against those evils which time in itself will generate. In the present system are there not certain circumstances which cannot last long as they are, and should be remedied without delay, lest they bring down the whole building with it?

I am, &c., &c.   C. JENKINSON.

THE EARL OF FIFE[1] TO MR. GRENVILLE.

Duff House, July 11, 1764.

MY DEAR SIR,—I had last post the honour of your letter. I do hope the commission to one Mr. Erskine appointing him Sheriff of this county, if granted, will be recalled.

I am informed he is a very improper person, and as there never has been any application made to me in that matter, there is no other view in it but just to hurt my interest in the country; a greater step could not have been taken against Mr. Wilkes, my friends in this corner will certainly believe me *expelled*. I have no connection with any but Mr. Grenville, and I am sure he will not suffer me to be so improperly treated. I will only beg your indulgence for being so troublesome, and offer Mrs. Grenville my respectful compliments, and remain, &c., &c.   FIFE.

[1] James, second Earl of Fife: he was made a British Peer as Baron Fife in 1790, and died in 1809.

MR. STUART MACKENZIE TO MR. GRENVILLE.

Castle Menzies, July 15, 1764.

SIR,—I had yesterday the honour of your letter of the 6th instant, the contents whereof I own did not a little surprise me; however, I shall forbear at present entering into any comment upon them, and shall only state to you the matter of fact concerning the Sheriff of Banffshire, as it really is; which I apprehend you will find a little different from what you imagined it to be, when you favoured me with that letter.

His Majesty having been pleased to promote Mr. Bruce (late Sheriff Depute for the county of Stirling) to the Bench, there immediately appeared several candidates for his Sheriffship, and, among others, Mr. John Erskine, Advocate, who having exerted himself in support of Government at a time when his services were of use, and never having had any notice taken of him for it, I resolved, though I was not even personally acquainted with him, to recommend him to succeed Mr. Bruce as Sheriff of Stirlingshire; but just at that time I received an application in favour of Mr. Cockburn, late Sheriff Depute of Banffshire, who was desirous to resign that office, and to obtain the Sheriffship of Stirlingshire; Mr. Cockburn being a man of an excellent character, and having had, in his sphere, great merit with Government, I was glad to embrace the opportunity of obliging him, especially as his request was so very moderate a one, as that of exchanging one Sheriffship for another of equal value, and I immediately informed Mr. Erskine's friends, that as Mr. Cockburn had thought it worth his while to apply for the Sheriffship of Stirlingshire, I could not avoid recommending him; but that in order to make amends in some degree to Mr. Erskine for his disappointment, I would recommend him to the vacancy which Mr. Cockburn's removal would make in Banffshire.

After these points had been thus settled, I received a very earnest application from Lord Deskfoord, both in his own, and in his father, Lord Findlater's, name, in favour of Mr. Murray, Deputy to the Lord Advocate, to be appointed Sheriff Depute of Banffshire; this recommendation was also strongly enforced by the Lord Advocate, who gave me a high character of the gentleman in question; however, I acquainted Lord Deskfoord and his father with the situation of the affair, and that it was merely a particular attention to Mr. Cockburn's request that occasioned any vacancy in Banff at this time; and that as Mr. Erskine had acquiesced in the arrangement in favour of Mr. Cockburn, I could not avoid recommending him (Erskine) to the Sheriffship of Banff; that I had already done it, and consequently that it was impossible for me to comply with their Lordships' request.

With respect to Lord Fife, I never heard a single syllable of any recommendation of his, or of any wish he had about that Sheriffship, till I read it yesterday in your own letter.

Now, from what I have said, Sir, you will observe that the alarm which Lord Fife has taken on the supposition that the person recommended by the Findlater family (Lord Fife's great rival in that county) was to be the Sheriff, has no manner of foundation; for Mr. Murray, whom the Findlaters recommended, is *not* made Sheriff, and Mr. Erskine, who has no kind of connection with that family, *is* appointed Sheriff; and being quite a neutral man his nomination cannot affect Lord Fife's interest in the county, no more than Mr. Cockburn's appointment did, who was the late Sheriff there.

With respect to certain unfavourable insinuations thrown out in your last letter, all I shall say, Sir, on this occasion is, that I did flatter myself that my conduct and behaviour towards you, from the first hour that His Majesty was pleased to call you to the office which you now hold, to this very day, had been uniformly such as must have freed me, or any man whatever, from the smallest imputation; and I cannot help thinking it very hard, to be, in some degree, charged with countenancing attacks on your friends, which God knows, I never even dreamed of, but on the contrary, have been constantly endeavouring, as I can call hundreds to testify, to gain friends to you by every method in my power. I will now detain you no longer, though I could say a great deal more on some of the points contained in this letter, but I will defer it 'till another opportunity. I have, &c., &c.

J. S. MACKENZIE.

P. S.—I have this minute received accounts of the Earl of Findlater's death[1].

MR. GRENVILLE TO THE EARL OF SANDWICH.

Downing Street, July 16, 1764, past 1 in the morning.

MY DEAR LORD,—I have just finished a long conference with M. de Guerchy, who has shewn me the French account for ours and their prisoners of war. They allow upwards of 15,000,000 of livres, or 667,000*l.*

[1] James Ogilvy, fifth Earl. He was Vice-Admiral of Scotland, and was succeeded in that office by the Earl of Hyndford.

sterling, to be due to us upon the balance. They strike off 255,000*l.* sterling for prisoners taken before war was declared, 15,000*l.* for prisoners who were passengers, and 121,000*l.* for articles about the prisoners not explained; and 113,000*l.* for English prisoners maintained by them. These sums make up 1,173,000*l.* sterling, the sum total of our account. I combated the first article of defalcation especially, and referred the whole to the Commissioners of the sick and wounded, but the most extraordinary part still remains. He proposed, when these deductions were allowed, to pay the 15,000,000 of livres in fifteen years. This I would not hear of, and think it full as bad as refusing to pay it at all. He wants to have us allow of the great article of deduction for prisoners taken before the war, and then for us to propose a shorter term for the payment, which I declared and insisted strongly that we had a right to have whatever was due paid at farthest in a year or two.

We ran through all the old argument about the prisoners taken before the war was declared, but neither of us were convinced.

He tells me that he is to see you to-morrow morning, and proposes from you to go to Woburn. Would you not write to the Duke of Bedford to apprize him of this strange proposal, which I think it would be impossible to hear of, or to admit of a delay in the payment of the whole which shall be due for above a year or two, especially if any doubtful articles are insisted upon being disallowed. I am ever, &c., &c.

GEORGE GRENVILLE.

M. de Guerchy goes directly from you to Woburn, and therefore your messenger must be ready to set out immediately after your conference, if you propose he should be there before M. de Guerchy.

MR. GRENVILLE TO THE EARL OF HERTFORD.

Downing Street, July 20, 1764.

My DEAR LORD,—The sincere desire which I have to give your Lordship a satisfactory answer to the letter which I had the honour to receive from you, has been the reason of my having hitherto deferred writing to you upon the subject of it. I knew the King's general resolution, not to make any promotion at present from the Earls' Bench, and notwithstanding the report to the contrary had the greatest cause to believe that His Majesty would not depart from it. This has been verified by the event, and I can assure your Lordship that, as far as I have been informed, there has been no foundation for what you have heard, except that several Peers of great distinction may have wished for that promotion, which I believe is true.

I thought, however, that when other requests of this kind have been mentioned, it would be more agreeable to your Lordship that your's likewise should be laid before the King, which I therefore determined to do, and the rather as it would give me an opportunity of doing justice to you, which I shall always embrace with the greatest pleasure. In consequence of this resolution I took an occasion of representing to His Majsety your Lordship's situation and services, and the many reasons which you had to hope for this mark of His Royal favour.

The King repeated to me his determination to make

no Marquesses at present, but I have the satisfaction to assure you that he was pleased to express his approbation of your Lordship in the most gracious terms; and as you seem to wish that this application should go through as few hands as possible, he ordered me to inform you that no other person whatsoever should be acquainted with it.

You will have heard of the many difficulties and disputes which we have had with M. de Guerchy; in some of them, which related to the introduction of prohibited goods, and of an unlimited quantity of wine duty free, I have been particularly concerned.

The notorious abuse which has been practised under colour of this indulgence, the particulars of which (though they are unhappily too publicly known) I would not willingly enter into, occasioned a great ferment here, and a body of six or seven thousand manufacturers came to the King to complain of it, and to desire that he would order the laws to be put into execution, which his Majesty solemnly directed to be done, and the orders were given accordingly. The rule which has been established with regard to Foreign Ministers for above a hundred years in this country, and which is confirmed at the beginning of every new reign, was ordered to be followed: by that rule Foreign Ministers are entitled to have their first entrys duty free, and that première entrée is limited to one tun of wine, their equipages, and the furniture of their house, but not to extend to any merchandize. The time for making this première entrée has been literally construed, and limited only to six months. M. de Guerchy, on the contrary, insisted on the reciprocity, that your Lordship had a right to bring in what you pleased at Paris, and that therefore he had the same right here, and upon this footing required that an order should be given by the Treasury for bringing in some clothes of his and of Madame de Guerchy.

No such order could be given, especially at this conjuncture, nor had it been usual to give such an order, though the introduction of these foreign goods may sometimes have been winked at when done by Foreign Ministers.

When this would not succeed, he presented a memorial to Lord Halifax to claim it, and to desire a positive answer, that he might apprize his Court of it, that an exact reciprocity might be observed towards you. This memorial was referred to the Treasury, who drew up an answer to it, stating the ancient rule which has been settled, and observed for these hundred years; that we did not purpose to make any new rule, but showed the necessity of not departing from that which had so long and so solemnly been established at a time when so many notorious abuses of it had been committed. We urged the impossibility of laying down the same rule in all countries, and that if it were done, the different laws and situations of different countries would make the favour and indulgence extremely unequal, particularly in the present instance between Great Britain and France. We therefore insisted that the reciprocity could only be to show the British Minister at Paris the same indulgence as was shown to all other Ministers of the same rank at that Court, which was what we practised here with regard to the French Minister, and that an alteration of the one would probably produce an alteration in the other. After some consideration and conversation with Lord Halifax, M. de Guerchy withdrew the memorial, and Lord Halifax the answer. He has since wished to have this packet containing his clothes, and Madame and Melle. de Guerchy's, restored to him on his return to Paris, which has been ordered by the Treasury accordingly.

I have troubled you with this long account of this trifling business, that you may know the particulars if you hear anything further about it.

You have received, I know, from Lord Halifax, a detail with authentic papers to verify what has passed about the taking up of his Ecuyer, and his confining the constables. I am fully satisfied that the wisest way is to let this mutual complaint drop likewise; as, whatever may be the case of the former, the Court of France can never justify the latter, and I really think that we have a sufficient number of disputes of a very serious nature between the two Courts, without laying hold of trifles and formalities.

This brings me to a matter which, I am convinced, is of the highest moment to the peace and good harmony between the two Courts. M. de Guerchy has communicated to us the defalcations proposed to be made from our accounts of the expenses of maintaining their prisoners of war. Your Lordship has so frequently answered the reasonings upon which the first article of those defalcations is founded, that it is unnecessary for me to repeat your answers in order to prove the impropriety and impossibility of making that allowance by admitting that the prisoners taken before war was declared were unjustly, or (to use M. de Mirepoix's words about the *Lys* and the *Alcide*) piratically taken.

We have always insisted, and, I think, rightly, that

the commencement of hostilities is the commencement of war, even though there should be no declaration of war at all. That this has been laid down by the most eminent writers on the law of nations, and that the practice has been agreeable to it, and that France herself approved of it by attacking Minorca without a declaration of war. The 2nd article, relative to the passengers, &c., is by no means of the same magnitude, either in its consequences or its value, but I believe the charge is in the usual manner.

The 3rd article of defalcation is in the general charge of expenses relating to prisoners, which certainly must be explained as the Court of France desires it. I can make no observations upon the French account of prisoners, as that will be more properly examined by our Commissioners of sick and wounded, and for the prisoners. But there is a question far more important than any, and which surprised me extremely. I mean the proposal as to the time of paying to us what shall be allowed to be due.

M. de Guerchy first named fifteen years, which would certainly amount to a refusal to pay it at all. The Treaty expressly provides that the prisoners shall be restored in six weeks at latest from the exchange of the Ratifications, "*each Crown paying* respectively the advances which shall have been made for their subsistence and maintenance, conformably to the receipts, stated accounts, and other authentic titles to be furnished on one side and on the other, and it is further stipulated that the execution of this article" shall be proceeded upon immediately after the exchange of the Ratifications.

Is it possible to contend, after a year and a half

already elapsed, and such large deductions insisted upon, that the demand of a number of years (I speak not now of fifteen, from which he himself departed, but of four or five years) can be deemed a fair and just performance of this article?

Lord Halifax, Lord Sandwich, and myself, had a long conversation with M. de Guerchy upon this subject, the day before yesterday, and endeavoured to convince him, by the most serious arguments, that the continuance of the peace and good understanding between the two Courts depended upon his Court's paying a stricter regard to the terms of the Treaty, in this as well as in the articles of the Canada Bills and of Dunkirk, than they seem at present to intend.

M. de Guerchy wished that we should first admit of the great articles of defalcation; that we should agree to postpone the payment for a number of years; and that we should then enter into the other articles and proofs of our account.

We insisted in the strongest terms upon settling the whole together; that if they expected any considerable deductions, to which we should show as much facility as could be consistent with the honour of the King and kingdom, and with common justice, they must, at least, deserve it, by a speedy payment of what should be allowed to be due.

To this M. de Guerchy urged the great difficulty of their finding the money. We replied that we could not believe that France, if she were so resolved, could not pay 600,000*l.* or 700,000*l.* in a year or two, when Great Britain could raise above double that sum, in all probability, and in a less time, for the payment of what we owed in Germany; and if there were any difficulties, that, after the great restitutions which had been so honourably performed on our part, they were, at least, as much bound to exert themselves for the payment of what they should admit that they justly owed to us.

We represented to him repeatedly how utterly impossible it was for us to consent to what he proposed, and desired him to represent to his Court, as he was not fully instructed to treat upon it himself, the great danger which there was of breaking the good correspondence and harmony which we had wished to cultivate, and of inflaming the minds of men by a proceeding which we could not attempt to justify.

It is, indeed, absolutely necessary that this matter should be fully and strongly stated to the Court of France, and you will, therefore, I am persuaded, excuse my writing to you so much at large upon a subject on which our future situation with that Court will, in a great measure, depend.

I do not look upon this in the light of a pecuniary transaction only; for, however welcome that sum of money may be to us, it is far more important from the consideration of it as a test of the intentions of France in the performance of the stipulations of that Treaty; and if she breaks them in the first instance that comes before the public, there is scarce a man in this country who will rely upon their good faith in those which still remain unperformed; whereas a fair and honourable conduct on this occasion would give a favourable impression of the whole.

Your Lordship knows what an effect the postponing the payments for four or five years would have, and therefore I need not enforce that argument; at the same time, it would be my earnest desire to settle this business amicably, if it could be done upon a reasonable footing. The importance of this question, and my desire to give you all the information I can of what has passed, as well as my own sentiments upon it, has been my inducement to trouble you with this long letter. I sincerely hope that, by your firm and able conduct of it, you will bring it to a happy issue for your own honour and satisfaction, and for the public advantage. I feel myself deeply interested in the latter from my duty to my King and country, and in the former from the sincere regard and respect with which I have the honour to be, &c., &c. GEORGE GRENVILLE.

THE MARQUESS OF CARNARVAN TO MR. GRENVILLE.

Minchenden House, July 21, 1764.

DEAR SIR,—Upon my return hither from Gloucestershire last night I found the favour of your letter of the 17th, acquainting me with His Majesty's determination in favour of Mr. Stanley to be Governor of the Isle of Wight.

I very sincerely hope that this appointment may in every shape answer the expectations of Government, and that Mr. Stanley may have weight and interest enough in the Island to render the power of the Crown as respectable there as it ought to be.

But as Mr. Stanley's connections and mine are very different in the county, it will be impossible for me or my friends to co-operate with him, or to give him that assistance we should wish to any person employed by His Majesty.

From this circumstance I find that it can be no longer

in my power to be of any service to Government from the offices I have now the honour to hold of Lord-Lieutenant and Custos Rotulorum, and as that was my only object, which now is frustrated, I must desire the favour of you to entreat His Majesty's permission for me to resign them : and as I am convinced of my own small consequence at Court, it is my intention to retire from it, and as soon as my waiting is finished next week, to implore His Majesty's leave to quit the Bedchamber, and thereby make room for some one that may have more power to serve him, though no one can have a stronger inclination.

As to the Woodward of the New Forest, before I troubled you with my application, I mentioned Mr. St. John to the Duke of Bedford, and received a very civil letter from his Grace, with his approbation of him. I then desired the favour of you to recommend him to His Majesty, as one approved of by the Duke, as a person of the largest fortune in the county, of known integrity, and one that had never spared his labour or his money in support of His Majesty's measures. These circumstances I thought sufficiently strong to authorize my recommendation, and which I apprehended when I had the pleasure of talking to you last, had been settled; and I still flatter myself that he will be approved of, as I am certain he is the properest man in the county for the office; and you may depend upon it that I should not have trifled with you (and I hope with no man living), in making use of one gentleman's name to serve another.

As to the timber of the New Forest, I fear it is a larger object on paper, and in conversation, than in reality, but this the Duke of Bedford must be the best judge of; I am certain that what there is, Mr. St. John will take care to preserve.

I have but one favour to ask of you, which I believe will be the last I shall presume to trouble you with, which is the continuance of your assistance in favour of the Irish Memorial, now depending before the Treasury Board, and which I flatter myself appeared fully to you as a matter of justice. I am, with great regard, &c.

CARNARVAN.

P.S. As I am very ignorant in matters of form, should be greatly obliged to you to let me know in what manner, after I have the King's permission to resign the Lieutenancy, I must proceed: whether by writing to the Secretary of State, and whether I should not send back the Patents to the Secretary's Office.

MR. GRENVILLE TO THE MARQUESS OF CARNARVAN.

Downing Street, July 22, 1764.

MY DEAR LORD,—I am extremely sorry as well as surprised to see by the letter, which I had the honour to receive from your Lordship last night, that His Majesty's appointment of Mr. Stanley to the Government of the Isle of Wight gives you so much uneasiness as to to make you think it proper and necessary to desire me to ask His Majesty's permission for you to resign the offices of Lord-Lieutenant and Custos Rotulorum of Hampshire, and to determine you to implore his leave to quit the Bedchamber as soon as your waiting next week is finished.

I mentioned some of the reasons for the appointment of that gentleman in my former letter, and intended to have explained them more fully to you, when I should have the pleasure of seeing you. In all my transactions with your Lordship I have endeavoured to contribute, as far as I was able, to your honour and satisfaction, and it is from the same motive that I now take the liberty to desire, that you would give some time to weigh this measure more maturely by yourself and with your friends before it is carried into execution, and to consider thoroughly upon what it is founded, and whether it has not been taken more hastily and warmly than the subject can require or justify. I owe this earnest request both to your Lordship and to the King's service; but if, contrary to my sincere wishes and unprejudiced opinion, you shall still persevere in this resolution, I must, in consequence of what you ask me, inform your Lordship, that as your office gives you personal access to His Majesty, I think that the properest and most respectful method to apprize the King of your intention both with regard to the Lieutenancy, as well as to the Bedchamber, will be from yourself, at an audience for that purpose, and there is no other formality I believe necessary. By this means your Lordship will best be able to explain your own motives for a step, which I am persuaded will much surprise His Majesty, and I cannot be blamed for not having done justice to your sentiments, which probably might be the case, as I must repeat to you that I do not see any sufficient reason for what you propose to do. Allow me once more to recommend this matter to your farther consideration, and to assure you that I do it from the same disposition, and from the same principles, upon which I have hitherto acted, and shall always wish to act towards you, and from the real regard with which I am, &c., &c.

GEORGE GRENVILLE.

P.S. I will take the first opportunity to consider what is further to be done about the Irish Memorial which you mention, and I shall certainly be desirous not only to do you justice in it, but to give the most favourable attention to that, and every other request of yours, which is consistent with my duty.

GENERAL CONWAY TO THE SECRETARY AT WAR (MR. WELBORE ELLIS).

Park Place, July 22, 1764.

DEAR SIR,—After the conversation I had with you in town, and the letter I took the liberty of writing to you on the subject of my dismission, I had flattered myself I might rest satisfied that my misfortune in having so greatly incurred His Majesty's displeasure was not owing to any blame laid on my conduct or behaviour in my profession. I thought I might conclude it, from your silence on the humble but earnest request I made, that if any such was against me I might be acquainted with it, and be allowed an opportunity of clearing myself; and I should not now have troubled you again on this subject if I had not seen in the printed papers, which seem to come out more immediately under the protection of Government, repeated insinuations that it is otherwise, and that my dismission was owing to some supposed crime, of which I have not the least knowledge or conception.

You must be sensible, Sir, that such a situation must

be very distressful to a man who has any sense of honour or conscience of innocence. I have lost my regiment, I have been robbed of His Majesty's countenance and favour, I must think (judging from the duty and veneration to his person) from some very unfair representation of my conduct; yet I had hoped my enemies would not have carried their malice to the attack of that character which I have endeavoured to preserve through a long course of service, with fidelity and zeal, to the utmost of my poor ability. I do, therefore, beg, Sir, as I owe it to myself not to part with that as long as it is in my power to maintain it, that you will lay before His Majesty my humble request, that if any crime, of what nature soever, in the course of my military service, is imputed to me, His Majesty would be graciously pleased to order that I may be informed of it; and if it be his pleasure, may have an opportunity given me of defending myself, and endeavouring to regain that good opinion in his Royal breast which it is my highest ambition to deserve. I am, Sir, &c., &c.

H. S. Conway.

I enclose the copy of a paragraph in a pamphlet just come to my hands, called the *Wallet*, which shows you my complaint is not without foundation:—

"Besides, as there were other gentlemen in the army that joined the minority in the same votes, that were *not* displaced, from whence does it follow that Mr. Conway was deprived of his places *merely or at all* on account of anything that passed within the impenetrable walls of St. Stephen's Chapel? Let the advocates for this gentleman examine his behaviour *without* doors, and see whether *there was any cause for his dismission there.*"

MR. WELBORE ELLIS TO GENERAL CONWAY.

July —, 1764.

SIR,—I have the honour of your letter of the 22nd instant, wherein you desire me to lay before His Majesty your humble request, "that if any crime, of what nature soever, in the course of your military service, is imputed to you, His Majesty would be graciously pleased to order that you might be informed of it; and if it be his pleasure, may have an opportunity of defending yourself, &c., &c."

This desire you ground on having seen repeated insinuations *in the printed papers, which seem to come out more immediately under the protection of Government*, and particularly on a late anonymous pamphlet, called the *Wallet*, of which you send me an extract. I know not that any papers are under the more immediate protection of Government, except the Gazette; and as to that anonymous pamphlet, the *Wallet*, which I have not read, I have some good reasons to believe that it is neither avowed, approved, or protected by Government. Abuse is very disagreeable to every man of sensibility; the scribblers, indeed, deal it out on both sides very plentifully; but I should think that I formed a hard judgment if I supposed that the gross misrepresentations and scurrility which I frequently see in the public papers and pamphlets against Government had the approbation and protection of any gentleman of rank, education, and principles, who differs with Administration.

This being my opinion, I cannot but be sorry that you seem to attribute more authenticity to scribblers on one side than I think just to allow them on the other, and especially that you have thought this a ground for preferring this request to His Majesty.

I have, however, in obedience to your desire, laid the same before the King, to which His Majesty did not think fit to return any answer. I have, &c.

WELBORE ELLIS.

MEMORANDUM OF THE PRINCESS AMELIA'S VISIT TO STOWE IN JULY, 1764[1]. [*In a contemporary but unknown hand.*]

July 22. Arrived, Earl of Ashburnham, Mr. Pelham, Sir Jeffry Amherst, and Mr. Offley.

July 23. Arrived, at one o'clock, Her Royal Highness, accompanied by Lady Mary (Harriet) Campbell, Lady Barrymore, Mrs. Middleton, Earl of Besborough, Earl of Coventry, and others whose names I could not learn. At three went to dinner, the first course consisting of twenty-one dishes, elegantly served and well arranged, a second course of twenty-seven dishes, the capital dishes in the first course twice removed, and a well filled side table of wholesome cheer all served on plate; Her Royal Highness ate off gold. Nothing can exceed the grandeur and order by which everything was

---

[1] In subsequent years the Princess Amelia frequently repeated her visits to Stowe. The writer of the above, probably Lady Temple's waiting-maid, seems much impressed with the "grandeur and order" of the ceremonies which she describes with such amusing minuteness. Some of the guests appear to have been not very well satisfied with their entertainment. In a letter from "Gilly" Williams to George Selwyn, dated July 30, I find the following:—"Coventry says the Stowe party ended but badly: the weather bad—the wine bad—and the ceremony intolerable." Horace Walpole describes another visit to Stowe by the Princess Amelia in 1770, when he was himself present.—See *Walpole Correspondence*, vol. v. p. 282.

conducted. Twelve gentlemen, well dressed, waited at table, and twenty-four in livery waited in the next room, and in the grand hall near the dining-room was a grand concert of music; the same evening, and every evening during Her Royal Highness's stay, the state apartments were illuminated with 120 wax lights. At half-past ten Her Royal Highness retired to her bedchamber, and the nobles to supper, consisting of twenty-one dishes and a fine dessert.

July 24. Her Highness, attended by the nobles, went round the gardens to view the curious works of nature and art, which were in great variety; the buildings, plants, and walks, together with the fine pieces of water, Her Royal Highness beheld with great astonishment and admiration, answering far beyond any former reports, descriptions, or conceptions. After dinner Her Highness went round the park, and returned highly pleased with everything she saw.

July 25. Her Highness walked in the gardens in order to take a second view, but was prevented in a great measure by a heavy shower of rain, which obliged Her Highness to take shelter in Venus's habitation.

July 26. Very rainy, which obliged Her Royal Highness and the company to keep all day within doors, but Her Highness came down stairs to inspect the offices, which seemed to give Her Highness great pleasure, and expressed her approbation of everything she saw, especially a basket of fine fresh mushrooms and some fish, and other provisions which Her Royal Highness saw in the kitchen.

July 27. All day a number of people were preparing the grotto and garden for Her Highness and company to sup there, the badness of the weather not permitting any entertainment there before. At ten the gardens were illuminated with above a thousand lights, and the water before the grotto was covered with floating lights. At the farther end of the canal on the ship, which was curiously figured with lights, was a place for the music, which performed all supper time. Upwards of a thousand people came from all parts to see the company at supper, which greatly added to the grandeur and magnificence of the place. This mixed assembly, which deserves a better appellation than a mob, behaved with the utmost discretion and civility. Her Highness walked down to the grotto at half-past ten, and was pleased and delighted with the grand prospect which was presented to her view; nothing was seen but lights and people, nothing was heard but music and fireworks, and nothing was felt but joy and happiness.

It's far beyond my power to give a proper account of all I saw in this delightful spot. In less than two hours no less than twenty gallons of oil was burnt, besides a vast number of other lights. Her Highness walked round through the people and lights with great satisfaction, then sat down in company to an elegant cold supper. Came home before twelve.

July 28. Her Royal Highness, and all the company, went away before eleven o'clock, highly delighted with it.

I never saw any entertainment conducted with more care, order, and decorum in all my days, every one endeavouring to outdo another in their places appointed them by their noble master and mistress, whose approbation and acknowledgment they in general received after the company departed.

MR. GRENVILLE TO THE EARL OF HALIFAX.

Downing Street, Monday, July 23, 1764.

MY DEAR LORD,—The despatch which you mention to have received yesterday from Lord Hertford, together with the letter from the Duke of Choiseul to his Lordship, have not yet been sent to me; and although I have read the French Arrêt upon the subject of the Canada Bills this evening, yet I am not able, without some farther explanation, to understand every part of it. But by the account which your Lordship gives of what I have not yet seen, and by what I can collect from what I have seen, this business seems to require a speedy and serious consideration. I wish that the answer from the Court of Spain about the logwood-cutters, which I read to day in the Gazette, had not contained the words *in the stipulated places*, as I am afraid that those words lay in a claim for a future dispute about what those *stipulated places* are, for which there seems to be no foundation in the Treaty. I saw M. de Blosset[1] to-day, and urged as strongly as I could the same arguments which were so often repeated in the conference we had with M. de Guerchy and him, in relation to the money due from the French Court for their prisoners of war. I did not expect any precise answer from him at present, nor did I receive any except the usual plea of the impossibility of their paying the whole of this debt so soon as they wished, and we had a right to expect. I shall be very glad to talk with your Lordship upon these important points when we meet to-morrow, and on

---

[1] The French Minister, in the absence of M. de Guerchy, who was gone to Paris.

Wednesday, as well as upon some other subjects which I will then mention to you. I am, &c., &c.

GEORGE GRENVILLE.

THE EARL OF HALIFAX TO MR. GRENVILLE.

Bushy Park, Monday morning, July 23, 1764.

DEAR SIR,—As the dispatch I received yesterday from Lord Hertford, and the letter from the Duke of Choiseul to his Lordship which accompanied it, puts it out of all doubt that the late infamous French Arrêt is meant to violate the stipulations of the Treaty of Peace, and defraud His Majesty's subjects, I believe you will agree with me in opinion that some speedy determination should be had on so interesting and important an occasion. I hope, therefore, you will turn the matter seriously in your thoughts before our meeting to-morrow. I am, &c., &c. DUNK HALIFAX.

THE EARL OF HERTFORD TO MR. GRENVILLE.

Compiegne, July 28, 1764.

SIR,—I have many acknowledgments to make for the very obliging manner in which you have laid my request before the King: I wish it had been conformable to His Majesty's views and inclination to have granted it: I should have received that mark of his favour with gratitude and very particular satisfaction at this time: it is, however, no small consolation to me, that His Majesty is graciously pleased to express his approbation of my poor services, and I am very sensible of the exactness with which you have executed my commission, and the delicacy with which you have accompanied the present refusal.

The Comte de Guerchy is arrived here: I have had a long conversation with him, in which he has, I believe, acquainted me with all that passed between the English Ministers and himself previous to his departure from London, and relative to the great points still depending between the two Courts. In this conversation, and from all I have heard of him, I must do him the justice to observe, that he seems well disposed to maintain harmony and peace between the two nations, and by his conversations with the Duc de Praslin since his arrival, I find he has made the same representations of the disposition of His Majesty's Ministers.

That I might be clearly understood to convey to this Court the language I had received in orders from my own, as well from Lord Halifax's last letter, as from what you have been pleased to communicate to me of your sentiments, I drew up a short memorial upon the three great points immediately in agitation, which I have sent to Lord Halifax, after having presented it to the Minister here.

I shall not trouble you with a copy of it, as you will have an opportunity of seeing it when you think proper in the office: I accompanied it, in my conversation with the Duc de Praslin, with every argument I could use, to show the necessity of making to England, in a reasonable time, the payments of the expense of prisoners: he told me in answer, with very unaffected warmth, as it appeared to me, that it was impossible to employ any argument on that head, of which he was not already fully sensible. He knew that the money had been long ago advanced by England for the most favourable, and indeed the most indispensable of all objects, the maintenance of prisoners, of Frenchmen, of those who had no other means of subsistence. But there was, on the other side, a consideration still more powerful than any other in the world; it was that of necessity.

The finances of the kingdom were in the utmost disorder; as this was no secret, it was needless to disguise it to me; the State was vastly in arrear in almost every branch of administration; public credit was at a low ebb; the refractory humour of the Parliaments augmented their difficulties, and the immediate payment of such a sum as our balance would probably amount to, he believed, to be an absolute impossibility. But be assured, my Lord, continued he, that we are really sincere in our intentions, not only of making payment, but of making as prompt payment as the nature of things will admit of. You may see by my frankness in confessing our necessities, the sensible confusion which I feel in requiring delay, and which I would alleviate by laying before you the reasons of my request. When I still continued to urge him, he told me he had already mentioned it in Council, that he should repeat it again on Sunday, when a Council of the finances was to be held; that he would lay the matter fully before them; that the Comptroller-General should have orders to consider it, and if human wit could devise a method of early payment, it should not be wanting: he added, that in seven or eight days he hoped to be able to make me a particular answer upon the subject.

The other two great points of Dunkirk and the Canada Bills I propose answering to Lord Halifax, with a copy of what I have wrote to you upon this subject; as his Lordship's letters are always free for your inspection, and you have not so minutely entered into either of those subjects, I think it unnecessary to trouble you very particularly upon them, and I will finish this matter by assuring you that my utmost zeal and attention shall be employed for the service of His Majesty, whilst I continue to have the honour of receiving his commands at this Court.

Having said thus much on public business in answer to what you have been pleased to write to me, you must give me leave once more to mention a subject to you, which I have often proposed with great anxiety.

It is that of Secretary to this Embassy, with which I must, from every motive, be desirous of seeing Mr. Hume invested.

To Sir Charles Bunbury I have no personal objection, as I have often said: when he was appointed, he was in a manner wholly unknown to me; I only learned that he was a young man who had no experience ; this alone was sufficient to make me resolve not to act with him in that station, if there had been no circumstances of his conduct towards me with which I had reason to be displeased. This resolution I have declared so publicly on all occasions, that I cannot now depart from it without drawing on myself the imputation of levity, or weakness.

From this situation I have been in some measure relieved by the assistance of a person who has abilities and experience to employ, when I have occasion for his services, but still I must beg you to consider that whilst he is without that character, I cannot leave this Court, even for health or business of my own, though there was ever so pressing an occasion for it ; the inconvenience of such a situation wants no colouring to show it: I ask for no leave to absent myself from my present duty; neither my health, thank God, nor my affairs require it, but I wish for that power in case of necessity; I am desirous, in friendship to Mr. Hume and for His Majesty's future service, to see so able a man invested in it, and it would be a satisfaction to me to think that the Secretary of the Embassy at Paris was appointed, as you are sensible those of all the other great Embassies have been, by the choice of the Ambassador.

His Majesty was pleased to take this matter into his Royal consideration, and to give me hopes that a remedy should be put to my complaint: if it was not just, I should not have so often renewed it; I apply, therefore, to you, Sir, to remind the King, at some proper moment, of his gracious intentions, and whilst you contribute to have this justice done me, you will serve a man who has great abilities, that may be made useful to his country, and you will at the same time oblige, Sir, with very great regard and respect, &c. HERTFORD.

The Comte de Guerchy has already given me notice that he must have a conversation with me upon the difficulties he has met with in England in regard to his *entrées*, in which he seems to think he has been more severely treated than his predecessors. I am sorry to observe, by the little he had time to say to me upon it, that he considers this matter as essential to his character of Ambassador: I shall, however, endeavour to soften that warmth, and persuade him that the true reciprocity between France and England is to treat the Ministers at the two different Courts with all the favour and indulgence that other Foreign Ministers receive there: to establish a difference at Paris in regard to the English Ambassador would be doing a very disagreeable thing to his person and character without serving the State.

THE EARL OF SANDWICH TO MR. GRENVILLE.

Hinchingbrook, August 4, 1764.

DEAR SIR,—Lord Buckingham in his last letter avoids naming any particular period for his leaving Petersburg, and as he expresses himself to be much pleased with the Empress's present behaviour to him, and to be flattered by the marks of distinction she now shows him, I am much inclined to think that he likes his situation so much better than he did that he will endeavour to spin out his stay in Russia as long as he possibly can. I have therefore wrote to desire he would recollect that his recall was sent him in consequence of his own repeated requests, and that as a person is destined to succeed him, it is necessary to know for certain when his Lordship proposes to take his leave of the Russian Court, that his successor may prepare himself for his journey. The Empress was expected back from Riga the latter end of the last month, and I have directed Lord Buckingham, immediately after her arrival, to fix the time of his coming away, and not to suffer himself to be any longer amused about the Treaties in agitation, which if that Court was in earnest, might be finished at any time in a very few days.

In this state of things about Lord Buckingham's recall, I should think Mr. Macartney [1] might kiss hands

---

[1] Afterwards Earl of Macartney. He married Lady Jane Stuart, daughter of Lord Bute, and died in 1806. He was employed in several diplomatic appointments, particularly in his well known Embassy to China.

now, in which case he would be able to set out in about two months (and less time he cannot have for preparation), and as he purposes to send his things by sea, he will be obliged to keep them 'till the winter is over, if they do not sail by the end of this month. He is now with me, and wishes much to have this matter terminated.

I tell you my opinion, but I will not proceed to carry it into execution 'till I hear from you in answer to this letter.

I think Lord Hertford has presented a very injudicious Memorial; I imagine you will think with me, when you see it, that it will do hurt to our affairs with France.

The enclosed memorandum was given me some time ago, as you will see by the date of it: I declined mentioning it to you, as I don't love being troublesome, and am not very solicitous about the event; but as I am applied to for an answer, I must beg of you to enable me to give one. I believe you know who Mr. Chamier is[1], and that he was to have gone with me as my Private Secretary to Spain in consequence of a recommendation from Lord Barrington; he is a man of fortune and merit, and the person he applies for is his brother, and is upon the spot; and as he tells me the office cannot be given but to one who resides in the country, probably it will not be much sought after. Yours, &c. SANDWICH.

---

[1] He was a clerk in the War office, and afterwards Deputy Secretary at War: in that office he was distinguished by the virulent abuse of *Junius*.

THE EARL OF SANDWICH TO MR. GRENVILLE.

Whitehall, August 8, 1764.

Dear Sir,—Lord Halifax, who is now with me, has apprized me of the contents of your letter relative to the French prisoners, but I flatter myself that the additional materials he will send you, in consequence of his conversation with Monsr. Blosset, will make you join with us in opinion that (with some very little alterations) the terms they now propose are not only admissible, but better than we had any reason to expect.

From the conclusion of our conference with Monsr. Guerchy at my house, I never imagined we could bring France lower than a term of three years for the payment of the balance; and I cannot think there is any very great difference in their present offer, as they agree to pay the large sum in the current year, and defer the discharge only of the smallest portion of the debt to the latest period. Indeed I now think we have the fairest offer we ever shall have upon this point; but I think it so material for the success of our general system, that we three should hold the same language, that I will decline explaining my sentiments in any conversation I may happen to have with Monsr. Blosset, and will not write to the Duke of Bedford upon this matter, 'till I know your sentiments upon the whole after due consideration.

As to what relates to Lord Buckingham's return, I cannot help thinking that he now wishes to protract it as much as possible; it will be two months before I shall have an answer to my last letter, and Mr. Macartney cannot be allowed less than two months from the day of his appointment to prepare for his journey: it was particularly requested by Monsr. Gros[1] on his arrival here, that his Court should not be left without an English Minister for any time, however short; therefore if he is now named, it will be four or five months, including his journey, before he can relieve Lord Buckingham: besides, I fear he will begin to be uneasy at the delay, though, indeed, considering the favour done him, if it answers any purpose, that may be got over without much difficulty; though I own I always love to do things with a good grace, if it draws on no ill consequences.

I am very sorry to say that I agree with you entirely in your apprehensions about the affair of Turk's Island[2]; something of the sort you propose must be done, otherwise the clamour will be great and universal; but I doubt whether Sir W. Burnaby must not be reinforced, as he has no ship of the line with him, unless you so call a bad 50-gun ship with her lowest complement of men; and if you send a reinforcement from hence, I fear it would operate upon our funds, but of that you are the best judge. I am, &c., &c. SANDWICH.

THE EARL OF HALIFAX TO MR. GRENVILLE.

Great George Street, Wednesday evening,
August 8, 1764.

DEAR SIR,—I thank you for the long letter you favoured me with, and the trouble you gave yourself in your retirement, of giving me your thoughts so fully

---

[1] Minister Plenipotentiary from the Court of Russia.
[2] A small island in the West Indies, on which were some English settlers. It had been seized by the French Squadron under Count d'Estaing, an act of zeal which the French Ministers were obliged to disavow, with a promise to restore the island and pay the damages.

upon the several points submitted to your consideration. I did not imagine I should have had occasion to trouble you again so soon, but my interview with Mons. Blosset this morning makes it necessary; and the French proposal, explained as it has been to me, I believe you will be of opinion with me, well deserves the consideration of His Majesty's principal servants. In my last I told you that if we could agree with the Court of France on other points of our demand, I much doubted whether it would be advisable to break off on account of the additional delay of sixteen months, beyond the three years to which my Lord Hertford stands limited, for the payment of the stipulated sum: and I gave that opinion, because I am satisfied that the payments as proposed in four years and four months, the largest payment to be made first, and the smallest last, was as good a bargain (though I have not arithmetically calculated it) as if the payment was to be made within three years, in six equal half-yearly sums. With me, therefore, the greatest objection did not lie there; it was that fifteen millions, to be paid us in full of all demands, was a sum too small to be listened to, especially as I have reason to believe that the East India Company's demand for the maintenance of prisoners, and the demand we are to make from the 11th of November, 1762, for the maintenance of prisoners to the time of their release, will prove to amount to considerably more than six millions of livres.

Early in my conversation with Mons. Blosset, I mentioned these two articles, and he immediately answered that I should have satisfaction with respect to both; that the French Court did not mean they should be comprised in the offer of fifteen millions to be paid in four years and three months (for so he computes the term), but that they should be separately considered, and justly and punctually paid, as soon as they should be liquidated and adjusted.

That their East India Company had some counter-claim, and that they expected a farther account from the West Indies; but he admitted both those articles on the part of France would be but trifling.

I told him this was new to me, for that my Lord Hertford had stated the matter differently, as well as Mons. de Guerchy.

He told me he could not be mistaken, and that he would read me that part of his letter from the Duke of Praslin, which he did, and what follows is the extract I took of it:—

"Les 15 millions que nous proposons de payer sont independants des deux autres articles qui n'étoient pas compris dans le compte d'Angleterre: viz., Prisonniers de la Compagnie des Indes: et l'entretien de nos prisonniers depuis l' 11me de Nov^{ro}. 1762, jusqu'au temps de leur élargissement."

This, Sir, being the case, you will perceive, that if they pay us faithfully (which Blosset tells me they will stipulate to do) the sum due on the two before-mentioned articles (which, when the French counterclaim is allowed, will amount to about six millions of livres, as I conceive), in addition to the fifteen millions proposed in full of the accounts delivered in by Lord Hertford, the whole sum to be paid us will probably not be less than twenty-one millions of livres.

I told Monsr. Blosset that we would never give up the charge of prisoners taken before the war, and that the accounts must be regularly stated.

He said they had nothing to say with respect to the

prisoners before the war, that we should state our account as we pleased, but that more than fifteen millions (excepting the East India article, and the other I have mentioned) they were absolutely unable to pay. That the agreement or convention they proposed was against themselves, and intended only to give proof of their sincerity by securing the proposed payment. That if nothing of that sort was settled, which would bind their Court, a change of Administration in France would render our payment precarious, but that such a convention, as is proposed, would bind the Crown of France, as well as the French banker who is to make it.

I told Monsr. Blosset that I would not take upon me to give him any answer to the proposal; that I was but one of His Majesty's servants; that I had not as yet talked with the King on the subject, but that I could tell him, that neither the sum nor the period of time for the payment were such as I had any reason to believe would be accepted; that he remembers well that one or two years at most were talked of at the meeting at Lord Sandwich's as an admissible delay. He frequently professed the good intentions of his Court, and their wish to give us every possible assurance of their having nothing so much at heart as the continuance of the Peace.

I should make my letter too long (it will be long enough to tire you as it is), was I to state to you some precautions and modifications, which I think will be necessary in case this matter shall be farther treated of. These I will trouble you with when we meet. Upon the whole, I will only say that I think we have a fair handle, if we make good use of it. The King thinks so, and so does my brother Secretary.

I agree entirely with you in regard to the monstrous and insufferable behaviour of M. d'Estaing. I have ordered a reference to the Board of Trade, who will meet on Monday.

I am not unapprized of our right to Turk's Island, but on so important an occasion I hold it necessary we should have a full opinion of it from the proper Board; after which we shall have a meeting, and if the Duke of Bedford and Lord Chancellor cannot attend it, I must ask and get their opinions by letter.

I think I have nothing further to add, but that Prince Masserano[1] has given a very erroneous account of what I said to him concerning the exercise of our right to cut logwood: for my language on that subject was nearly the same as yours was; and it was on your ideas, and the account you had given me of your conversation with him, that I talked.

Bothmar, likewise, as you must have observed, has represented my brother Secretary and myself in foolish colours you do not think we deserve to be painted in.

I am, &c., &c.   DUNK HALIFAX.

MR. GRENVILLE TO THE EARL OF HALIFAX.

Wotton, August 9, 1764.

MY DEAR LORD,—I have returned the public despatches which you sent to me, by the messenger who brought them, and am very sorry to see that they likewise relate to a dispute with France, upon another encroachment made by them in another part of the world, which confirms me in my former opinion of the indispensable necessity to put

[1] The Spanish Ambassador.

a stop to these unjust proceedings by firm and temperate measures before the fire is lighted in so many parts, and fed with so much fuel as to make it impossible to extinguish it.

I defer, however, troubling you with any more observations upon this subject, or with anything relative to the proposals made for the payment of the money due for the subsistence of the French prisoners. I find by your Lordship's letter that some precautions and modifications will, you think, be necessary if the latter of these subjects shall be farther treated of; and as you propose to communicate them to me when we meet, I shall refer myself to what shall appear when the materials are fully before us both upon this business; and what seems to me still more important, the act of violence committed by M. d'Estaing in the West Indies. I shall certainly be in town, if nothing extraordinary prevents me, on Monday evening next, and will do myself the honour of calling upon you in Great George Street by half an hour after eleven on Tuesday morning, if I hear nothing from you to the contrary. I am, &c., &c.

GEORGE GRENVILLE.

MR. GRENVILLE TO THE EARL OF SANDWICH.

Wotton, August 9, 1764.

MY DEAR LORD,—I propose to be in town on Monday evening, and therefore, as I shall have the pleasure of seeing you so soon, I will defer 'till then entering any farther into the business relative to the French prisoners, especially as Lord Halifax writes me word that there are some farther modifications and precautions necessary, which he will explain to me when we meet.

I agree perfectly with you that it is of the greatest consequence, that in the various disputes which have arisen, or may arise between Great Britain and the Crowns of France and Spain, we should all hold exactly the same language, as I am fully convinced our representations will not otherwise be attended with that success which is necessary for the whole, and all the firmness we can show will be necessary to put a stop to proceedings so destructive of that peace and harmony which it will be impossible to maintain if they are suffered to go on much farther. I hope you will excuse my not answering the other parts of your letter at present, as I am extremely engaged, and we shall meet in a few days, when they may be more easily settled.

  I am, &c., &c.   George Grenville.

THE DUCHESS OF QUEENSBERRY[1] TO LADY TEMPLE.

Ambresbury, August 13, 1764.

My most dear Lady Temple,—Having received yours under the shade of Italian shutters, I read first in your words, the Bill comes to 35*l*. 0*s*. 7*d*., without

[1] Catherine Hyde, wife of Charles Douglas, third Duke of Queensberry. The beauty of this celebrated lady was the theme of many poets. She was the friend and correspondent of Pope, Prior, Swift, and Gay, and the kind and affectionate patroness of the latter. It was one of her eccentricities that through a long life she retained the dress of her youthful days, which rendered her appearance very remarkable. Horace Walpole, describing the coronation of George the Third, speaks of the Duchess and her "milk white locks," and that it was "her *affectation* on that day to do nothing preposterous." He uses the same figure upon the occasion of a ball given by the Duchess in 1764, that "the only extraordinary thing the Duchess did, was to do nothing extraordinary," and he adds some amusing anecdotes of her in his letter to Lord Hertford, dated March 11, 1764. The Duchess died in 1777.

discerning the extreme faint dots between the pounds and shillings: thus you see the enclosed bill instantly became a pennyworth, without the aid of foreign art to enhance the valuableness of our own dear country manufacture; and I may truly add, in the style of the *Rehearsal*, your news is welcome whatso'er it be: so that pray send the ruffles to our house in London, and when they come they will certainly find me not half enough ruffled. If they can be sent soon, a friend of ours, who goes to London this evening or to-morrow, can return here with the ruffles in his pocket, unwashed by the too profuse rain for harvest now falling; worse by half than all your Christmas weather, as cold is never counted bitter where much sunshine abounds. The Duke and I would gladly swim to Stowe forthwith; but we came so much later than we meant that we are now tied by the leg, so cannot promise ourselves when we can have that pleasure; in the mean time shall certainly keep up the intention in store as a pleasure to come; but lest I should first die in your debt, and my personal estate be not worth a straw, it seems best for me to refund the sum you have been so good to advance for my ruffles hereby. The Duke and I each desire our kindest and best respects to dear Lord and dear Lady Temple, whose most faithful and affectionate humble servant I am. C. QUEENSBERRY.

The ruffles may be directed to the Porter, at the Duke of Queensberry's, Burlington Gardens, London, with a word to bid him send it to me by the first safe and dry opportunity.

MR. CHARLES TOWNSHEND TO EARL TEMPLE.

Adderbury, August 14, 1764.

My dear Lord,—I did not send you the manuscript yesterday, because I could not persuade myself to lay it before you without the advantage of the notes, and I felt confident the post would, in the evening, bring me the pamphlet itself[1]. I was not mistaken, and I now enclose it to you. If the diligent Almon should have sent your Lordship a copy, you will be pleased to return mine, and I am sure I need not bespeak your candour or partiality in reading it. Your Lordship will recollect I designed it as a remonstrance, not a pamphlet, and thought it most prudent, in so great and good a cause, to assume the temper and deportment of a serious and impartial man, writing from principle, and arguing from facts, and therefore studied brevity, simplicity, and the general strength of composition resulting from them, rather than amplification, brilliancy, or inflammatory passages.

At the same time I confess I preferred the sobriety and candour of this plan, because I thought it the most likely to be effectual.

They tell me the representation already begins to have effect, and I am called upon to second the blow; but I should hope others will contribute to maintain whatever advantage ground this fair and full state of

---

[1] Entitled *The Defence of the Minority*: "Charles Townshend's prodigious parts," says Horace Walpole, "must not be judged of by this, or indeed by any of his few writings. He never was an author in proportion to his abilities. His thoughts flowed in too rapidly to give him time to digest them; nor was he ever enough in earnest about anything to consider it deliberately."

this important matter may give us in the public judgment.

Tell me freely where you are pleased, and where you differ from me in reading it, that I may take your better taste for my future guide, and be *thus* rewarded for my labour in the common cause.

It is not unpleasant to see the virtuous and popular Halifax pursued through all his mazes of essoigns, privilege, and fines, ordinary and extraordinary[1]; and, if I am not deceived, this detection of his, and their unexampled imposition on the Commons and the public, so proved by this comparison between their conduct in Parliament and judicature, will put an end to their last dream of union, and all hope of confidence.

I have this paragraph in a letter from London :—

" The Ministry are alarmed by private letters, confirmed by their own intelligence, which give an account

---

[1] An allusion to the means used by Lord Halifax, in order to evade the consequences of the action brought against him by Wilkes. The following is a curious history of the "law's delay" upon that question. "Original was issued, tested the first day of June, and returnable from the first day of the Holy Trinity, in three weeks (19th of June, 1763), and the Earl being summoned, cast an essoign, which was adjourned until the 18th of November. Then he availed himself of his privilege, which being at an end, and all the essoigns expired, a distringas was taken out, tested the 9th of May, being the first day of Easter term, 1764, returnable from the day of Easter in five weeks (27th of May): the Sheriff returned forty shillings issues. The Earl did not appear; the court directed fifty pounds issues. An alias distringas was taken out, tested the 30th of May, and returnable on the morrow of the Holy Trinity (18th of June); the Sheriff returned his issues. The Earl still refused to appear: the Court ordered five hundred pounds issues. A pluries distringas was taken out, tested the first day of Trinity Term (22nd of June), and returnable in three weeks of the Holy Trinity (8th of July). In November following, Mr. Wilkes was outlawed: then the Earl appeared and pleaded the outlawry." — *History of the late Minority.*

of thirty-six English vessels taken and confiscated in North America by an Admiral of France, and Mr. Grenville came to town upon it last night."

I shall be happy to hear your Lordship's lameness continues to lessen, and I desire you will believe that no friend you have is more anxious for the health and happiness, nor more attached to the honour of the family at Stowe than, my dear Lord, your affectionate humble Servant, C. TOWNSHEND.

MR. ALMON TO EARL TEMPLE.

Piccadilly, August 14, 1764.

MY LORD,—I took the liberty of sending your Lordship, per last post, the *Defence of the Minority*[1], and a few posts ago the *Counter Address*[2], on the dismission of General Conway, both of which are esteemed excellent performances; but as there is now-a-days no certainty in the post, I have likewise sent them by this surer way, together with Mr. Churchill's last pieces, lest the others should have miscarried.

The several pamphlets lately published cannot but do great service to the cause.

The *Budget*[3] still keeps going off, and it is amazing how it has opened the eyes of the public. The *Letter from Albemarle Street*[4] is as highly commended as the

---

[1] By Mr. Charles Townshend.

[2] *The Counter Address* was written by Horace Walpole, in reply to *An Address to the Public, on the late dismission of a General Officer*, which Walpole says was prepared by Dr. Shebbeare under George Grenville's direction.

[3] David Hartley was the author of *The Budget: inscribed to the man who thinks himself Minister*. It was for some time attributed to Sir George Savile.

[4] Lord Temple was the Author of *A Letter from Albemarle Street to the Cocoa Tree*.

Budget by those who have read it with attention. There has been nothing else published of consequence, owing, I am afraid, to the late verdicts at Guildhall.

The violence and partiality of the Chief Justice in those causes was not only astonishing, but is shocking to think of. His charge entirely consisted of a reply to the defendant's counsel, grounded upon and enforced by the most infernal principles which ever disgraced any nominal free country. He affirmed the jury were only judges of the *fact;* he charged them on that single point, and added with an emphasis, that if they believed the evidence (which only swore to the *selling* the *North Briton*), they must find guilty *of the fact*, or be perjured. Upon this strange and unheard-of charge, the jury, on Williams's trial, found a special verdict, or rather no verdict at all. The case was this: the foreman and another were strongly for bringing in a verdict of *not guilty;* but one Page, a tool of, and personally known to Lord Bute, was obstinately and resolutely bent on finding the defendant *guilty.*

In this struggle he brought over nine of the jury, urging (as is said), that as the Minority had left Mr. Wilkes, they certainly looked on that paper as a libel, &c.

Still the foreman and the other man stood out; at length they capitulated and consented to meet each other half-way, and brought in a verdict in these words, *Guilty of publishing the North Briton, No.* 45.

Now, my Lord, it seems to be matter of the highest importance to consider well, whether a Chief Justice *can,* in so essential a point as this, abridge the fair right of jurymen to judge the *law* as well as the *fact,* as clearly and strongly laid down by the best law authorities, and which is one of the first principles of the Revolution?

And if he *cannot,* whether (upon one or two of the jury's making affidavit that they found such a verdict, which by the bye, many precedents show to be no verdict at all, *in consequence of that charge*), this is not proper and highly just matter for impeachment?

In the course of Kearsley's trial, the Chief Justice stopped Glynn, the counsellor, when he told the jury they were judges of both law and fact, and said that if he (Glynn) asserted *that,* he would have the opinion of the twelve judges upon it; but Glynn cowardly withdrew his assertion, and only said that *he had conceived it so.*

The carrying this favourite point of convicting the *North Briton* in the City, has struck such a panic into the printers, &c., that I am afraid I now stand alone in the resolution to publish with spirit; however, I am determined to persevere, and whatever may be my fate, I hope that in case of persecution (which I hear is threatened me, with the addition of the heaviest vengeance of the Administration), I shall have the assistance and support of all those who call themselves friends to the liberties of their country; at least, I will endeavour to deserve it, by acting with that prudence, firmness, and fidelity, which can never injure a good cause, nor hurt them who shall choose to be my friends.

I hope the *London Evening* pleases; it has been very spirited lately. I have contributed as much as possible to the public cause, in order to keep up a proper spirit during the summer, but am sorry to remark that there are few other persons who write in the papers, and it is a pity, for the people in general are in a very good humour.

It is impossible they should abhor the Administration more than they do, and they like the Minority as well as one body of men could another; but they would like them better if they would take more pains to instruct them. Everybody believes that there will be a warm winter, and that the Minority will act with great spirit. I am, my Lord, your Lordship's most obliged and most dutiful Servant, J. ALMON.

THE EARL OF SANDWICH TO MR. GRENVILLE.

Whitehall, August 22, 1764.

DEAR SIR,—The last letter from Lord Buckingham (which you will see among the papers which will be brought to you by this messenger) mentions his desire to remain where he is till the spring; this, I own, I have long expected, as it has been plain to me that something or other has happened that makes him like his situation more than he did; however, I can see no reason for indulging him in this request, and His Majesty is of the same opinion, as you will see by the public letter which I had orders to send by the last mail; to which I have added a private one in my own hand, a copy of which I herewith inclose (and which you will be so good as to return) in order to leave him as little reason as possible to complain.

I have had another letter from the Duke of Bedford, in answer to mine, containing a communication of what passed at our meeting, which he entirely approves, and seems thoroughly pleased with everything that has been done. I am, &c., &c. SANDWICH.

Since writing what is above, I learn that orders are given to add 30 men to the complement of all the guardships now in commission, and that it is intended to replace the two ships that are to go to the West Indies by two new guardships: these arrangements will occasion a considerable addition of expense, therefore it is proper you should be timely apprized of it.

MR. GRENVILLE TO MR. JENKINSON.

Wotton, August 22, 1764.

DEAR JENKINSON,—The outrageous insult committed by the smugglers at Deal requires the most effectual and speedy remedy. I approve, therefore, of every step that can be taken for that purpose. There seems to me but three things to be done. The first is to have the offenders prosecuted and punished as severely as the law will allow. The second is to reinforce the Lieutenant of the cutter by a sloop and a man-of-war who may be fully sufficient to keep that gang in order. The third is to send some troops, particularly dragoons, upon that part of the coast. Your letter to the Commissioners of the Customs is a proper one, but I would add to it the advertisement which you mention, of a reward for discovering and apprehending the offenders, which should be put into the Gazette by the Admiralty Office, and the Commissioners of the Customs, that it may carry the more terror by both offices taking it up, though I think the prosecution should be carried on, as it is for a smuggling offence, by the Commissioners of the Customs. Directions should likewise be given to them, by your letter, or otherwise, to inquire what the last East India ship was, and who was the captain, and to prosecute him likewise, if it was an English East India ship, as I take for granted. The East India Company should likewise be applied to, that they may punish him by dismission, if he had any part in this infamous transaction, which it seems impossible to me but that he and his officers must have been principally concerned in, and all who were, ought to share in the punishment. Should not the East India Directors be told that the breaking bulk in this notorious manner, before the ship is delivered into the care of the Custom House officers, incurs the penalty of forfeiture, and therefore, if that is the case, it is doubly incumbent upon them to punish the offenders with the utmost rigour? At all events, I desire to know what the ship is, the name of the captain, and what steps can be taken in this business with the Directors of the East India Company. I asked Mr. Pitt[1] whether any orders had been sent by the Admiralty to reinforce Lieutenant Prittie, which most certainly should have been done immediately, from any of the neighbouring stations, as the whole ship might otherwise be unloaded in a few days. Mr. Pitt did not know that any such orders had been given, but told me he would write to Mr. Stephens about it to-day. I think the Commissioners of the Customs should be asked why they have sent us no account of this transaction, and that they should be directed to write to Lieutenant Prittie, to encourage him in the execution of his duty, to tell him that they have orders to prosecute the offenders with the utmost severity, that he will be supported both by a land and sea force, and to desire him to give them an exact account of the farther proceedings of the East India ship, and of the measures

[1] Thomas Pitt, one of the Lords of the Admiralty.

which he shall take with regard to her. I think you should write an answer to Mr. Stephens, to inform the Admiralty of what we have done, to press them to strengthen the sea-guard there, and reinforce Lieutenant Prittie as soon as is possible, if it is not already done, and to let them know of the orders to march troops to the coast, which you should write to the Secretary at War to hasten with the greatest expedition.

What I have traced out above will, I hope, be sufficient to restrain so daring an act of violence under our eyes, which it imports us to repress effectually in the first instance, if we mean to preserve, much more if we mean to increase, the revenue of the Customs. I am much surprised that we have not heard from the Commissioners upon this subject. I am, &c., &c.

GEORGE GRENVILLE.

THE EARL OF SANDWICH TO MR. GRENVILLE.

Whitehall, August 29, 1764.

DEAR SIR,—Lord Halifax has communicated to me the letter he has received from you concerning the affair in the Bay of Honduras: I entirely approve of every word you make use of, and I have the satisfaction to find that there is not the least difference of opinion among us, as Lord Halifax, I believe, intends to inform you by this night's post.

It is absolutely necessary for me to give soon a final answer, whether any money should be given for the support of what is called our party in Sweden; it is very plain that France means, if they carry their point in the approaching Diet, to engage part of their fleet for future occasions, and if they should execute that scheme (considering the lowering aspect of our affairs both with France and Spain), should not we be justly blamed for not having used every means in our power to obstruct their measures? Turn this matter in your thoughts, and let me know your determination when next we meet: you best know whether the money requisite is to be had, and whether, if it is, it should be so employed; at all events, it is advisable that whatever is done should be done on mature consideration, and be decided by your advice, and that of others of the King's servants, as it is too much for me to determine by my own weak judgment. I am, &c., &c. SANDWICH.

MR. GRENVILLE TO THE EARL OF SANDWICH.

Wotton, August 31, 1764.

MY DEAR LORD,—I am extremely glad that you agree with me in opinion upon the necessity which there is of taking effectual measures to set right what has happened to our logwood cutters. The more I consider the state of things in that part of the world, the more convinced I am that the squadron at Jamaica should be reinforced not only with two ships of the line, but with four or five ships of the line, as soon as is possible. The sending a small force may be attended with very great inconveniences, as it is possible that upon this alarm France and Spain may steal out two or three ships of the line, and it is of the highest importance to extinguish this spark of fire at once, lest it should kindle into a blaze, which probably may be the case, if our force, and that of France and Spain, shall be nearly equal in those seas.

I hope, therefore, that Lord Egmont has been spoken or writ to, that he may make the necessary preparations upon this subject as soon as it is possible. I have not heard from Lord Halifax, but beg the favour of you to make my best compliments to him and to Lord Chancellor, at whose house I suppose this letter will find you both, and where I sincerely wish you all every circumstance of health and pleasure which can render your excursion agreeable to you. I defer giving you any opinion about what you mention with regard to the affairs of Sweden, but will as you desire turn it in my thoughts, that we may talk of it the first time we meet, that some determination may be come to in a matter of this consequence. I am, &c., &c. GEORGE GRENVILLE.

THE EARL OF HALIFAX TO MR. GRENVILLE.

Bushey Park, Sunday, September 9, 1764.

DEAR SIR,—With this you will receive a letter from Lord Hertford to me, with other papers which accompanied it, and by them you will find that the French Court promises to give ample satisfaction for the outrage committed on Turk's Island, in every particular required, except the punishment of Monsr. d'Estaing, who gave, and Monsr. de Guichen, who executed the order. Upon the receipt of Lord Hertford's dispatches, I immediately desired Lord Egmont to stop the sloop which was on the point of sailing to the West Indies with preparatory orders from the Admiralty to Sir William Burnaby. I am, &c., &c. DUNK HALIFAX.

MR. WILKES TO EARL TEMPLE.

Paris, Rue St. Nicaise, September 9, 1764,

MY LORD,—Monsr. de Beaumont[1], who has merited so highly of humanity by employing the powers of a most persuasive eloquence in the cause of the unfortunate Calas' family, is so happy as to be going to England.

The many great public and private virtues of Lord Temple have excited in him the ambition of paying his respects to your Lordship, and I beg to have the honour of introducing him where I always found everything equally noble and engaging. He is no less amiable in the private walk of life than distinguished and admired by the public, and I am sure I cannot do your Lordship a more acceptable service than by presenting a gentleman of the first genius and merit to the best judge and patron of both.

May I beg that, under your Lordship's auspices, Monsr. de Beaumont may pay his respects to Mr. Pitt, and to Lord Chief Justice Pratt? All his wishes will then be gratified, and he will return after having seen the true riches of our island with no unpleasing account of the *fiers insulaires* to this polite capital, and to the most amiable French lady I know, whom he has had the

---

[1] M. Elie de Beaumont had a very high reputation as an Advocate at the French Bar. He appears to have gratified his wishes in sightseeing during his stay in England. Horace Walpole mentions him in a letter to Lord Hertford. " He breakfasted here (Strawberry Hill) t' other morning, and pleased me exceedingly : he has great spirit and good humour. It is incredible what pains he has taken to *see*. He has *seen* Oxford, Bath, Blenheim, Stowe, Jews, Quakers, Mr. Pitt, the Royal Society, the Robin Hood, Lord Chief Justice Pratt, the Arts and Sciences, has dined at Wildman's, and I think with my Lord Mayor, or is to do." M. de Beaumont died in 1786.

happiness of marrying, and I wish to have the powerful advocate of our nation here.

As to myself, I will only say that I am adversis rerum immersabilis undis, and that the warmest sentiments of my heart are those of veneration for your Lordship's character, and gratitude for the steady support which the cause of liberty has ever received from you.

I hope the day is not very distant when I shall be able to demonstrate with how much respect and attachment I am, my Lord, &c., &c. JOHN WILKES.

Miss Wilkes joins with me in respectful compliments to Lady Temple.

MR. GRENVILLE TO THE DUKE OF BEDFORD.

Downing Street, September 12, 1764.

MY DEAR LORD,—I have not yet seen Lord Sandwich or Lord Halifax since my return to town last night, but I had the pleasure of receiving the day before an account of Lord Hertford's last dispatches, by which I find that the Court of France has consented to make restitution of Turk's Island, to disavow any orders given for that act of violence, and to make satisfaction and reparation for the damages sustained by it. I wish that she had completed the whole by there call of M. d'Estaing, who, after having committed one very unjustifiable and dishonourable act in the East Indies against this country, should not have been so soon in a situation to have committed a second in the West Indies, and I hope will not be allowed to commit a third. I flatter myself, though there are many articles which remain unadjusted, that by degrees they will all be settled in the manner which they ought to be; but, as I imagine that it will very probably be necessary to have more meetings upon the subject of them, I most earnestly wish that we may have your Grace's assistance and advice, whose experience in business, and whose particular knowledge of the temper and disposition of the Court of France, will enable you to furnish lights in our disputes with that Crown, which will be of the greatest utility to His Majesty's service. I do not know that any time is yet fixed upon for a meeting, but whenever it is, I hope it will not be inconvenient to your Grace to be present at it; for although I have heard with very great pleasure from Lord Sandwich, that your Grace in general approves of the several steps which have been taken, yet it must have been more satisfactory to His Majesty, and more agreeable to us all, to have had the advantage of your Grace's presence and opinion, as well as the honour of your concurrence. I have, &c., &c.

GEORGE GRENVILLE.

THE LORD CHANCELLOR TO MR. GRENVILLE.

Grange, September 18, 1764.

DEAR SIR,—I had the honour of your letter Sunday, signifying the fitness of attending at St. James's on the Coronation day, the 22nd instant, and the meeting of the King's servants, the 21st. I must confess I was so bad a courtier that I did not know that annual day was particularly observed, but I now see the propriety of your not quitting London before.

As I find both from yours and Lord Halifax's letter, that my presence is desired at this meeting, I think it my duty to attend, and propose being in London Friday morning. I understand, by Lord Halifax's letter, that the principal subject of the meeting will be Lord Hertford's last dispatches, I suppose that part of them which relates to the maintenance of the prisoners, and the Canada Bills, for the affair of the island [1] seems disposed of.

With regard to the first, it seems an important point; for the sum proposed is to be paid in full, exceptis excipiendis, and if so paid, it must be so received.

As to the second, I own it hath never been dilucidated to me, or by me; for though it is very certain that the French Arrêts cannot bind the King's subjects, or expound the Treaty, yet I don't flatter myself that we shall ever attain for the Canadians so great and so dangerous a distinction between them and the French subjects, and I don't clearly see the justice on which we are to support it.

As these are matters much out of my department, and as I retain a particular friendship and respect for Mr. Grenville, I only throw out my own difficulties, that if anything occurs to you for my information, you may advise me of it, before we meet at the Earl of Halifax's.

I shall necessarily return Sunday, and if your great and assiduous employment will permit you to visit this place as intended, I can bring you down with great pleasure, and to a very cordial reception. I have the honour to be, &c., &c. NORTHINGTON.

[1] Turk's Island.

THE EARL OF SANDWICH TO MR. GRENVILLE.

September 22, 1764.

Dear Sir,—In Mr. Wolter's advices of this day, it is said from Brest, that in that port they have thirty-three ships, fifteen of which want rebuilding, or thorough repair, which with us is equivalent to rebuilding; the French word is *refondu*, but that they wait for wood to begin the works.

I dare say that those we were talking of the other day reckon thirty-three ships at Brest as fit for sea; and that method of calculation will account for the formidable state in which he represents the navy of France and Spain. I am, &c.

Sandwich.

THE KING TO MR. GRENVILLE.

5 min. past 10, a.m, Saturday, Sept. 22, 1764.

Mr. Grenville, I wish you would call at St. James's at a quarter past twelve, that I may know the event of last night[1] before I see any of the *others*.

MR. CHARLES TOWNSHEND TO EARL TEMPLE.

Adderbury, Thursday evening (October 4, 1764).

My dear Lord,—I am sorry to inform you that we last night heard, from Lady Dorothy Cavendish, a most melancholy account of the Duke of Devonshire, who has suffered another stroke of the palsy, by which he has entirely lost the use of one hand and one side. You

---

[1] The meeting of the Cabinet Ministers upon the several subjects of dispute with the French Court.

may imagine she writes in the utmost grief, but, I think, it is evident, from Lord John Cavendish's letter to her, and her manner of speaking of her father's situation, that we are to entertain no hope of his Grace's recovery. It is impossible to enter upon the train of fatal consequences which necessarily follow this unhappy event, while the sense of it is so fresh and strong upon the mind; but certainly it requires immediate and serious consideration, as it will, believe me, entirely change the disposition of many individuals, and much vary, if not reverse, the general and former order of things. If you agree with me in this, and wish to have any discourse upon the subject, I will come to you in any morning of this week.

I should have set out for Stowe this day, if I had not found my mind too much overcome by this calamity, so severe to me, from every consideration of private and public life. I am, my dear Lord, &c., &c.

C. TOWNSHEND.

MR. CHARLES TOWNSHEND TO EARL TEMPLE.

Adderbury, October 6, 1764.

MY DEAR LORD,—I have ordered a servant, in his return from Buckingham, to inquire after your Lordship's and Lady Temple's health, and we hope to hear you are both well.

I send you the report of the Board of General Officers merely as I thought you might like to read the issue of a matter in which Sir R. Lyttelton was a party[1].

[1] Sir Richard Lyttelton was Governor of Minorca, and this relates to a dispute with his deputy, Colonel Johnston. See a letter from Sir Richard Lyttelton *infra*.

Our last letters give still less hopes of the Duke of Devonshire[1], who has lost the use of one arm absolutely, and of one side almost entirely. His mouth is much contracted, and he cannot move out of his chair without the aid of two servants.

Ranby[2] went express to Newmarket to attend the Duke of Cumberland on Friday last, where he had that day been taken very dangerously ill. I have not since heard how he found him, but Sir George Rodney left his Royal Highness on that day very little likely to recover.

Mr. Grenville has lately opened himself to a person[3], much my friend, upon the subject of my situation, and in a manner not a little singular and artful. He said, among other things, that he heard I am more warm than Mr. Pitt, who, it is said, was very moderate; that he adhered to his original resolution not to solicit any man to accept high office; that he now looked upon all accommodation as impossible, and that Government must be contended for. He assumed great cheerfulness and ease, and spoke of me very handsomely, though as the only individual supposed to be determined.

Not one word of Mr. Yorke, or any other man, beyond the suggestion of Mr. Pitt's reported great moderation, and separate situation[4].

[1] The Duke died at Spa, on the 2nd instant.
[2] He was Sergeant Surgeon to the King, and had been long in the confidence of the Royal family.
[3] Mr. Morton, of Tackley, M.P. for Abingdon.
[4] Mr. Pitt's *separate situation* was alluded to by himself in a letter to the Duke of Newcastle, dated October—(see *Chatham Correspondence*, vol. ii. p. 296), in reply to some openings which had certainly been made about this time towards a reconciliation with the Government. There had been for some months past a coolness between Lord Temple and Mr. Pitt. Walpole had observed it, and found out that

I do not relate this as a passage of much consequence, but merely that I may preserve my rule of communicating the very letter of whatever is thrown out to me. My wishes upon a topic much too delicate for me to stir otherwise than as it *now* becomes so essential a part of the general state of things, are well known to your Lordship, and indeed every day, and every incident which that day produces, convinces me still more that no good is *now* to be expected, either in individuals or the public, upon any other plan of conduct than that which you permitted me to touch upon when I had last the honour of seeing you[1]. Consider what the summer has taken from us: the fatal effects of the Duke of Devonshire's dangerous illness, the manners of the times, the result of the winter, the characters of some of the considerable men who remain, the state of parties, Mr. Pitt's infirmities—forgive me if I venture too far, the autumn draws near to its conclusion. Some resolution should be taken, *at least by us*, and I own I think delay and indecision immediate and ignominious ruin.

there was scarcely any correspondence between them. (*Memoirs of George the Third*, vol. ii. p. 27.) This would account for Mr. Pitt's *separate situation*. In his letter to the Duke of Newcastle, he says, " As for *my single self*, I purpose to continue acting through life upon the best convictions I am able to form, and under the obligation of principles, not by the force of any particular bargains." And again— " Your Grace will not, I trust, wonder, if after so recent and so strange a phenomenon in politics, I have no disposition to quit the free condition of a man standing *single*, and daring to appeal to his country at large, upon the soundness of his principles and the rectitude of his conduct."

[1] It would seem that a coalition of parties had been a subject of discussion between Mr. Townshend and Lord Temple. The conclusion of the letter evidently points in that direction, and it will be seen in a subsequent letter that Mr. Townshend was not unwilling to support Mr. Grenville's Administration.

The moment my house is free from strangers I propose to have the pleasure of waiting upon you, and I am, &c., &c. C. TOWNSHEND.

Lady Dalkeith desires her compliments to your Lordship, and we both join in presenting our best respects to Lady Temple.

LORD CLIVE TO MR. GRENVILLE.

Rio Janeiro, October, 1764.

DEAR SIR,—I wish I could send you a better account of this first part of our voyage, which I believe has been the longest ever known where no accidents have arose to prolong the passage.

Upon our arrival at this place, to our great surprise, we found Commodore Byron in the *Dolphin*, and Captain Monat in the *Tamar*, who left England a month after us, and anchored here nearly a month before us. Had the situation of affairs permitted you, Sir, to suggest to me the Commodore's destination, it would certainly have saved me much time; however, I propose embarking upon the *Dolphin* at the Cape of Good Hope, which will shorten my passage six weeks or two months.

I cannot as yet form any idea about the politics of India.

By the *Osterly*, who arrived in England a few days after we left it, we learn that the troubles in Bengal were drawing towards a conclusion; but by the *Liverpool*, who was spoken with by the Commodore at sea, and who left that place so late as the 5th of April, we are given to understand that affairs still continue in some confusion. If we are happy enough to recover our lost reputation, and the confidence of the natives, and can adopt some solid plan, supported upon such principles of moderation as are consistent with the true interests of a trading company, my utmost wishes will be accomplished; but if this cannot be effected, we shall at last be reduced to the necessity of making such strides towards power and dominion as must, I should think, end in a parliamentary inquiry and a national jurisdiction.

As a well-wisher to my country, I cannot avoid representing to you the deplorable condition of this capital and rich settlement of the Portuguese; indeed, I should think myself deserving of everlasting infamy if I did not, with one battalion of infantry, make myself master of Rio Janeiro in 24 hours. They have nothing here that deserves the name of fortification; an unflanked wall, a miserable rampart, and a few unserviceable honeycombed guns, constitute the chief strength of this place; their regulars do not exceed 500 men, and if their capital be thus defenceless, what are we to think of their other subordinate settlements on the coast of Brazil? Bad as the Spaniards are, they could not fail, in another war, of making a speedy and easy conquest of all the Portuguese possessions in this part of the world, which would be of much more consequence to Spain than the conquest of Portugal, and the Reformation already begun there, extended to the coast of Brazil, it might possibly be the means of preventing these valuable possessions from falling into the hands of the French or Spaniards.

If India afford any curiosities which would be acceptable either to Mrs. Grenville or yourself, I beg you will lay your commands on, dear Sir, your obliged and devoted humble Servant, CLIVE.

LORD HOLLAND TO MR. GRENVILLE.

Kingsgate, October 14, 1764.

DEAR SIR,—You very kindly encouraged me to apply to you where I was personally concerned. I cannot be more so in anything than in the success of my endeavours to assuage the incurable wound given to my brother by his daughter[1].

Mr. O'Bryen is gone with her to New York, and the keeping him there in credit is all that can be done, whilst we, if possible, forget them here. I hear there is a complaint made against Mr. Lambert Moore, who may probably in consequence of it, be removed; in that case, I beg you to make Mr. O'Bryen Comptroller of the Customs at New York in his room.

I will be security that the public shall not suffer. His Majesty has shown so much compassion on this unhappy occasion, that I flatter myself he will have no objection.

Let me intreat you then, dear Sir, to propose it, as a most essential and lasting obligation to a whole family, ever to be most gratefully acknowledged by your most obedient, &c., &c. HOLLAND.

[1] The marriage of Lady Susan Fox, Lord Ilchester's daughter, with O'Brien, the actor. See a letter from Horace Walpole to Lord Hertford, in *Walpole's Correspondence*, vol. iv. p. 404.

MR. MORTON TO MR. GRENVILLE.

Tackley, October 15, 1764.

DEAR SIR,—I flatter myself that you will not have imputed my silence to a neglect of the business you did me the honour to entrust to my discretion in our last walk at Wotton.

Before I went the circuit, all my attempts to see the gentleman[1] proved ineffectual, and 'tis now only within these few days, at a visit at my own house, that I have received any intimations from him that would justify the interruption of a letter.

After repeated conversations on the subject, I have his leave to assure you, that all reports of his engagements or inclinations to continue adverse measures are without foundation or truth.

That he is most sincerely inclined to give all possible assistance to Government, and would be particularly happy could this be done by means in every respect most (agreeable) to you.

That the time and circumstances of carrying this into execution must be the result of a more particular discussion than a letter will admit of, need not be observed.

Indeed, a subject of this kind is in every point so delicate, that I should not have trusted any part of such a commission to paper, had it not been his wish that you should know thus much as soon as possible, and that 't was both our opinions, that no overtures of this kind should have been made through more hands than one.

My return to town cannot now exceed a fortnight, and therefore hope an interview with you before that

[1] Mr. Charles Townshend.

time will not be necessary. I will embrace the first moment of my being in town to wait on you, and explain everything that has passed on this occasion. In the mean time, if anything should seem proper in your judgment to be mentioned to him, you may depend on the punctual observance of all directions you may please to give me. Your most obliged, &c. JOHN MORTON.

SIR RICHARD LYTTELTON TO MR. GRENVILLE.

Richmond, October 15, 1764.

SIR,—The Decision of the Board of General Officers, to the astonishment of mankind, appears by their report to have acquitted Colonel Johnston of some of the accusations referred to their consideration, whilst other articles of charge of disobedience or neglect have been passed over by them unnoticed, such seems to have been the weight of Court influence and power exerted in his favour.

Petitions from the Magistrates or Universities of Mahon, &c., containing matter of high charge against Colonel Johnston, for arbitrarily and illegally, and of his own authority solely, laying impositions upon shipping, to the great prejudice of His Majesty's subjects, and the trade and navigation in Minorca, and for other matters of very serious nature complained of by them, have been transmitted through me, as their Governor, to the Earl of Halifax, to be laid before the King in Council, which petitions I conceive have not as yet been attended to; and I am told that it has been signified to Colonel Johnston that he may forthwith return to Minorca, and re-assume the government of that island.

Is Mr. Grenville Minister, or even one of the Privy Council, and can these things be possible? if this be so, I hope I may, with all dutiful submission and humility towards His Majesty, be allowed to retire from a situation that has been productive of so much vexation to me, and in which under these circumstances I can no longer continue; and as most general officers, and very many who are my juniors, have not only regiments, but governments and other emoluments,—if, Sir, His Majesty should be graciously inclined to think that, after having made three volunteer campaigns at the expense of my little original fortune, and of my health, without having ever, in the course of near thirty years' service, received even the common emoluments enjoyed by others, I may deserve to be placed upon an equality with them, I shall contentedly wait the event of such a gracious disposition, and of that friendship you have so long professed for me. I am, &c., &c.

RICHARD LYTTELTON.

EARL TEMPLE TO MONS. MICHELL[1], à Berlin.

À Stowe ce 18 Octobre, 1764.

MONSIEUR,—Je saisis avec empressement le premier moment pour vous témoigner le plaisir que je ressens de

[1] Michell had been very lately recalled from his post as Ambassador in England, by desire of the British Government, and in accordance with the precedent of Sir Charles Hanbury Williams having been recalled from Berlin by desire of the King of Prussia. The above letter is from a copy in the handwriting of Mrs. George Grenville, and as at this time no communication existed between Lord Temple and his brother, it was probably obtained either in its transit through the Post Office, or from being intercepted in some other way. Mr. Grenville being aware of the interference of the Prussian Ministers

vous féliciter sur la reception distinguée dont le grand Roi votre maître vous a honoré à Potsdam, en y ajoutant titre d'honneur, gratification, et pension honnête ; récompenses de vos services dans la bonne cause. Je me flatte, pour le bien de l'Europe, qu'avec le temps la situation des affaires pourront se réduire où elles doivent naturellement être, et d'où ils n'auront jamais dû se départir ; mais si ce n'est qu'un souhait, c'est au moins un souhait que je voudrois entretenir aussi long tems qu'il est possible. Le compte que vous me rendez de la santé parfaite de Sa Majesté, et des arrangemens civils et militaires qui font l'occupation de la Paix glorieuse qui a terminé de sa part une guerre non moins périlleuse qu'éclatante, me donne une satisfaction vive.

Le Prince Héréditaire de Brunswick m'honore beaucoup en se souvenant de moi. Vous sçavez de longue main tous mes sentimens quant au dehors, et je suis sur que vous me rendez justice.

J'ai le plaisir de vous apprendre que par les dernières lettres de Hayes, il paroit que Mons. Pitt jouit d'une santé parfaite. J'ai eu d'abord en arrivant ici une entorse à la jambe, dont les suites m'ont duré jusqu'au présent.

Je suis pourtant quasi entièrement rétabli, et jouissant

in the affairs of the British Government, and their active encouragement of party writers, with whom Lord Temple was known to be connected, it is natural that he should wish to ascertain the purport of any correspondence between Lord Temple and the Court of Berlin. Both the Postmasters, Lord Hyde and Lord Trevor, were the most intimate friends of Mr. Grenville, and therefore he could easily obtain all the information he desired from that quarter. The practice of opening letters at the Post Office for political purposes was so common at this time, and so generally known or suspected to be so, that Lord Temple would not be likely to commit himself by writing anything intended for the Post, which he wished to conceal.

de la meilleure santé possible. Vous connoissez assez, et vous sentirez de même tout le malheur de la perte que nous venons d'essuyer dans la mort du Duc de Devonshire: nous jouons de guignon, mais la cause étant bonne on ne doit jamais se décourager ; au moins ce n'est pas la mode à Potsdam. TEMPLE.

MR. NUGENT TO MR. GRENVILLE.

Bath, October 20, 1764.

DEAR SIR,—By a letter lately received here, General Durouse, Governor of the Castle of St. Mawes, is dying or dead in France. My son, who is just returned from Cornwall, is very urgent with me to extend my request to you upon that subject, and to beg you may be pleased to recommend him to succeed to the vacancy, as he finds that the part which he and I took in the Cyder Bill has given the Boscawen family some advantages over us among his constituents[1].

The Lords of the Manor of St. Mawes have formerly, in many instances, been appointed to that Government, although not military men ; and I am not only Lord of the Manor, but proprietor of at least four-fifths of the town. There are other circumstances which, if I should die before Mr. Newsham[2], may render it very useful to my son's interest to have this weight thrown into his scale ; as in that event, the property which I possess in the borough would be divided with Newsham during

[1] Colonel Nugent was subsequently appointed Governor of St. Mawes. He was one of the members for the borough.

[2] Mr. Nugent married Mrs. Knight, formerly the widow of a Mr. Newsham, consequently the person here mentioned was his son-in-law.

his life. After having said all this, I must say, what I sincerely feel, that if a grant of my extended request should expose you to any difficulties worthy of your attention, I had much rather depart from it than have mine, or my son's interest, served at your expense. Upon this principle I never have, and I think I never shall again trouble you with a request for anything in Cornwall, which by the bye, may serve as one answer to Lord Falmouth, who under every Administration has had an ample share in favour of his friends.

The Duke of Bedford is in excellent spirits and good humour, and the Duchess is in love with you. I am not quite clear, from the things she has said to me, whether she does not mean I should be a convenient person between you. It is true she talks much of the inviolable union subsisting between the Duke and you, as if that were a bias upon her inclinations: but this is an old device, not to be imposed upon a man of my gallantry.

I paid her in her own coin, and told her that if she answered for the Duke, I could answer for you, from the things I had heard you say of him.

Prowse[1] is here, not at all well, and lives very much retired. I have heard some things of him, which I do not entirely like, although they are only symptomatic.

Hunt[2], who voted constantly against us last year, is I think in better temper, and declares himself personally very much your friend, but with a *But*, which will not serve our purpose. Suppose you was to write me a letter containing a paragraph relating to both, or either of them, fit for them to see, in answer to this letter?

[1] M.P. for Somersetshire.
[2] George Hunt, M.P. for Bodmin.

The eldest Buller is I think in a dying way, swelled as if he had drunk a hogshead of cyder; or rather, as if he had swallowed the apples whole, for his belly is as hard as a board.

Lord Strange is much better, but not quite so well as you and I wish him: we drink your health sometimes together, and I wish he drank it only with me, but he will dine at the Tons, and he loves jollity. Sturt[1] has been here, and continues firmly yours, as does my good uncle Colleton[2].

At Bristol I do not believe now there is one single discontented man; but from the circumstance of the present Mayor being brother-in-law to Lord Westmoreland, which adds to his influence in the corporation, I do not care to press the choice of a steward to succeed Lord Hardwicke. Lord Botetourt and I have talked this over, and he is of my opinion. I have seen a friend of Conolly's here, lately come from Ireland, who tells me that he has heard him express hopes that his presence may not be necessary the next session; a letter from you will, I dare say, bring him, and I should think the sooner it is writ the better. If Drax[3] does not come to me, I have thoughts of making him a visit. My son begs leave to join his respectful compliments and good wishes with those of, dear Sir, your, &c., &c.

G. NUGENT.

MR. WILKES TO EARL TEMPLE.

Boulogne, November 1, 1764.

My Lord,—I cannot express the gratitude of my heart to your Lordship and Lady Temple for the most

---

[1] M.P. for Dorsetshire.   [2] M.P. for Lostwithiel.
[3] Thomas Erle Drax, M.P. for Wareham.

obliging message by Mr. Cotes. Give me leave to say that I will *deceive* even your Lordship's penetration in one point; a point in which I know you wish to be *deceived*, my real attention to finances. I feel as I ought all your goodness to me. I will make you the only return you desire, the acting up to the truest prudence and economy. I have talked the whole over with my two friends here[1]. I consent to Miss Wilkes's leaving me and coming to England.

I will quit the expensive and luxurious Paris, where I have been more fêté than has done me good. I will cross the Alps, live quite alone in some town of Italy, neither seen nor known, visiting nor visited, boarding in a good family, and I will confine myself to whatever Mr. Cotes sends me. I will never exceed it one shilling. I shall employ this active mind in an employment I am not totally, perhaps, unqualified for, I mean the History of my own Country since the Revolution[2]. I will try to equal the dignity of the ancient historians, and as I shall bring it down to my own times, I shall have an opportunity of telling my own story, and of doing justice to the very few friends I love, and their country ought to adore. With these resolutions, *fixed as fate*, or the foolish Lord *Batitort*, I shall not die of the pip. My pen will every day be adding to my fortune, and I will not return to England while I am a shilling in any man's debt. For this great work I shall have the letters of the French Ambassadors in England, of which Monsieur Suard procures me copies, and the

[1] Churchill and Humphry Cotes. They had gone together to Boulogne on a visit to Wilkes. Churchill was suddenly attacked by a fever, from the effects of which he died, three days after the date of this letter.

[2] Of which he only wrote the Introduction.

Journal of James II.[1] to the day of his death, which Abbé Arnaud gets me. It is in three vols. folio, entirely the handwriting of James II. This will be a good parade to the public, and to booksellers.

I shall find it some expense to clear Paris, but I will set about it immediately on my return, after I have recovered poor Churchill, whom I stay to nurse in this wretched town. Mr. Cotes will explain these and other particulars to your Lordship. I finished *a letter to the Electors of Aylesbury*[2], which I have read twice to Mr. Dunning at Paris, and to my two friends at Boulogne. I have profited by their lights, and therefore I shall now send it on the wings of the wind, as it has their full and entire approbation.

This vile town almost anticipates my *outlawry*. It is composed of *outlawed smugglers*. My dear Churchill and I are, however, very well lodged in a worthy merchant's house, a friend of Mr. Cotes's.

When I think of England, I am pretty well weaned from it, and I am not sure that I do not more execrate the *Minority* than the *Majority*. Now my two friends are here, England only contains Lord and Lady Temple, which to me consecrate my native country. I shall be happy everywhere if their kindness extends to my dearest daughter. I am ever, my Lord, your most obliged and devoted humble Servant, JOHN WILKES.

[1] Since published, from the Original preserved with the Stuart Papers: 2 vols. quarto, 1816: edited by Dr. Stanier Clarke.
[2] See *Wilkes's Correspondence*, by Almon, vol. iii. p. 86.

MR. HARRIS TO MR. GRENVILLE.

Treasury Chambers, November 2, 1764.

Sir,—The office of Pannel Painter to the Crown being now vacant by the death of Mr. Hogarth, I do not presume to recommend, but only to remind you of Mr. Stuart, Editor of the *Antiquities of Athens*, whose excellent taste in painting and architecture is universally known[1]. I have the honour with great respect to subscribe myself, &c. JAMES HARRIS.

MR. ALMON TO EARL TEMPLE.

Piccadilly, November 12, 1764.

My Lord,—I did not advise your Lordship of what passed between Mr. Fitzherbert[2] and Sir William Baker[3] (when they dined together a few weeks ago, in order to consult upon business, as I mentioned in a letter to your Lordship written about the same time), because nothing material was done. They agreed indeed that a weekly political paper ought to be set up, but the want of a proper writer or writers has hitherto prevented it. Mr. Fitzherbert told me that if six papers were wrote, the publication should not be delayed one moment; but although one Member of Parliament (I am not at liberty to mention his name) has wrote two papers—and excellent ones they are—yet there is such a backwardness, or rather shyness, in the others who can write, that nothing has been done. At the request of four or five of those who were most

---

[1] James Stuart was soon after appointed Sergeant Painter.
[2] M.P. for Derby.   [3] M.P. for Plympton.

anxious for it, I applied to Mr. Horace Walpole, begging he would contribute a paper or two to begin with. He approved of the scheme, said it was absolutely necessary, but added, the leaders who are to be benefited by it will disapprove of it, and what can we do without them; upon the very first scrape you get into (meaning me as publisher) the leaders will immediately disavow it. He enforced this prediction with arguments which were too convincing to be resisted, and he concluded with the example of Mr. Wilkes; therefore he excused himself from assisting, and said that he was disheartened by the languor which appeared in those who, as leaders, ought to show an encouraging spirit. Good God! said he, two or three times, did ever anybody see an Opposition acting on the *defensive* before? He assured me positively that General Conway will not deceive the Minority; and in all his remarks on the backwardness of certain people, he always excepted your Lordship, and repeatedly said that if Mr. P.[1] and Mr. T.[2] had the same spirit, and the same hearty desire of going forward as Lord T., the Ministry would be entirely defeated in a fortnight. There are very few who do not say and think the same. The Ministry take advantage of this supineness, and are indefatigable in spreading reports that the Opposition is all a farce, dead, dispersed, broken-hearted, &c. A few days since one of their people had the assurance to ask Sir William Baker, " how long the Minority intended to carry on this farce." " A farce do you call it?" said Sir William, " you will find it such a farce as you never saw in your life."

Your Lordship knows that there was an embryo

[1] Mr. Pitt.   [2] Mr. Charles Townshend.

intention of inviting the Minority to the Lord Mayor's feast[1]; the manner in which it was frustrated was thus: Mr. Beardmore applied to the Mayor for tickets. His Lordship said that if any of the Minority had a mind to come he would give them tickets to the number of twenty. Mr. Beardmore told it to Mr. Fitzherbert, who instantly observed that when twenty of the Minority had sent their names, his Lordship might probably refuse to deliver the tickets, and then it would look as if the Minority wanted to come and could not, upon which no more was said about it, for it is feared the Mayor is a little in the interest of Lord Sandwich.

Mr. Cotes was not returned last night from Boulogne, owing to the unfortunate illness and death of Mr. Churchill, who was seized with a scarlet fever on Monday, the 29th of October (the day before he was to have come away), and died at Boulogne on the Sunday following. Although he was very much out of humour with the Minority, and intended very soon to attack some of them upon their *moderation*, in a poem to have been called *Moderation*, inscribed to Mr. Pitt, yet his death will be felt as a real loss, for the public admired his writings, and whatever he might have said of the Minority, he would certainly have said much worse of the Ministry.

I have received another pamphlet from *Candor*, which is very long, very severe, and very good; it is upon juries, libels, warrants, &c. I have likewise received an *answer* to the *Defence of the Minority*[2];

[1] Alderman Sir William Stephenson was now Lord Mayor.
[2] Almon attributes the *Defence of the Majority* to Charles Lloyd, and he says that it was in reply to this Defence of the Majority that the celebrated *Letter on Libels and Warrants* was written. See *Biographical, Literary, and Political Anecdotes*, vol. ii. p. 109.

the author of which is a Member of the House of Commons, but I have not permission to name him. And what is better still, I have received also Mr. Legge's papers, I mean those relative to the Hampshire election, which he desired might be published. I am at liberty to say I had them from Lady Stawell[1]. This week I will send your Lordship a printed copy, but they are not to be published to the world till Christmas or January. The other two pamphlets will be published as soon as possible; therefore, notwithstanding the terrible panic which has seized all the printers and publishers both in and out of the City, I continue to go on, and will continue, so long as I am permitted to go at large. It is true I will avoid danger if I can, but if I cannot I will not fly from it. I am, my Lord, with the truest sense of gratitude, &c., &c. J. ALMON.

P.S. This moment received a letter from Sir Wm. Meredith, another from G. Onslow, Esq., both in high spirits.

MR. WHATELY TO MR. GRENVILLE.

Lincoln's Inn, November 14, (1764), 7 o'clock.

DEAR SIR,—I have seen Mr. Wedderburn, who has very readily undertaken to deliver the message to Mr. Yorke this evening, in the terms you desire, and will wait upon you in his way to Westminster to-morrow morning.

He only desires that his name may not be mentioned

---

[1] Mr. Legge's widow. The publication in question was edited by Dr. Butler, afterwards Bishop of Hereford, who also wrote a Biographical account of the Right Honourable Henry Bilson Legge.

to anybody, as he fears it might be thought officious in him, and possibly give offence. I am, &c.

THOMAS WHATELY.

MEMORANDUM BY MR. GRENVILLE, RELATING TO A NEGOTIATION WITH MR. CHARLES YORKE[1].

A FRIEND of Mr. Yorke having talked with Mr. Grenville upon this occasion, as he had frequently done before on the mutual good will they bore each other,

[1] It has been supposed, in the absence of the more authentic information which these Papers supply, that Mr. Charles Yorke did not upon this occasion solicit the office of Master of the Rolls, or that of Attorney General, and that had they been offered to him he would not have accepted either. Sir Thomas Clarke, the late Master of the Rolls, having been seized with Apoplexy on Sunday, the 11th of November, died on the Tuesday following. "The same evening," says Mr. Grenville, in his Diary, "Mr. Yorke went to my Lord Chancellor, and opened to him the dispositions he was in to fill either of the two great posts in the law. He desired that a Peerage should be annexed to the Mastership of the Rolls, and that a considerable addition should be made to the salary, and it was his wish also that he should be enabled to state to his friends, that it was by the express command of the King that he accepted office under this Administration." With none of these stipulations was the King willing to comply, and after many days wavering between acceptance and refusal, with all that fatal irresolution which seems to have been his peculiar characteristic, he at last declined both the Rolls and the Attorney-Generalship, and only asked that he might have a Patent of Precedence over the Solicitor General, at the same time declaring his intention of taking a part in support of Government. The effect of Mr. Yorke's acceptance of a Patent of Precedence is very clearly described by Mr. Croker, in a note to one of Walpole's letters. It appears that when Mr. Yorke was made Solicitor General in 1756, he was not a King's Counsel: he succeeded to be Attorney, but on his resignation in 1763 he lost the precedence which his offices had given him, and he returned to the outer Bar and a stuff gown. This arrangement was convenient to him for the conduct of his business in Court, but gave him no addition of either rank or profit.

Mr. Grenville said that if Mr. Yorke thought that his situation would admit of it, he would be very glad to see him at nine o'clock to-morrow evening, in order to speak to him upon the subject as far as related to himself, and his sentiments upon the occasion, and that he authorized his friend to tell him so.

This passed at the Treasury at four o'clock with Mr. Whately, and the message was delivered to Mr. Yorke, by Mr. Wedderburne, on Wednesday, November 14th, 1764, at nine o'clock in the evening of the same day, after Mr. Yorke returned from Lord Chancellor's, to whom he went without being sent for, to speak upon the same subject.

MR. GRENVILLE TO THE LORD CHANCELLOR.

Downing Street, November 16, 1764.

MY DEAR LORD,—I have been, since I left you, at St. James's, and have made my report to His Majesty of what passed last night, who is by no means inclined to make any alteration in the office of the Master of the Rolls, but approves very much of your seeing the Attorney General[1] this evening, and directed me to recommend it particularly to you to bring the matter to bear with him in the manner in which your Lordship and I talked of it this morning, if possible. The King will be extremely glad to hear of its success, and is persuaded that you agree with him in wishing it, and that this matter is therefore in the best and properest hands to procure it. I have, &c., &c. GEORGE GRENVILLE.

[1] Sir Fletcher Norton.

THE LORD CHANCELLOR TO MR. GRENVILLE.

Lincoln's Inn Fields, November 16, 1764.

My dear Sir,—I had the honour of yours of this day, wherein you report that His Majesty is not inclined to make any alteration[1] in the Rolls, which corresponds entirely with our Royal Master's early and yet sound judgment.

I have, in consequence of the King's approbation, seen this evening his Attorney General, to receive his deliberate determination.

He answered, "That the answer he gave me before, he considered as conclusive to himself, though he found it was not so good as he thought, which, if it came to him without prejudice" (meaning, I suppose, to the chiefs, should they drop), "he did not regard that." I then said that I thought the place should be mended, by an alteration of the Act to renew at the end of five or seven years, which I believed you agreed with me, but this to be done on all accounts when the place was full, and to be a measure not to be talked of, but to yourself. This gave the fullest satisfaction, and I have absolute authority, at all events, to lay this resolution before the King, which I purpose to do Sunday next. He desired to know whether he might communicate what passed between us to you. I told him, everything; and he will desire an audience of you to-morrow for that purpose.

This negotiation, I think, ends perfectly satisfactory to the King's wishes, and to the ideas of his servants.

I should do injustice to Mr. Attorney, did I not add

[1] The addition to the salary which Mr. Yorke had required.

that his whole conversation was big with zeal to the King, and attachment to his Administration. I have, &c., &c. NORTHINGTON.

THE LORD CHANCELLOR TO MR. GRENVILLE.

(Monday, November 19, 1764).

DEAR SIR,—Though I was not well enough at night yesterday to see company in general, yet I let in Mr. Yorke, who had called on me, without admission, the evening before.

I had a very long, and a very unexplicit conference on his side; on mine it was very frank, and very personally kind and obliging to him, which he very fully acknowledged.

The substance, which you ought to know, it is impossible for me to write. Perhaps I could give you some idea of it in discourse. One thing I thought very singular, as I did not hear it from you; viz., that he had told you he intended to take the Duke of Newcastle's opinion along with him in this transaction.

In short, it makes one sick, and I write now only from particular friendship, and a desire that nothing should by surprise, or for want of information, lead you into any steps wherein you may be disappointed.

I am not able to go out; if you can come hither, I would be alone to your appointment. I am, with real truth, &c., &c. NORTHINGTON.

DR. HAY TO MR. GRENVILLE.

Admiralty, Monday, Nov. 19, 1764.

SIR,—I have seen Mr. Yorke, who was as much surprised at the expression in the Chancellor's letter as you was. His visit to the D. of N. is for communication, not judgment, and to satisfy him that the affair at Cambridge will be honourably disposed of.

The Chancellor most certainly mistook Mr. Yorke[1].

I am, Sir, &c., &c. G. HAY.

MR. JENKINSON TO MR. GRENVILLE.

(November 20, 1764).

BINDLEY has just been with me. He has been with C. Townshend for six hours.

He found him in the best humour imaginable both with respect to himself and to Government.

He told Bindley that he entirely approved of the part he had taken, and that he had nothing to do but to act a manly part, and to do all he could to support Government: that he believed every sensible man would now do the same.

With respect to himself, Mr. Townshend said that the Pay Office, and being a Cabinet Councillor (which he was, he said, before) would satisfy him.

I rather understood that he would be content to wait for Lord H.'s[2] death. He said he wished him dead, and so he believed did everybody. He intends going to Court to-morrow. I should think that a good reception there would increase his present good-humour, and be of use. He said he desired only to be second in the House of Commons. You will judge how far all this is to be relied on, and what use should be made of it, but Bindley will call on you to-morrow between nine and ten, and if you admit him will tell you more.

[1] See Mr. Grenville's Diary, *infra*.
[2] Lord Holland, who was still Paymaster General of the Forces.

Bindley told me that Lady Townshend came in to Mr. T.'s after the above conversation, and a little before he left him, and said that Mr. Yorke was to be Attorney General. This was her Ladyship's information just at that time, for I have been told that she said at dinner that Mr. Yorke would not take that office. C. T. spoke in high commendations of Sir Fletcher Norton.

I see that Bindley wishes for his brother[1] the Stamps, rather than the Receivership.

THE EARL OF SANDWICH TO MR. GRENVILLE.

Friday evening, November 23, 1764.

DEAR SIR,—You love Lord Townshend, and will therefore be pleased at reading the enclosed letter, where his good heart and his attachment to the Government appear in full colours. You will observe that I have *sufficient* though not *full* powers to treat in his name, and that it is not from any unnecessary scruple of mine that I cannot consent to give up the interests of my friends. You will also observe the postscript about Draper and his claim in favour of Caius College, which goes unanimous with Government, chiefly on Lord Townshend's account.

This letter will, however, facilitate rather than obstruct my agreement with Mr. Yorke, if he really means to agree; I expect him, and the Bishop of Chester, and Mr. Montagu, at eight o'clock. Be so good as to return me Lord Townshend's letter, and believe me, &c., &c.

SANDWICH.

---

[1] James Bindley was for many years a Commissioner of Stamps, and well known for having formed an extremely curious and valuable collection of books and prints, which at his death were sold by auction.

You will perceive that Lord T. seems to take it for granted that the agreement with Mr. Yorke will take place, but my letter to him only mentioned it as probable, in order to know his full sentiments upon the occasion.

THE LORD CHANCELLOR TO MR. GRENVILLE.

London, November 26, 1764.

MY DEAR SIR,—In consequence of our conversation yesterday, I saw Mr. Yorke to-day, and I had as strong an answer to report to the King should he ask, what yesterday I supposed he might, as could be received. I had this answer at three o'clock, and a permission to say not only where he was not to go, but if necessary what was to be his situation, to the Attorney General, with whom I could not speak without that permission.

I immediately sent to the Attorney General, and saw him a little after six, and he hath just left me; I found him very much dissatisfied with the delay of this transaction, which I expected; and which he said (and I believe truly) had raised so many reports to the disadvantage of his character.

However, I told him I had sent for him, not knowing, 'till within an hour, what were the fixed wishes of Mr. Yorke, assuring him that both you and myself had only considered all along those wishes as they might be reconcileable to his, the Attorney's. That I was to inform him now that Mr. Yorke had difficulties which made him not wish for either of those places. He replied, he did not doubt that, was of that opinion from the beginning, and believed I thought the same. I said this being the case, I had sent for him to know his sentiments, for that now it became material to Government that his abilities should be employed in the office of Attorney. He was, he said, unable to answer so new a proposition entangled by the delay and its consequences, and in which he thought his honour and character concerned.

He then asked of course what was to become of Mr. Yorke. I told him, in secrecy, and upon honour to be kept so, that he would have no mark of favour but inferior to the Attorney General.

This seemed to make impression, and pleased, and he added, if I was certain of that:—I added,—he might.

I then told him again his honour had not been committed, and that he had never been mentioned by me, and I believed not by you, as asking the Rolls, but as willing to take it to accommodate the King's affairs; and therefore if he remained in a greater post to the King's satisfaction, and for the service of Government, I thought it contributed both to his honour and weight.

He then asked who was to go to the Rolls. I replied that this being the hour which had left it open for others, I knew no more than himself. Upon the whole he has taken to-morrow night for his answer, and to see you to-morrow. I have therefore sent you the detail of what has passed between us, as necessary for your information and interview. I have only to add, that though he is out of humour, he seemed manageable:—my opinion of the whole is known to you. I am, &c., &c.

NORTHINGTON.

MR. GRENVILLE TO THE LORD CHANCELLOR.

Downing Street, Monday, November 26, 1764.

MY DEAR LORD,—Just before I received the honour of your Lordship's letter, Dr. Hay came to me by Mr. Yorke's desire to deliver to me a declaration in writing of what passed between your Lordship and him.

I send you a copy of it, together with the answer, which I returned to it in writing, to prevent any mistake in a matter of this nature, and the rather because I understood from your Lordship yesterday that the manner in which this business was to be laid before the King was, that your Lordship and I were convinced by our conversations with Mr. Yorke that in desiring you to lay before His Majesty his wishes to receive this public mark of the King's favour by a Patent of Precedency for life between the Attorney and Solicitor General, Mr. Yorke proceeded upon a determination to give a cordial and friendly support to His Majesty's measures.

I sincerely hope that this business will be properly settled by your Lordship without any farther difficulty, as I find by the beginning of your letter, that the answer which you was to report to the King was as strong as could be received.

I am sorry to hear that Mr. Attorney General expressed so much uneasiness, but I flatter myself from the good dispositions which he has shown in the course of this transaction, and from what you now tell me, that he will not suffer that to add to the embarrassment which has hitherto attended the other parts of this business.

I am much obliged to your Lordship for the trouble

you have taken to give me the information of what has passed, and am ever with the truest respect and regard, my dear Lord, &c., &c.

GEORGE GRENVILLE.

If any more difficulties arise would it not be better for you and me to meet with Mr. Yorke together, and put an end to them one way or the other?

[*The following are the inclosures referred to in the above letter.*]

November 26, 1764.

Mr. Yorke has seen Lord Chancellor, and desires me to tell Mr. Grenville, that there being various difficulties as to either of the Offices, Lord Chancellor approves of the Patent of Precedency between the Attorney and Solicitor General, as a mark of the King's personal grace to Mr. Yorke for his past services, without any stipulations for the future.

And that the King will be pleased to permit Mr. Yorke to thank him in a personal audience.

G. HAY.

Mr. Grenville having received from Dr. Hay the paper containing Mr. Yorke's declaration of what passed between Lord Chancellor and himself with regard to the Patent of Precedency between the Attorney and Solicitor General, desires Dr. Hay to acquaint Mr. Yorke that Mr. Grenville saw Lord Chancellor yesterday morning, and from his conversation with Lord Chancellor he cannot help thinking that Mr. Yorke hath misunderstood Lord Chancellor in some parts of that declaration. In order, therefore, to prevent any mistakes, Mr. Grenville will send this account to Lord

Chancellor, and in the mean time desires to be excused from expressing his sentiments with regard to it.

[*On the back of the letter, addressed to the Lord Chancellor, Mr. Grenville has written the following note.*]

N.B. This letter, with the two inclosed papers, were delivered to Dr. Hay, who brought Mr. Yorke's account of what had passed, and who promised to send this letter with the inclosures the next morning to Lord Chancellor, unless Mr. Yorke, whom Dr. Hay was to see first, should agree to withdraw the paper which he had sent, and accordingly the next morning, November 27th, Dr. Hay came again to Mr. Grenville, and informed him, that to avoid any altercation upon the words *for his past services without any stipulation for the future,* Mr. Yorke consented to withdraw his paper, and wished that the letter should not be sent, and said that he meant to tell the King that he would give a cordial and friendly support to his measures, as far as he possibly could with his real opinions. This letter and inclosed papers were therefore returned to Mr. Grenville by Dr. Hay, and never sent to the Lord Chancellor.

MR. DE GREY[1] TO MR. GRENVILLE.

November 30, 1764.

Sir,—I am certain you would think me unworthy of the station I have at present the honour to be in if I was insensible to the recent instance of indignity the office of His Majesty's Solicitor General has received in

[1] Solicitor General.

the appointment of a gentleman to the office of the Rolls, inferior in rank, without not only an offer, but not even the condescension of a message or communication upon the subject to me, but especially to that which he is now about to receive, and also without any notice, of introducing a Patent of Precedence of a gentleman now happening to stand without the Bar, immediately before His Majesty's Solicitor General.

I believe neither of these circumstances has ever happened before. A resigning Solicitor has preserved his precedence before a Solicitor newly appointed. I am at a loss to know to what account to place this misfortune of mine, unless I have unknowingly offended His Majesty, or given you, Sir, some cause of displeasure.

Whatever it may be, I thought it incumbent upon me, before this last mark of public disgrace was received, to lay my sentiments before you, that whatever may be the result of it I may, as far as the thing admits of it, be able to vindicate myself to my friends, particularly to those by whose means I flattered myself with having, though undeservedly, some share of your favour. I have the honour to be, &c., &c. WILLIAM DE GREY.

MR. GRENVILLE TO MR. DE GREY.

Downing Street, November 30, 1764.

SIR,—I am very sorry to find by your letter that you feel so much uneasiness at the appointment of Mr. Sewell to be Master of the Rolls, and at the Patent of Precedency intended to be given to Mr. Yorke. You must be sensible that I never had the least intimation from you that you wished to be appointed Master of the Rolls, though that office has now been vacant a considerable time, nor has my Lord Chancellor, through whom the recommendation to the great offices of the law must necessarily pass, ever heard anything from you upon this subject that I know of. In this situation I take it for granted that my Lord Chancellor was persuaded that you had no thoughts of it, and therefore did not think it necessary to send to you upon that subject. As to the Patent of Precedency to Mr. Yorke, I did understand that you declined having any competition with him, and would very willingly have seen him Attorney General, and therefore I did not imagine that a Patent of Precedency to him would have been the subject of such complaint from you, much less that you would look upon it as an indignity to you, and a mark of public disgrace. When you come to consider the situation and circumstances of this transaction more coolly, I am persuaded that you will see it in another light; in the mean time I can only assure you that I have been desirous, ever since I had the pleasure of knowing you, to give you proofs of my regard and good will, and consequently cannot see without concern and surprise that you have so greatly mistaken my conduct and dispositions towards you upon the present occasion. I avoid entering into the detail of all the particulars which you mention, as I trust that upon farther consideration you yourself will see that it is unnecessary, and that you will do more justice to the sentiments with which I am, &c., &c.

GEORGE GRENVILLE.

THE REV. DR. MARKHAM[1] TO MR. GRENVILLE.

Durham, December 4, 1764.

SIR,—I was obliged once before to trouble you with a letter of the Bishop of Rochester[2], in which (after he had some days before advised me to decline the preferment that was offered, because he would certainly resign at Michaelmas,) he said, that on second thoughts he wished that I would accept it, if it was not too late, because it was possible he might change his mind.

After that time I saw him often, and was as often told by him that, notwithstanding what he had said in his letter, he still held his resolution to resign before Christmas. He used the same language to the Dean of Christ Church, except that, in their last conversation, he took a longer term, and said it might possibly not be 'till between Christmas and Easter. This I own begot in me a worse opinion of his sincerity than I had before.

I came into the North early in July; and as I heard nothing from him in the course of five months, I last week thought it prudent to write to him, and said to him, in the civilest terms, that if he was yet come to any determination on the subject of his Deanery it would be very convenient to me to know it. The reason of my writing was, that from the knowledge I had of him I thought it very possible that, though he might have changed his intentions, he would not be manly enough

---

[1] In the following year he was Dean of Rochester, and afterwards of Christ Church. In 1771 he became Bishop of Chester, and was made Preceptor to the Prince of Wales. He was subsequently Archbishop of York, and died in 1807, at the age of 89.

[2] Dr. Zachary Pearce: he also held the Deanery of Westminster; the latter he resigned soon after.

to acquaint me with it, but would suffer me to continue in my ill-founded expectations.

I received his answer to-day, and have sent you a copy of it. I shall make no comment upon it, except that I can no longer entertain any reasonable hopes from the kind arrangement which you made in my favour.

I have now only to hope, that as you were pleased unsolicited to destine me to a station of so great distinction as well as emolument, the same favourable disposition may still continue, and to assure you that you can never take any one under your protection who will retain a juster sense of his obligations.

I must now ask your forgiveness for passing to a very different subject.

I happen to be situated in the midst of the coal country: an opinion prevails here that some regulations in that trade will be made in the approaching session.

I happen to know some people who, though not coal-owners, nor any ways interested, are perfectly acquainted with the whole mystery of the trade, both on the Tyne and Weare.

If you think that any informations which I can procure may be useful to you, I shall use my best endeavours to satisfy you: my own opinion is, that they may be considerable, and will probably pass through purer channels than you usually receive them by.

I should have been afraid of troubling you on a subject so much out of my walk, if I had not been writing to you on another occasion. I hope you will not call it impertinence, but rather ascribe it to its true cause, the perfect and invariable zeal which I shall always feel, where your honour or interest are any way concerned.

I am, &c., &c. WILLIAM MARKHAM.

THE LORD CHANCELLOR TO MR. GRENVILLE.

December 14, 1764.

DEAR SIR,—I think it proper to inform you that I had a visit last night from the Attorney General, who was very dissatisfied with a transaction concomitant to the late promotion, and in which he represents himself much disappointed, and was going to resent it accordingly.

Though this collateral business, in its progress, had never been communicated to me, like other things, I thought it my duty to the King, and my regard to you, to submit it to consideration. I have the honour to be, &c., &c. NORTHINGTON.

EARL TEMPLE TO MR. WILKES.

[*A fragment*].

December 21, 1764.

. . . . . There is no union, to be sure, betwixt the D. of N. and us; but if there be an union of sentiments concerning public matters, there must follow an union of conduct.

THE EARL OF MANSFIELD TO MR. GRENVILLE.

Bloomsbury, December 24, 1764.

DEAR SIR,—Since I saw you I have heard from the King in general, and afterwards more particularly, but very indistinctly, from some persons who visited me last night, of a complaint concerning a civil government and judge sent to Canada.

Is it possible that we have abolished their laws, and

customs, and forms of judicature all at once?—a thing never to be attempted or wished. The history of the world don't furnish an instance of so rash and unjust an act by any conqueror whatsoever: much less by the Crown of England, which has always left to the conquered their own laws and usages, with a change only so far as the sovereignty was concerned.

Where other changes have happened, as in Ireland, they have been the work of great length of time, many emergencies, and where there was a pale of separation between the conquerors and conquered, and the former only conquered by their own laws at first.

Berwick, the conquests made by Edward III., and yielded by the treaty of Bretigny, retained their own municipal laws. Minorca does now. Is it possible that a man sans aveu, without knowing a syllable of their language or laws, has been sent over with an English title of magistracy unknown to them, the powers of which office must consequently be inexplicable, and unexecutable by their usages?

For God's sake learn the truth of the case, and think of a speedy remedy. I was told last night that the penal statutes of England concerning Papists are to be held in force in Canada.

The fundamental maxims are, that a country conquered keeps her own laws, 'till the conqueror expressly gives new.

A colony which goes from hence to settle in a waste country, if they have an express constitution by charter, (or so far as that is silent), carries with them such part of the laws of England as is adapted to, and proper for their situation.

A very small part of the Common or Statute Law of

England is law there by this maxim. Ecclesiastical Laws, Revenue Laws, Penal Laws, and a thousand other heads, do not bind there by implication, though in force here at the time of their settlement.

Perhaps the principal parts of this Report may be untrue, but I am so startled at it that I cannot help writing to you: you may easily learn from the Board of Trade whether there has been any Act from hence to send them over in a lump a new and unknown law.

I have thought of the observation you made yesterday from looking into the charters of some of the Charter Governments.

Though the question certainly does not want this, or any other authority, yet it will be a striking alteration to ignorant people, and an unanswerable argument ad homines; and, therefore, I wish you would employ somebody to look with this view into the origin of their power to tax themselves and raise money at all.

As to the Charter and Proprietary Governments, it can only be found in the Letters Patent from which it must be derived.

As to the King's Government, it can only be derived from the King's Commission, and Instructions to the Governors of an early date, which may be found at the Council Office or the Board of Trade. I would particularly look into that of New York, which was taken from the Dutch, and in a few years often changed her master.

Their first commission by a King of England is by Charles II.

I am just going out of town for the holidays. I could not help troubling you, for which I hope you will forgive me. Yours, most affectionately, MANSFIELD.

THE EARL OF SANDWICH TO MR. GRENVILLE.

Woburn, December 27, 1764.

DEAR SIR,—I find that the Duke of Bedford has strong objections against Bishop Robinson, and thinks him a very unfit person for the Primacy, that it would be imprudent in Government to confide in him; that if he could have been fixed by ties of gratitude, he ought to have been so from the favours he received from the Duke of Bedford, who promoted him to the Bishopric of Kildare: instead of which, in the very moment of translation, he refused to give his interest in a borough belonging to his former Bishopric, according to the Duke of Bedford's recommendation, and forced him to take the disagreeable alternative of contesting it with him, and carrying it by force against him: that, besides, he has no superiority of abilities or character to give him a claim to the preference, and that any other person of a decent reputation would do infinitely better than him: in short, I think the Duke of Bedford's chief point in this business is the exclusion of Robinson, and that he will be hurt if a person who behaved to him with such notorious ingratitude should be raised to the highest dignity in the church of Ireland[1].

You will be sorry to hear that the Duke of B. is this morning taken with a fit of the gout in one of his hands; that we are all apprehensive that it will extend itself, and perhaps confine him for a considerable time.

The enclosed letter is from Mr. Crespigny, who I mentioned to you in the summer as having an intention to oppose the Duke of Grafton at Thetford, and with

---

[1] Dr. Robinson, nevertheless, was made Archbishop of Armagh, as was supposed through the influence of Lord Bute.

great probability of success; you then authorized me to tell him that any assistance Government could give him in the execution of his plan, might, on application, be obtained.

Mr. Crespigny married the heiress to a person who had managed the borough of Thetford for the late. Duke of Grafton for many years, by whom he acquired an estate of 1200*l.* a year at that place, besides about 4000*l.* of debts from the principal people of the Corporation.

With this foundation, and living on the spot, he doubts not of carrying his point, and he is, I do most sincerely assure you, a very sensible and decent young man, and one that will not discredit Government, if he is taken by the hand. His request is, I hope, attainable (it would be attended with no difficulty if there had not been an abuse which ought not to be suffered, of pricking two people unqualified to serve, by which the Clerk of the Assize in a manner names the Sheriff), and I beg of you to lose no time in applying to Lord Chancellor to excuse this gentleman: if you will trouble yourself to write to Mr. Crespigny to tell him the success of your application, you will oblige him much, and attach him to you; if you choose to convey it through my channel, you will please to send me your commands.

    Believe me, &c., &c.   SANDWICH.

MR. GRENVILLE'S DIARY:

(Continued from page 242.)

Monday, January 2nd, 1764. Mr. Grenville dined at Kenwood with Lord Mansfield, and came to town in the evening.

Tuesday, January 3rd. Mr. Grenville saw the King, who made many inquiries about the party at Woburn.

Wednesday, 4th. The King spoke with great warmth and cordiality to Mr. Grenville; told him there was no man in his service whose sentiments so perfectly agreed with his own, as his, and no man to whom he could speak so openly and confidentially.

Mr. Jenkinson was at Luton on Sunday. He says Lord Bute is vastly pleased with the successful state of the King's affairs, and always speaks in high commendation of Mr. Grenville.

Friday, January 6th, 1764. Lord Halifax dined with Mr. Grenville. After dinner they talked upon American matters, and upon the appointment and salaries of the officers appointed for the Colonies. Mr. Grenville would not consent to their having salaries from England. Lord Halifax was against this regulation, and was extremely heated and eager. Lord Thomond was present at a great part of the conversation, and Lord Hillsborough and Mr. Jenkinson heard it all.

Tuesday, 10th. The King told Mr. Grenville that Mr. Charles Townshend had, by the means of Mr. Bindley, desired that Lord Halifax and Mr. Grenville might know that he respected their abilities and talents, and was desirous they should know that he did so; that he saw there was nothing to be done in Opposition; that as to Mr. Pitt, he was a man nobody could act with; that he neither thought Lord Temple a good man, nor an agreeable man, and that as to such creatures as Tom Walpole and such as him, it was beneath him to act with them. Mr. Bindley said at the same time that he had no message to bring, but only that Mr. Townshend wished that Lord Halifax and Mr. Grenville should be acquainted with his sentiments concerning them.

Wednesday, Jan. 11th. Lord Halifax told Mr. Grenville the same that he had heard from the King in re-relation to Mr. Townshend, and in the evening Mr. Jenkinson told Mr. Grenville that Mr. Bindley had been with him, with an express message from Mr. Charles Townshend to him, containing the expressions of regard and esteem already mentioned for him and Lord Halifax, saying that he did not like the rest of the Administration, but these were the people he should like to act with; he enlarged upon his approbation of Mr. Grenville, and expressed great regret for the words of heat that had passed between them in the House of Commons just before the holidays, when Mr. Townshend had attacked Mr. Grenville with warmth, and declared that he should, in all probability, be seldom or ever of the same opinion with that gentleman, to which Mr. Grenville had replied, that no threats could intimidate him, that he neither courted that gentleman's assistance, nor feared his talents, &c. To this message of Mr. Bindley's Mr. Grenville only returned, that he was obliged to Mr. Townshend for his good opinion, and should always be glad to see his talents employed in support of the King's measures.

Mr. Townshend had been much offended at the King's not speaking to him when he carried the Duke of Buccleuch to Court, and tried to find out whether or no the King would speak to him when he went again. Mr. Grenville said, as to that he could say nothing, but that in general, in the violence of these times, it was natural as well as advisable for the King to give his countenance to such as stood in support of his Government, and to look cold upon those who endeavoured to disturb it.

Saturday, January 14*th.* Mr. Grenville went to Somerset House to pay his compts. to the Hereditary Prince, who came to town the night before.

Sunday, 15*th.* Mr. Grenville dined with the Hereditary Prince.

Monday, 16*th.* Mr. Grenville went to the marriage, and after the ceremony, had a long conversation with the Duke of Bedford upon the following subject.

His Grace told him that Lady Bute had sent to Lord Gower to desire to speak to him; that she had told him that Lord Bute had heard that the Duke of Bedford had said, that whenever Lord Bute should think of returning to London, that would be to him a signal for resigning his office; that Lord Bute thought this proscription too hard, and did not know what he had done to the Duke of Bedford, to deserve this behaviour from him; that he was tired of staying in the country, and besides, had daughters to marry, and other business, which made it necessary for him to come to town. This Lord Gower was to deliver as a message to the Duke of Bedford, who answered that he never had made a declaration that he should take Lord Bute's return to London for the signal of his own resignation; that it was very true that he thought his return might be very prejudicial to the King's affairs, as it would be difficult for people to see his Lordship here, without thinking he took a lead in business, notwithstanding the strong declarations he had made of his resolution against ever intermeddling any more; that to this opinion he, the Duke of Bedford, must adhere. He asked Mr. Grenville what he thought of it? Mr. Grenville commended the temper of the Duke's answer, and said that he perfectly agreed with him in it.

Thursday, 19th. The House of Commons sat 'till four o'clock in the morning upon the expulsion of Mr. Wilkes, and other questions relating to his absence, &c. There were four divisions, in each of which the Court gained in their numbers, and the whole was very triumphant on that side of the question. Mr. Grenville wrote the King word what had passed after he came home, and received a note from him, expressing his satisfaction, which he enforced when he saw him.

Friday, 20th. The Opposition made a motion concerning the breach of privilege of Mr. Wilkes. Mr. Grenville desired, by all means, that it should come on immediately, and proposed the Monday following; but they desired it might be postponed 'till Thursday, to which Mr. Grenville consented.

Mr. Charles Townshend took occasion, in this day's debate, to make a personal attack on Mr. Grenville, insinuating that some transactions during the summer made it particularly necessary to be watchful upon every breach of privilege, and the liberty of the subject. Mr. Grenville, in his reply, took notice of these words, and said he had but one answer to give, which was to desire the instances might be named which deserved such an insinuation; and that, for his own part, whenever he was attacked, he desired no better than to have an opportunity given him to lay open his conduct for his justification, and that he therefore repeated again that he desired the Right Honourable Gentleman would name them.

Mr. Townshend sat silent, and that very evening repented of what he had done; went home in low spirits; said he had spoke very ill, and had given some offence in his speech to Mr. Grenville, for which he was very sorry.

The Duke of Bedford came to Mr. Grenville in the evening. In the course of conversation he told Mr. Grenville that the man in all England who hated him the most was Lord Holland, because he was unable to fill the station he held himself, and could not bear to see Mr. Grenville in it. The Duke of Bedford complained of want of participation in the distribution of offices, instancing the nomination of Lord Cathcart and Lord Marchmont, the latter to succeed the late Duke of Athol, and the former to succeed Lord Marchmont, and likewise in the destination of Dr. Markham to the Deanery of Christ Church, in case Dr. Gregory should be made a bishop by the Bishop of Rochester's resignation.

Mr. Grenville showed his Grace how ill founded such a complaint was against him, that the Scotch promotions were made upon a former destination long before his

Grace came into the office of President, and that in regard to Dr. Markham, he had been recommended to Mr. Grenville by his Grace; that he had sent Dr. Markham to his Grace for his approbation of that promotion in case it could take place, but that if he wished it for any other person, Mr. Grenville was willing to alter it at his Grace's desire. Mr. Grenville always avoided coming to the point of partition of patronage, and upon the whole the Duke seemed to go away in good humour and satisfied.

Sunday, 22nd. Mr. Grenville went to the Drawing Room, where the Hereditary Princess spoke to him about her pension, and desired him to come to her at Leicester House, at seven o'clock that evening. After the Drawing Room he went to the King, who told him the Duke of Bedford had just been in to ask for the Deanery of Christ Church for Dr. Markham, and to recommend Sir Richard Wrottesley to the Deanery of Windsor whenever that should be vacant. His Majesty consented to the promotion of Dr. Markham, but told the Duke that Windsor was promised to Dr. Barrington, at which the Duke seemed to be displeased. This had been settled by Mr. Grenville for Dr. Barrington some time ago.

At seven o'clock Mr. Grenville went to Leicester House, where the Hereditary Princess executed the papers necessary for her pension, and then entered into a great deal of cheerful talk with Mr. Grenville; spoke very affectionately and gratefully of the King, and in great praise of the Hereditary Prince, both for his military glory, his behaviour to her, and the wise conduct he had held here, entering into no party, and carrying himself with equality and civility to everybody. She said a woman ought to be proud of nothing but her husband, and she was very proud of hers. Her Highness told Mr. Grenville that, as to herself, she never meddled with politics, that she thought it did not become her; that her connection with Lady George Sackville was the mere chance of meeting her often in Kensington Gardens, and that the generosity of her own mind would not suffer her to abandon her in her misfortunes, but that she had never taken any part in favour of Lord George, always having told Lady George that she could not enter upon that topic where her grandfather had taken so strong a part; that she had asked if the Hereditary Prince would speak to Lord George. The Princess said she would endeavour to find an opportunity to ask him, which she did; and the Prince said yes.

Lord George went up to him at the Levée, which her Highness said he had better have let alone; but the Prince spoke civilly to him. She said Lady George was desirous to see her Highness alone before she left England, but she said that could not be, for she saw nobody except Lady Bute.

Her Highness told Mr. Grenville that the Duke of Cumberland and Princess Amelia had reproved her for speaking to Mr. Pitt, after the indecent behaviour in the City on the Lord Mayor's day; that since affairs were changed, she had inquired of them both how Mr. Pitt did, and had embarrassed them by the question. Notwithstanding this conversation, the Hereditary Prince went early that same morning to visit Mr. Pitt, at Hayes: he went on horseback. Lord Temple sent an express at five o'clock in the morning, to acquaint Mr. Pitt that the Hereditary Prince was coming.

Wednesday, 25th. Lord Holland came to take his

leave of Mr. Grenville, and had a great deal of talk with him. His Lordship told him he thought the Administration strongly established; that nothing could hurt it but a division amongst themselves, or a change in the King's mind; but, if that should happen, His Majesty was in fetters for life. Mr. Grenville could easily perceive, by his discourse, an averseness to the Duke of Bedford; he said he believed Lord Bute to be a perfect honest man; that he respected him as such; and that in the intercourse between them, Lord Bute had never broke his word with him.

Thursday, 26th. When Mr. Grenville went to the King, he told His Majesty that the visit to Hayes made a great noise. The King said the first he had heard of it was from the Duke of Bedford, and asked Mr. Grenville if he thought it was true; he told His Majesty he had great reason to believe it, and that the Hereditary Prince had likewise been to drink tea with the Duke and Duchess of Newcastle, at all which the King seemed much displeased.

Saturday, 28th. Mr. Jenkinson asked Mr. Grenville how matters stood between the Duke of Bedford and Lord Bute. Mr. Grenville said he understood they had had a sort of explanation through Lady Bute. Mr. Jenkinson asked if he thought the Duke would resign in case his Lordship returned; that as to Lord Bute himself, he knew his Lordship wished to live upon civil terms with the Duke of Bedford, but he did not know how the Duke stood affected towards him.

Mr. Grenville said he could say nothing to that. Mr. Jenkinson then asked what Mr. Grenville should think of his return, to which Mr. Grenville answered, that he had not been the means of Lord Bute's retreat, nor could he be so of the keeping him in exile, but that his opinion was that his return might, in many ways, be prejudicial at this time to the King's affairs, and that he had always understood that his Lordship meant to absent himself during the sessions of Parliament. Mr. Jenkinson said he thought it likely that Lord Bute might possibly return privately for a day or two, and then go back to the country.

A scheme was proposed, chiefly by Lord Sandwich (at this time), for the two Secretaries of State, the Duke of Bedford, and Mr. Grenville, to dine together once a week to talk upon business; to this Mr. Grenville agreed, as often as the business of the House of Commons would allow of his coming to it. Lord Sandwich named it to the King, who when he saw Mr. Grenville asked him about it, and advised him to treat of nothing there but public business only, and not to come upon the arrangements for offices, in which he would be overpowered by the other three. Mr. Grenville assured his Majesty that it was his intention to do so, knowing that the Duke of Bedford and Lord Sandwich would always join upon that head against him. The King said he thought he would do well to join the Chancellor into this weekly meeting.

Monday, January 30th. The King had a great deal of confidential easy talk with Mr. Grenville; His Majesty told him Lord Mansfield had been with him, that he was extremely well pleased and satisfied with the language he had held to him: that he had spoke a good deal to him upon his Ministers, telling His Majesty that he thought them now strongly and firmly established: that he looked upon it as the hand of Providence which had directed His Majesty to the wisest choice he could have made, to deliver him from the greatest of all dangers in the treaty begun with Mr. Pitt: that he must own, from the timidity of his own nature, he had doubted of the permanency of the Administration, but that he no longer did so now. The King repeated all this with great eagerness and seeming satisfaction. Mr. Grenville saw the Duke of Bedford, who told him that a person on whom he could rely had informed him that he knew for a certainty that the Dukes of Grafton and Devonshire had said that it was in their power to come into office in a week's time whenever they pleased, with Lord Bute in their hands.

Thursday, February 9th. The King told Mr. Grenville that he was informed that the Duke of Cumberland had had an apoplexy, and that he believed him to be very ill; but that he did not send to inquire after him, because, after the Duke's behaviour to him, nobody could suppose he could inquire out of regard to him.

Sunday, February 12th. Mr. Jenkinson told Mr. Grenville that Mr. Beckford told him that he intended to speak in the House of Commons upon the complaint made in behalf of Mr. Wilkes of a breach of privilege, and that he should take occasion to express his regard to Lord Bute. Mem.—Mr. Jenkinson did not tell Mr. Grenville that Lord Bute is to come to town next Thursday, though Lady Bute says it publicly.

Tuesday, February 14th. The House of Commons sat upon the legality of the warrants for apprehending Mr. Wilkes. The House continued sitting 'till past seven o'clock the next morning. The first question, viz., for adjourning the House and the farther matter of complaint, was put at two o'clock in the morning, and carried by the friends of Government, in the negative, by ten. The second question, for discharging the complaint against Mr. Wood, Mr. Webb, and the three messengers, for a breach of privilege, agreed. Question put for adjourning carried again in the negative, but by twenty-four only.

The King wrote to Mr. Grenville on Tuesday morning, to desire an account of the debate in writing, as soon as he came home, which Mr. Grenville accordingly wrote on Tuesday morning. The King's answer expressed great warmth and resentment at the defection among those who professed themselves his friends, and desired to see Mr. Grenville early.

When Mr. Grenville went, he found His Majesty angry, but not alarmed, saying the Opposition might, for what he knew, carry the question upon the warrants on Friday, when it comes on again, but that would make no change in him in regard to this present Administration, which he meant to support to the utmost; he had no job to ask of his people, nor nothing to conceal, and therefore was not afraid, and that firmness and steadiness was what alone could get the better of the state of anarchy which seemed to threaten Government, and that it must be shown.

His Majesty told Mr. Grenville that he had seen the Chancellor, who seemed much alarmed and sunk, and told His Majesty that Mr. Grenville was betrayed, and had not fair play. Lord Sandwich, His Majesty said, seemed to make more light of it, and said it would go much better on Friday. The King held a very firm and confidential language to Mr. Grenville. Lord Denbigh said that Lady Bute had told him on Tuesday that no time was fixed for Lord Bute's return.

Friday, February 17*th.* The House of Commons

sat 'till seven o'clock the next morning. The question of adjournment was carried by the friends of Government by fourteen votes.

When Mr. Grenville went to the King on Saturday he found him not in the least alarmed, though the Minority were 220; he still held the same firm language, displeased at those in his service who went against the question, but very temperate and not inclined to any precipitate measure, telling Mr. Grenville he would follow his advice in such steps as he, Mr. Grenville, should think necessary to be taken.

Mr. Grenville told his Majesty he thought it would be unwise to dismiss any person upon a question seemingly so popular; the King agreed with him, but told him he would find the Duke of Bedford (whom His Majesty had already seen) eager for making examples.

Sunday, 19th. The Duke of Bedford told Mr. Grenville that he had found the King perfectly steady, and in no sort of alarm; he had spoke with the same firmness to his Grace as to Mr. Grenville, and upon the Duke telling His Majesty how much the Opposition was elated, and how sure they thought themselves of a change in the Ministry, the King told him if that was their hope they would find themselves deceived.

Friday, Feb. 24th. The King told Mr. Grenville that he heard he had outdone himself in the House of Commons on the Tuesday preceding, that His Majesty was sorry he had so empty a House to speak to. He added many other gracious expressions of approbation.

Sunday, Feb. 26th. Mr. Grenville took occasion to ask the King if he would be graciously pleased to give him his picture and the Queen's as a testimonial to his family of the honour he had of being in his service.

His Majesty told him he would do it with the utmost pleasure; that he was well entitled to a mark of his favour, having served him so entirely to his satisfaction, and with so much distinction to himself, and added, I know the difference between you and the rest of my servants; they have many purposes to serve, you have none but my service, and that of the public.

Tuesday, Feb. 28th. Mr. Jenkinson told Mr. Grenville that Lady Bute had told him that her Lord intended to come to town immediately. Mr. Jenkinson seemed very desirous of knowing how Mr. Grenville intended to behave to him, and said that Sir Henry Erskine seemed earnestly to wish that the intercourse between Lord Bute and Mr. Grenville should be renewed. Mr. Grenville said it had been rather broke off by Lord Bute than by himself, that he should always desire to live civilly with his Lordship, but that in regard to an interview, the past transactions had better never be touched upon, and Lord Bute had declared he never would intermeddle with the future. Mr. Jenkinson seemed to press the advantages to be derived from Lord Bute and his friends; Mr. Grenville said he did justice to the assistance the latter had given him in Parliament, but as to the rest confined himself to general terms.

Tuesday, 6th of March. When Mr. Grenville went to the King he found him very eager against the Opposition, concerning the question they had endeavoured to bring on in the House of Commons, against the Post Office; he said they were endeavouring to take away every power that was necessary towards carrying on the Government, and to tie his hands in such a manner as must prevent his being able to do his duty; His Majesty used this comparison, and said, it is, Mr. Grenville, just as if, when I appointed you First Commissioner of the Treasury (who I wish to be there more than any man living), I should at the same time hinder everything you found necessary in the execution of the office. His Majesty talked a good deal of Lord Sandwich, with whom he always seems displeased, spoke of his eagerness in the pursuit of the Stewardship of the University of Cambridge, and the likelihood there was of his endeavouring to debar Lord Halifax of the Chancellorship when it should be vacant. He told Mr. Grenville that in regard to the recall of Mons. Michell, the King of Prussia refused it, and Lord Sandwich was for letting it rest there, but that he could never consent to that, and hoped Mr. Grenville was of the same opinion, which he assured His Majesty he was.

The King read a letter to Mr. Grenville, which he had received from Lord Scarsdale, expressing disgust at Lord Granby's appointment to the Lieutenancy of Derbyshire, and seeming to insinuate that he had been deceived by hopes from some of the Ministers. It appears that Lord Sandwich had given him some hopes, and then thrown the failure upon Mr. Grenville.

Wednesday, March 7th. Mr. Jenkinson told Mr. Grenville, that Mr. Beckford went down some days before to Mr. Marshe Dickenson's[1], and from thence sent over to Luton to desire leave to wait upon Lord Bute, who excused himself from seeing him, and sent word he was not well. It is supposed that he was sent there by Mr. Pitt, charged with some negotiation from the Opposition.

[1] M.P. for Brackley, and Chairman of the Committee of Ways and Means. He was also an Alderman of London.

Mr. Beckford is joked with by his friends upon this idea, which he neither confirms nor refutes; but says, he was at liberty to go to see Lord Bute either of his own accord, or if desired by his friends.

Saturday, the 10*th of March.* Lord Mansfield came to Mr. Grenville this morning, and related a conversation he had had with the King, in which His Majesty had expressed himself with great approbation of Mr. Grenville; and talking of Mr. Beckford's journey into Bedfordshire, the King said he did not believe that any transaction had passed between the Opposition and Lord Bute, but that if any had, His Majesty gave him his honour that he knew nothing of it.

When Mr. Grenville went to the King, he found him highly pleased with what had passed the day before in the House of Commons concerning the supplies of the year; His Majesty kept him a great while in conversation, and in the course of talking of what was thought to be the plans of the Opposition, the King told Mr. Grenville that he heard that Mr. Pitt had promised Mr. Charles Yorke that he should be Chancellor over Lord Chief Justice Pratt's head, if they had come to cut and carve for themselves, which (said His Majesty) *now* is impossible, but it would have been likely enough for the Lord Chief Justice to have consented to it.

Sunday, 11*th.* The King told Mr. Grenville that he heard from everybody that no man had ever spoke so well as he had done, the Friday, in the House of Commons; that it gave him great pleasure to see his Administration so ably conducted by the man, of all others, in whose hands he wished to see it.

Mr. Jenkinson again renewed the conversation relative to Lord Bute's return, saying he would expect a degree of consideration, and his friends thought he ought to have it; Mr. Grenville said, he did not know what Lord Bute wished; was it to come into office again? he understood that his engagements had been solemnly to the contrary.

Mr. Jenkinson said, he did not believe he meant it. Mr. Grenville left the discourse again upon the general footing he had done the former day.

Wednesday, 14th. The King told Mr. Grenville that Mr. Worsley[1] had told him that Lord Temple was much cast down, and had said to him that he heartily wished the negotiation of the 29th of August had succeeded. Mr. Worsley told Lord Temple he did not doubt it. The King said he heard the Opposition seemed now without hopes, and added, "how can it indeed be otherwise, for the distinguished and able manner in which you, Mr. Grenville, have acquitted yourself, must (even independent of the partiality and favour I have to you) give the greatest strength to my Government."

The King speaks daily with more and more averseness to Lord Sandwich, and appears to have a settled dislike to his character. When he names Lord Halifax he blames the hurry and precipitancy with which he does his business, but complains of nothing else.

Saturday, 17th. Mr. Grenville went to acquaint the King with the death of Lord Macclesfield, by which the reversion of the Teller's place, for George Grenville, jun.[2], took place. The King told Mr. Grenville he was

---

[1] He was Surveyor General of the Board of Works. Walpole says of him also that he was "a sort of Riding Master to the King."

[2] Afterwards Earl Temple, and Marquess of Buckingham. He died in 1813.

very glad of it; that he was happy to give him that mark of his favour, adding that he had long known his abilities, and always wished to employ them; that they were now manifest to all the world, that he was sensible how much weight was derived to his Government, by his able and prudent conduct in the management of his affairs, and that his talents and wisdom were confessed by everybody, and that he was glad to have everybody know how highly he esteemed them.

He was going into his Closet, and turned back to bid Mr. Grenville tell Mrs. Grenville that he wished her joy of the Teller's place, which he knew must give her great satisfaction, and that he hoped, as she had been ill a great while, this event would do her good.

Sunday, 18*th*. Mr. Grenville told the King that Mrs. Grenville had endeavoured to come to Court, to testify her grateful sense of His Majesty's great goodness, but that a fresh attack of her complaint had made it impossible. The King bid him tell her that he desired her to take care of herself, and not to attempt to come to Court, 'till she was quite recovered.

Monday, 19th.—Mr. Jenkinson told Mr. Grenville that he went on Saturday to Luton, that when he came there he found the House door shut, and a bell fixed to it, which he rung; the servants let him in and carried him into the Dining-room. Lord Bute was some time before he came to him; when he did come he found him in the lowest dejection of mind, scarce speaking a word, saying two or three civil words about Mr. Grenville, and then addressing himself chiefly to Lady Bute and Mr. Hume. He at last told Mr. Jenkinson that he thought himself very ill used; he complained of the

Duke of Bedford and Lord Sandwich, and said he would never forgive the former. As soon as dinner was over he went upstairs, and continued in this gloomy mood the next morning. Mr. Jenkinson told Mr. Grenville he thought Lord Bute meant to come to town in a few days.

On Monday evening Lady Blandford met Lady Bute at the Duchess of Montrose's; she asked how Lord Bute did, to which her Ladyship answered he was very well, and was come to town with her that day.

When Mr. Grenville went to the King he found His Majesty easy and cheerful, and full of the same gracious expressions to him which he had so often used to him. His Majesty told him that he heard Lord Sandwich was to decline the contest at Cambridge, and that Lord Halifax was to stand, at which he seemed very glad.

Tuesday, 20th. Mr. Grenville dined with the three other Ministers at Lord Halifax's. The Duke of Bedford mentioned Lord Bute's return with temper, but said he heard from undoubted authority that he had been with the King that morning from seven till eleven.

The Ministers all agreed to go to see him the next day, and if they found him, to talk on general topics only, and no business; and in regard to recommendations, if he wished to make any in their several departments, to pay the same attention to that as they would in the same case to any other Peer.

Wednesday, 21st. Mr. Grenville went to visit Lord Bute; the porter said his Lordship was not at home.

Mr. Grenville saw Mr. Jenkinson afterwards in the House of Commons, who showed him a letter from Lord Bute, expressing the greatest anger imaginable at his servants, who had had the absurdity and stupidity to deny him to Mr. Grenville (whom he above all others wished to see), at the same time that Lord Sandwich and some other person was with him, and desiring Mr. Jenkinson to inquire of Mr. Grenville when he could see him, adding that he would have gone the moment he knew it, to have endeavoured to find Mr. Grenville at home, had he not taken something that obliged him to stay at home.

Mr. Grenville desired Mr. Jenkinson to tell Lord Bute that he would call upon his Lordship the next day.

Mr. Jenkinson seemed to wish that Mr. Grenville would have wrote.

Thursday, 22nd. Mr. Grenville went to Lord Bute at ten o'clock in the morning: he received him with great civility, said the King had spoken to him of Mr. Grenville with the highest praise and satisfaction; that he, Lord Bute, knew that the only safety for the King's affairs was to put the Administration into Mr. Grenville's hands; that the event had justified his opinion; that he meant himself to give every support to Mr. Grenville that was in his power, which indeed could only be by speaking to his friends, for that he was a private man, and meant to remain so.

Mr. Grenville answered him with great civility, but no overstrained professions.

Friday, 23rd. When Mr. Grenville went to the King, His Majesty talked to him with more than ordinary goodness; said he was sensible of the weight and authority that he had given to his Government, that it was always his opinion that it would be so, but that now, all the world confessed it as well as himself; that it was necessary to lodge the power of government in one man alone, and that Mr. Grenville was the person in whom he wished to see it; that when Lord Egremont was alive, it was necessary from particular circumstances to make that power more equal in the three Ministers; that he meant it should be in him; that to him he gave, and would give his confidence; that it would be necessary for Mr. Grenville to keep certain managements with the two Secretaries of State and the Duke of Bedford, but that must be at his own discretion, for that it was his desire and purpose that all recommendations and appointments should come through Mr. Grenville; that when Lord Bute had left him he told His Majesty he had now put his affairs into the hands of an affectionate and able servant, who would take him out of the difficulties he was under; that Lord Bute had now told him he had heard with joy and satisfaction how ably Mr. Grenville had gone through this difficult session, and had spoke of him in the most cordial manner imaginable.

The King enlarged this discourse with many gracious expressions, and told Mr. Grenville he looked upon the Opposition as nothing; that the firmness Mr. Grenville had shown—when they run him so near as 14, when instead of coming to treat with them, he had stood firm to his purpose—had quite overthrown them. The King spoke at different moments of his other Ministers, and said the Duke of Bedford had told him Lord Sandwich had tried the Stewardship at Cambridge with a view to being Chancellor. His Majesty threw out a hint of this to Lord Halifax, who said Lord Sandwich, he believed, would not trust the Duke of Bedford, with the particulars of the situation between them two.

Mr. Charles Townshend conveyed expressions of civility to Mr. Grenville within these few days, saying opposition was at an end; that he could act with Mr. Grenville in any situation, and complimented him two days following in his speeches in the House of Commons.

Saturday, 24th. Lord Bute came to return Mr. Grenville's visit; he was very good humoured, but formal: nothing remarkable passed in the conversation.

Wednesday, March 28th. When Mr. Grenville went to the King he found him very uneasy, and expressing great eagerness upon the publication of Monsr. D'Eon's book; he asked if the House of Lords would not take notice of it; said that he had mentioned it to Lord Halifax, but that he found him averse to stirring in it; that the same would have happened in Mr. Wilkes's affair, had that been in the House of Lords; that it was to Mr. Grenville's firmness and spirit that he owed all that had been done on that head, and that he could never say enough upon the manly conduct he had held through the sessions of Parliament, which had brought him through all his difficulties. The Queen held the same language to Lady Egremont.

The Duke of Bedford was very angry at the Red Ribbon being given to Lord Clive in preference to Col. Draper, for whom he claimed a prior promise. He wrote an angry letter to Mr. Grenville, who was then at Lord Botetourt's, upon this subject; Mr. Grenville answered it mildly but firmly, pleading the necessity and propriety of Lord Clive's having this mark of distinction, considering the important service he was going upon. Mr. Grenville found the Duke much softened at his return to London.

Mr. Grenville mentioned to the King how desirable it would be, after having given the Garter to Lord Halifax, to distinguish the Chancellor with a mark of His Majesty's favour by making him an Earl. He pressed it strongly before he went to Bath, but did not make the impression he wished upon His Majesty; but upon resuming it again at his return to London the King consented to do it, and ordered Mr. Grenville to go and acquaint him with it. The Chancellor was highly pleased with this mark of the King's favour, and with the friendship Mr. Grenville had shown to him upon this occasion.

Friday, June 8th, 1764. The King spoke with great kindness to Mr. Grenville, told him that the rest of the Ministers acted against him; that he would have incontestable evidence of this upon the subject of a complaint M. de Guerchy made in relation to some contraband goods; that he would find that he, Mr. Grenville, was disavowed both by Lord Halifax and the Duke of Bedford. Mr. Grenville was a good deal surprised, and told His Majesty that his reliance was upon the gracious promise made to him by His Majesty that he would support him, which he hoped, as long as he did his duty, he would continue to do. The King assured him he would, and commended his firmness in the transaction with M. de Guerchy.

Mr. Grenville had afterwards a warm discourse on the

subject, both with Lord Halifax and Lord Sandwich, upon the unfairness of such a proceeding.

Mr. Grenville again renewed his instant exhortation, which he had often before made to Lord Halifax, to press Lord Hertford to insist upon the money being paid by the Court of France upon account of the prisoners.

Lord Halifax says he has done it, but is neither so warm nor so pressing in that affair as Mr. Grenville wishes.

Tuesday, June 12th. Mr. Grenville dined with Lord Halifax at Lord Sandwich's, and resumed the conversation relating to M. de Guerchy's complaint, and his representation of the disavowal of Mr. Grenville by the other Ministers. Lord Halifax denied the fact having the least foundation of truth, and put it all upon the constant misrepresentation made on all subjects by M. de Guerchy.

Thursday, June 21st, 1764. Mr. and Mrs. Grenville went to dine at Northumberland House, where the French Ambassador and Ambassadress were expected. They came very late, and M. de Guerchy informed Lord Halifax that a constable had come with a warrant to take up Chazal, his Ecuyer, in the court of his house; that he looked upon this as an insult, and contrary to the law of nations; that his servants had taken the warrant from him, and had locked the man up in his cellar. Lord Halifax told him that what he had done was against the law, that he could not imprison a man in his house for executing a warrant, nor was his house an asylum to his servants for a breach of the peace. In this Lord Halifax was supported by the other Ministers then present, and with some difficulty they prevailed with him to set the man at liberty. M. de Guerchy was extremely angry, and the Ministers very uneasy at the wrong-headed step he had taken.

Tuesday, June 26th. Mr. Grenville obtained leave from the King to go for ten days to Wotton. His Majesty granted it with great expressions of kindness to Mr. Grenville, and desiring him to take every opportunity he could of doing what was so necessary to his health.

Mr. Grenville set out the next day, and the newspapers were immediately full of reports of an intended change. Mr. Pitt came to the Levée during Mr. Grenville's absence: this strengthened the report, though all who were present said the King received him with great coldness.

Many people affirmed there had been a meeting and conference between Mr. Pitt and Lord Bute, but no symptoms of this appeared at Mr. Grenville's return; the King received him with great seeming satisfaction, talked with great confidence to him, but continued the same language which he had held to him often for some time past, of the disinclination Mr. Grenville's colleagues in the Ministry seemed to have towards him, and in particular Lord Halifax.

Several people told Mr. Grenville that Mr. Pitt's language had become extremely temperate; that he disclaimed the Opposition, and talked as if he wished to act in office with the Government, and that his language in regard to Mr. Grenville was, that he was necessary to any Administration, and had conducted the King's business wisely through the last session of Parliament.

Thursday, July 12th. Mr. Stanley having expressed

his desire of succeeding Lord Holmes in the government of the Isle of Wight, came to Mr. Grenville to discourse upon the subject. Mr. Grenville suggested that if he still thought of going forwards in the line of business, his present wishes should be no hindrance to him, provided it was understood that he was to relinquish this government, whenever the King should think proper to employ him elsewhere. Mr. Stanley received this with great thankfulness and professions to Mr. Grenville, and which he again renewed by letter.

The King continues more than usually cheerful; seems pleased with the conduct and success of his affairs; and gives not the least reason to suppose that there could be any foundation for the report of an intended change of Ministry; but, on the contrary, speaks with great slight and disregard of the most considerable people of the Opposition.

Monday, July 16*th.* Mr. Grenville had a conversation with M. de Guerchy, which lasted 'till one o'clock in the morning, concerning the satisfying the debt claimed by England, for the prisoners taken in the late war, and before the commencement of it. M. de Guerchy endeavoured both to lower the sum and to postpone the payment, requiring the term of fifteen years for the performance of it. Mr. Grenville strongly represented against the unreasonableness of this proposition, stating the violation of the Treaty both in this and the two other articles of the payment of the Canada bills, and the demolition of Dunkirk, all expressly stipulated, and not one as yet performed; and would by no means listen to the very long term of fifteen years proposed by the Ambassador for the payment of the debt; but, on the contrary, insisted upon one year or two as the longest term that could be allowed by England. After the conference was over, Mr. Grenville, understanding that the Ambassador was going to Woburn, wrote immediately to Lord Sandwich to give him an account of what had passed, and to desire his Lordship would take care to apprise the Duke of Bedford of it, that his Grace might be prepared before he saw the Ambassador to resist this proposal of the fifteen years, as Mr. Grenville had done.

Tuesday, July 17*th.* Mr. Grenville gave the King an account of what had passed the night before, which His Majesty entirely approved of.

Wednesday, July 18*th.* Mr. Grenville and Lord Halifax dined with Lord Sandwich. In the evening M. de Guerchy came to them by appointment, and had a very rough remonstrance made to him by them all three upon the subject of the payment of the money. He still continued the same language, and even went so far as to say that France had not the money to satisfy the demand.

Mr. Grenville laughed at that, and advised him not to urge the Court of England too far, nor to push it to extremities, for his Court would find us not inclined to bear beyond what was reasonable.

M. de Guerchy pleaded the Duke of Bedford's having given him hopes that a longer term, as far, perhaps, as five years, might be complied with, but that he gave that as his own thought only, not knowing whether the King himself or the rest of his servants would be of the same mind. The two Secretaries and Mr. Grenville absolutely disclaimed any such concession. It was true that the Duke of Bedford had not kept up his language high enough in talking with M. de Guerchy, which Mr. Grenville knew from a letter which Lord Sandwich had from the Duke of Bedford.

The disputes with France concerning the money due upon account of the prisoners and the Canada bills gave Mr. Grenville great uneasiness, seeing that Government in no disposition to fulfil the conditions on which the Peace was made, though, at the same time, he saw no likelihood of their being willing to begin another war.

Spain, on the other hand, returned an unsatisfactory answer to the complaint made of their having driven away the English from the cutting of logwood at the Bay of Honduras.

Tuesday, July 24th. Mr. Grenville had a long conversation with the King upon these points, in which he advised His Majesty to be firm and steady in his conduct, and temperate in his language, through his Ministers, to those of France and Spain, as the best means of maintaining the Peace. The King agreed perfectly with Mr. Grenville in this opinion. Mr. Grenville at the same time laid before His Majesty the state of his Civil List, with his thoughts upon the best methods to proportion the expenditure to the receipt. The King seemed disinclined to lessen any part of what he appropriated to his own use. Mr. Grenville left the papers with him for his farther consideration.

He told His Majesty of his intention to adjourn the Treasury for five weeks from the 25th. His Majesty approved of it, but told him he hoped he himself did not intend to make so long an absence without returning to London. Mr. Grenville told His Majesty he proposed never to be absent above a fortnight at a time, and then to return for a few days, at which the King seemed highly satisfied, saying it was what he himself wished.

Wednesday, July 25th. Mr. Grenville went in the evening to the Duke of Bedford, with whom he had a long conversatiou. They differed in opinion concerning the time proposed for the Court of France to pay the money due, which Mr. Grenville said ought not to exceed one year, or two at the most, and the Duke of Bedford was for allowing them five, but in all other points they perfectly agreed, and the interview passed with great temper and good humour, but they parted, each adhering to his own opinion.

Thursday, July 26th. Mr. Grenville went to the Drawing Room before he went to the King. In passing through the rooms he met the Duke of Richmond, and had some talk with him, at the end of which Mr. Grenville told the Duke that he supposed his Grace knew that his (the Duke of Richmond's) name had been made use of in a paper which he had lately seen. The Duke said he knew it had, but that Mr. Walpole had mistaken him, and as he understood had rectified the mistake: Mr. Grenville said he had, but that he (Mr. Grenville) begged leave to ask his Grace whether, upon his entering the room in Downing Street, where his Grace and Mr. Conway were, he did not immediately inform them that Mr. Walpole had greatly mistaken him in saying that he had any message to send to General Conway. The Duke of Richmond said he remembered that Mr. Grenville had said so. He then asked his Grace whether he did not likewise remember that he had asked them whether or no he was to understand the conversation they were then going to have, as passing between three people in private only, or as to be repeated to the world: they all agreed, as in private only, which his Grace likewise said he remembered. Mr. Grenville then asked him if he did not remember that when they were going to part, Mr. Conway desired to know what part of the conversation might be related to such of his friends as might be entitled to know something of it, and that it was then agreed, that where it was necessary to make any report of what had passed, that nothing was to be related except General Conway's declaration that he had taken no systematical engagements with the Opposition, but did not mean to draw a line between himself, the Duke of Grafton, and the Duke of Devonshire, with whom he lived in friendship.

The Duke of Richmond said he did remember it, and then began to talk to Mr. Grenville upon the general idea of separating the military officers from the civil, and disapproving the removing an officer from a military employment for his conduct in Parliament.

Mr. Grenville said, the removing a man either from civil or military for his parliamentary conduct, was a language unfit to be held, but he made no distinction between the one and the other where it was a uniform opposition, in and out of Parliament, to the King's Government.

The Duke said, Mr. Conway had said, that it was a silly dispute of words only, and his Grace took up Mr. Grenville's words of an opposition out of Parliament, which Mr. Grenville still said could very well be.

The Duke of Richmond was very civil, and upon Mr. Grenville's blaming Mr. Walpole's conduct, the Duke said, he did not mean to say whether that was right or wrong.

Mr. Grenville desired the conversation his Grace and

he had then held might be to themselves alone, to which he assented.

When Mr. Grenville went in to the King, His Majesty was extremely gracious, and spoke with great confidence to him, desiring him to come to him the next day before twelve o'clock, that he might hear from him the first account of the very important meeting that was to be held at Lord Halifax's that night, between the two Secretaries of State, the Chancellor, the Duke of Bedford, and Mr. Grenville, that he might know the particulars in case their accounts should differ.

The meeting passed in good humour, though with difference of opinion in regard to the time required by the Court of France for the payment of the money, which Mr. Grenville would by no means suffer to exceed one year, or two at the most. The Duke of Bedford was for allowing them five years, agreeable to what he had dropped to Monsr. de Guerchy. To this opinion he adhered, urging very strongly that they would bring a fresh war upon themselves by insisting upon a shorter time, to which Mr. Grenville replied, with some warmth, that it was his opinion never to suffer France, after having been conquered, to speak to England in the terms of conquerors, and that he was persuaded that the way to avoid mischief was to hold a firm language to her; that he did not mean to drive her to extremities, nor to propose what was unfitting for her to grant, but that England could never be justified in yielding to her in one demand after another; that the way to make her fulfil the conditions of the Peace was to keep her to them. The Duke of Bedford answered with great temper and good humour, that he was as unwilling as any man to make unfit concessions to France, as Mr.

Grenville knew by the conversation he had had with him the preceding night, but in this point he must differ from him. It was agreed that a private letter should be writ to Lord Hertford directing him to require the payment in the space of one year, and to agree to two as the ultimate time that would be allowed. In regard to Spain they were all of one mind.

His Majesty, in his first conversation with Mr. Grenville, directed him to admit of no longer a term than two years at the utmost, but that a twelvemonth must be first proposed; but when he talked with the two Secretaries upon it, His Majesty allowed as far as three.

The Duke of York made application to the King, through Mr. Grenville, for some money to assist him in defraying his expenses in Italy. The King ordered four thousand pounds to be sent to him, and the Duke of York writ to Mr. Grenville to make his dutiful acknowledgements to the King, which Mr. Grenville did.

His Majesty then asked Mr. Grenville which way the Duke proposed coming home? He told His Majesty that he did not absolutely know, but that since he asked him, it was his duty to tell him that he had reason to believe that he meant to go to Marseilles, and so all through France. The King started at this, expressed surprise and displeasure, and said sure he could not think of it. Mr. Grenville said that he feared that he did.

During the time Mr. Grenville stayed at Wotton he had many proofs of the two Secretaries of State, but particularly Lord Halifax, holding a language to the foreign Ministers much less firm than had been agreed upon between their Lordships and Mr. Grenville, and endeavouring to cast the odium of any strong measure upon him; Mr. Grenville took notice of this in a letter to Lord Halifax, who denied the fact.

Mr. Grenville went to London *August* 13*th*, (1764). The King received him with great good humour and confidence, talked much to him upon the two Secretaries of State, greatly blaming their conduct towards Mr. Grenville, and concurring himself in sentiments with Mr. Grenville upon his foreign business. Mr. Grenville finding His Majesty in these gracious dispositions, took an opportunity to apprize His Majesty that there was a grant of a Light House in the disposal of the Treasury, which was to expire in four years, held now by Lord Leicester's executors. He humbly asked of His Majesty to bestow this upon him as a provision for his younger children, who, from various circumstances relating to the unhappy state of his own family, might be left in difficulties.

The King was graciously pleased to grant it, and did it with expressions of great kindness to Mr. Grenville.

Mr. Grenville had a warm remonstrance with Lord Halifax and Lord Sandwich; they both denied the charge, but Lord Halifax's conduct and behaviour to him in general was very unsatisfactory.

There was a Council at Lord Halifax's, *Friday*, 17*th*, upon the affair at Turk's Island, &c.

Saturday, 18*th*. Mr. Grenville returned to Wotton, and brought my Lord Chancellor down with him, who professes the warmest attachment to Mr. Grenville. He went away the Monday following.

Wednesday, 22*nd*. The Primate of Ireland came to Wotton; in part of his conversation he seemed to prepare Mr. Grenville for some additional pensions upon the Irish list. Mr. Grenville told him he was very sorry to hear it; that he thought Lord Northumberland had determined to add none, but that if that resolution was broke through in Ireland, he could no longer resist, as he had hitherto done, in England.

Mr. Grenville returned to London, *Monday, September 3rd*, 1764. He found the King more and more gracious to him, speaking to him with great confidence upon all his business, and ever complaining of Lord Halifax and Lord Sandwich. He seemed much surprised to hear they had not been at Wotton; said they did wrong in not going; that he had asked Lord Halifax if he did not mean to go, to which his Lordship had replied he would take another opportunity.

The King told Mr. Grenville that the Duke of Bedford had wrote to him to ask for a commission in the army. He ordered Mr. Grenville to write his answer, meaning to show by that, that he ought to have applied through Mr. Grenville. His Majesty seemed to think his Grace had absented himself very much this summer, and had not attended the Cabinet Councils. Mr. Grenville touched upon that subject in his letter to the Duke, who answered temperately and civilly as to the commission, which was engaged, and, in regard to his absence, pleaded his health in some instances, and his having received no summons to the last Cabinet Council; he said his health had been so bad that he must be under a necessity of asking His Majesty's leave to go to Bath this autumn.

The Duke of Bedford came to town *September, 21st.;* was in perfect good humour with Mr. Grenville, and assisted at a Council the same evening.

The Chancellor likewise did the same; he dined with Mr. Grenville on that day and the following, and went to the Council the 21st, at Lord Halifax's, with Mr. Grenville.

The King's servants who met there were unanimous in their opinions, though neither Lord Sandwich nor Lord Halifax took the part of delivering their sentiments, but rather receiving them from the other Lords present, particularly Lord Halifax, who merely held the pen to write down the minute, calling incessantly upon Mr. Grenville to dictate.

Saturday, 22nd. The King sent Mr. Grenville a note early in the morning, desiring him to come to him before twelve, that he might learn from him what had passed the preceding night, before he saw any of the others. When Mr. Grenville waited on him, His Majesty received him with the greatest good humour, and talked with the greatest openness to him. He constantly complains of the two Secretaries of State, particularly Lord Halifax, whose eagerness and precipitation on the one hand, and inattention to his business on the other, highly displeases him. Lord Halifax is discontented with Lord Hertford; says he is cold and insufficient, and wants to have him recalled: the King is by no means disposed to recall him, in which Mr. Grenville entirely concurs in opinion with His Majesty.

The King sometimes observes to Mr. Grenville, that there are not among his servants too many people of decent and orderly characters; that Lord Hertford is respectable in that light, and therefore not lightly to be cast aside.

Mr. Grenville has great difficulty in combating Lord Halifax's eagerness upon this subject, as well as many others.

The Chancellor is, upon all occasions, friendly in his attachment to Mr. Grenville, and blames Lord Halifax.

Sunday, September 23rd. Mr. Grenville went to the Grange with the Chancellor, where he stayed 'till Tuesday evening.

Mr. Grenville received a letter, rather in an angry tone, from Lord Halifax, in a few hours after his arrival at the Grange, in answer to one sent to his Lordship the morning Mr. Grenville set out.

Wednesday, September 26th. When Mr. Grenville went to the King, His Majesty told him that both the Chancellor and the Duke of Bedford had complained to him of the deadness of Lord Halifax at Council. Mr. Grenville agreed that it was wrong, and said it was the part of the Secretary of State to open the subject on which the Council met; to deliver his own opinion, and then ask that of other Lords. His Majesty expresses great approbation of Mr. Grenville's conduct, talks to him with great confidence, and increases in good humour to him daily.

Thursday, September 27th. The Duke of Bedford, Lord Sandwich, and Lord Halifax, dined with Mr. Grenville. The Duke of Bedford seems in perfect good humour, and cordiality to Mr. Grenville. Lord Sandwich went away early, the Duke of Bedford soon after. When Mr. Grenville and Lord Halifax were alone they had a little warmth upon the subject of Lord Hertford. Lord Halifax wished, if he was not recalled, that some of his friends should write to advise him to ask to come home. Mr. Grenville said no friend of Lord Hertford's would do so, and besides, who had Lord Halifax to replace him? his Lordship named nobody. Whilst this conversation was going on despatches arrived from

Spain, bringing duplicates of the orders sent to the Spanish officer at the Honduras, relating to the complaint made by our logwood-cutters, admitting our complaint, reprimanding the officers, and restoring what they had taken, but not repairing the damages done. The Spanish Ambassador here finds the Secretaries of State much less tenacious than Mr. Grenville, who, he says, would lose all he has in the world rather than suffer diminution of the honour of the King his master, or of the commerce of the kingdom.

Friday, September 28th. The King was extremely pleased with the answer from Spain; Mr. Grenville had a long conversation with His Majesty upon many subjects, and among others, mentioned a successor to the Primate in case he should fail. His Majesty heard him make an enumeration of the English Bishops, being before determined not to have an Irishman in that station, though His Majesty said he thought it likely Lord Northumberland should try to recommend a person of that country. Mr. Grenville named the Bishop of Chester as the best nomination the King could make, to which His Majesty assented, and said he would try to prepare Lord Northumberland for it.

Lord Northumberland had writ to Mr. Grenville to desire him to recommend Lord Warkworth to His Majesty, to be his Aid-de-Camp in the room of Colonel Carpenter, to whom he had given a regiment, which Mr. Grenville did accordingly.

Wednesday, October 3rd. The King told Mr. Grenville he would make Lord Warkworth his Aid-de-Camp, if Mr. Grenville wished him to do so: Mr. Grenville told His Majesty Lord Northumberland was very desirous of it; to which the King replied that he would have him tell Lord Northumberland that he had named it to the King, who seemed to have some difficulty, but that he believed it would succeed ; in order, as His Majesty said, that he might see it was done through Mr. Grenville, and be obliged to him for it.

The King said Lord Halifax was almost out of his wits with joy, at the answer from Spain.

The King was desirous that Mr. Grenville should take the transaction with M. de Guerchy, relating to the payment of the money for the French prisoners, entirely into his own hands, saying, at the same time, how sensible he was of Mr. Grenville's assiduity in this business, compared to that of any of his other servants; and this being a business relating to money, it more properly belonged to him. Mr. Grenville said he would endeavour to do it, and would have some conversation upon that head with Lord Halifax.

Mr. Jenkinson told Mr. Grenville that he knew from the best authority that Mr. Legge, about two hours before his death, had sent for Lady Stawell, and delivered to her all the papers giving an account of his transaction with Lord Bute upon the Hampshire election, directing her to publish them after his death, saying he did it to serve his Whig friends. Lady Stawell, it is said, has given them to Mr. Buller, Mr. Legge's executor.

Wednesday, October 31, 1764. Mr. Grenville received a card from Colonel West, signifying to him that the Duke of York desired to see him the next day at eleven o'clock.

Thursday, November 1*st.* Mr. Grenville waited upon the Duke of York, who opened to him the necessity he was under of desiring to have an increase of income, stating that it was impossible for him to live upon his present allowance from the King, to whom he was daily necessitated to apply for different sums to enable him to discharge such debts as he could not but incur; that though His Majesty was very good to him, yet he never spoke to him upon money matters, which ought to come from His Majesty to him, rather than the contrary; that his brothers were likewise much straitened in their expenses; that he himself had hoped hitherto, that in some shape or other, the King would have thought fit to make a provision for him, either by putting him at the head of the Admiralty, or by the Bishopric of Osnaburg, either to him or one of his brothers; but seeing both pass by them, he found himself obliged to make this application, choosing to do it by means of the King's Ministers as the proper channel, and seeming to wish for a parliamentary provision, but stating, at the same time, that two other ways remained, viz., either out of the King's Civil List, or by a grant upon Ireland.

Mr. Grenville told His Royal Highness that whatever concerned the King's Royal family was of too delicate a nature for him to presume to touch; that he took the liberty to observe to H. R. H., that a matter of this kind, especially, ought certainly to come to the King directly from himself; that he therefore advised him to speak to His Majesty of it; but if H. R. H. thought it proper, he would mention to His Majesty that he had spoken to him (Mr. Grenville) upon it, and intended to name it himself to His Majesty the next day; that H. R. H. said very rightly that there were but three methods of doing it, which were those he had taken notice of, but that he must observe to H. R. H. that the King was himself in great difficulties.

The Duke upon that took notice of the great number of pensions granted to many people by the King; to which Mr. Grenville said, whatever that might be, they had not been since he had been in the Treasury; those since his time were only the continuation of Lord Effingham's pension to his children; seven hundred pounds per annum to Mr. Weston, who had been an old servant to the Crown; four hundred pounds to Lady Susan Stewart at the recommendation of the Hereditary Princess; and that he could venture to say that the list of pensions and gratuities had never been so low for many years as it was last year.

The Duke still recurred to the great grants that had been made by the King, and many of them to people who had shown no gratitude; one indeed, he said, had been a coup de parti, and very skilfully given as a damper, which was the annuity to Mr. Pitt. Mr. Grenville said he must take the liberty to differ from His Royal Highness in thinking that a damper; on the contrary, he thought it the highest and most honourable testimony which the King could bestow, or a subject receive, at the moment of quitting the King's service, upon differing with his whole Administration. The Duke touched several times upon bringing his provision before Parliament, saying it had been done for the Duke of Cumberland. Mr. Grenville said the circumstances of that were not quite present to his recollection, but that he rather believed Parliament had only enabled the late King to give him the 15,000*l.* after his death. The Duke said his present Majesty paid less out of his Civil List to his royal family than his grandfather had done, in which Mr. Grenville said His R. H. was mistaken, that it was more.

The Duke, in many parts of the conversation, disclaimed disaffection to the present Government. Mr. Grenville said, God forbid it should be otherwise, and quoted to him a passage from Cardinal de Retz, of the Prince of Condé, who, being pressed by some of the malcontents farther than he chose to go, said "Oubliez-vous que je m'appelle Louis de Bourbon?"

The conversation ended by the Duke desiring Mr. Grenville to name his request to the King, which he accordingly did the same day.

The King paused, said he would consider of it, and desired Mr. Grenville to give him his advice in what manner he thought it could best be done, saying he believed his brothers were strait enough; that he must at the same time do something for Prince William, but desired to have Mr. Grenville's opinion as to the manner.

Mr. Grenville told His Majesty he would consider of it, but begged, before His Majesty took his resolution, that he would allow him to lay the whole state of his Civil List before him, to which the King consented.

Lord Hyde told Mr. Grenville in the morning that Mr. Walsingham had told him that the day before, at dinner, the Duke of York had bid somebody guess who he had been writing to, and said it was to Lord Bute.

Upon the death of Mr. Buller, to whom Lord Gower had, at Mr. Grenville's request, given the office of Groom Porter, Mr. Grenville proposed to Lord Gower to dispose of it to Mr. Frederick Montagu, whom Lord Halifax had recommended to Mr. Grenville, and who entirely approved of this nomination, to which Lord Gower most obligingly consented; but when this matter came to be named to Mr. Montagu, he at first desired a day to consider of it, and then absolutely refused it, saying it was no office of business, which was the line in which he wished to move. Lord Halifax was much displeased at his refusal, as he had been before at his declining to vacate his seat at Northampton, in order to stand for Cambridge in the room of Mr. Edward Finch, which would have been serviceable to Lord Sandwich, and would have enabled Lord Halifax to bring in Sir George Osborne for Northampton.

Lord Halifax and Lord Sandwich dined with Mr. Grenville; the latter expressed great uneasiness at Lord Mansfield so frequently going into the King's closet, telling Mr. Grenville he ought to beware of it, and prevent it if possible. Mr. Grenville said *that* was not in his power, nor did he wish to do it; he took no umbrage at it; Lord Mansfield seemed cordial in his support of the Government, and his (Mr. Grenville's) maxim was, in these kind of affairs, to live and let live.

Monday, November 5th. Mr. Grenville waited upon the King with the full account of his Civil List, and his expenses, all which he laid before His Majesty. The King saw the state of it, and seemed to approve of such savings as Mr. Grenville had been able to make compared with others. Mr. Grenville shewed his Majesty that these were singly in Lord Talbot's department and his own, and at the same time shewed him the excess in some of the other branches, all which the King admitted, and said reformation must be made in them. Mr. Grenville then stated to him the disgrace it would be in the beginning of his reign to apply to Parliament for his brothers' maintenance, besides that it would be making them at once entirely independent.

Mr. Grenville mentioned the seven thousand pounds a year allowed by the late King to the Princess for the whole of the young Royal Family, exclusive of His Majesty and the Duke of York, saying Her Royal Highness would soon, by the marriage of the Princess Caroline with the Prince Royal of Denmark, and the establishment intended to be made for Prince William, have only three of her children to maintain. The King said that was very true, but that he always understood that allowance was to be continued to her. He determined, in the end, to augment the Duke of York's establishment to fifteen thousand pounds a year, by adding a pension of three thousand pounds a year upon the Irish establishment, and wished to do the same for Prince William, who was to be created Duke of Gloucester.

Mr. Grenville advised his Majesty to defer that 'till some other opportunity, as the putting at once six thousand pounds a year upon Ireland might give uneasiness.

The King acquiesced, and said for the present Prince William should have only 12,000*l.* a-year, as the Duke of York had at first, and that it should be paid out of some of the Civil List revenues.

Mr. Grenville had several times named to the King some gentlemen strongly recommended to him for Prince William's family, particularly Mr. Duff, Lord Fife's brother, and Captain Bellew, recommended by Lord Thomond. His Majesty made general answers, saying he did not mean to constrain his brother in the choice of his servants, and the more as the number was confined to two grooms and two equerries. Mr. Grenville said that was too reasonable to be combated, but the King said, however, that he would name those persons to Prince William.

When Mr. Grenville saw Prince William at the Drawing Room on Sunday, the 11th, his Highness returned him thanks for having forwarded his business with the King, and said it was perfectly to his satisfaction.

The Master of the Rolls was seized with an apoplexy that same day, and it was thought he could not recover.

Tuesday, 13th. Mr. Grenville received intelligence from good hands that Mr. Charles Yorke seemed disposed, in case of the Master of the Rolls' death, to resume his former place of Attorney-General, or to take that of Master of the Rolls.

Wednesday, 14th. When Mr. Grenville went to the King, His Majesty told him Prince William's household was settled; that he had named the persons recommended by him, but that none had succeeded.

Mr. Grenville seemed a good deal surprised, and desired to know who were the persons appointed. The King told him Colonel Clinton, Colonel Ligonier, Mr. Cox, and Mr. Blackwood, the last recommended by Lord Bath. Mr. Grenville had some expostulation with His Majesty upon it, saying that had the appointment been of young people well known to Prince William he should not have had a word to say, but none of these had any such appearance, and that where recommendation was to prevail, he thought he might have hoped for better success. The King seemed embarrassed, said he would do anything for them that Mr. Grenville could wish, but that the family was settled, at which Mr. Grenville seemed mortified.

His Majesty talked with him afterwards upon several things very confidentially, and, amongst others, told him that he plainly saw that Lord Mansfield wished and meant to be Chancellor in case of Lord Northington's death, and that His Majesty having asked him why he declined it before, he told him he had done it both from the uncertainty of the Ministry, at that time the Duke of Newcastle being upon the decline, and Mr. Pitt, who was his mortal enemy, in power. Lord Mansfield, in conversation both with Lord Northington and Mr. Grenville, very lately, had used the words " as long as I continue where I now am."

Upon the death of Lord Poulett, Mr. Grenville went to the King to remind His Majesty of his promise to give the Lieutenancy of Somersetshire to Lord Thomond, to which the King readily consented, saying, he was very glad to do what was agreeable to Mr. Grenville, as well as to show a mark of regard to Lord Thomond, and to Lord Egremont's family.

Prince William sent Mr. Le Grand to Mr. Grenville, to desire him to speak to the King to allow him two thousand pounds to set out with when his establishment should take place. Mr. Grenville endeavoured to decline this by mentioning how much more properly such an application would be from H.R.H. to the King; but being strongly pressed, he at last consented, and accordingly named it to His Majesty, who consented to do it.

Thursday, 15th. Mr. Grenville again remonstrated to His Majesty upon the subject of Prince William's family, showing him how much he was distressed by being able to comply with none of the recommendations which had been so strongly made to him. The King still combated this point, but said at last that he would speak to Prince William to see if there was an equerry undisposed of.

The Master of the Rolls was seized with an apoplectic fit on *Sunday, the* 11*th of November,* and died on the Tuesday following.

The same evening Mr. Yorke went to my Lord Chancellor, and opened to him the dispositions he was in to fill either of the two great posts in the law.

The Chancellor told this conversation to Mr. Grenville, and Mr. Wedderburn also told Mr. Grenville that he had seen Mr. Yorke, who seemed surprised to have heard nothing from Mr. Grenville upon the death of the Master of the Rolls. Mr. Grenville told Mr. Wedderburn that he meant no slight to Mr. Yorke, and would be glad to see him to talk upon the subject.

Mr. Yorke came to Mr. Grenville on *Thursday,* 15*th,* and staid with him three or four hours, making a long deduction of the state of things, and expressing his willingness to take a part in the King's Government in either of the posts of Attorney-General or Master of the Rolls, stating the great loss the latter would be to him, as the salary barely exceeded two thousand pounds a year, and that at present he made six thousand of his business; and therefore, that in case of his acceptance of that office, he should hope the King would be pleased to make the salary up to four thousand pounds a year, and give him a Peerage. Mr. Grenville gave him no reason to hope that this would be complied with, and endeavoured to put him off of it; but he still desired it might be named to the King, and that the preliminary article for his coming again into the King's service must be the putting an end to the contest at Cambridge in favour of his brother, Lord Hardwicke. He seemed very desirous to have it understood that the King had called him to his service. Mr. Grenville said he had no message to him from the King whatever, but that the conversation would not have passed between them if Mr. Grenville had not thought it would be agreeable to the King. Mr. Yorke still seemed to wish to have the King's commands to plead, that he might have that ground to stand upon to his friends, by whom he should be arraigned as having deserted them, though at the same time he said he knew what his friends were, and how very unmeritorious they had been to him. He seemed willing, in case the arrangement mentioned did not take place, to return to his former situation of Attorney-General; but that, even though he should not come into either of those offices, he meant to take part in support of the King's Government in the next session of Parliament.

Friday, November 16th. Mr. Grenville went to the King, to relate to him what had passed between Mr. Yorke and him; his Majesty approved it very much, but would not hear of the proposition of the Peerage and additional salary, and therefore desired Mr. Grenville to signify to Mr. Yorke that he wished to see him in his service again in his former station.

Saturday, November 17th. Mr. Yorke came to Mr. Grenville, with whom he had a very long conversation; he opened it by saying he meant to take one of the great offices in the Law, but still insisted much on the necessity of his having the King's commands for returning into his service; held up his own pretensions very high, and throughout the whole conversation endeavoured to preserve to himself a situation of independency, though in Court.

Mr. Grenville endeavoured to combat his distinctions, which obliged him many times to ask Mr. Grenville if he mistrusted him, or thought him not an honest man; but his declarations never seemed to be such as not to leave Mr. Grenville room to doubt how far his support would be strong and uniform. Mr. Grenville declared many times that no necessity obliged either the King or his servants to wish to see him in employment, otherwise than as respecting his talents and character; that the office of Master of the Rolls could be very honourably filled by Judge Wilmot, whom Lord Mansfield had recommended to the King. This seemed to make an impression on him, but upon the whole he seemed rather inclined to that office than that of Attorney-General, contrary to his opinion in the former interview, and upon the strength of which Mr. Grenville had mentioned the exchange to Sir Fletcher Norton, who was disposed to agree to it; he seemed to wish much for the promise of being Chancellor in case the seals became vacant, or of having the certainty of a compensation, but Mr. Grenville gave no encouragement to either of these proposals. Upon the whole, he desired to have 'till Wednesday to consider of it, and to go in the interval to Claremont to disengage himself from the Duke of Newcastle, proposing to take Lord Lyttelton with him as the witness of what should pass there.

Monday, November 19*th.* Mr. Grenville received a letter in the morning from the Chancellor, informing him that he had had, the night before, a very inexplicit and unsatisfactory conversation with Mr. Yorke, with which the Chancellor was much dissatisfied, and said, amongst other things, that Mr. Yorke told him that he had told Mr. Grenville that he must go to Claremont, to take the Duke of Newcastle's opinion in this transaction, to which Mr. Grenville had consented. Dr.

Hay was with Mr. Grenville when he received this letter, who, being a friend of Mr. Yorke's, he shewed it to him, and desired him to go to Mr. Yorke to tell him that he had mistook Mr. Grenville entirely, if he thought that he understood that the Duke of Newcastle was to be in any way a party to this transaction; that he (Mr. Yorke) had told Mr. Grenville that he meant to go to Claremont to disengage himself from the Duke; but that if his Grace's opinion was to be taken in this affair, Mr. Grenville must at once put an end to the transaction.

Dr. Hay in a short time wrote to Mr. Grenville, acquainting him that the Chancellor had quite mistaken him, that he meant to go to Claremont for communication, and not for judgment.

Wednesday, November 21. Mr. Grenville showed the Chancellor's letter to the King, who seemed to think his Lordship might possibly have been too warm in his expostulation with Mr. Yorke; Mr. Grenville endeavoured to soften the King's mind towards the Chancellor, who he said had great merit in his service, and that if Mr. Yorke was to come into His Majesty's service upon doubtful ground, he would ruin his affairs; the King said he thought him too honest a man for that.

Thursday, November 22nd. Lord Halifax told Mr. Grenville that Mr. Yorke had been the day before at Claremont, that Lord Lyttelton not being able to go with him, he had taken Mr. Frederick Montagu with him, who had been shy of repeating the conversation; but upon Lord Halifax saying he could repeat what had passed, and made a speech for each of the parties, Mr. Montagu assented to what he said. Mr. Yorke's tended to detach himself, and the Duke's to prevent it, and to dissuade him from taking an office; they parted with discontent.

Mr. Yorke called on Lord Besborough on his way to Claremont, and was desirous that he should have gone with him, but Lord Besborough desired to be excused, and did not care to have any thing to do with it.

Mr. Yorke came to Mr. Grenville in the evening; his language was more inexplicit than before, and still stronger in the plan he seemed to have laid down to himself, of drawing a line in government between himself and the rest of the King's servants, all which was rather to be collected from his discourse than that he himself avowed it, except upon the subject of the general warrants, which question, when Mr. Grenville touched upon, he (Mr. Yorke) said he should not depart from the conduct he had held last year, and which would have been the same had he then been Attorney-General.

Mr. Grenville said he must excuse him if he told him he thought it impossible that, in the situation of Attorney-General, he could have differed from the rest of the King's servants in a matter of that importance, neither could he now come into Government under that declaration; this question was long discussed between them; the conversation lasted 'till near two o'clock in the morning, and ended by Mr. Yorke desiring to have further time to consider upon his final answer.

The first part of the conversation was a long discussion of Mr. Yorke's upon the mode of his entering into the King's service at this juncture, whether it should be in the office of Attorney General, or Master of the Rolls, or whether he should only ask the King for a patent of precedency.

Another long part of the discourse was upon settling the affairs relating to Cambridge with Lord Sandwich, with whom he had at first declined a meeting, but was now to have one the next day, desiring Mr. Grenville to tell Lord Sandwich that he should expect him to give up Cambridge entirely, and promise never to engage in any contest against Lord Hardwicke.

Mr. Grenville told him it was a great deal too much to ask; that for his own part, was he himself in the case, he should enter into no such engagement, and therefore could not carry a message to ask what he himself would not grant.

Friday, November 23rd. Mr. Grenville related the sum of his conversation with Mr. Yorke to the King, who seemed dissatisfied with his demands, but still much inclined to see him again in office.

Saturday, November 24th. Mr. Grenville was assured, from those who said they knew it to a certainty, that Mr. Yorke had seen Mr. Pitt, who was in town the day before.

Mr. Yorke came in the evening to Mr. Grenville, and declined either of the two offices, but wished to receive a mark of the King's grace by giving him a patent of precedency. He declared his resolution of taking a part in support of Government, and said he should wish to have an audience of His Majesty (if he was pleased to confer that grace upon him) to thank him for it. He was very temperate and good humoured, and in the course of the conversation Mr. Grenville took an opportunity to ask him when he saw Mr. Pitt; he said not since last winter, and then only one single time after he had quitted the office of Attorney General.

Mr. Yorke seemed very thoroughly to disclaim farther

connection with the Opposition, saying it was bad enough to be a deputy Minister, but to be a deputy in Opposition was what he could not submit to.

Monday, November 26th. Dr. Hay came to Mr. Grenville from Mr. Yorke, bringing him a paper from him, in which he gave account of a conversation he had had with the Chancellor, who had said that he entirely approved that His Majesty should grant to Mr. Yorke a patent of precedency, as a reward for his former services. These words occasioned some surprise in Mr. Grenville, who understood from the Chancellor that he did not mean to acquiesce to those words, and a letter he received at the same moment from his Lordship still confirmed him in this opinion. This occasioned some altercation, and Mr. Grenville wrote in consequence of it to the Chancellor, and showed his letter to Dr. Hay, who desired him to suspend the sending it 'till he (Dr. Hay) should have seen Mr. Yorke, to which Mr. Grenville consented.

Tuesday, November 27th. Mr. Yorke withdrew his paper, and Mr. Grenville did not send his letter.

Mr. Yorke declared his wish to the Chancellor to obtain the patent of precedency, and spoke very fully in regard to his design to support the Administration, as he had likewise done to Mr. Grenville, and accordingly he was to kiss hands on Friday.

Wednesday, November 28th. Mr. Grenville told His Majesty what had passed, who seemed to think Mr. Yorke had hurt himself in men's minds by his irresolution, but consented to give him the patent.

Friday, November 30th. Mr. Yorke sent to Lord Chancellor to state some difficulties about the patent, and desired to consider farther upon it 'till the Wednesday following, probably not caring to kiss hands on so public a day as the Princess of Wales's birthday.

Wednesday, 5th December. Mr. Yorke kissed the King's hand for the patent of precedency. He had afterwards an audience of His Majesty, at which he made the strongest declaration of his intentions to support the King's Government, and did not mean to have any leanings to those in Opposition, though he reserved always to himself the claim of differing from the King's servants in any matter that should be really contrary to his opinion; and whenever that should be the case, he would endeavour to show His Majesty that it was from opinion only, unmixed with any party connection whatever. He threw out general words disclaiming the giving any contradiction to his former conduct by his future, meaning, as it is supposed, in regard to the question upon the general warrants.

The King still complains in many instances of Lord Sandwich and Lord Halifax, and tells Mr. Grenville that they do not act fairly by him, for that they are continually pushing him (Mr. Grenville) upon increase of expense, and favouring everybody's demands, and holding back at the same time every facility they could give to him in business relating to the Treasury. Mr. Grenville could not deny it.

Monday, December 17th. Mr. Grenville went to the King, to speak to him about drawing his Speech, and mentioning to His Majesty that it would be proper to take notice of the election of the King of the Romans, and the King of Poland: His Majesty from thence talked a good deal upon the present situation of Europe. Mr. Grenville took occasion to observe to him how advantageous it had proved His Majesty's having stood entirely neuter, without the expense of a shilling of money to bring about either of those desirable events, and begged His Majesty to remember it had ever been his advice to him to let his mediation and assistance be courted by all the Powers in Europe, rather than offered; that this advice he gave him, both as to foreign affairs and those of his own kingdom, never to seek others, but to put himself in such a situation as should make him be sought; that it had been his opinion in regard to Prussia; it was equally so in regard to all the other Powers.

The King said, he was perfectly convinced of the wisdom of this conduct, though another had been proposed to him in that very room (at the Queen's House) by Mr. Pitt, who wanted to put him à la suite of the King of Prussia, and in mentioning the treaty with Russia, had said it ought to have been obtained through the mediation and interposition of the King of Prussia. Mr. Grenville said, the greatness of the King of Prussia's situation could never be but temporary; that England and France, being the two greatest Powers of Europe, would ever be courted by Russia and Prussia, and in proportion as the one got in closer alliance with France, it would throw the other into the scale of England. His Majesty seemed to approve extremely of this reasoning, entered into it very fully, and brought the instance of King William, who had been precisely in the situation of being sought and applied to by all the Powers of Europe.

Wednesday, December 19*th.* The Primate of Ireland died at ten o'clock.

Mr. Grenville went to St. James's, where he met

Lord Halifax and the Duke of Bedford. They talked together upon a successor to the Primate.

Lord Northumberland was desirous it should be Dr. Robinson, brother to Sir Thomas and Sir Septimus, who is an Irish Bishop. The Duke of Bedford proposed Dr. Carmichael. Mr. Grenville had some time before named the Bishop of Chester (Dr. Keene) to the King, who seemed to approve of him; but upon sounding the Bishop upon that head, he rather seemed disinclined to it. He renewed this proposal to the King upon the Primate's death, and in case that should not succeed, he named Dr. Newton, Bishop of Bristol, who did not disapprove it, but seemed rather more inclined to Dr. Robinson. Lord Granby wrote a very pressing letter to Mr. Grenville in favour of Dr. Ewer, Bishop of Llandaff.

The Duke of Bedford had a great deal of very friendly talk with Mr. Grenville, and, among other things, told him that after this session of Parliament he must withdraw from public affairs to go to live at Bath. Mr. Grenville told his Grace he should be very sorry to see that day, and hoped he would not quit the King's service, which could not but be very prejudicial to it. The Duke told him it should not be whilst the King's affairs were in any distress, nor whilst he could be of service in establishing Mr. Grenville in his present situation; but that nothing but his duty to the King, and his friendship personally to Mr. Grenville, should keep him there a moment longer, and that he only meant to stay 'till he (Mr. Grenville) had overcome all his enemies, and thoroughly strengthened himself where he was.

The Bishop of Chester came to Mr. Grenville in the evening, to decline the situation of Primate, which he could not bring himself to think of, from his unwillingness to enter upon so public a scene.

Mr. Grenville sent to the Bishop of Bristol to sound his inclinations upon the same head, but found him equally averse to it upon account of his health. Mr. Grenville had a second letter more pressing than the first, from Lord Granby, to solicit for Dr. Ewer. The King pauses upon appointing any one to it as yet, and in that and some other instances of delays in some things, and averseness to what Mr. Grenville proposes in others, he feels the effects of some inferior persons who get about His Majesty, and seemingly indispose him to his principal servants.

END OF VOL. II.

LIBRARY OF DAVIDSON COLLEGE

Books on regular loan may be checked out for **two weeks**. Books must be presented at the Circulation Desk in order to be renewed.

A fine of **five cents** a day is charged after date due.

Special books are subject to special regulations at the discretion of library staff.

MAR 0 6 1990
ILL
JAN 9 '91